The New Zealand
Experiment

The New Zealand Experiment

A WORLD MODEL
FOR STRUCTURAL ADJUSTMENT?

Jane Kelsey

AUCKLAND UNIVERSITY PRESS
BRIDGET WILLIAMS BOOKS

*For my mother
and others of her generation
who feel angry and betrayed.*

Published 1995 by Auckland University Press with
Bridget Williams Books, University of Auckland,
Private Bag 92019, Auckland, New Zealand
Reprinted 1996 (January, March)

Also published 1995 as *Economic Fundamentalism: The New
Zealand Experiment — A world model for structural adjustment?*
in the International Labour Series by Pluto Press, London and
East Haven, Connecticut

ISBN 1 86940 130 1

Printed by GP Print Ltd, Wellington

Contents

Abbreviations

ACC	Accident Compensation Corporation
ACT	Association of Consumers and Taxpayers
APEC	Asia Pacific Economic Co-operation forum
BIL	Brierley Investments Ltd
BNZ	Bank of New Zealand
CEO	Chief executive officer
CER	Australia NZ Closer Economic Relations Trade Agreement
CHE	Crown Health Enterprise
CPI	Consumer Price Index
CRA	Credit rating agency
CRI	Crown Research Institute
CTU	(New Zealand) Council of Trade Unions
DPB	Domestic purposes benefit
DPMC	Department of Prime Minister and Cabinet
DSW	Department of Social Welfare
ECA	Employment Contracts Act
EMTR	Equivalent marginal tax rate
FCL	Fletcher Challenge Ltd
FEC	Finance and Expenditure Select Committee
FPP	First-past-the-post (electoral system)
FRA	Fiscal Responsibility Act
GATT	General Agreement on Tariffs and Trade
GDP	Gross domestic product
GMFI	Guaranteed Minimum Family Income
GPS	Government Property Services
GRI	Guaranteed Retirement Income
GST	Goods and services tax
HNZ	Housing New Zealand
IIE	Institute for International Economics
ILO	International Labour Organisation
IMF	International Monetary Fund
LATE	Local authority trading enterprise
MMP	Mixed-member proportional representation
NBR	*National Business Review*
NZF	New Zealand First
NZIER	New Zealand Institute for Economic Research
NZP	New Zealand Party
NZQA	New Zealand Qualifications Authority
NZTUF	New Zealand Trade Union Federation
OECD	Organisation for Economic Co-operation and Development
OIC	Overseas Investment Commission
PFA	Public Finance Act
PSA	Public Service Association
PTA	Policy Targets Agreement
RHA	Regional Health Authority
SCI	Statement of Corporate Intent
SOE	State-owned Enterprise
SSC	State Services Commission
TCE	Trans-national corporate enterprise
TNC	Trans-national corporation
WTO	World Trade Organisation

Preface

In 1995, as the disciples of economic fundamentalism proclaim the New Zealand 'success story' across the globe, some will consider it disloyal to suggest that 'the emperor has no clothes'. Critique is not a well-established tradition in this country. In recent years the hostile reaction to public critics, especially those who take their analysis off-shore, suggests that the much-heralded recovery of New Zealand's economy is more fragile than its proponents are willing to concede.

It is essential that the peoples and governments upon whom the New Zealand model is being pressed have access to both sides of the story. There are important lessons for them to learn. For the peoples of Aotearoa New Zealand many of those lessons have come too late. Our task for the years ahead is to identify how we might realistically achieve a more socially just society, what the price of further change will be, and on whom it will fall.

This book seeks to serve the needs of both those groups. The analysis is presented in three parts. Part One looks at how and why economic fundamentalism took hold in New Zealand after 1984. Part Two examines what was done, and the attempts made to embed the neo-liberal regime against change. Part Three describes the economic, social, democratic and cultural deficits that were left in its wake. The book concludes by exploring the alternatives to economic fundamentalism, and the strategies that might help to achieve them in Aotearoa New Zealand and overseas.

The book reflects my passionate belief that all people have the right to live in dignity, to determine their own visions for the future and to play a role in bringing those about. It would not have been written but for the insistence of Arthur Lipow, editor of the Pluto International Labour Series, that the myths of the New Zealand 'success story' should be exposed. Support came from colleagues and contacts in the United Kingdom, Canada, Sweden, Australia, India and South Africa.

Many people have contributed ideas and information to the book, although they bear no responsibility for its content or conclusions. I thank Toni Ashton, Joe Atkinson, Jonathan Boston, Paul Dalziel, Grant Duncan, Ian Eagles, Maxine Gay, Ray Harbridge, Rua Rakena, Keith Rankin, Robert Reid, Bill Rosenberg, Susan St John, Chris Trotter, and others who must remain nameless, for their valuable comments on specific parts of the book. Others in government agencies and community organisations have been generous with their time and information. I am especially grateful to Brian Easton for his careful and detailed comments on an earlier draft, and to Simon Collins and Marilyn Waring for their observations on the final draft. The willingness of all these people to contribute testifies to the wealth of analysis and critique which is available in New Zealand, but which today is too rarely heard.

I must also thank the University of Auckland for granting me sabbatical leave to work on the book, and to St Anne's College, Oxford, for providing a haven in which to write. Once again, my supportive and trusting publisher Bridget Williams and editor Andrew Mason have eased the way. My thanks also to Gillian Kootstra for the typesetting and Eleanor Opai for setting the graphs. Finally, I am indebted to my friends and family who, as always, have been there when I needed them.

J. K.
September 1995

Introduction

WHY SHOULD NEW ZEALAND—a small, geographically remote group of islands in the South Pacific, with a population of just 3.4 million people—be of interest to the rest of the world? New Zealand used to claim credit as the first country to give women the vote, as the birthplace of the welfare state, for a harmonious multiracial society and, more recently, for being 'clean, green and nuclear free'. Today, it is becoming infamous for what is known as the 'New Zealand experiment'. This model of pure neo-liberal economic theory was first applied by a Labour government from 1984 to 1990, and has been continued with equal, if not greater, fervour by a National government thereafter. In 1995 it is being hailed by the World Bank, the *Economist*, the Organisation for Economic Co-operation and Development (OECD) and other like-minded guardians of the global economy as an example for the rest of the world.

What is so significant about the New Zealand experiment? Four factors stand out.

- This radical exercise in structural adjustment was not implemented by a 'third world' government as a condition of securing credit from the international financial institutions, but was unilaterally undertaken by a democratically elected government within an advanced capitalist economy.
- Successive governments applied pure economic theory to a complex, real-life community, with generally cavalier disregard for the social or electoral consequences.
- The programme was implemented in 1984 by a Labour government, whose party had traditionally embraced a social democratic philosophy, and was continued after 1990 by a purportedly free-enterprise, but traditionally interventionist, conservative National government.

1

- The 'fundamentals' of the programme—market liberalisation and free trade, limited government, a narrow monetarist policy, a deregulated labour market, and fiscal restraint—were assumed to be 'given', based on common sense and consensus, and beyond challenge. These fundamentals were systematically embedded against change.

Overview

The basic formula for the New Zealand experiment mirrored the structural adjustment programmes implemented in the poorer countries of the world.

The fourth Labour government took office after a snap election in July 1984. The currency was immediately devalued by 20 percent. In rapid succession, the finance markets were deregulated, exchange controls removed and the New Zealand dollar put on a free float. Controls on prices, wages, interest rates, rents and credit were replaced by a monetarist anti-inflationary regime, operated through a policy of high interest and exchange rates. The overriding goal of price stability was legislated for in the Reserve Bank Act 1989; previous references in the legislation to production, trade and employment were removed. The bank was insulated from direct political control. Wage restraint and structural unemployment became key elements of monetary policy, with the Reserve Bank determined to keep inflation down when the economy eventually returned to positive growth.

Export and domestic subsidies were eliminated. Import licences were abolished and dramatic tariff reductions imposed. The Closer Economic Relations (CER) free trade agreement with Australia, first signed in 1983, was expanded. Both Labour and National governments urged other members of the General Agreement on Tariffs and Trade (GATT) to open up their economies and create a level playing-field of free trade, especially in agriculture; they enthusiastically pursued that goal through the Asia Pacific Economic Co-operation (APEC) forum. Restrictions on foreign investment were removed for almost all transactions under $10 million, while Overseas Investment Commission approval for investments above that amount became virtually automatic. New laws for business competition dispensed with considerations of employment and consumer well-being, and focused on competitive efficiency within the deregulated marketplace. Pressures to tighten takeover and securities laws following the 1987 stock-market crash met sustained resistance from the corporate élite.

The emphasis moved from direct to indirect taxation. A universal goods and services tax (GST) was introduced in 1986, covering all final domestic consumption, including food, and excluding only financial services, real estate transactions and very small businesses. Personal income tax rates were flattened and reduced, along with corporate tax rates, making the top personal income tax rate among the lowest in the OECD. The Fiscal Responsibility Act 1994 required fiscal policy to maintain a budget surplus on average, reduce public debt, increase government's net worth and keep tax rates stable. Governments deviating from the new norm would be required to justify themselves, and indicate when they would return to a 'fiscally responsible' path.

Labour markets were progressively opened up. Under the Labour government, compulsory arbitration was withdrawn, unions were required to consolidate to secure recognition, and bargaining shifted progressively from industry to enterprise agreements. In 1991 the National government's Employment Contracts Act replaced the system of national awards and collective bargaining with individual employment contracts covering both state and private sector employment. Unions were renamed 'employees' organisations' and required to secure explicit authorisation to negotiate on their members' behalf. All statutory privileges for unions were removed. Occupational health and safety became increasingly self-regulated through market incentives. The no-fault accident compensation system was redesigned to shift the funding burden for non-workplace accidents from employers to workers and other individuals. Although eligibility for accident compensation was cut and pay-out levels were reduced, the right to take civil action for personal injury, which had been abolished when the scheme was introduced in 1974, was not restored.

From 1986 any state activity with a potentially commercial function was corporatised, placed in the hands of a government-appointed board of entrepreneurial directors and required to run as an equivalent to private sector business. A majority of state-owned enterprises (SOEs) and other assets were later fully or partly privatised, including three state banks and the trustee savings bank system, state insurance company, railways, the national airline, local transport, shipping, telecommunications, electricity distribution, petroleum and natural gas reserves and refineries, forests, fisheries, hotels, housing mortgages, computing services and the Government Printing Office. Foreign buyers were actively sought, mainly in Australia and the United States.

Most government scientific research was split up into commercial Crown Research Institutes (CRIs), which were forced to charge full-cost recovery for their services and compete with the private sector for a contestable research fund whose amount and priorities were set by the government. Public hospitals were converted to commercial Crown Health Enterprises (CHEs) and required to run as successful private sector businesses. They, too, were to compete with private providers to secure a share of the contestable public fund. The former Housing Corporation, renamed Housing New Zealand, was placed in charge of a declining state rental housing stock and required to produce a return on its assets. Its role as first supplier to those with priority housing needs was abandoned.

In education, responsibility for school administration was transferred to local school boards, who were 'freed' to determine their spending priorities from government-allocated budgets, to employ teaching staff of whatever quality they thought appropriate, and increasingly to negotiate staff wages. Tertiary institutions were recast as delivering private benefits to fee-paying students, in order to justify reduced government funding and force the institutions to respond to market demand. While enrolments in professional courses boomed, low spending on trade training left the labour force seriously underskilled.

State expenditure was cut back and the bureaucracy reorganised to increase efficiency and introduce entrepreneurial discipline. Government departments were separated into operational and policy units. Operational functions were run along business lines and frequently contracted out to private enterprise. The core ministries were put in the hands of chief executives on fixed-term performance-related contracts. Managerial autonomy was monitored through output-based reporting requirements in the Public Finance Act 1989. Policy work was increasingly contracted out to a flourishing industry of private consultants and management firms. Private sector labour laws were applied to the rapidly diminishing permanent public sector staff.

The amount and extent of entitlement to welfare benefits were cut back as the numbers forced to depend on them grew. Following

National's 'mother of all budgets' in 1991, the population was classified as earning low, medium or high incomes, as the basis for differential rates of subsidy for state-provided health services (these categories were later reduced to two). Schools levied 'voluntary' fees on their students and sought to supplement their budgets in an entrepreneurial fashion. Tertiary students, facing rising fees and reduced allowances, accumulated debts to be repaid at commercial interest rates through a compulsory earnings levy. Subsidised state housing rentals were progressively raised to full market values, with a supplement available for tenants in public and private rental accommodation or home buyers who met a strict eligibility test.

Institutions for the mentally ill, elderly and young closed their doors in the name of community care. Women were called upon to perform a traditional role as volunteer carers to fill the void left by the state. Maori were assumed to have tribal and family support systems to fall back on. Churches and charities were expected to cover the government's withdrawal from social and income support. Expenditure on police, courts and prisons continued to grow.

International success story

From its inception, this radical adventure captured the imagination of the international economic community, whose institutions and organisations provided a chorus of support. Typical was the OECD's report on New Zealand in 1993. Its analysis ran along the following lines.

New Zealand's economy since 1950 had been the most highly protected in the OECD: it lacked a skilled labour force, had rigid labour, capital and product markets, high effective tax rates and was prone to respond to external shocks in an inflationary way. The result was an uncompetitive, 'cost-plus' economy.

In 1984 the new Labour government embarked on a programme of regulatory reform designed to generate sustained economic growth through increased competition, reduced rigidities and low inflation. The result was 'one of the least distorting tax systems in the OECD area, the lowest OECD producer subsidy equivalent in agriculture, substantial trade liberalisation, and a more efficient public sector. Finally, the Reserve Bank Act (1989) gave the central bank increased autonomy in the pursuit of a single goal—to achieve and maintain price stability.'[1]

Unfortunately, the Rogernomics experiment (named after Minister of Finance, Roger Douglas) failed to work for the two terms that Labour was in power. The OECD conceded that, after six years of declining economic performance and concentrated pain, there was very little apparent gain.

> Overall, continuing macroeconomic imbalances, high debt levels, inflexible labour markets, and pressure in the tradeables sector were all elements in stalling the broader economic benefits of the reforms adopted during the 1980s. By the time of the October 1990 general election, the economy was still suffering from sluggish growth, high and rising unemployment, and high real interest rates. This created a difficult investment environment, which was sufficient to stall the shift of resources to areas of greatest future potential.[2]

The OECD offered various explanations for this. First, whether by technical error or force of circumstance, Labour had deregulated the finance markets while imposing restrictive monetary policies through high interest rates. This produced a high exchange rate which undercut exports and a binge on imports following the rapid liberalisation of trade. Second, 'economic policy credibility was slow to be established' as strong wage growth, introduction of GST and user charges kept inflationary expectations high. Third, the speculative boom in property and equities investment meant asset values failed to 'adjust' as predicted to removal of industry protections. Fourth, the global stock-market crash in 1987 exposed weak (and fabricated) corporate balance sheets and contracted demand for financial services. Finally, the Labour government's commitment to reform, especially cuts to spending and deregulation of the labour market, slackened after 1988. So, in the eyes of the OECD, the failure of Rogernomics to produce the promised returns was not really its architects' fault. Nor was it the fault of the structural adjustment model.

In 1990 the new National government stepped into the breach and 'relaunched economic restructuring, with an intent to restore balance to the macroeconomic policy settings'. These focused on cuts to government spending and radical labour market reform. Unfortunately, National plunged the country into even deeper recession. 'The New Zealand economy entered a recession during 1990, which intensified in early 1991. . . . Real domestic expenditure fell 6.6 per cent in 1991, after being essentially flat in 1990, with both private and public consumption growth declining. Public investment fell by 27 per cent and private investment by 13 per cent.'[3] The likelihood that cuts to benefits, government spending and wages had turned the economic screws too tight was of less interest to the OECD than the up-side of recession: deflation in both wages and prices through 1990–91 contributed significantly to New Zealand's improved competitiveness and export performance. Out of gloom came recovery. After nearly a decade of painful restructuring, it seemed that the long-awaited recovery had arrived.

Private sector economic analysts and international credit-raters offered their enthusiastic support. The 1994 report on New Zealand by Moody's Investors Services observed:

> The reorientation of New Zealand economic policy after 1984 represented one of the most ambitious and comprehensive structural reforms undertaken by any OECD country. . . . At the time, many expected that the reform process would be relatively short and painless. As it has turned out, the reform process has proved somewhat tortuous and quite painful for many segments of New Zealand society. . . .

Despite this, investors were assured that the future of the structural adjustment programme was secure.

> Moody's believes that economic fundamentals are solid, and both major traditional parties seem to be committed to the existing parameters of policy. Minor changes are not seen as threats to the policies already in place. Because it will be more difficult in the future to create electoral majorities [under the new electoral system of MMP], it will also be increasingly harder to overturn reforms already in place. . . . The risk . . . is that success could breed complacency and/or policy shifts that could jeopardize all the gains made to date. The political forces both in power now, and in the future, will probably not want to reverse the virtuous cycle presently in place, however.[4]

The international media joined the refrain. A special correspondent commissioned by the *Economist* in 1985 to investigate the early reforms seemed enthralled by the Labour government's 'exhilarating dash for economic freedom. . . . Delighted progressive businessmen hardly dare believe that a Labour government is doing these things, while bewildered old trade union leaders loyally pretend that it isn't.' Asking, 'Can this free-market experiment in socialist sheep's clothing succeed?' the correspondent replied, 'During his 36 years as a newspaperman your correspondent has visited most major countries, but he can remember no economic experiment that he has been more eager to see succeed than that of this brave New Zealand Labour government.'[5]

Subsequent reports in the *Economist* carried such epithets as 'New Zealand's free-market socialists',[6] 'the sort of socialism of which millionaires approve',[7] 'New Zealand's brave recipe',[8] 'out-Thatchering Mrs Thatcher',[9] 'trail-blazing economic reforms',[10] 'an international model for economic reform',[11] 'a paradise for free-marketeers — if not for those New Zealanders who have lost their jobs',[12] and 'the most thoroughgoing economic reform in the OECD'.[13] In the lead-up to the 1993 election, the *Economist* sympathetically reviewed the state of the experiment:

> During the past decade New Zealand has implemented free-market reforms more radical than any other industrial country's. . . . On November 6th New Zealanders will decide whether they want the experiment to continue. Their verdict will send an important signal to the rest of the world's economic reformers.[14]

The *Times*[15] and *Financial Times*[16] of England, Toronto's *Globe and Mail*,[17] the *Wall Street Journal*,[18] among many others, mirrored the *Economist*'s theme. Successive Labour and National governments basked in their plaudits while hoping to ignite a similar degree of enthusiasm at home.

Counter-versions of New Zealand's 'success' story were rare. Some Canadian journalists pointed out that New Zealand in 1984 was very different from Canada in the past or present day,[19] and the Canadian Broadcasting Corporation carried several documentaries which highlighted the down-side of the New Zealand experiment.[20]

A full-page feature in England's *Independent* in March 1994 detailed the social costs of New Zealand's structural adjustment programme. Headlined *What happens when you scrap the welfare state?* its lead comment opened: 'New Zealand has, and its economy is stronger. But there is a dark side: one in seven below [the] poverty line; record numbers of people in jail; armed police on the streets; queues at charity "food banks".' After cataloguing the social distress and decay in poorer New Zealand communities, the story concluded 'there is the feeling that something irreplaceable has already been lost. For 40 years, New Zealand tried to build a civil society in which all its people were free from fear or want. That project has now lapsed. In its place is only a vague exhortation for individuals to go and get rich.'[21]

The Australian press were even more cautious, and often caustic, about what New Zealand had to offer. The Australian Liberal Party's policy embraced aspects of the New Zealand model, notably labour market deregulation during the Victoria state election in 1992, and a universal goods-and-services expenditure tax in the federal election of 1993. These were met by horror stories in the Australian media condemning the 'New Zealand disease'.

Irrespective of their logic or empirical substance, these criticisms were unlikely to dislodge the increasingly pervasive, and constantly reinforced, perception of New Zealand's 'success' among those economists, politicians, financial analysts and journalists who formed the vanguard of the new world economic order.

Rethinking 'success'

But what did these people mean by 'success'? If they had been defining 'success' in terms of positive economic indicators, the New Zealand experiment would not have been receiving glowing accolades throughout the years of prolonged stagnation and recession, well before there was evidence to cite in support.

Between 1985 and 1992 total growth across OECD economies averaged 20 percent; New Zealand's economy shrank by 1 percent over the same period.[22] Other objective indicators showed that between 1984 and 1993 productivity growth in New Zealand averaged around 0.9 percent, and this was mainly due to labour cutbacks. Inflation averaged around 9 percent a year. Real interest rates remained excessively high. Unemployment rose to unprecedented levels. Net migration flows were negative. Overseas debt quadrupled. New Zealand's credit rating was downgraded twice. Investment as a percentage of GDP halved, and spending on research and development fell to half the OECD average.

After seven years spent in varying degrees of stagnation and recession New Zealand had finally shown signs of vigorous economic growth in 1993. The 1994 budget celebrated the results: low inflation (between 0.5 and 1.5 percent), declining interest rates (short-term rates around 6 percent), impressive growth in GDP (estimated at 5 percent for 1994/95 followed by 3.5 percent in 1995/96 and 1996/97), record export receipts (export volumes were up 29 percent in the past four years), job growth (3.9 percent in 1993/94, with another 90,000 jobs predicted in the following three years), sustained high business confidence, reduced government expenditure (from 39.3 percent of GDP in 1991/92 down to an estimated 34.8 percent in 1994/95 and a projected 30 percent by 2000), a forecast budget surplus ($730 million in 1994/95, with $2.49 billion forecast for 1995/96 and $4.53 billion for 1996/97), reductions in net public debt (from 48 percent of GDP in 1990 to 42 percent in 1994 and 30 percent forecast for 1996/97, with a goal of 20 percent by 2004) and the prospect of tax cuts for the 1996/97 year.

The 'turnaround economy' became the toast of the global economic community. Yet three years into the much-heralded economic recovery some of the key indicators, such as public debt, were just returning to their pre-1984 levels. Others, notably unemployment, were nowhere near that. While a number of indicators had improved, critics argued that the country was significantly worse off than it would have been under a different economic approach. Moreover, a sustainable economic recovery was far from guaranteed. By 1995 there were signs that the economy was weakening once more.

Social critics insisted that, whatever the economic outcomes, the country and many of its people were a great deal worse off. Unemployment and poverty had become structural features of New Zealand life. The Labour government had been responsible for the early decline, with rising unemployment, failure to keep benefits and family assistance in line with inflation, and favourable tax treatment of the rich at the expense of the poor. Its National successor had further fuelled unemployment and deregulated the labour market to force wages and penal rates down. It had slashed benefit levels and tightened eligibility criteria, imposed new user charges, and suspended inflation-indexing for family assistance and income support.

The number of New Zealanders estimated to be living below the poverty line rose by at least 35 percent between 1989 and 1992; by 1993 one in six New Zealanders was considered to be living in poverty. Even if unemployment returned to the level of the mid-1980s— still very high by New Zealand's historical standards—poverty and hardship were expected to remain about the same.[23] Both National and Labour ignored the political, economic and human cost of these social indicators.

The political verdict was equally damning. The electoral fortunes of the Labour and National parties see-sawed throughout the decade. In the 1993 general election National saw its return reduced from 69 to 50 seats in a 99-seat parliament, thus retaining a one-seat majority despite winning just over 35 percent of the total vote. Its historical competitor for power, the Labour Party, still feeling the wrath of voters for its policies and practices in government, secured just under 35 percent of voter support and won only 45 seats. Minority parties saw their share rise to almost 30 percent, although due to the vagaries of the first-past-the-post electoral system they secured only four seats. Referenda on electoral reform in 1992 and 1993 reinforced the message. Disillusioned with the lack of accountable government, and deprived of meaningful choice between the traditional political parties, the majority voted to change the electoral system itself to mixed-member proportional representation (MMP).

The message was clear: even if the New Zealand economy was showing some signs of recovering, many of the people were not.

What the self-authorised attestors of success—the major industrial powers, the self-interested players in the capital markets, the evangelical libertarian intellectuals and free-market economists, the financial journalists of trans-national media, the credit rating agencies with their own vested interests, and the like—were really applauding was the unimpeded imposition of a particular ideological model to which they adhered, notwithstanding its economic and social consequences. This interpretation of 'success' remained largely unexplained, and independent evidence in support of their claims was rare. Constant repetition and mutual reinforcement helped elevate the rhetoric beyond effective critique.

The mission of New Zealand's change agents had been to initiate and entrench the 'right' policies, not to secure socially acceptable outcomes. According to their theory the two would ultimately coincide. In the process, they rationalised the costs to individuals, families and communities as inevitable and short-term. They ignored the divergence between prevailing social values and those of the market, and the implications for social coherence in the years ahead. They failed to recognise the tensions between limited government, market power, political stability and the legitimacy of the state. And they remained oblivious to the impact of an individualised, privatised and internationalised society on human development, cultural identity and the sense of belonging to a community that cares.

The success of the New Zealand experiment must be evaluated in its broader context, including the short-term effects of the process itself, and its legacy for domestic economic life, social development, governance and cultural identity in the years ahead. This book seeks to begin that task.

PART ONE

THE PROCESS

CHAPTER ONE

Setting the Scene

BECAUSE THE NEW ZEALAND experiment was embarked on voluntarily, and not imposed by the international financial institutions, its international context tends to be ignored. But the pressures that drove many countries into structural adjustment were not confined to the third world.

There is a tendency in New Zealand, common to most Western democracies, to assume that the idea of a national economy has existed since time immemorial. Yet it is a relatively recent creation, born of particular economic conditions. The colonisation of Aotearoa (New Zealand) in 1840 was part of the nineteenth-century British, American and German expansion that aggressively promoted the economic interests of these countries throughout the world. The recession of the 1880s, the emergence of mass production and the growth of trade unionism prompted these powers and the interests of capital to retreat into self-contained domestic economies. As Joseph Camilleri and Jim Falk record:

> By the end of the 19th century, all capitalist states were in varying degrees involved in regulating the business cycle, overseeing industrial relations, supplying credit and subsidies to industry, funding scientific and technological research, organising energy, transport and communications systems, and managing the external relations of the economy. The functions of the state did not derive so much from the logic of sovereignty or the will of the sovereigns as from the needs of national economic expansion.[1]

It is important not to overstate the extent of that autonomy. Metropolitan states may have enjoyed a large degree of economic autonomy, but the majority of the world's states at this time were trapped within exploitive and subordinated colonial economic relations.

For the first half of the twentieth century, expanding industrial capitalism was protected and promoted by governments within their domestic economies. Border barriers were erected to protect the developing economic base, while full employment and wealth redistribution through progressive taxes and the welfare state ensured a viable consumer base. In the picturesque terms of historian Eric Hobsbawm, 'world capitalism retreated into the igloos of its nation-state economies and their associated empires'.[2] The image of the world became centred on individual political units, each with a supreme authority enjoying the allegiance of its citizens and, in theory at least, exercising an unlimited capacity to dispose of the territory and resources of that society.[3]

In many ways, this period of economic nationalism can be seen as a temporary interlude. As Hobsbawm observes, classical liberal writings, such as Adam Smith's seminal anti-mercantilist treatise on *The Wealth of Nations (1776)*,[4] saw no place for protectionism or national economic development strategies in a world market committed to free trade. But the goal of a single global economy was not yet attainable. Large-scale states, limited by the 'threshold principle' to those which were economically viable, were thus conceived of 'by the ideologists of the era of triumphant bourgeois liberalism [as] part of liberal ideology . . . because the development of nations was unquestionably a phase in human evolution or progress from the small group to the larger, from family to tribe to region, to nation and, in the last instance, to the unified world of the future . . .'[5]

By the 1970s, that interlude appeared to be ending. The simple model of the sovereign nation-state with its national economy, national polity, national legal system and national identity no longer fitted the global reality. Major corporations were outgrowing their national boundaries. The number of companies operating multi-nationally expanded rapidly as they sought out new markets and innovative ways to circumvent domestic barriers. International trade between nation-states increasingly gave way to global economic transactions between and within trans-national corporate enterprises (TCEs). Their inherent flexibility, and their superior access to finance, technology, skills and economies of scale, enabled these firms to dominate a national economy and evade its regulatory regimes. Inflows of overseas capital could crowd out smaller domestic investors who were more likely to be committed to the particular industry, workforce, domestic economy and local community. TCEs had little interest in the social and economic consequences of their decisions. Whether they were locally controlled ultimately made no difference.

The dominance of trans-national enterprise, the ascendancy of finance capital, and the rapid expansion of the services sector were all boosted by advances in technology. Governments found it difficult to regulate the flow of money and capital across their boundaries, and to control economic activities through domestic regulation. This, in turn, restricted their ability to gather taxes and maintain their physical and social infrastructure. Threats by capital to disinvest, often backed by warnings of credit rating downgrades, imposed additional constraints on national governments.

The global economy was further shaped by the election of conservative free-market governments in the United States, United Kingdom and Germany—countries that could apply significant leverage in the rest of the world. The demise of the Soviet Union removed the West's main strategic and ideological combatant. Institutions like the OECD, International Monetary Fund (IMF), World Bank and credit rating agencies pressed conformity with the 'free market' model. Neo-liberal economics and philosophy dominated intellectual discourse, radiating out primarily from the United States.

Western capitalist democracies faced a dilemma. Tensions had emerged between the need of capital to accumulate profits, the need of the state to administer its increasingly large and costly machinery, and the need of government to secure loyalty and co-operation from the mass of its citizens by providing a reasonable standard of living, paid employment and political participation. Minor adjustments, it seemed, were no longer enough. Major structural changes were required.

Western governments saw themselves facing a stark choice between the promotion of profit through the free market, and the protection of the welfare state through government intervention. Pressure and encouragement from international economic interests made the latter increasingly difficult, even for governments of a social democratic stamp. The neo-liberal model implemented through structural adjustment became dominant. Attributing this solely to the hegemony of international capital is too easy. Governments of individual countries, especially those free from 'conditionalities' attached to loans, still had policy choices about which path to take and how far and how fast to move.

The Washington consensus

In 1990 United States academic John Williamson set out what has been termed the 'Washington consensus' of key elements in a structural adjustment programme.[6] These are:

- *fiscal discipline*: keeping government budgets small enough that, after debt servicing, the operating deficit is no more than 2 percent of GDP;
- *public expenditure priorities*: redirecting expenditure from politically sensitive areas and 'white elephants' towards neglected fields which are economically productive, strengthen the country's infrastructure, or have the potential to improve income redistribution, such as primary health and education;
- *tax reform*: reducing marginal tax rates to sharpen incentives for companies and individuals to earn more, and broadening the tax base to improve horizontal equity;
- *deregulation*: abolition of regulations which impede entry of new firms or restrict competition, while ensuring that all other regulations can be justified by criteria such as safety, environmental protection, or prudential supervision of financial institutions;
- *foreign direct investment*: removal of investment barriers impeding foreign firms, with all receiving 'national treatment' (the same treatment as domestic firms);
- *financial liberalisation*: progressively move towards market-determined interest rates within a less constrained financial marketplace;
- *exchange rates*: a single exchange rate that is set at a level that encourages expansion of non-traditional exports and managed in a way that assures exporters of continued competitiveness;
- *trade liberalisation*: rapid conversion of quantitative trade restrictions, such as import quotas, into tariffs, and the progressive reduction of tariffs to between 10 and 20 percent;
- *privatisation*: of state enterprises and assets;
- *property rights*: ensuring security of property rights under law without excessive costs.[7]

Williamson observed that within this 'consensus' there was room for differences in some areas: the desirability of maintaining capital controls; the extent and pace of inflation reduction; the usefulness of incomes policy and wage and price freezes; the need to eliminate indexation; the propriety of attempting to correct market failures through such techniques as compensatory taxation; the proportion of GDP to take in tax and expenditure by the public sector; how far income should be redistributed in the interests of equity; whether there is a role for industrial policy; the model of market economy to be sought (Anglo-Saxon laissez-faire, European social market, Japanese-style responsibility of corporations to multiple stakeholders); and the priority given to environmental preservation.[8]

Even within the 'Washington consensus', therefore, a range of positions was available. Choosing a point on this spectrum would depend on the economic, social, political and cultural conditions of the particular country and the inclinations of those responsible for its economic policy. Countries similar to New Zealand, notably Australia,[9] chose quite different paths in the 1980s. So, despite the frequent claims by those driving the New Zealand experiment that 'there was no alternative', there clearly *was*. On behalf of the people of New Zealand, the Labour government *chose* to take the 'Washington consensus' to its neo-liberal extreme.

The laboratory

New Zealand in 1984 provided almost perfect political, economic and intellectual conditions in which to experiment. It had a small, relaxed Pakeha (of European origin) population of just over three million people. As a British colony, it had developed a deep dependence on, and expectation of, major power paternalism. The historically high standard of living and quality of life bred a complacency that the world would always stay the same. The bulk of the Pakeha population were ill equipped to respond to, let alone struggle against, the onset of radical change. For indigenous Maori, who had a long history of resistance to the colonial state, economic fundamentalism was a variation on the theme. Their opposition, while more persistent, never threatened to derail the structural adjustment programme.

New Zealand culture

Until after World War II Pakeha had no strong culture of their own. The dominant identity during the nineteenth century combined rugged settler individualism with enduring colonial ties, and defined itself in opposition to the indigenous Maori.[10] As labour economist Nigel Haworth explains:

> New Zealand *pakeha* society was more than the search for a new identity by rugged individualistic pioneers seeking freedom from the apron

strings of Victoria's Britain. Language, literature, song, popular culture, educational processes, sporting ties, familial contact, military service, religious observance, gardening habits, and a host of other ties suspended the settler society between the old and the new. In a sense, the identities of person and policy were similarly Janus-like, confronting the new yet constrained by the old.[11]

This cultural ambivalence changed only slowly over the years. What altered more rapidly was the relationship of the individual to the state. The welfare state introduced from 1935 fostered a social democratic ideal of the harmonious classless society based on the conformist, upwardly mobile, two-parent, consumption-oriented family unit, cosseted by a benevolent government. Although this provided only a palliative to structural inequalities for Maori, women, workers and the poor, the ideals of welfarism became deeply embedded in the Pakeha self-image.

A more mature self-image of the New Zealander gradually emerged. From the 1970s, the influence of feminism gave women more visibility and voice. Maori challenged the monocultural status quo and asserted their tangata whenua (first nation) rights over the land. Immigrants, first from the Pacific Islands and later from Asia, broadened the country's cultural base. This diversity, in turn, made unity and national identity increasingly hard to find.

There was a corresponding void in independent critical thought. Most academics did their post-graduate training overseas, which tended to perpetuate dependence on theories and perspectives developed in quite alien contexts. The small market for local publications, and limited media outlets, also accounted for the weak development of a national intellectual tradition, or even a strong contest of ideas.

The one point of apparent unity was sport. Despite periodic troughs, New Zealand maintained a high profile on the international sporting stage. The dream of high performance, or just the comradeship and adrenalin of the match, provided an escape from people's daily lives. It had a genuine levelling effect. The status of rugby, netball or athletic star was attainable by all, irrespective of race and class (although not gender). Sport also provided one of the country's most divisive points of conflict, as the tension between sport and politics split the country in 1981, with often violent mass demonstrations against the Springbok rugby tour.

Despite such episodes, at the popular political level Pakeha lacked a strong history of class struggle, resistance to external domination, or militancy on which to call. Over the years, the sectors of potential opposition among labour and women had become deeply integrated into the two-party political system. This left them unable or unwilling to mobilise effectively against major structural change.

The strengths and the weaknesses of the New Zealand union movement stemmed from the landmark Industrial Conciliation and Arbitration Act 1894 and its successors. The state had encouraged the formation of employer and employee unions, given them monopoly rights in industrial organisation and bargaining, imposed what was in effect compulsory unionism, and incorporated them into a state-controlled conciliation and arbitration process. Organisations of state employees, although unregistered and not compulsory, enjoyed broad support from postal and telecommunications workers, teachers, nurses, police, fire-fighters, railway workers and public servants. Rare outbreaks of union militancy in the 1890s, 1910s and early 1950s were brutally suppressed.

The alliance between the political and industrial limbs of the labour movement came with the formation of the Labour Party in 1916. This provided the foundations for what political commentator Bruce Jesson termed the 'historic compromise', a 'long term reconciliation with capitalism, not just by the Labour Government but by the entire New Zealand working class'. Labour came to power in the post-Depression election of 1935. 'Instead of using the state to overthrow capitalism as they had originally intended, the Labour leaders used the state to stabilise it. . . . Most of the country's social and political forces benefited from the welfare state and the regulated economy, but in return they moderated their political aims.'[12] The result was a solid union movement, but one that was occupationally based, geographically dispersed, and politically dependent on the Labour Party.

The organised women's movement was primarily liberal, Pakeha and middle class, mobilising around campaigns on abortion, pay equity, health, peace and anti-nuclear issues. A well-executed feminist infiltration of the Labour Party forced these issues onto the mainstream political agenda. Deteriorating social and economic conditions in the late 1970s led to a more decentralised form of politics through women's refuges, rape crisis centres and childcare networks, which had an important impact on many women's lives. These strategies remained outside, but generally vulnerable to, the power of the state.

Although Pakeha largely remained docile through the welfare state

years, they did resent being pushed around by their own governments, or by a foreign power. The 1960s saw the emergence of
protest movements which ran strong and successful campaigns
against apartheid, the Vietnam war, nuclear weapons and destructive environmental projects. But these movements tended to be based
on a single issue, diffuse and frequently short term. In the 1970s
and early 1980s Prime Minister Robert Muldoon, out of touch with
the changing times, provoked confrontations over Maori land occupations, sanctioned police raids on immigrants, short-circuited environmental legislation, refused to intervene over French nuclear
testing and split the country down the middle by insisting that the
1981 Springbok rugby tour went ahead. Muldoon's authoritarian
response bolstered demands from diverse groups for political, economic and cultural change.

The election of the fourth Labour government in 1984 made
social movements feel more secure. Labour was, after all, the party
of the workers, of women, of the peace movement and of the greens.
They promised to—and did—close the South African embassy, tell
the French to stop their nuclear tests, and declare New Zealand
waters nuclear-free. Few social activists knew what Labour's economic policy was, and probably not many cared. Some applauded it,
accepting the claims that 'there was no alternative'.

The Treaty of Waitangi

In contrast to Pakeha, Maori had an enduring vision of politics,
economics, society and identity, located within residual tribal entities which commanded great loyalty. This made for a sharper critique of the role of the state, of welfarism, and of claims to social
equality and multiracial harmony. It also guided the quest for forward-looking alternatives, which frequently required radical economic and constitutional change—although there was also diversity
among Maori views.

While Pakeha tended to see New Zealand in 1984 as an independent, post-colonial state governed by a Westminster-style Parliament and the rule of law, for many Maori, Aotearoa[13] was still
occupied by a colonial power. They had resisted through military,
extra-legal, legal and political means the usurpation of tribal sovereignty for almost 150 years. Their main point of reference was the
Treaty of Waitangi, signed in 1840 between representatives of Maori
tribes and the British Crown. The treaty had guaranteed the tribes

tino rangatiratanga—continued exercise of independent authority over their lives and their land—a promise that settler governments systematically breached. Observers from outside New Zealand tend to be surprised that the treaty occupies such a prominent position in political discourse. Yet in a country as small as New Zealand, Maori politics is an inescapable part of political life.[14]

Since the 1970s the resurgence of Maori activism centred on the treaty had been sustained, high profile and intense. Yet very few Pakeha in 1984, including politicians, technocrats, economists and media, understood the complexity of the issues or that their responses were often counter-productive. The National government's reaction between 1975 and 1984 had been to dismiss and repress the revitalisation of Maori movements. This fuelled the grievances and intensified Maori demands for their resources and power to be restored. Before the 1984 election, Labour promised to honour the Treaty of Waitangi and set in train a process to settle outstanding grievances. When Labour failed to deliver, and refused to engage with the issue of political power, expectations turned to frustration and various forms of resistance were renewed. For most of the restructuring period, however, Maori remained no more than an irritant to be neutralised.

The economy
Economic conditions also provided fertile ground for the experiment. The New Zealand economy was intrinsically vulnerable. Historically, the colony had offered a home for Britain's surplus population and a garden in the south seas, built on resources taken from Maori. Its agricultural base, sustained by guaranteed markets, provided a high standard of living for most of the white settler population, and deep impoverishment for Maori.

During the twentieth century the state harnessed the natural resources of land, forests, coal, geothermal and hydro power for commercial and social purposes. Like most Western liberal democracies after the Depression, the Labour government from 1935 to 1949 pursued orthodox Keynesian economics, with limited nationalisation, social welfare and employment protection. Infrastructural services like rail, communications and banking were expanded to serve economic, employment and social development goals. Protection of the domestic market, introduced by Labour in the late 1930s, was continued with some ambivalence under National governments in the 1950s and 1960s, in order to support the fledgling industrial base. Full employment became the central plank of economic and social policy. The state emerged as the country's major employer. While government played an active role, the economy remained heavily dependent on domestic agriculture, foreign finance and the British market.

In the late 1960s this protected, state-centred, vulnerable agricultural economy was set adrift as Britain sought more fertile pastures within the then European Economic Community. As the world economy changed rapidly, so did New Zealand's capital base. In the 1970s, major companies in the key forestry, construction, insurance and finance sectors merged. The traditional oligarchy was being replaced by a new generation of entrepreneurs. External crises, notably the oil shocks, and the changing international economy fed increasing demands for domestic and trade liberalisation. There were some moves during the Muldoon years to deregulate aspects of the economy, but these were partial and ad hoc. Costly attempts to build energy self-sufficiency and Muldoon's resistance to change saw debt, inflation, economic stagnation and unemployment rise. Fewer than 3000 people had been registered as unemployed in 1975; by 1980 there were nearly 21,000.

Despite the economic situation, National continued its policy of tax write-offs and subsidies, most notably the supplementary minimum price guarantee to farmers. The political advantage outweighed the economic costs. The deepening problems with the economy brought further intervention from Muldoon by way of the wage, price, rent and interest rate freezes of 1982. By 1984 the number of unemployment beneficiaries had topped 50,000. Early that year an IMF report condemning Muldoon's approach was leaked to the press. Mutiny was stirring within his party's ranks. At the same time economic fundamentalism was becoming firmly established within the Labour opposition, the Treasury and the corporate élite.

Parliamentary politics

The process of structural adjustment was made easier by the shallowness of New Zealand's political system—a classic single-tier Westminster-style Parliament, elected on first-past-the-post (FPP), with an entrenched two-party monopoly. A reform-minded Cabinet was virtually guaranteed the unimpeded power to rule. There was no formal written constitution or supreme Bill of Rights by which the courts could constrain the Executive's powers. The burgeoning state bureaucracy was increasingly, though not always fairly, ridiculed for its inefficiency. The comprehensive welfare system was largely taken for granted, while benefit support had been extended since 1968 to single mothers and others whom many viewed as the 'undeserving poor'.

Party politics was a tame affair. During the welfare era, political factionalism had consolidated into a rigid two-party system with strong internal discipline. National had been in power for 29 of the 49 years since 1935. Labour had spent three spells in government, 1935–49, 1957–60 and 1972–75. The political system was traditionally stable. National took the rural vote, Labour the working class, and the two parties contested the middle ground of provincial towns and middle-class city suburbs with a pragmatic policy mix. In theory, the two major parties reflected conflicting class positions. National, supported by farmers and business, was committed to a conservative, free-enterprise platform; Labour, representing mainly working class and Maori, espoused first democratic socialism, then social democratic politics. In practice, both parties pursued pragmatic interventionism. Large, national sector groups such as farmers and trade unions were incorporated into policy-making and became active participants in party and government machines. The result was ad hoc, captured decision-making of the kind so criticised by the later public choice theorists. But this corporatist approach also consolidated the foundations of state power.

Social, economic and political changes disturbed that equilibrium in the early 1970s. National was unattractive to the educated, affluent younger voter and the new entrepreneurs. Muldoon's focus on conservative social policies and economic security appealed primarily to the less educated and the elderly. The more he depended on them, the less room he had to embrace the 'more-market' approach.

By the early 1980s a new policy mix crossed traditional boundaries. Industry, financial institutions, Maori, home owners and workers were all impatient with Muldoon's economic interventions and political authoritarianism, although for quite different reasons. Party politics were also volatile. The formation of the Values Party in 1972 was an early indicator that the two-party system was breaking down. Values secured 5 percent of the vote in 1975. Continued support for the Social Credit Political League, which gained around 16 percent of the national vote in 1978, was another. In the 1981 election its support rose to 21.7 percent, although the league won only two seats. This fell away to 7.6 percent in 1984.

Party and parliamentary leadership of both Labour and National became dominated by professionals divorced from the traditional class base. Many of the well-educated political and social activists, interested primarily in non-economic issues, had in the 1960s and early 1970s gravitated to the Labour Party, where they occupied something of an organisational vacuum. A number rose rapidly through the party's ranks and formed part of the new intake of MPs in 1984. This generation of activists were more modernisers than socialists, and had a sceptical or even hostile attitude to the state. Given that Muldoon was deeply identified with the strong, interventionist central state, it was not surprising that anti-Muldoon sentiments were often also anti-state.

Pressures for change were reinforced by a growing band of free marketeers within Muldoon's own caucus. In 1983 three National MPs, including later finance minister Ruth Richardson, crossed the floor of Parliament to oppose a Bill that enshrined mortgage rate controls in legislation. These dissidents pushed through a number of changes. The CER agreement, providing for greater trade harmonisation with Australia, was signed in 1983. Transport and trade began to be deregulated. An agreement between government and industry to convert import licences to tariffs was signed. Voluntary unionism was introduced. But progress was slow.

In 1984 the frustrations of the new generation of market evangelists came to a head. The neo-liberal New Zealand Party (NZP), led by entrepreneur Bob Jones, played a pivotal role in Muldoon's downfall. This was a new phenomenon in New Zealand politics. Jones's campaign has been likened to Ross Perot's in the United States presidential election in 1992: the combination of 'money, colorful personality, and blunt talk made the NZP an overnight sensation'.[15] The party's anti-state, pro-market platform confused the traditional left–right configuration of Labour and National by condemning the welfare state and economic interventionism, while endorsing a nuclear-free New Zealand and attacking Muldoon's authoritarianism. NZP secured 12.3 percent of the vote, but no seats (see Figure 12.1). The party also loosened traditional allegiances. Most of its votes came from National, and turned a narrow Labour victory into a landslide.

Outgoing Prime Minister Muldoon refused to follow convention and hand over power immediately after losing the July 1984 snap election, thus preventing the new Labour government from devaluing the dollar. A rush of speculators' money out of the country created a liquidity crisis and a sense of economic emergency. This opened the way for economic fundamentalists in Treasury and the Reserve Bank, their fellow-travellers in the new Labour government, and supportive individuals and lobby groups in the corporate sector, to implement the strategy they had been working on for several years. With almost evangelical fervour, those driving first the Labour and then the National governments set about redesigning the economic and social structure of New Zealand.

CHAPTER TWO

Capturing the Political Machine

CONDITIONS IN NEW ZEALAND in 1984 may have been conducive to fundamental economic change, but structural adjustment, as distinct from pragmatic reform, required something more. There had to be a systematic programme, carried out with precision and discipline by a group of strategically placed individuals, and supported by institutional power.

A 1993 colloquium, sponsored by the Washington-based Institute for International Economics (IIE), examined the political factors that made the implementation of structural adjustment possible in a range of developing and advanced capitalist countries, including New Zealand.[1] The goal of the IIE's colloquium was to devise a manual for technocrats (defined as 'those who advocate organisation and management of a country's industrial resources by technical experts for the good of the whole community')[2] and technopols (technocrats who have assumed a position of political responsibility) involved in implementing structural adjustment programmes.

The IIE study tested a number of hypotheses formulated by its convenor John Williamson. Societies, he suggested, have a natural tendency to become sclerotic and their flexibility declines. When a major crisis occurs within the existing system, it creates new opportunities for actors who until then have been prevented from taking the initiative. Where a crisis does not occur 'naturally', it might make sense to provoke one to induce reform. The most effective time for the reforming government to act is the honeymoon stage immediately after taking power, when the need for, and costs of, reform can be blamed on previous governments. Alternatively, the reforming government could seek a mandate and disclose the agenda in an election campaign. The problem of sustaining the changes until they bear fruit might be overcome by deliberately creating a group of beneficiaries likely to fight to protect the reforms. Structural adjustment is likely to be easier where the opposition can be discredited and disrupted, or repressed.

Successful implementation, according to the hypothesis, also requires a team of technocrats who have a common, coherent view of what needs to be done and who command the instruments of executive power. They need a leader with a vision of history who is unconcerned about the political or personal fall-out from radical and unpopular reform, and who will preferably be a technopol. Rapid and comprehensive reform will be more appropriate in some situations than others. Because 'theoretical merit and internal consistency in a reform programme are not enough to generate political support',[3] those who implement the programme need to appeal to the general public through the media, and bypass vested interests (such as unions) which can be expected to oppose change.

Williamson's review of the twelve case studies strongly supported three of these hypotheses: the need for a strong political base, visionary leadership and a coherent economic team.[4] The possibility of exploiting crises or honeymoons, and the importance of developing a comprehensive programme, occurred frequently enough to justify being 'borne in mind'. Profound economic reforms, he noted, need not be the product of authoritarian governments, but could be achieved by democratic governments, sometimes from the left of centre.

Preparing the ground

The New Zealand experiment was a model of orthodoxy in Williamson's terms. The unstable political and economic conditions in which the 1984 snap election was called seemed almost scripted to facilitate urgent and radical change. Some believe that Roger Douglas deliberately precipitated the crisis when he 'accidentally' released a background paper several weeks before the election saying that Labour would devalue the currency by 20 percent.[5] David Lange subsequently confirmed the significance of the crisis for the structural adjustment programme:

> The circumstances of those first few days in government gave Roger the opportunity to do what he had always wanted to do anyway. But he wouldn't have been able to do that had we gone through the orthodox

routine of an election in November, then a budget in June. . . . When the crisis hit in July 1984 it was Roger Douglas who, above all, had thought through the economic issues—so when the Cabinet needed to fall back on an economic philosophy, it was Douglas who had one.[6]

Douglas operated as a classic technopol, committed to the project irrespective of the electoral consequences.[7] Although Alan Bollard suggests that Douglas had no long-term commitment to a political career, his distaste seems to have been more for democratic process than for political power. He was heavily influenced by, and dependent on, his economic advisors, and probably had a less systematic and sophisticated understanding of economic issues and the overall programme than at times was made to appear.

Douglas had a strong Labour pedigree. His father and his maternal grandfather had been Labour MPs. In 1993 he still claimed: 'My political beliefs and my general philosophy of life are all products of that Labour line.'[8] But his approach to Labour politics had always been unorthodox. Back in 1971, the accountant-turned-politician had called for the abolition of double taxation on company profits, the abandonment of various state activities, and the establishment of an efficiency measure similar to the private sector yardstick of profit.[9] Douglas carried these objectives into the 1972 Labour government. As a junior minister, he divided the then New Zealand Broadcasting Corporation into three competing state-owned enterprises and introduced an income-related contributory pension scheme. Concerns over the state's accumulation of such a large superannuation fund were exploited by Muldoon to help the National Party win the 1975 election. Labour and Douglas were returned to the opposition benches.

He refined his emerging vision in a paper prepared for the Labour Party in 1979, but it made little impact. Dissatisfied with Labour's direction, Douglas unilaterally issued an alternative budget in June 1980, expanded in his first book, *There's Got to Be a Better Way!*[10] This break with party discipline, coupled with his role in the unsuccessful attempt to replace Labour leader Bill Rowling with David Lange, saw him dropped from the shadow cabinet in 1980. With some reluctance, he agreed to stand again for election in 1981.

Labour lost that election. Douglas, assisted by a handful of other Labour MPs, several leading businessmen, an economist in the Opposition Research Unit and a Treasury official seconded to his office, set about preparing an economic blueprint for Labour's re-election in 1984. At this stage Douglas's vision became more concrete, although he depended heavily on his advisors. The team produced a 51-page 'Economic Policy Package' which sought to reduce the role of the state in the economy and foster the operation of domestic and international markets. Their strategy promoted detailed fiscal, monetary and price–income policies, radical changes in export assistance, employment, tax and industry support, and 'fairer distribution of the country's wealth' mainly through more precise targeting. According to Douglas, the package contained 'every step subsequently taken by the fourth Labour Government when it was elected to office'.[11] Some have suggested that, '[i]n the lead-up to the elections, bureaucrats from the Treasury and the Reserve Bank assisted this group and their party beyond accepted norms'.[12]

When Douglas placed his 'Economic Policy Package' before the Labour caucus and the party's policy council in 1983, in effect he asked them to turn their back on what the party stood for. This was a classic confrontation between the defenders of welfare capitalism and corporatist democracy, and the disciples of neo-liberalism and market forces. The caucus and policy council first considered the package in November 1983. Douglas claims they were split. Their position by the time the snap election was called in June 1984 remains unclear. Some say the policy was unresolved.[13] Others, including Douglas, argue that there was a deliberate muddying of future intentions.[14]

Labour's economic policy statement at the time of the election was vague. The 'foundations for economic recovery' were described as:
* consensus on the programme of economic and social reconstruction;
* a fair prices and incomes policy;
* an investment strategy to help restore full employment and reduce the external deficit;
* reform of industry assistance;
* a fair tax system;
* monetary policy that underpins a balanced growth strategy;
* fiscal policy that tackles problems caused by the internal deficit;
* the re-targeting of public resources to ensure more effective delivery of services to those in greater need.

Douglas was made Minister of Finance in the new government. His intentions soon became clear as he set about implementing the radical programme set down in Treasury's post-election briefing to the incoming government.[15] With hindsight, this might have been anticipated, as Labour's pre-election policy warned that only after the promised post-election opening of the books would the full magnitude of the country's economic problems be revealed.

Between 1984 and 1990, with a brief hiatus in 1989, Douglas oversaw the Rogernomics programme. As Bollard notes, however, Douglas 'was not a strong traditional politician. He was a poor speaker and a poor debater and was without a traditional support base.' The support of Douglas's two main associates was vital. 'David Caygill, [an] ex-lawyer, was the more intellectual, able to present the case for liberalization in its theoretical terms. Richard Prebble, yet another ex-lawyer, was forceful and streetwise, able to argue the case with dissenting groups inside and outside the party. The ministers proved to be a most effective trio.'[16] Other members of the Cabinet played a supporting role.

The honeymoon
Labour's 1984 pre-election policy statement had promised 'a more democratic approach to economic management', including summit meetings on prices and incomes and on employment. The government made a show of consultation in its first few months, convening a multi-sectoral economic summit conference at Parliament in September 1984. Australia's Prime Minister Bob Hawke had made a similar move the previous year as part of Labor's 'Accord' to gain support for a more gradual and pragmatic programme of economic reform. Many New Zealanders assumed their Labour government was following the same path. The summit proceedings resounded with talk of unity and self-sacrifice. There were calls to maintain the pace of reform, with participation by all sectors at all levels in public decision-making, and on-going consultation and distribution of information to build on the new-found spirit of co-operation.[17]

Whether the summit was a deliberate smokescreen or reflected a genuine desire for participatory decision-making by some within a divided Cabinet remains unclear. Douglas initially denied that it was a stage-managed affair, but did admit 'it was designed to dramatise the problems of the economy to the nation and create the right climate for change' leading up to his first budget.[18] After his retirement and Labour's defeat in 1990 he gave a more forthright, if retrospectively tinged, explanation. In a speech to an accountants' conference where he attacked the practices of lobby groups, Douglas stated that '[b]lunting their power was the real role of the summit conference in that year'.

> By giving them nationwide television exposure, in a sense, we put them on public trial. Under such a spotlight they had enough sense to realise that if they persisted in seeking their own selfish, short-term interest at the expense of the wider community, then they would instantly lose the support of the public. . . . Having forced them into a commitment to put New Zealand first, or at least publicly to do so, we used the 1984 budget to hit the privileges of all the interest groups at once.[19]

The economic summit epitomised the honeymoon period of 'consultation with no real action'. That continued through 1985, and into 1986 with the establishment, under protest from the Treasury, of a Royal Commission on Social Policy. Consultations with Maori followed a similar line. A hui (meeting) to discuss Maori concerns and treaty policy was held at Ngaruawahia in October 1984, followed by discussions at Waitangi in February 1985. But inexperience, arrogance and the primacy of the structural adjustment programme saw any commitment to dialogue with Maori quickly fade. The general appeal of consultation soon worn off. People recognised that the rapidly accumulating economic changes bore no resemblance to the views being so assiduously harvested from their communities. The pretence largely stopped.

The blitzkrieg
The honeymoon phase, and the sense of economic crisis, gave the technopols the breathing space to get the programme under way. By early 1985 they were firmly in control, and began moving as far and as fast as the few institutional constraints allowed. Easton has called this the 'blitzkrieg' approach: 'In each case the lightning strike involved a policy goal radically different from the existing configuration, to be attained in a short period, following a surprise announcement and a very rapid implementation.'[20] Critics and opponents were always on the defensive and left debating last week's reforms. The major decisions would already have been taken; any consultation was limited to details. Bollard suggests that even faster implementation was constrained by the speed at which the technopols could work, not 'by any self-imposed requirements to consult with industry, or other groups, or by major concerns about correct sequencing'.[21]

Douglas used this approach equally with the general populace and with his Cabinet colleagues.[22] Speaking to the Reform Party convention in Saskatoon in 1991, he reportedly explained: 'consensus for "quality decisions" is achieved after they are made. He advised them not to reveal their program—but if elected, to implement it as quickly as possible to overwhelm the opposition.'[23] Douglas offered similar political lessons to would-be structural adjusters in his 1993 book *Unfinished Business*:

- Do not try to advance a step at a time. Define your objectives clearly and move towards them in quantum leaps. Otherwise the interest groups will have time to mobilise and drag you down.[24]
- Once the programme begins to be implemented, don't stop until you have completed it. The fire of opponents is much less accurate if they have to shoot at a rapidly moving target.[25]
- Consensus among interest groups on quality decisions rarely, if ever, arises before they are made and implemented. It develops after they are taken, as the decisions deliver satisfactory results to the public.[26]

As for consultation, Douglas observed: 'People cannot co-operate with the reform process unless they know where you are heading. Go as fast as you can but, where practicable, give the community notice in advance.'[27]

Treasury's 1984 post-election briefing papers had a similar two-stage view of 'effective' communication. 'First, before any major decisions are taken there is often a need to develop a constituency for the proposed policy change.' Where a policy area affected a range of interest groups a broad consultative process might be constructive—provided it was 'carefully handled to avoid encouraging the belief amongst particular sector groups that consultative processes will provide a vehicle for furthering their particular interest'.[28] Second came the need to publish analyses which justified policy decisions already made. Both stages sought to impart information and bring important interests on board, not to consult them about the nature and direction of change.

Despite this highly undemocratic approach, the media rarely held the new government to account. Muldoon had been notorious for his intolerance of public debate, media scrutiny and investigative reporting. Journalists were regularly subjected to intimidation and ridicule. The ascent of Lange, Douglas and the Labour government in 1984 was enthusiastically embraced by the media. Many journalists were seduced by the glamour and excitement of the pre-crash bonanza, and some turned into little more than sycophantic propagandists for Rogernomics. 'State of the market' reports and economic updates became regular features of evening telecasts. Specialist business journals like the *National Business Review* (*NBR*) moved (unsuccessfully) to daily publication. The *NBR* became an important vehicle for the ideologues to attack obstacles, denounce critics, float new ideas and prepare the ground for the next round of change. At the same time, however, the *NBR* provided an important source of information to outsiders about the current thinking of the inner élite.

Following the stock-market crash, the euphoria began to wear off. Pro-market journals like the *NBR* and less supportive columnists like Bruce Jesson in *Metro* had already begun to investigate questionable corporate activities, often with a close connection to government. But it was several more years before the run of corporate collapses, court cases and embarrassing excesses of the Rogernomics era received substantial—and still very cautious—media scrutiny.

Capture of the party machine

As Williamson hypothesised, the capture of a Labour Party historically committed to social democracy proved a major political coup and helped neutralise opposition from the left.

Labour's regional party conferences during 1985 debated and rejected the market-led approach. Few beyond the inner circles of the policy council seemed to grasp the transition that had already occurred. As the Rogernomics agenda became more widely understood, and party remits which condemned it were brushed aside, the extent of the takeover became clear. The Labour government became the vehicle for a programme which neither its members nor the electorate had endorsed, and which was irreconcilable with the basic tenets of social democracy. Those responsible were unrepentant about their arrogation of power. In Richard Prebble's words: 'You have to put politics aside. What's needed is a sensible pragmatic approach that puts the good of the country first . . . and focuses on good sound economic management.'[29]

During the government's first three-year term many of Labour's activists focused on non-economic issues, and the disaffected kept their criticism largely in-house. There were among the Labour MPs confirmed social democrats who felt increasingly ill at ease. But these were not old-fashioned socialists. Many were young, educated, middle-class professionals with a focus on anti-nuclear, defence and disarmament issues, abortion, homosexual law reform, environment, education, and health, rather than economics.[30] Many of the feminists, peace activists and environmentalists who chose to work within the Labour Party concentrated on their sectoral concerns. While they secured significant advances in specific areas, these were always limited in their scope, effect and permanency, and never seriously threatened the restructuring programme.

The left of the party seemed torn between reasserting traditional policies and forcing an electorally damaging public split, or working behind the scenes for change and re-election. The trade union movement, in particular, refused to take on 'its own' Labour government, fearful of a fate similar to the British unions under Thatcher if they lost. Lacking any coherent alternative, the left were frequently out-manoeuvred and marginalised. The institutional framework within which they were operating had been replaced by a new set of imperatives which had little respect for traditional party lines or concerns.

As the gap between traditional Labour and Rogernomics grew wider, party membership fell from around 45,000 before the election in 1984 to 11,000 in May 1988.[31] Herman Schwartz explains how this worked to the technopols' advantage in the August 1987 election:

> The inner cabinet members could afford to ignore this fall because they received NZ$3.7 million in campaign funds directly from the newly concentrated financial sector, and this allowed them to launch an American-style, capital-intensive, media-oriented electoral campaign. Strict spending limits on campaigns for individual parliamentary candidates made them dependent on the inner cabinet's 'generic' advertising.[32]

Labour was re-elected in 1987 with crucial support from former New Zealand Party voters and the *nouveaux riches*. The party's full manifesto was only issued two weeks after the election. Treasury's post-election briefing papers reinforced suspicions that Rogernomics would be extended to social policy during Labour's second term. Aware of the risk that reaction to the October 1987 share-market crash might derail the programme, Douglas, reappointed as Minister of Finance, launched a new offensive.[33] His December 17 economic package centred on a flat income tax rate and radical changes to social support, most of which Prime Minister Lange subsequently renounced.

Lange's attempts to hold the line against what he termed 'the excesses' in Labour's second term failed. Although Prebble was dismissed from the Cabinet in November 1988, and Douglas was forced to resign the next month, the respite was short-lived. The technopols' grip on executive power was confirmed when Douglas was re-elected to Cabinet eight months later, although he was not reinstated as Minister of Finance. Lange's position became untenable, and he resigned. Prebble regained his Cabinet seat in early 1990.

Conflict within the party also spilled into the public arena. At the 1987 party conference a loose coalition called the Broad Left had won the majority of party positions, owing mainly to trade union votes. But their influence remained marginal. The public sector unions were hit without warning with the State Sector Bill which in effect privatised their workforce. Promises made to the 1988 conference that the party would be consulted about any departure from the manifesto were undermined or ignored. Sydenham MP and former party president (1979–84) Jim Anderton resigned in protest at privatisation of the Bank of New Zealand and Postbank, and formed the NewLabour Party, based on old Labour principles.

Public conflict broke out between Backbone Club supporters of Rogernomics and the Broad Left, who sought to reinstate the social democratic line and protect union voting rights in the party. Prebble and the Backbone Club wanted affiliated union participation confined to the national, rather than electorate, level. The resulting changes to the party's constitution were more moderate. They introduced new requirements covering union affiliation ballots, reduced union representation at national policy council and electorate committees, and tightened rules governing participation in selection processes at electorate level. By then active union participation in the party was falling anyway.

Labour's fortunes internally, and in the opinion polls, were in decline. In November 1990 the party's mailing list was only 37,000, with financial membership perhaps less than a third of that figure. There was no money for a big election campaign in 1990. Labour spent just $1 million, and even that left it $400,000 in debt.[34] Just six weeks short of the election, with more than half of the Cabinet predicted to lose their seats, a new leader, Mike Moore, was brought in to attract back the traditional Labour vote.

Despite Labour's claim to have rediscovered its roots, many of its former supporters remained unconvinced. Labour had lied to them. It had promised to maintain social services, but it cut them. It had promised to retain state assets, but it sold them. It had promised full employment, but it produced record unemployment. It had promised constitutional government and the rule of law, but it circumvented, overrode and treated with contempt the democratic processes of representation, participation and accountability.

The political promoters of Rogernomics saw the writing on the wall. They had achieved all they could through the Labour Party. Several of the mainstays, including Douglas, opted to retire. Many others lost their seats in a humiliating defeat for which they were justifiably blamed. Only a few diehard supporters were left. But they were severely weakened by the parliamentary wing's attempts to distance itself from Rogernomics, and outnumbered in the caucus by the economic 'wets' foisted on them by the Labour Party hierarchy.

Prime Minister for most of Labour's turbulent six years, David Lange, later reflected on the time:

> The risk of being a reforming government, being a radical government, is that you develop a taste for, in fact an enormous appetite for the adrenalin of change and you take it beyond what is acceptable and rational. We got thrown out of office because we went beyond that which was essential and we started to pursue things for their own sake and for the sake of ideology. That is an outcome which I regret. I apologise however for nothing of what we did to begin with. . . . The outcome was that in the course of about three years we changed from being a country run like a Polish shipyard into one that could be internationally competitive. . . . [T]here is something fairer about a society which is transparent in its reward to people who work and doesn't preserve for those who don't an inevitable flow of money.[35]

After 1990 the Labour opposition tried desperately to create a new image which appealed to the markets, the political middle ground, and its traditional support, by keeping the 'good' and divesting the 'bad' of the Rogernomics years. But the markets were nervous once political and electoral considerations had returned to Labour's agenda. Popular opinion and the media were equally suspicious, observing that most of Labour's leaders had played a central role in imposing the structural adjustment programme, or at least had not publicly stood out against it.

Capturing the National Party

National's fortunes followed a reverse pattern. After Muldoon's landslide election defeat in 1984, the party faced a long period of leadership instability and factional struggles for control between the interventionists and the free marketeers. There was the added problem that Labour had stolen National's traditional ground as the party of individual liberty and free enterprise.

Outraged that he was denied the chance to stand down as leader on his own terms in 1984, Muldoon waged public war on his successor, Jim McLay. Muldoon, as a backbencher, and his 'Sunday club' supporters ridiculed and undermined McLay at every turn. Almost two years of poor performance and disastrous poll ratings prompted a leadership coup in March 1986 which brought farmer Jim Bolger to power. A survivor of the Muldoon Cabinet, Bolger had pro-market sympathies, pragmatic politics, a solid, saleable public image, good organisation skills and an ability to talk to each side.

Within the party, president Sue Wood and general secretary Barrie Leay set about turning the ideological tide. Wood's image as a young, urban, educated, capable and forward-thinking woman helped rejuvenate the party's flagging base. After taking over in 1982 she set about neutralising the damaging effects of Muldoon, strengthening the party's relationship with the caucus and rebuilding local support. Strong international connections and local business contacts played a critical role in the party's transformation. National developed links with what party historian Barry Gustafson called an 'international alliance of anti-socialist political parties'. A formal alliance and close working relationship emerged with overseas conservative parties, including the Republicans in the US and the British Conservatives, where they 'started to exchange information about policies, techniques, strategies and organisational structures'.[36] Party organisational leaders met several times a year. The inaugural meeting of the International Democratic Union, organised by British Prime Minister Margaret Thatcher, was attended by Wood and Leay in 1983. Others who became leading National technopols became involved in its youth wing.

When Wood stood down in August 1986, she was replaced as president by businessman Neville Young. The momentum waned. The 1987 party manifesto reflected the continued internal policy battles and the difficulty of staking out political ground which distinguished the party from Labour. Funding and votes became a problem, as many of National's key supporters, and corporate sponsors, withdrew their support.

The tide finally turned in early 1988 with Lange's rejection of

Douglas's December 1987 economic package. Business leaders now looked beyond Labour. National's new finance spokesperson and former Federated Farmers legal advisor, Ruth Richardson, began doing the rounds of the major corporates, and secured a foothold in the commercial community. With improved resources, including secondment of a Treasury official to her office, Richardson set about constructing an alternative economic vision which would surpass Douglas's for ideological purity. She built around her a team of enthusiastic like-minded young MPs who would later become National's technopols. Political columnist Denis Welch observed that, by mid-1988, 'Richardson's team is the engine-room of party policy direction and growth'.[37]

Young was replaced as president in 1989 by John Collinge, recently retired chair of the Commerce Commission, pro-market and an experienced political campaigner. Collinge supported the substance of Labour's structural reforms and was instrumental in bringing the National Party on-side. But he was more an old-school Tory than an economic fundamentalist, and publicly cautioned against extreme viewpoints and the social harm an unduly polarised society could cause. While Collinge was in favour of privatisation, he created considerable disquiet by warning of the risks should public monopolies be taken over by private monopolies before genuine markets had been created.

The ideological battle continued within caucus ranks. Populist National MP Winston Peters campaigned on a platform of economic interventionism and anti-corruption, and topped the public opinion polls as preferred Prime Minister. At the other extreme, Richardson and her team of ideologically driven colleagues were vowing to finish the job Labour had begun, and bring National's traditional constituencies of farmers and employers back into the fold.

In 1990 National won 67 of the 97 seats. The new intake was predominantly from the professions.[38] The 1990 manifesto promised a pragmatic government, with Bolger as Prime Minister and his senior colleagues Bill Birch and Don McKinnon in control of the parliamentary team. Richardson had been kept off the public platform in marginal seats. But business interests made it clear that they expected her to be appointed Minister of Finance in return for supporting National, both financially and electorally; and she was. Richardson was dedicated to her task and, borrowing a phrase from Thatcher, declared 'this lady's not for turning'. Her contempt for electoral democracy was even more overt than Prebble's had been:

> The myth is that the democratic method is that institutional arrangement for arriving at political decisions which realises the common good by making the people themselves decide. The reality is the process of arriving at decisions through a competitive struggle for the people's vote. Party politicians are the response to the fact that the electoral mass is incapable of action other than a stampede.[39]

Richardson enjoyed considerably more strategic Cabinet support than Douglas initially had. Observers estimate that at least twelve of the 1990 Cabinet were free-market ideologues, giving them effective control.[40] Whether that was a deliberate move by Bolger remains unclear. Under National, Cabinet membership reflects the Prime Minister's choice. But he may have had little option. A number of key technopols were among the most competent and experienced National MPs, and could hardly have been left out in a caucus of newcomers.

As Douglas found with Labour, not all Richardson's colleagues supported her programme. The unwieldy government caucus contained widely differing views. Peters remained publicly outspoken, despite the restraints of a Cabinet position. Minor deviations in policy were made to placate MPs who feared that broken election promises on superannuation and rural postal delivery would lose them their seats. Some MPs who remained unhappy with the Cabinet's programme defected. Peters was finally expelled from the caucus and the party in 1993 and created his own party, New Zealand First. The purge of Peters put an end to the public division and, under a new presidency, the party appeared united behind the fundamentalist line.

National's electoral committees complained, to little avail, that the continuation of Rogernomics was not what they had campaigned for.[41] Traditional constituents, especially the elderly, felt betrayed by a series of broken promises and were angry at the dismissive arrogance many ministers displayed. Farmers, who had returned to the National fold in 1990 and generally supported the liberalisation programme, mobilised at party conferences against the social impact of other aspects of the reforms. Conservative attitudes to immigration and foreign ownership confronted National's liberal commitment to an open economy, for which imported skilled labour and capital were pre-requisites. Attempts to portray New Zealand as part of Asia further unsettled National's insecure traditionalist base. National's moves to placate Treaty of Waitangi claims drew allegations of special treatment from some MPs and party stalwarts, and blanket assertions of 'one people, one nation, one law'. These reactions were accommodated by minor adjustments to the government's programme. But so long as private enterprise was securely in support of structural change, the technopols remained unconcerned.

In 1993 National's electoral fortunes flagged. The binding referendum vote in favour of electoral reform foreshadowed a turbulent three-year term as individuals and parties repositioned themselves for MMP. With a narrow one-seat election victory, political pragmatism re-emerged. Bolger brought into Cabinet people of more pragmatic or moderate stance. Richardson was sacrificed as Minister of Finance, having lost most of her power in, and support from, the business community earlier in the year. Unwilling to remain impotent on the back benches, she resigned in 1994—but not before steering through the select committee process a 'fiscal responsibility' package which she hoped would cement her legacy in law.

Richardson was replaced by an economic pragmatist with deeply conservative social beliefs. Bill Birch had been Muldoon's right-hand man in the decade before 1984 and Bolger's closest ally for years. He was probably the most competent administrator in the parliamentary hierarchy. Having overseen labour market deregulation, the (largely unsuccessful) restructuring of the health system and accident compensation, and continuing state-sector reform from 1990 to 1993, Birch was determined to continue with the few remaining elements of the structural adjustment programme.

Bypassing the democratic process

Both the Labour and National governments were assisted in implementing the programme by the unsophisticated nature of New Zealand's political system. The single-house, first-past-the-post, two-party system meant the winning party had absolute power to rule. By maintaining a strategic ratio of ministers to MPs, the Cabinet was able to dominate decision-making in the caucus, while a rigid system of party whips ensured that all its MPs followed the Executive's line. A small number of ministers dominated the Cabinet, the Cabinet dominated the caucus, and the caucus dominated the Parliament.

The changes were implemented by both governments at a blistering pace. Parliamentary conventions were frequently ignored. The constant use of urgency powers enabled the technopols to force through controversial legislation, and avoid the inconvenience of scrutiny before or by a select committee. Under Labour this almost became the norm. In the first half of 1989, for example, Parliament sat under urgency for a third of the time. Often there were not enough, or sometimes even any, up-to-date copies of the measures available for those taking part in the debate. Despite its criticisms of Labour's practices, National behaved no differently. The July 1991 budget debate saw Parliament sit continuously for 101 hours. In addition to the Appropriation Bill, the government used the cover of urgency to push through a number of major and controversial measures which severely eroded the welfare state.

Much of the time, legislation was made on the hoof. The changes moved so fast that bills were introduced before the fine print had been settled, with details added part-way through the parliamentary process. One commentator's description of the process in Thatcher's Britain applied equally to New Zealand: 'The volume and complexity of new legislation . . . caused the Government to use parliamentary procedures mainly as an opportunity to tidy up the rough drafts submitted for ratification.'[42]

Numerous other devices were employed to avoid public scrutiny and criticism. Bills were often debated in parts, rather than clause by clause. When particularly controversial matters arose, the government curtailed debate by moving for closure. Major changes were introduced by Supplementary Order Paper (SOP), usually tabled in the committee-of-the-whole-House after the report from the select committee, and so the debate was not recorded in Hansard. Sometimes the select committee collaborated in this process, as with inclusion of the controversial 'principles of fiscal prudence' by SOP in the Fiscal Responsibility Act 1994.[43]

The government had an automatic majority on select committees. A committee's recommendations could be reversed in the parliamentary caucus, which the Cabinet effectively controlled.[44] Other measures did not even get to a select committee hearing. National, for example, directed the social services select committee not to take public submissions on a controversial proposal affecting welfare benefits for people over 55. The minister explained that the measure needed to be passed urgently to ensure the package of reforms could be implemented on schedule. There was simply no time for submissions.[45] Important changes to select committee procedures following the public finance reforms in 1989 increased the transparency of departmental operations, and provided for cross-examination of chief executives and ministers. But bad publicity and political pressure were the only effective sanctions the select committees had.

A review of the standing orders of Parliament, completed in 1992, offered little agreement on more substantial change. MPs on both sides expressed disappointment. One National member frankly observed: 'In my view, the reason for the widespread public disillusionment with this institution is that the public very correctly understands that the Executive has got too much power and that the process of checks and balances does not operate adequately.'[46] Technopol Richard Prebble concurred: 'having looked at the Standing Orders and listened to the various arguments that are raised, in my view many of them miss the point that Parliament is a debating chamber. No alteration to the Standing Orders will suddenly make us, as members of Parliament, into the Government. We are not the Government; Cabinet is the Government.'[47] And that, he clearly believed, was as it should be.

The political fall-out

In one respect the political management of the New Zealand experiment differed from Williamson's formula. He hypothesised that 'successful' structural adjustment required its architects to create a credible image of a reasonably just and attractive society.[48] Despite government cultivation of the media and vast sums spent on public relations consultants and advertising, many New Zealanders remained hostile to the structural adjustment programme. The wild swings of electoral fortune in 1984, 1987 and 1990 testified to their dissatisfaction. Each government had been elected on a minority of total votes, rendering their mandates dubious. By-elections, always an opportunity for anti-government protest votes, confirmed the incumbent's unpopularity. But people found that changing the party in government had little effect.

Deprived of any real political choice under the existing system, people expressed their dissent by voting the electoral system out. In 1992 an indicative referendum overwhelmingly rejected the first-past-the-post regime, and returned a preference for the German-style MMP. The National government reluctantly ran a binding referendum on the issue at the 1993 election. After an intensive anti-MMP campaign funded by big business, a small but significant majority (54 percent) voted for change. Maori dissent went further.

The Maori Council of Churches had sponsored an election boycott campaign in 1990. Calls for constitutional dialogue to address tribal sovereignty gained momentum in the following years.

In the lead-up to MMP, a number of MPs who were unlikely to be selected by their party under the new system went out on their own, wiping out National's formal majority in Parliament. By 1995 the National government was torn between completing and cementing in the structural adjustment programme before the advent of MMP in 1996, and avoiding a humiliating and confidence-damaging defeat by pushing through controversial changes which its short-term allies opposed.

CHAPTER THREE

Empowering the Technocrats

ROBERT BATES AND ANNE KRUEGER, in a 1993 study of structural adjustment, observed how the state and its economic actors generally become more powerful through the restructuring process, not less. Radical

> economic reform clearly leads to an increase in the power of the execu-
> tive branch of government and, in particular, of its financial units. It
> is important to savor the irony embedded in this finding. Many who
> advocate economic policy reform in the Third World advocate an ex-
> panded role for markets and call for a reduction in the role of the state.
> In their rhetoric they pit the market against the state; expansion of the
> role of one implies, in their conception, a reduction in the scope of the
> other, as through privatization, cutbacks in public spending, and a re-
> duction in regulatory powers. And yet, as suggested in the country
> studies . . . economic policy reforms are not 'anti-state'; rather, they
> appear to strengthen the powers of the core of the state, the executive
> branch, and to enhance its control over key economic policy variables
> which affect the outcome of economic activity . . . ; the expansion of
> the role of markets requires a strengthening of the state and especially
> of its financial bureaucracy.[1]

Securing control of the state's economic policy-making machinery in the hands of technocrats was equally critical to the New Zealand experiment's 'success'.

The change agents

Implementation of the programme rested with a small group of key civil servants who 'moved among key institutions, putting reforms in place and preventing bottlenecks'.[2] Most had economics qualifica-tions, but few came from professional backgrounds or had practical experience of the particular activities of which they took control. Hailed as change agents *extraordinaire*, these invisible hands shifted from one job to the next with little apparent on-going accountability for what they had put in place.

Prime among them was Rod Deane. After four years with the IMF, Deane returned to New Zealand in 1979 as chief economist at the Reserve Bank, and soon became its deputy governor. He was a major intellectual contributor to the economic policy debate in its formative years. In 1986 Deane moved to the State Services Commission (SSC) to oversee state sector reform. He then became chief executive of corporatised Electricorp, which was expected to be the most troublesome of the state-owned enterprises (SOEs). In 1992 he was appointed chief executive of the privatised Telecom. In 1994 Deane was named Deloitte/*Management Magazine* Executive of the Year, and joined the board of Fletcher Challenge (FCL), one of New Zealand's largest trans-national corporations. Throughout this period, he was an active member of the powerful corporate lobby group Business Roundtable and in the 1980s was a trustee of the Hayekian-oriented Centre for Independent Studies.

Graham Scott was Secretary to the Treasury in the critical years 1986 to 1993, and a close Douglas ally. Scott had a PhD from Duke University in the US, and spent from 1969 to 1973 at the National Planning Association in Washington, DC. A private sector consultant from 1974 to 1976, Scott worked in the Prime Minister's Department under Muldoon from 1976 to 1979. Shifting to the Treasury in 1980, he was responsible first for medium-term economic strategy issues, and subsequently for Treasury's overall economic policy during Muldoon's final years. Scott took over as chief executive of the Treasury in 1986. He retired and established an international consultancy in 1993.

Another key technocrat of the early Rogernomics years was Roger Kerr. Kerr moved from Foreign Affairs to the Treasury in 1976, where he frequently clashed with Muldoon. As director of Treasury's think-tank 'Economics II', Kerr worked closely with colleagues Scott, Rob Cameron and Bryce Wilkinson in formulating the alternative economic strategy, and co-wrote the Treasury briefing paper *Economic Management* in 1984. Kerr left the Treasury in 1986 to become director of the Business Roundtable, on the recommendation of Rod Deane. His links with government continued: Labour appointed him to the board of Electricorp, alongside Deane and fellow Roundtable activist John Fernyhough; the National government appointed him to the Victoria University Council. Kerr remained close to Douglas, who acknowledged him in his 1993 book *Unfinished Business*.

Individuals from the private sector also played a vital role. Sir Ron Trotter acted as Labour's chief advisor for the economic summit conference in 1984. He chaired the government steering group on privatisation during the formative stage of the programme from 1987 to 1988, and served on the Reserve Bank board during the critical years 1986–88. Trotter also chaired the Telecom board from 1987 until just before it was privatised in 1990. During this period, he served as chair of the Business Roundtable and was a founding trustee of the Centre for Independent Studies. He was knighted by Labour in 1985. Recognising his allegiance to the overall agenda rather than to any party, National appointed Trotter to oversee the restructuring of the health system in 1991. In the private sector, Trotter was managing director of Fletcher Challenge until he retired in 1987 and chaired its board until 1995.

Alan Gibbs's progress followed similar lines. He chaired the establishment board and then the board of state-owned Forestcorp from 1987 to 1990. He presided over a review which promoted a radical restructuring of the health services in 1987,[3] and which formed the basis for National's subsequent health policy. He, too, was a leading member of the Business Roundtable and executive board member of the Centre for Independent Studies. Gibbs was equally active in pursuing his commercial interests. He made initial contacts with Bell Atlantic and Ameritech, and put together the consortium which included merchant bankers Fay Richwhite to buy Telecom in 1990. Gibbs became a director of the privatised corporation. He was also co-owner of Freightways which, among other activities, ran the country's major network of courier firms. Gibbs purchased the New Zealand broadcasting rights for the BBC World Service, which was used to propagate neo-liberal views. The venture failed financially and was sold to a group of entrepreneurs and journalists of an even more extreme ideological persuasion, although the BBC was not prepared to be associated with the new venture.[4]

Others in the state and private sectors played similar roles. The tight circle of key players was neatly encapsulated by Anthony Hubbard in a *Listener* article in 1992. Fernyhough, as the chair of Electricorp, had asked Kerr who would made a good chief executive, and Kerr had recommended Deane. 'Rod [Deane] helped Roger

[Kerr] get the Roundtable job; Roger helped Rod get the Electricorp position. Roundtable stalwart Ron Trotter has held a bewildering number of positions under Labour as under National. This is a like-minded elite which is always taking in each other's washing.'[5]

The control agencies

At the institutional level, the role of the Treasury was pivotal. It had always wielded considerable power. Back in 1958 a senior civil servant observed, 'Treasury's influence is greater than that of any other department, because, as the controller of finances, it is at the centre of the administration, and its financial decisions and recommendations pervade every aspect of government activity.'[6] But Treasury did not have a monopoly on economic decisions at that time. A three-tier committee structure for economic policy-making had been established in 1952, comprising a Cabinet committee, an officials committee and various working parties of officials. This required Treasury to share its power. Some government departments had their own facilities for economic advice, ensuring that economic policy was generally the product of inter-departmental consensus. There were also outside economic policy-making bodies, such as the Economic Stabilisation Commission which, although chaired by the Secretary to the Treasury, enabled sectoral representatives to have their say.

In 1985 a comprehensive overhaul of the Cabinet machinery saw this structure replaced by a new framework to co-ordinate economic and social policy. The Cabinet Policy Committee was officially charged with ensuring the clarity and coherence of all policy. With the Prime Minister, Deputy Prime Minister and Minister of Finance as members, it effectively assumed control of the government's resources, and hence of the restructuring programme.

The new structure was serviced by the two 'control ministries' of Treasury and the SSC. Advice would come to Cabinet via the Cabinet Policy Committee from specially constituted Cabinet co-ordinating committees. Treasury, as gatekeeper, could thus prevent access by other departmental officials. Because every submission placed before Cabinet or a Cabinet committee which had economic, financial or revenue implications required Treasury endorsement or a separate report, Treasury could effectively kneecap unacceptable policies from other departments and agencies. Those affected had no reciprocal right to challenge the Treasury view. Most major task forces, officials committees and reviews also had Treasury representation and/or were serviced by them. Treasury claimed that the new structure was necessary to eliminate ministerial capture by self-maximising bureaucrats.[7] As custodians of the nation's economy, only they could be trusted to provide independent and objective advice. Douglas argued that it was Treasury's constitutional function to provide independent economic advice 'free of any party political positions or narrow ideology'.[8]

New procedures for expenditure control further entrenched Treasury's power. From 1985 departments were required to produce three-year expenditure forecasts. Any new policies would be funded from compensatory savings unless exceptional circumstances were agreed. Ministers had to determine spending priorities within their own departments and remain within their budgets. Yet Treasury seemed immune from such restrictions. As its powers increased, it built up a specialist staff of financial and policy analysts, which in turn reinforced its control. In 1985 Treasury officials were offered highly attractive salary packages and retention incentives at the same time as they were supervising staffing and spending cuts in other departments. It was 1988 before it was even required to file an annual report, which then came under select committee review as a result of the Public Finance Act 1989.

Treasury had the distinct advantage of working to its own agenda in a Cabinet dependent on its guidance. As early as 1986 political scientist John Roberts observed that Treasury's advice probably outweighed any other single source.[9] Brian Easton qualified this. When alternative advice was presented, Treasury's view did not always prevail.[10] But that did not happen often, especially in core areas of economic policy where there was no alternative government agency. Jonathan Boston noted that 'any policy analysts . . . who reject the prevailing Treasury orthodoxy are at a major disadvantage. For in order to have their views taken seriously they must first demonstrate the validity and coherence of their own analytical framework, and this is no mean feat, particularly if it has to be done in the face of determined Treasury opposition.'[11] Treasury was, without doubt, the driving force behind the structural adjustment programme. Its influence waned somewhat in the later 1980s, in line with that of Labour's technopols; under Richardson's patronage in the early 1990s that influence revived.

The second 'control' agency, the SSC, provided vital support for the programme, taking responsibility for corporatisation and restruc-

turing of the state sector. Its power over other departments was divested to arm's-length chief executives. But the SSC still set the
boundaries within which the executives could operate, exerting control while generally disclaiming responsibility. The SSC was also the
agency responsible for monitoring departmental performance under
the new state sector regime. This gave it oversight of a vast array of
matters designated as departmental outputs. The SSC's policy preferences differed at times from those of Treasury—mainly over how
far the state should abdicate in favour of the market. Treasury took
the more extreme position of abandoning state responsibilities to the
market, while the SSC wanted to retain some central state control.
But these were variations on a mutually agreed theme.

Moves to establish a third 'control' agency in the Prime Minister's
Department reflected an attempt by David Lange to balance Treasury's power, with limited success. The Prime Minister's Department
was replaced in 1987 by the Prime Minister's Office, comprising the
Prime Minister's advisory group, press office and personal staff, and
a separate Cabinet Office. The fragmentation of government departments, deteriorating inter-departmental relations, Treasury's assumption of a leading rather than co-ordinating role, and the need for
contestable advice, saw these reintegrated in 1989 to form the Department of Prime Minister and Cabinet (DPMC). The new department was intended to focus on specialist policy advice, special
projects, long-term planning and co-ordination of ministries and
departments.[12] The Prime Minister retained a small private office
with press staff and contracted advisors. As a way to counter Treasury, the strategy proved largely ineffective. Under National, however,
the DPMC became the powerhouse for implementing a number of
key reforms, notably in labour market deregulation, accident compensation and health. This was generally, although not always, in co-
operation with the Treasury.[13]

The fourth, and crucial, agency was the Reserve Bank. Key
personnel in the bank, notably Rod Deane, played an integral role
in shaping the programme. While monetary policy was central to
economic policy during the early years, its nature and effects were
not widely understood. As these became apparent, the preoccupation with inflation policy came under pressure. In 1988 it was decided
to insulate the Reserve Bank from direct political control. The government would set the target range for inflation within a specified
period, and that target would be written into the Governor's con-

tract. This policy and the Reserve Bank Act 1989 are discussed in detail in Chapter 7.

While the technocrats directed the programme from the control agencies, its implementation was rarely entrusted to the existing bureaucrats. Like-minded chief executives were gradually appointed to departments and ministries to restructure and run them on managerial lines. In many cases new agencies, guided by private sector boards of directors, were invested with the authority to implement market-based reforms and insulated from political interference. State commercial enterprises were placed in the hands of autonomous, ministerially appointed boards drawn from the private sector. The new SOEs (covering civil aviation, telecommunications, electricity, postal services, banking, railways, public works, coal mines, forestry, land and property holdings) and similar agencies (the Crown Health Enterprises, Crown Research Institutes and Housing New Zealand) were designed to keep politicians at arm's length, eliminate non-commercial considerations, and in most cases prepare state businesses and assets for sale. Transitional local government agencies were created to ease the commercialisation and privatisation of local body utilities and services. Elected decision-makers were replaced by ministerial appointees on local health boards and electricity supply authorities.

Business leaders were commissioned to oversee policy reviews which prepared the ground for controversial change. Education, for example, was the subject of numerous reports which were led variously by the head of a retail distribution chain;[14] the director of the Institute of Policy Studies;[15] the former general manager of a major rubber and carpet manufacturer;[16] and a senior partner in Price Waterhouse,[17] who also chaired the superannuation task force on private provision for retirement.[18]

These various agencies and agents performed an essential role in the transitional stages of the programme. Once the transfer of assets, resources and responsibilities to the private sector was complete, so generally was their task. Some agencies continued in a limited management or monitoring capacity, but their role was circumscribed by the narrow range of activities over which they exercised control.

Setting the agenda

The technocrats and their allies set about applying pure neo-liberal theory to a continually expanding range of government policies and activities. Alan Bollard explains that, whereas finance minister Roger Douglas in 1984 saw a practical need for liberalisation,

[t]he Treasury economists were interested in the range of theoretical microeconomic developments of the preceding decade and anxious to try them in practice. They shifted their focus away from macroeconomic policy (for several years the Treasury cut its macroeconomic divisions and ceased formal forecasting). This also coincided with a change in policy focus from traditional New Zealand ones of stabilization and equity to a primary focus on efficiency. The Treasury argued that the government should rethink all its traditional economic roles. . . .[19]

This work began in the later 1970s. Economist Geoff Bertram traces the first significant New Zealand divergence from the Keynesian line to two reports of the New Zealand Planning Council. In 1979 *The Welfare State? Social Policy in the 1980s* introduced the idea of public sector overload. In 1980 *The Stabilisation Role of Fiscal Policy* argued against fine-tuning the economy through fiscal policy. The latter was co-authored by Rod Deane. Bertram says the study quickly became conventional wisdom among New Zealand policy commentators and a staple of the Reserve Bank position.[20]

In the three years to 1984, the Reserve Bank produced a series of research papers which circulated widely among professional economists, and helped to shift the thinking of many on macro-economic policy.[21] The formula included deregulation of market interest rates, full funding of fiscal deficits by borrowing from the private sector at commercial rates, and a flexible exchange rate which was adjusted to prevent the balance of payments having any direct effect on monetary conditions.

By the 1984 election a strong body of thinking had consolidated within Treasury and the Reserve Bank in favour of economic deregulation, exchange rate flexibility and tight monetary policy. The technocrats portrayed their position as part of the new economic orthodoxy, backed by a widely held intellectual consensus. Brian Easton challenged this, claiming that the influence was primarily American and 'not from its mainstream, but from a particular section; Chicago and its satellites. Even then it was a particularly normative approach, not subject to Chicago's high standards of empirical research. Since the same thing did not happen in Australia, it seems likely that the phenomenon reflects peculiarities here rather than some universal imperialism.'[22] The existence of conflicting paradigms in North America had been ignored.

The Secretary to the Treasury during the early years of Roger-nomics, Bernard Galvin, agreed that US theories were used selectively. But he pointed to important influences beyond Chicago, such as Australian work on the exchange rate, IMF experience in indirect taxation, and British, Canadian and European ideas on state-owned enterprises. In other cases, solutions such as the removal of labour market rigidities had been considered 'obvious' and trade liberalisation was already in place.[23]

Treasury officials also referred to sources outside the United States, notably the OECD, IMF and GATT (all of which were heavily influenced by US economists), as well as developments in the UK and Australia.[24] But they generally conceded that the primary influence came from the US, in particular the micro-economic theories of Demsetz and Coase on the nature of the firm, Williamson on transaction costs, Baumol et al. on contestability theory, Alchian on property rights, Buchanan and Tulloch on political influence and public choice, along with Friedman's monetarism and the rational expectations theories of Kydland and Prescott. A Reserve Bank official acknowledged the bank's reliance on US theories since the late 1970s.

New US models with supply side shocks gained influence. In particular, the monetarist framework relating to inflationary control of monetary targeting was most influential. In the 1980s rational expectations in new classical theories in the US gained more credibility, teaching lessons such as the futility of monetary policy for fine tuning, the importance of credibility and reputation, and the need to control fiscal deficits as well as the money supply.[25]

The US influence had entered New Zealand economic policy in various ways. Some prominent change agents were graduate students in the US in the 1960s and 1970s. Feminist academic Phillida Bunkle, a student in the US at the same time, observed how many of them seemed embarrassed about New Zealand's quaintness, its social uniformity and lack of sophistication, and were determined to bring New Zealand into the global village.[26] Later, as the structural adjustment programme was being developed, key members of the 'change team' spent time in the US to update their analysis.[27] There was a regular exchange of Reserve Bank officials with the IMF and World Bank.[28] Some US experts were imported by Treasury to act as consultants and Treasury recruits were sponsored to study at leading North American universities.

The US influence was so pervasive that these theories were implemented in almost undiluted form. In 1988 Bollard offered the 'simplified but generalised conclusion that . . . there is a rich diversity of theory and applied economic research in the US, but only part of it has been tapped for application in New Zealand, sometimes without adequate adaptation.'[29] Some theories had been transmitted directly from the US polity into Treasury's economic policy without any of the filtering by New Zealand researchers that one might expect. Even more dangerous was the application of American theory, such as the radical deregulation of the finance sector, to New Zealand policy without its ever having been adopted as policy in the US.

Treasury briefing papers
The basic blueprint was set out in the Treasury's briefing papers to the incoming government in 1984 and 1987, with further contributions in 1990 and 1993. Practicalities and details were developed during the implementation process. Others key individuals contributed, and new concepts and theories were incorporated along the way. At times this led to modification, but rarely to significant change. Political barriers occasionally caused delays or the need to implement change in stages. After a decade very little on the blueprint for change remained undone.

Economic Management
The micro-economic foundations of the programme, backed by a monetarist macro-economic policy, were set out in Treasury's briefing to the new Labour government in 1984. Published in book form as *Economic Management*, this combined a detailed analysis of the country's current economic plight with a clear agenda for change. The Labour government's exercise of 'opening the books' made public Treasury's 'comprehensive, independent and professional assessment of the state of New Zealand's economy'.[30] Because Treasury could not be certain which way the new government would go, the argument was grounded on economic necessity. Reliance on intervention and control by past governments, it argued, had caused economic stagnation, coupled with inflation, massive overseas debt and internal inefficiency. The current economic outlook 'adds to the evidence in the statistical record over many years that the economy is beset with serious structural difficulties and that we have continually failed to make the best of the circumstances we find ourselves

in'.[31] Hence, 'the New Zealand economy continues to display one of the most lacklustre performances among countries in the developed world.'[32]

Past governments had focused on ad hoc responses to the symptoms, refusing to tackle 'the underlying causes of our economic malaise'.[33] Urgent remedial action was required. Resources locked into unproductive and inefficient investment by high taxes and government spending needed to be liberated to find their most valued use.

> Put simply, policies for faster adjustment allow changes in international prices to be reflected in the domestic economy. Ultimately this is the only way to ensure that the country's resources are continually being allocated so as to achieve the highest national income available. . . . In the short term the government can only borrow to cover the deficit and/or squeeze domestic expenditure causing lost production and unemployment. The income loss can be offset only by reallocating resources and is prolonged by delaying this adjustment.[34]

By deregulating the economy and controlling money supply, demand could be checked and wages and prices kept down. Inflation could be brought slowly under control without the need for counter-productive short-term interventions. Targeted benefits and market delivery of social services would reduce government spending and promote efficient resource use. Flexible labour markets would allow productivity to increase and real wages to fall in response to rising unemployment. Commercial state activities could be operated on market terms, or where appropriate sold. Non-commercial functions of government should develop efficiency and management performance mechanisms to replicate the private firm.

The economy was portrayed as an aggregate of individual contracts which allocated scarce resources efficiently and was co-ordinated through freely operating markets. The society comprised individuals making these contractual decisions about different aspects of their daily lives. People needed to accept realistic limits on what the government could deliver and what it could protect them from. The inherent efficiency of markets meant 'the government is more likely to achieve its ends effectively by harnessing and supplementing markets rather than suppressing them'.[35] In some situations society may wish to trade efficiency for other goals that it considers desirable. 'In all cases, however, there is a need to select the appropriate form of intervention, and to minimise any unwarranted effects on incentives to firms or individuals so that associated costs can be kept to a minimum.'[36]

Attention was also paid to management of the economic programme.[37] Treasury argued for a more systematic approach to developing and implementing economic policy within a broad policy framework. Proposals included a policy review committee of core ministers, sitting between Cabinet and its committees to discuss 'the large issues' with officials from the Treasury and Prime Minister's Department.[38] Other Cabinet committees would be streamlined. The existing departmental structure could be reorganised to minimise interest-group capture of government agencies and self-maximising bureaucrats. By merging departments, competing client bases could be brought within the one agency; alternatively, policy and operational functions could be separated to improve their efficiency in the longer term. Transparency of government decisions, and improving community understanding and acceptance of government policy, were also required.

Of Treasury's 1984 proposals, only some aspects of the tariff regime, formal endorsement of the privatisation policy, completion of state sector restructuring, deregulating the labour market and securing popular acceptance of the government's polices remained to be achieved by the October 1987 election.

Government Management

The 1984 briefing paper was a textbook application of micro-economic theory to the New Zealand economy. By contrast, the two-volume, 750-page briefing for 1987, called *Government Management,* was an extraordinary ideological tract. *Economic Management* was about restructuring the economy; *Government Management* was about restructuring the state.

In setting their objectives, Treasury argued, governments had to recognise the competing interests of equity, efficiency and freedom, and the trade-offs involved in each. There were five basic constraints on achieving social goals:

- *scarcity* of physical and human resources relative to the demands placed upon them;
- *interdependency,* whereby one person's actions affected another;
- *uncertainty* created by the bounded rationality of individuals when planning for the future;
- *information* problems arising from availability and cost; and

- *opportunistic* tendencies of individuals, which required people to minimise the adverse effects of others' acts and created incentives to align their interests with one another.

The first 40 pages of *Government Management* redefined the role of the state from Treasury's preferred starting-point of 'decentralised voluntary contracting based on the price mechanism and competition'.[39] This pro-market bias was reinforced by the theories used throughout: property rights, transaction cost analysis, agency and public choice.

According to Treasury, a system of enforceable, tradeable property rights offered the best way to allocate scarce resources, resolve conflicting claims and provide incentives to increase the resource pool. These rights should be exercised through private voluntary contracting or market exchange—the system which existed before the state assumed responsibility for housing, health and education. Private contracts allowed information to be used efficiently, co-ordinated individual actions and guided resources to where they were valued most. The price mechanism provided a low-cost way to measure relative worth. Concerns about exploitation, unfair trading and monopoly practices could be met by ensuring opportunities for competition. Actual competition was unnecessary. Contestability theory showed that the mere potential for rivals to emerge, or for the government to regulate, would act as a check on inefficiencies and abuse. Voluntary associations offered another way to provide benefits for members of the wider community, tailored to local needs.

Treasury acknowledged that equity problems could result from the way property rights were defined, from unequal information costs, and from opportunistic exploitation of circumstances. Addressing these by redistribution would deprive people of the right to choose between possible outcomes, and fail to reward risk, skill and effort. Trying to address them through fair process raised problems of identifying a consensus approach. Treasury insisted that:

> A full evaluation of the justice or fairness of a society through time requires an assessment not only of outcomes, and processes of distribution, but also the starting point of individuals. This requires an appreciation of such factors as the history, socioeconomic background, and physical or natural abilities of an individual.[40]

It also recognised that loss of dignity and alienation might have social consequences and become matters of public concern. But public policy needed to ascertain where that was most important, and what the possible safeguards were, recognising the costs and trade-offs involved. Private voluntary contracting assumed an initial distribution of resources and natural talent. Attempts at redistribution by redefining rights or reallocating resources imposed efficiency costs.

> Thus a tax or subsidy may lead people to underinvest or work less. . . . [M]arkets perform an important allocational task. Through changes in prices, changes in demand and supply are signalled to resource owners and resources are guided to more highly valued uses. This process assists growth and improves welfare for all. By interfering too much in the income received by owners the Government may adversely affect incentives to efficiently allocate and use resources. The necessity to evaluate trade-offs between efficiency and equity cannot be over-emphasised.[41]

Treasury considered this 'comparative systems approach is "level headed" about the limits of Government, and the limits of private arrangements, eschews the blind pursuit of ideal worlds by recognising trade-offs between goals, and places emphasis on a detailed microanalytic approach or, simply, attention to detail including empirical evidence and argument'.[42] In saying this, Treasury seemed oblivious to its own blind pursuit of an ideological paradigm and to its own failure to offer any such detailed empirical work.

Other constraints on efficiency, Treasury argued, could be minimised by replicating the approach of the private firm. Private sector firms run the risk of agency costs because the interests of owners (shareholders) may diverge from those of managers and other employees. The owner must induce the manager to act in the owner's interest. Important restraints include share-market pressures, takeover mechanisms, boards of directors which exercise delegated authority on behalf of shareholders, performance monitoring by major lenders, competition and the threat of insolvency. Similar inefficiencies and conflicts arise, by analogy, between state bureaucracies and their taxpayer or citizen owners, represented by their elected representatives in government. State sector reforms modelled on the for-profit sector would improve the efficiency and accountability of state agencies, although they could never replicate the disciplines and incentives of the private sector.

Treasury acknowledged that private markets also faced problems of uncertainty, information and opportunism. But those applied equally, if not more, in the centralised state. Central planners were hampered by inadequate information, weak incentives and poor accountability for the costs of their decisions. Invoking public choice theory, Treasury argued that capture of regulatory decisions came from external sources like lobby groups, and from within the bureaucracy itself, whose superior hold on information over that of elected representatives 'creates the potential for opportunism or subgoal pursuit by the bureaucracy including shirking, budget maximisation and generally inefficient policies for society as a whole'.[43]

Failure of markets to address social costs and provide public goods, Treasury noted, had often been used to justify intervention by the state. This argument had been applied to externalities like pollution; to free-rider situations where non-paying users could not be excluded, as with street lighting; to provision of coercive public goods, like defence; and to natural monopolies, which required regulation for the common good. But Treasury insisted that all these involved trade-offs, not absolutes. The failure of the market reflected the excessive costs of providing these services privately. If the regulatory regime was adjusted to alter the existing constraints, incentives and contracting costs, the market could provide much more.

Under Treasury's model, the proper role for the state was to provide the correct policy settings in such areas as government expenditure, taxation and money supply. It should enforce property and contracting rights and relations between individuals. And it should set legislative frameworks and regulatory regimes. Where possible, decision-making should be devolved to local control, either by voluntary associations or by local bodies, provided their funding was also decentralised so that they faced incentives against waste. By targeting expenditure and providing consumer choice in education and housing, efficiency and quality would improve. Expenditure cuts would offer positive opportunities for flexibility, diversity and developing the capacity of social organisations. 'This is particularly visible where state funded social services, or consumer protection legislation reduces the amount private individuals invest in market or self-insurance (for example for old age).'[44]

In an annex to the briefing papers, Treasury officials developed a composite *rational ethical human position* from which all government activity should be derived.[45] Reflecting on three variations on liberal philosophy—libertarian (Friedman and Nozick), contractarian (Rawls) and utilitarian (Bentham and J. S. Mill)—it adopted its own position, which was basically a Hayekian line. Society, Treasury argued, is made up of interdependent individuals motivated at least in part by self-interest and opportunism. Ways must be found to limit any negative impact of unrestrained self-interest, so that the interests of different individuals can co-exist. To ensure freedom and liberty of the individual, however, the society must not inhibit the right of those individuals to follow their desired path. That includes the freedom to exploit, alter and trade their private property, unless they are impeding someone else's exercise of their choice or preference.

Well-designed policies should align individual self-interest with the common interest. A society that is willing to take risks, and to organise itself accordingly, is more likely to be innovative, ready and able to seize and exploit the opportunities thrown its way by chance and circumstance. This encourages greater 'equity, efficiency and freedom'. A society that is excessively averse to risk, however, that tries to protect and insulate its members from all the adverse consequences of a changing external environment, or improving technology, is unlikely to adapt constructively to change. It is also much less likely to seize the opportunities that could provide higher incomes and additional jobs.

Government does have responsibilities beyond those of individuals and must pursue all the objectives of efficiency, equity, liberty, public morals and human dignity. But all such rights are relative and political, not natural. Government must make some choices. Before it imposes any constraints on individuals, government must calculate the comparative costs of different options, and make only carefully selected interventions. These require prudent assessment of the trade-offs between dignity, output and wealth.

Treasury concluded that government's social policy should reflect a rational ethical human position wherein 'the interests of the most disadvantaged are the first concern of policy'. But that is to be achieved in a way that will 'maximise the social well-being and minimise the threat to those individual rights . . . which derive their authority from a social consensus. . . . Those rights must reflect New Zealand society as it is currently structured. . . . The rights need not be the same as those we might have defined 50 years ago [at the birth of the welfare state]. Similarly, the rights are not some absolute right which the individual takes but are instead socially agreed rights which are offered for the individual.'[46] The state should not altogether abandon its responsibility to the most disadvantaged. But it should deliver their basic needs through the mechanisms of the market.

Political analysts Shaun Goldfinch and Brian Roper observe that, taken to its logical extreme,

> the ideal world as portrayed by the Treasury briefing papers would be one inhabited by independent rugged entrepreneurs, where markets were allowed free reign [sic] largely unencumbered by consumer and environmental laws, and free from the influence of unions and other interest groups. Social services would be provided by the market, and access to them would be through direct income transfers or private charity. The functions of government would be limited to controlling the money supply in order to maintain price-level stability, distributing limited income transfers, guaranteeing the legislative and institutional framework for the efficient operation of markets, and defending the 'free enterprise system' against internal and external threats (maintaining 'law and order' and 'national security').[47]

This rational ethical human position was applied to education, health, housing, income maintenance, the labour market and Treaty of Waitangi policy. The second volume of *Government Management* was devoted entirely to education. While the emphasis was on social policy and the role of the state, Treasury also reinforced the micro-economic and monetary policy arguments made in the 1984 briefing, with special attention to labour market reform.

The 1987 briefing provided the formula for replacing the welfare state, and its commitment to comprehensive entitlement from 'the cradle to the grave', with a number of targeted and market-driven minimal safety nets—although full implementation had to wait until National's finance minister, Ruth Richardson, produced her 'mother of all budgets' in 1991.

1990 briefing papers

The 1990 and 1993 Treasury briefing papers reaffirmed and expanded the themes of the earlier documents, with special emphasis on the labour market, fiscal policy, public management and the welfare state. As economist Paul Dalziel points out, the 1990 briefing was overshadowed by the National government's 'Economic and Social Initiative' which was released on the same day and announced benefit cuts and the introduction of the Employment Contracts Act.

The 1990 approach was particularly interesting because Treasury now had to confront the full impact of its policy failures since 1984. This was just being felt by election time in 1987; by 1990 major deterioration was evident. The briefing papers acknowledged that the current employment situation did not meet the country's expectations: in 1990 New Zealand had minimal employment growth when the OECD countries averaged 12 percent; the lowest productivity growth in the OECD, with gains due mainly to 'shedding' of labour, not higher output; rapidly rising unemployment levels; marked geographical differences in employment rates, with higher unemployment among people with little or no educational qualifications; and rapidly increasing long-term unemployment levels. Rather than treating this as the cumulative effect of the past six years, however, Treasury blamed the country's 'economic fragility' on factors outside government control. Recession was seen as inevitable whatever policies were adopted. Treasury's response was to target increased international competitiveness as a source of future wealth.

A second significant feature of the 1990 briefing papers was the abrupt shift in Treasury forecasts from those given in the July 1990 budget, especially the trebling of the projected budget deficit. This 'alarming fiscal situation' was used to justify the austerity campaign of benefit and spending cuts on which National immediately embarked. Because there had been no hint of this crisis in the 1990 budget, most economic commentators and potential critics were caught by surprise. Once more the Treasury model was able to prevail virtually unopposed. Dalziel notes the irony that, 'while the remainder of the country was engaged in a General Election which was ostensibly about economic strategies, officials in Treasury were putting together a consistent and coherent economic programme based on choices they had already made about the best economic development option available to New Zealand'.[48]

The other major feature of the 1990 briefing was the demand for policy coherence across all areas and the harmonisation of economic instruments. Proposals for monetary, fiscal, social, labour market and regulatory policy were all to be made consistent with monetary policy and the goal of price stability.[49] Dalziel noted that Treasury was arguing for the very situation it opposed during the price and incomes freeze under Muldoon.[50] Any pretence of a balanced economic policy that considered such objectives as economic growth, full employment, external balance and income distribution had by this time disappeared.

The 1993 post-election briefing was much less strident, doubtless reflecting Treasury's uncertainty about which party would be in government and what ideological agenda and policy programme it would pursue.

The critical void

Treasury maintained a strong internal position, and was impatient with dissenting views. Its briefings were published and other documents circulated, but this exposure was selective and usually took place after the policy decisions had been made. Those outside the inner circle had no effective opportunity to participate in policy-making. Dalziel notes that Treasury economists were forbidden to reply publicly to criticism, except through their ministers.

> This constitutional arrangement means that on the one hand, the politicians can pick and choose what, if anything, they will tell us of the advice they receive from their economists in Treasury. On the other hand, the economic analysis of Treasury economists is hidden from independent checking and critical comment by other economists outside Treasury. This is a dangerous set-up, especially with the Executive having so much power in our system of government.[51]

Institutional critique of Treasury's position was rare. Old-style government departments were progressively abolished. A number of quasi-governmental agencies were closed down; only a few 'quangos' remained. The New Zealand Planning Council continued to produce a range of reports, some of which reflected alternative ideological perspectives and economic theories. On Treasury's recommendation, the Planning Council fell victim to National's cost-cutting drive in 1991.

Other specialist centres played a more supportive role. The Institute of Policy Studies at Victoria University in Wellington provided a high-profile platform for numerous advocates of the restructuring programme. It also offered a research base for the genesis of new policy initiatives, such as work on information-sharing, privacy and the smart-card,[52] 'open regionalism' in the Asia-Pacific,[53] and redesigning the welfare state.[54] Although not all the institute's research could be classed as neo-liberal, those who were critical of the new orthodoxy report that it was a difficult environment in which to work.[55] Another consistent non-government contributor to the debate was the New Zealand Institute of Economic Research. While supporting the economic liberalisation agenda, it provided useful information and on occasion questioned the failure to address the transitional costs which had accrued.

Although New Zealand's economics profession as a whole had not endorsed the neo-liberal agenda, academic critique was surprisingly restrained. There had been some dialogue on future economic policy in 1983 which saw 'academic economists of broadly new-Keynesian or structuralist persuasion set against Government officials with a generally monetarist or new classical approach'.[56] No consensus emerged, and Douglas later criticised the academics' unwillingness to commit themselves.[57]

The 1984 briefing papers came in for trenchant criticism at the New Zealand Association of Economists meeting in February 1985, where Treasury was accused of treating the real world as though it matched the pure theoretical neo-classical model, and expressing conclusions from the abstract model as though they were statements of empirical fact. In so doing, '[Treasury] is in danger of misleading its political masters into believing that the facile solutions . . . which are attainable in neoclassical models are characteristic of the real world with which they have to deal.'[58] A paper shortly afterwards warned of the danger that tight monetary policy would lift the exchange rate and undermine the profitability of traded goods. Another predicted slow growth and high unemployment as a consequence of these policies. Bertram notes that those predictions proved essentially correct.[59]

After 1984 opportunities and academic enthusiasm for debate and challenge declined. Brian Easton attributes this to the intrinsic limitations of New Zealand's academic community. In the economics departments there had been little teaching before 1984 of the new micro-economics used by Treasury, although some macro-economic courses were being taught. Not many New Zealand academic papers had been published in the area. Few university economists had been trained in North America, although quite a number had come from Britain, and students who had gone to the United States for postgraduate study had usually not returned.[60] Economist Suzanne Snively, who immigrated from the US in the 1970s, observed the cultural cringe which pervaded the academic world.

The economics departments at New Zealand universities in the 1970s reflected the typical lack of confidence of an insular group. With some exceptions, the lecturers and professors looked to the overseas economic journals for their affirmation. The mark of success was to write an article which could be published overseas in a 'learned journal'. . . . The trouble is, the American economic journal articles that they tended to respect were written from the perspective of the American economy which has very little history of innovative social policy. Some New Zealand social economists were miles ahead and could have told the Americans a thing or two. Despite this talent, the mainstream economics profession here was rather more interested in imitating their overseas counterparts and adopting universal prescriptions than in analysing ways of maintaining the pleasant social conditions that prevailed [in New Zealand].[61]

This left a limited pool of experienced economists who could readily challenge the US-derived agenda. The small size of the New Zealand economics community, the lack of institutions within which its members could develop and publish alternative theories, the shortage of funding for independent research, and enormous pressures to conform also explain the one-sided nature of the debate.

Those who voiced opposition to the neo-liberal project were generally dismissed as vested interest lobbyists, outmoded Keynesians, or radicals intent on subverting the interests of the nation. Nevertheless, some continued to speak out. One of the most telling critiques came from Easton in 1988, in a detailed analysis of the influence of US micro-economic theory in the papers and positions prepared by the economists driving the restructuring programme.[62] Easton attacked their narrow theoretical base, and their interpretation of the data they did use. He accused them of failing to acknowledge the institutional context in which empirical evidence was produced, and in which theories were to be applied. For example, American deregulatory approaches to security law, which involved fiduciary obligations on major shareholders and class actions by minority shareholders, would mean 'importing the culture of the American litigation system into New Zealand'.[63] Similarly, theories of labour market deregulation derived from the larger American labour market ignored the vast geographical, institutional and cultural differences between the two countries. Easton also condemned the technocrats' position on welfare, which was based on an objective of efficiency or aggregate wealth maximisation and treated as value free. 'Efficiency only looks at whether the policy change increases GDP, irrespective of its consequences on the income distribution and social wellbeing. In fact quite small allocative gains can be associated with massive changes in the income distribution.'[64]

Given the absence of sustained critique, the self-appointed agents of change were able to hold the floor, claiming legitimacy and orthodoxy for what they were doing, and dictating the terms of the debate for most of the decade. The political appeal of Treasury's package lay in its simplicity. Incomes policy could be abandoned. The blame for unemployment could be sheeted home to organised labour, and the need to maintain close contact with unions was reduced. Government intervention was seen as powerless to correct any failings in the market other than inflation. 'In a nutshell, the new classical policy package gave politicians the chance to abdicate, with a clear conscience, many of the responsibilities which the State had assumed in the preceding decades. . . . Politicians in many countries seized eagerly upon the alibi thus offered for their failure to meet the economic expectations of their electorates.'[65]

Critics were concerned not just about the content of the Treasury's position, but about the apparent ease with which it came to dominate the debate and construct the image of economic orthodoxy. Snively commented: 'Perhaps the Treasury views in *Economic Management* reflect a development of a separate school of thought in New Zealand about the labour market. This would be a healthy and exciting development if Treasury's role was simply that of adviser to governments. Unfortunately, in the absence of economic debate and a New Zealand version of introductory economic texts, they have also become the perpetrators of what is supposedly mainstream economic thought in New Zealand.'[66]

These economic theories and the presumed failure of existing models and policy frameworks prevailed, Bertram suggests, not because of their intrinsic merit but because they corresponded with some very crude empirical generalisations that were widely accepted at the time. The public prestige of any body of economic doctrine was heavily influenced by the number of major vested interests it could attract as adherents. Key defections from Keynesianism, especially by financiers and industrial firms, in the 1970s provided electoral or external support for the economic restructuring of the 1980s. 'But intellectual ascendancy achieved by this essentially political route needs always to be distinguished from the ascendancy of a scientifically superior theory over its competitors, as in the traditional fable of scientific progress.'[67] The lack of effective contest exposed what Bertram saw as a deep and worrying reality shared by many countries facing pressures for major structural change:

New Zealand's small size and limited research establishment have always resulted in a tendency to import key economic ideas from elsewhere, and to concede substantial authority to the international climate of opinion. . . . The critics of the New Right, like the New Right themselves, drew much of their theoretical ammunition from the overseas literature, and the resulting debate had a rather second-hand quality which gave an edge to the well-funded lobbying organizations supporting the New Right programme, who were able to bring a long series of 'overseas experts' to New Zealand to legitimate their case in the eyes of politicians and the public.[68]

CHAPTER FOUR

Embedding the New Regime

THE NEW ZEALAND EXPERIMENT matched almost every element of Williamson's manual for technopols:

- a core of politicians committed to the structural adjustment pro-gramme, irrespective of the electoral risk, who were able to cap-ture their party machines and steer through the changes with minimal obstruction or effective dissent;
- a team of technocrats with a common, coherent view, who com-manded the instruments of executive power;
- an inflexible, sclerotic economy widely perceived as being in need of radical change;
- a foreign exchange crisis accompanying the transition of power (partly provoked by Douglas himself);
- an extended honeymoon, with adjustment costs easily blamed on the previous administration;
- a compliant media and information network for disseminating propaganda about the restructuring programme;
- political opposition which was disorganised and philosophically confused;
- intellectual opposition which was harassed, discredited and marginalised;
- isolation of sectoral groups, especially organised labour, likely to oppose and disrupt the programme;
- pacification of Maori opposition with promises to address treaty grievances;
- diversion of other sectoral groups with promises of social or foreign policy reform; and
- a pool of well-resourced and powerful private actors who would provide and protect the new regime.

That explains how the structural adjustment programme was implemented. To be 'successful', however, the changes also had to be entrenched.

Consolidation of structural change

In a 1992 study Stephen Haggard and Robert Kaufman identified two stages to the structural adjustment process: the initiation and then consolidation of change. They observed that the initiation phase was best secured through relatively autonomous, free-floating, technocratic 'change teams', and requires a more activist and capable state than classical liberal theory contemplates—paradoxically, the state needs to be strengthened before the government can reduce its role in the economy and extend market forces. This means creating new bureaucratic structures or significantly reorganising existing ones to operate outside routine decision-making channels. The authors concluded that 'reform initiatives are more likely where and when political institutions insulate politicians and their technocratic allies from particular interest group constraints, at least in the short run'.[1] The period of consolidation, by contrast,

> involves stabilising expectations around a new set of incentives and convincing economic agents that they cannot be reversed at the discretion of individual decision makers. Consolidation is most likely where governments have constructed relatively stable coalitions of political support that encompass major private sector beneficiaries, and have secured at least the acquiescence of the major political forces competing within the political system. Without such tacit or explicit alliances between politicians, technocratic elites, and those gaining from the policy change, reform attempts will necessarily falter.[2]

Consolidation also required considerable 'social learning'—described as the 'evolution of a broader ideational consensus among leaders, interest groups, party elites and attentive publics that sets some boundaries on the range of economic debate'.[3] This provides a constituency of support among private sector beneficiaries. Citizens and firms are encouraged to lower their expectations and make individual, non-political adjustments. When demands for relief do become politicised, they are often directed at the government in power rather than at the system as a whole. State agencies which had been responsible for the initiation phase retain control over bureaucratic recruitment, the definition of the state's mission, and the boundaries governing the state's relations with social groups. The result is what Haggard and Kaufman termed 'embedded autonomy'.

The greatest political risks to the consolidation phase lie with party fragmentation, unstable coalitions, populist appeals, favouritism and wide policy swings. Terry Moe points out that the first-past-the-post system of majority rule makes controversial reforms especially vulnerable until they are consolidated, because the government that instituted the changes, or a future government, can reverse them at will.[4] Changes cannot be formally insulated from this possibility, short of constitutional entrenchment. However, the risks can be minimised by instructing change agencies

> to hit the ground running—getting benefits in the hands of recipients, organizing recipients into support groups, . . . and otherwise building a powerful clientele that will strongly resist any attempt by the government, whether this one or those that follow it, to change anything about programs or structure. The more quickly and effectively this can happen, the more durable the deal will prove to be in practice. . . .[5]

This analysis describes the process of structural adjustment in New Zealand with remarkable accuracy. An ideological consensus had emerged among many, even most, of the key actors in politics, the economy and the media, which saw the norm of Keynesian interventionism replaced with that of a deregulated, internationalised market economy. Key agencies and agents remained in effective control of the economic decision-making process and the machinery of government. Both traditionally dominant parties had been instrumental in initiating the changes; their subsequent policies offered variations within the neo-liberal paradigm. The reaction of most of the people, for most of the time, was to grumble but acquiesce. When the public did rebel, they sought adjustments to the electoral system, not a radical redistribution of economic and political power.

The role of private capital

A further, critical, factor to the experiment's 'success', as Haggard and Kaufman point out, was the construction of a powerful base of beneficiaries, committed to initiating the changes and determined to resist any move to alter significantly or abandon the new regime. The understanding that benefits will accrue to the private sector is implicit in orthodox analyses of the structural adjustment process, but this integral relationship between the technocrats, politicians and business interests is rarely acknowledged. Neo-liberal theory instead claims to reflect objectivity, neutrality and science. It elevates technocrats and technopols to the status of selfless technicians acting in the public interest, even where the public do not agree, and assumes that private markets inherently promote the public good. This approach, taken by analysts such as John Williamson, sits uncomfortably with the perception of bureaucrats and politicians as motivated by self-interest. Equally, the obvious private benefits that accrue to many of those directly involved are difficult to reconcile with the condemnation of rent-seeking behaviour by special interest groups.

Other neo-liberal theorists more realistically acknowledge the pivotal role the private sector plays in the structural adjustment process. Economic technocrats become powerful, they argue, because politicians choose to make them so. Restructuring would not be possible without them. Equally, the technocrats would be powerless without the political patronage that creates the space for them to act. But external benefactors hold the key to sustaining the new regime. Robert Bates explains:

> Economic technocrats become powerful, and thus reform becomes politically sustainable, when they serve the interests of powerful groups: industries, sectors, or regions of the economy. Over time, the fortunes of powerful groups become dependent upon the maintenance in place of a policy regime; they develop a vested interest in keeping the reforms in place.[6]

Policies that involve conflicting interests will necessarily produce winners and losers. 'An agreement to change policy is an agreement to favor some constituencies over others.' Agencies which are designed to implement and defend those changes must be responsive to the constituencies who will benefit from them.[7] 'Through these decisions, political actors assure that the influence accorded to different constituents is not random: indeed, by controlling the details of procedures and participation, *political actors stack the deck in favour of constituents who are intended beneficiaries of the bargain'*.[8] This ensures that they continue to benefit under different administrations, and will act as 'fire alarms' to raise the alert and mobilise resistance if new regulators look like changing course. In the process, politicians reduce not only their opponents' opportunities for future control, but their own as well. Yet this is seen as a reasonable price to pay: 'because they get to go first, they are not really giving up control—they are choosing to exercise a greater measure of it *ex ante*, through insulated structures that, once locked in, predispose the agency to do the right things.'[9]

'Stacking the deck' and cultivating a pool of private sector beneficiaries of the restructured economy come very close to the 'rent-seeking' behaviour or capture that public choice theory so abhors. To avoid the problem, 'rent-seeking' is pragmatically redefined. In the IIE study, Williamson rejected outright any suggestion that 'the chances of successful reform will be enhanced if losers are provided with compensation, rather than abandoned to become impoverished and embittered opponents'.[10] But he seemed less tied to philosophical principles in considering the possibility of 'accelerating gains to winners':

> Despite the absence of corroborating evidence from our case studies, the idea of trying to make sure that some form of 'indirect compensation' comes on stream soon enough to sustain support for a reform program seems eminently sensible. It is important that this not be debauched into buying votes, thus yielding the moral high ground that justifies undertaking the reforms in the first place, but it is almost equally important that technopols not adopt a priggish disdain for political realism such as to doom them to political irrelevance.[11]

Both these approaches ultimately concede that conferring special benefits on powerful élites is part of the strategy for locking in the structural adjustment programme.

The government–business relationship

In New Zealand the link between the economic liberalisation policies, the benefits of which rapidly accrued to the corporate sector, and the strategic influence of that sector in the restructuring process is manifest. During the implementation phase key private sector actors, industry organisations and business lobby groups collaborated with the technopols and technocrats to initiate change. In the consolidation period key individuals continued to support the changes through their residual role in state agencies, such as SOEs and CHEs. Financial analysts and 'free market' ideologues dominated the economic debate. Powerful lobby groups remained vocal in their support. The economic interests of corporations and finance capital made them the first line of defence against any suggestions of retreat.

It is impossible to tell how far 'stacking the deck' was a deliberate strategy on the part of the architects of the programme and how far it was intrinsic to the structural adjustment process. Those who were responsible for the experiment were quick to claim the high ground for themselves and one another. Douglas praised the objectivity and selflessness of the Treasury and Business Roundtable, while they and their supporters in the media, academia and lobby groups applauded the technopols for their sacrificial dedication to the cause. There are certainly grounds for scepticism about such claims. Yet, even if the technocrats and technopols deliberately installed fellow-travellers in places from which the latter could advance and defend the new regime, and even if these individuals or the companies they worked for benefited from the restructuring, that does not prove either a conspiracy or that those involved were motivated by personal gain.

Documented examples of direct personal benefits are rare. One leading corporate figure was candid about his financial support for Labour. Former chief executive of Equiticorp, Alan Hawkins, later jailed for multi-million-dollar corporate fraud, described a donation of $250,000 to Labour, routed through Roger Douglas, as 'recognition for the good work he had done in deregulating the economy, something Equiticorp had benefited tremendously from'.[12] Direct political pay-offs channelled through individual politicians were not accepted political practice in New Zealand, however. Most of the politicians and officials involved in the process would have viewed such motives as distasteful, politically risky and corrupt.

Party funds, however, relied on business patronage, and there was direct financial support from the corporate sector for the project. Based on interviews with leading political, state sector and corporate actors in the Labour years, US analyst Herman Schwartz recorded how the capital inflow from 1985

> facilitated a centralization of economic power that in turn created a new social base for the Labour party. The party's financial market deregulation enabled takeover artists, using Euromarket funds, to gobble up firms stricken by the tight monetary policy. The newly emergent financial empires then provided the Labour party with both election cash and a series of chief executive officers who were willing to run New Zealand's newly corporatized SOEs.[13]

In 1992 the Wellington regional division of the National Party called for a funding drive directed at business, claiming: 'Those who benefit directly from the policies of the Government must be encouraged to support the Government by their donations.'[14] Securing such donations was a part of political life. Yet, unlike most of its Western counterparts, New Zealand had no rules requiring political parties to make public their source of funds. The refusal of both major parties to agree to such a move, recommended by the Royal Commission on the Electoral System in December 1986, reinforced suspicions that the major parties, especially the government, may have been unduly close to big business.

A June 1992 poll showed that a massive 81 percent of those surveyed believed there was corruption in New Zealand politics.[15] The Chief Ombudsman suggested establishing an anti-corruption commission, alongside early and more complete release of official information and greater personal financial disclosure by ministers, MPs and senior officials. Neither Labour nor National was impressed. But corruption was not really the right word to describe the corporate–government connection. In a country like New Zealand, with a government circle as small as that in Wellington and a business community where directorships and commercial activities were closely interlocked, conspiracies and graft were not necessary. Like-minded people and agencies, constantly interacting with one another in business and social settings, had much the same effect.

Business Roundtable

The most influential of these networks was the lobby for big business, the New Zealand Business Roundtable. The Roundtable began informally in the later 1970s, and became more organised with the advent of Rogernomics in 1984. In 1986 it set up office in Wellington under the direction of former Treasury technocrat, Roger Kerr.

Membership of the Roundtable was by invitation only, ensuring a consistent ideology and minimum of conflict. In 1995 the Roundtable comprised 57 chief executives from the country's largest companies, and four associate members. Not all major chief executives were members—Hugh Fletcher, the chief executive of Fletcher Challenge, criticised its extreme position, although FCL chair Sir Ron Trotter played a leading role from 1984. The share of stock-market capitalisation among companies run by Roundtable members in 1991 was estimated at 85 percent of the national total.[16] The proportion of members from the financial sector also increased during the 1980s, reflecting recent changes in the structure of New

Zealand capital. Throughout the structural adjustment programme, the Roundtable used its resources, public profile and corporate power to fortify and accelerate the rate of change, and to condemn any suggestion of retreat. At one time under Labour almost half the SOE directors were members of the Roundtable.

The Roundtable published a multitude of reports, usually prepared by overseas consultants, on a range of economic and social issues. It also offered several all-embracing blueprints for the future. Many of its reports were initially dismissed by commentators as extreme. But there were striking similarities between many Roundtable proposals and the policies of both Labour and National governments. The Roundtable and its supporters attributed this influence to the quality of its work and its economic orthodoxy. According to Kerr:

> I have found it an extraordinary experience to have been associated with a business organisation which has consistently, through immensely difficult economic times, adhered to those principles and avoided self-serving lobbying. I know of no other business organisation in the world that has stayed committed to promoting long-term national interests in this way. Nor am I aware of any other country where the relationship between business and politics is as free from corruption as New Zealand.[17]

Douglas applauded the Business Roundtable 'for having put self-interest and privilege aside in the national interest'. Instead of 'surreptitious lobbying', it had 'issued reasoned, researched discussion papers in the full glare of public debate'. This had driven 'the level of policy debate up to internationally respectable levels of excellence'.[18] A rather different assessment came from labour economist Nigel Haworth, who described the Roundtable as 'simultaneously the purveyor of ideology and policy and the locus around which key national players in the business world develop their project for the integration of New Zealand into the globalisation process on the basis of comparative advantage'.[19]

Industry lobbies
Considerable input and influence was also enjoyed by major industry lobbies. Immediately after Labour's election in 1984, a submission was presented to Prime Minister Lange from the Top Tier Group—the presidents of the Chambers of Commerce, Employers' Federa-

tion, Manufacturers' Federation, Federated Farmers and Retailers' Federation—urging radical economic reform. Major sectoral groups usually found it difficult to reach a common policy stance. The submission was therefore seen as remarkable, and a clear indication that widespread support for a laissez-faire economy had been building among New Zealand's major business associations since the late 1970s.[20]

Once the Labour government so fervently embraced the structural adjustment programme, active lobbying and structured consultation were rarely required. The Top Tier organisations continued to work together to pressure government and create a climate for change on issues of mutual concern. The Employers' Federation's determination to lower the cost of labour and break the unions had wide business appeal. The employers had abandoned their long-standing support for centralised wage bargaining and compulsory unionism in the late 1970s, once it proved ineffective to hold wages down and prevent industrial disputes. By the mid-1980s, encouraged by international employer militancy, they were arguing for contract-based employment, enterprise bargaining and voluntary unionism under a national code of minimum conditions. The effective privatisation of the public sector workforce through state sector restructuring and the creation of the SOEs, followed by the Employment Contracts Act, significantly increased Employers' Federation power. By the early 1990s, the federation represented two-thirds of all employers, and 80 percent of those in the private sector.[21] It became an outspoken advocate for the entire structural adjustment package.

Specific sectors pursued their own concerns. Deregulation of the financial markets spawned an industry of merchant bankers and financial analysts. Their survival depended on the free movement of capital and labour, while inflation eroded the value of their financial assets. These voices of the market constantly warned of the dire consequences of retreat. The Retailers' Federation, Bankers Association and Finance Houses Association all urged liberalisation in their particular realms, as well as supporting stability in inflation and exchange rates, fiscal restraint, labour market deregulation and tax reform.

The Manufacturers' Federation endorsed most areas of the structural adjustment programme, except tariff reduction and the monetary regime. Its opposition there was portrayed as vested interest lobbying to protect its own interests ahead of 'the economy as a whole'. Even then, there was conflict between the large, trans-national, export-oriented companies, which supported trade liberalisation, and the small and medium-sized companies, which produced for the domestic market and depended on protection. The latter reluctantly acceded to progressive tariffication and reductions which went beyond the government's obligations under the GATT.

The traditionally conservative farming sector provided probably the strongest, most sustained support for radical change. Again this predated Labour's election in 1984.

> In the early 1980s a change took place in Federated Farmers' economic policy with a return to the full-blown economic liberalism which had been the Federation's official philosophy prior to the 1970s. This coincided with changes in personnel in the top three presidential positions. [The policy change] created tensions between Federated Farmers and the Muldoon Government. Indeed Federated Farmers' general election policy statement of 1984, *Agriculture: The Anchor of the Economy*, reads like an agenda for Rogernomics.[22]

The farming community bore the brunt of the removal of subsidies, tax concessions and concessionary loans in the first two years of restructuring. Nevertheless, the leadership continued to support Labour's policy at the 1987 election, demanding that other sectors be subjected to the same disciplines to bring their cost structures into line. In 1990 they switched their allegiance back to National, where farming interests remained at the heart of the government. Federated Farmers consistently supported the Uruguay round of the GATT, labour market deregulation and removal of producer board monopolies. The three federation presidents during this time (Elworthy, Chamberlin and Jennings) all became evangelists for the structural adjustment line, and continued to promote the cause after they retired.

Contracting and consultants

At a more subtle level the interplay between public and private sectors provided a seamlessness in strategies, practices and values. State sector restructuring and labour market deregulation meant senior and middle management moved freely between the public and private sectors. Former Treasury economists and change agents left the public sector to join or establish private consultancies from which they continued to support the programme. For example, Secretary to the Treasury Graham Scott, when he retired in 1993, formed a consultancy which provided economic and financial advice for government and business in New Zealand and abroad. Three senior SSC officials formed a private consultancy in 1993 specialising in labour market and state sector policy advice.[23] Public and private sector roles often overlapped. For example, in 1988 the Treasury commissioned two former Treasury officials, then at Jarden Morgan investment bank, to review the Commerce Act. The same year, these former officials prepared reports for the Business Roundtable on privatisation and on Commerce Act reform.[24]

Not only the technocrats played this role. Senior politicians in parliamentary and party ranks, after retiring from office, also set up or joined consultancies. These included Sue Wood (president of the National Party 1984–87), Rob Campbell (unionist and Labour policy council member 1980–86), Jim McLay (National Leader of the Opposition, 1984–86), Richard Prebble (Labour Minister for SOEs and related portfolios, 1984–88, 1990), Roger Douglas (Labour Minister of Finance, 1984–88) and Ruth Richardson (National Minister of Finance, 1990–93). Campbell was not the only former unionist to see the opportunities for negotiating agents under the Employment Contracts Act. Others also swapped sides, advising government on key areas of structural change and formulating strategies to neutralise union opposition.

Commercial confidentiality makes it impossible to determine exactly how pervasive the government's use of consultants became. In response to a series of parliamentary questions, 32 departments reported spending more than $44 million on consultancy assignments valued at over $5000 during the National government's first year.[25] Treasury has disclosed that between 1987 and 1994 a total of $120 million was paid out in consultancy fees for the asset sales programme.[26] Consultancies also became a significant new export earner. In 1992 alone New Zealand consultants reportedly earned between $70 and $100 million advising agencies such as the World Bank and overseas governments embarking on their own restructuring programmes.[27] Other agencies were employed as public relations advisors to sell major government reforms. As journalist Bruce Jesson observed: 'These consultancy and public relations firms work for government departments. They organise political campaigns for government. They represent business to the government and provide business with political advice. . . . These political consultants have become the new mediators in an age of commercialised politics.'[28]

Redefining capture

While those who actively supported structural adjustment were generally treated as neutral and objective, those who opposed the changes were dismissed as vested-interest lobbyists seeking to capture the policy-making process. As a consequence:

> Beneficiaries, unemployed organisations, the traditional public service, community groups and even local bodies, all have proved powerless to prevent damaging changes to their situations. Consensus and pluralism are—for the moment—a dead letter in New Zealand politics, with the balance of influence shifting to business and finance in a culture of thoroughgoing commercialism.[29]

While the role of individual actors, corporations and lobby groups was important to its implementation, New Zealand's structural adjustment programme was only one small part of a much broader reconfiguration of economic and political power, and was driven by forces beyond its control. The programme was intended to integrate New Zealand's economy into the new global order, and did so very successfully. The economy became dominated by foreign- and 'New Zealand'-owned trans-national enterprises and finance capital. International political co-operation, led by the powerful leaders of the United Kingdom and United States, fostered dialogue and created alliances at an inter-party level between free-market conservatives, including the National Party. The network of neo-liberal and libertarian think-tanks around the Western world arranged exchanges, conferences and speaking tours for leading ideologues—in New Zealand's case through the Business Roundtable and the Centre for Independent Studies, which had its heyday in the second half of the 1980s. The ideological influence of neo-liberal theory, emanating mainly from the United States, became pervasive and operated in a largely unadulterated form in New Zealand. Overseas consultants were imported to assist this country's technocrats. As New Zealand assumed a more prominent role in the global structural adjustment industry, consultants eagerly cashed in on the export opportunities, while the technocrats in turn offered their expertise overseas.

The New Zealand experiment was prosecuted in the name of the 'public good' and the 'national interest'. In practice it oversaw the systematic transfer of power over the country's economic, social and political future to individuals and institutions of private capital, driven by profit and market forces, devoid of any ethical or moral responsibility for the social effect, and backed by the institutions and agencies of international capital, who remained shadowy figures in the background.

PART TWO

THE SUBSTANCE

CHAPTER FIVE

Market and Trade Liberalisation

NEW ZEALAND'S STRUCTURAL ADJUSTMENT programme centred on five 'fundamentals': liberalisation of domestic markets and trade; reduction of the size and scope of the state; monetary policy, driven by an overriding goal of price stability; labour market deregulation and deunionisation of the workforce; and fiscal restraint, through broadening the taxation base and cutting state spending and social support.

The deregulation of domestic markets and liberalisation of international trade was perhaps the least politically fraught element of the programme. Early moves towards industry deregulation, reduction of import licensing and closer economic relations with Australia had taken place under Muldoon. With both Labour and National fully committed to the policy, the debate centred on how far and how fast it should be done.

The Labour government had secured general support for deregulation at the 1984 economic summit, although the detailed implications were never spelt out. Action after that has been described as 'swift, involving less consultation and going further than some of the summit conference delegates would have wished'.[1] In short order, the government

- removed import licensing;
- removed exchange regulations;
- reduced tariffs;
- removed price controls on almost everything;
- removed production and distribution controls in individual industries and services;
- deregulated finance markets;
- amended the Commerce Act to focus on efficient competition;
- repealed the Economic Stabilisation Act to limit ministerial powers of intervention;

- abolished many consultative and advisory organisations; and
- transferred responsibility for regulatory control increasingly from the legislature and Executive to the judiciary.[2]

The strategy for exposing 'fortress New Zealand' to the global competitive market-place centred on three elements: eliminating industry assistance; withdrawing border protection from domestic producers and financial institutions; and shifting the regulation of capital, goods and labour from the state to the market.

The deregulation agenda

In 1984 almost every part of the economy was heavily regulated. A complex system of trade protections—mainly tariffs, import licensing, and export incentives and subsidies—had been built up over the years in response to various balance of payments, revenue, employment and industry needs. Competition and trade practices law, including provision for price controls, also served a range of efficiency and welfare goals. Other regulations applied to land and resource use, labour, health and safety, environment and product quality. Various methods of regulation were used, including ministerial discretion, government-established industry bodies, and self-regulation by trade and professional bodies.

By the 1980s there was a growing literature criticising regulatory intervention. Regulation was accused of hampering innovation and flexibility, impeding efficient resource allocation and international competitiveness, and encouraging industry capture. In 1984 Treasury talked not of deregulation but of 'shifting government intervention'. A market-driven approach to regulation would allow market signals to guide investment, minimise administrative and compliance costs, and encourage adaptation to the constantly changing international environment.

Treasury side-stepped the equity implications of such change. According to its 1984 briefing papers 'there are areas in which the achievement of equality (or more broadly equity) may be regarded as being subservient to other considerations such as efficiency, or where gains in one must be traded off against losses in the other'.[3] The interventionist approach, Treasury claimed, had its own negative equity effects. Ultimately, the market would align private incentives with social goals. Any residual inequities were best left to redistribution through tax.

In 1987 *Government Management* offered a deeper philosophical justification, using voluntary transactions as the starting-point.[4] Regulatory regimes, Treasury argued, should seek to maximise efficiency and liberty. 'Regulation should largely be restricted to the definition of rights to use resources in order to facilitate private contracting to minimise interdependencies. There is a fundamental need to be wary of detailed regulatory interventions restricting rights to contract. Such interventions may hinder dynamic efficiency.'[5] The focus on market failure as a justification for intervention, Treasury argued, ignored the equal, or greater, likelihood of government failure. An institutional bias in favour of intervention had resulted from poor information, industry capture of the advisory process and administration, and agency problems caused by vested interests in the bureaucracy and government. Treasury's solution was to replace the direct control of the state with the purportedly unbiased contractual mechanisms of insurance, common law and the market-place.[6]

Deregulation of finance markets

One of the Labour government's first moves was the comprehensive deregulation of the financial sector, 'taking it, in short order, from among the most regulated of the OECD countries to probably the least regulated'.[7] Foreign investment was considered the key to New Zealand's economic growth. Foreign capital has always played a large part in the country's economy, owing partly to its colonial history and partly to the small size of the domestic capital market. Historically, Britain invested in primary industries and Australia in finance. Increased domestic protection in the 1950s drew new investors seeking to circumvent domestic trade barriers, especially from the US. Controls on foreign investment were always weak, but restrictions on foreign exchange movements and high transport and internal costs limited New Zealand's attractiveness. Removal of exchange controls and deregulation of the finance markets rapidly changed that.

Economic Management had tagged exchange controls and financial regulations, such as restrictions on borrowing overseas, holding overseas assets and entry into banking, as matters requiring urgent attention. These controls had developed over time to meet equity, efficiency and stability goals. Treasury now argued that they retarded the development of open money markets and distorted product development and competition. They also produced inequities between savers and borrowers.

Economists David Harper and Girol Karacaoglu have described

the scope and speed of changes to financial policy after July 1984 as unequalled in the OECD or the Pacific region over the previous two decades.[8] Within two years of Labour's election, all price regulations in the financial sector and controls on the structures of financial institutions' balance sheets had been removed. The government had committed itself to improving contestability in financial markets and removing artificial entry barriers. Its advisors had devised a system of prudential oversight which they claimed would minimise the systemic effects of failure by individual institutions. Monetary control was being pursued through open market operations.

Most existing financial institutions seized the new opportunities with alacrity. Firms rapidly diversified to build on their information, skills and market base. As competition squeezed profits from traditional financial transactions, new products and niche markets were created. Financial information services expanded rapidly. Merchant and investment bankers became important intermediaries in internationalised capital markets. The speculative futures market took on a life of its own. Property trusts provided opportunities for real estate investment, while unit trusts serviced consortia of small investors and investment funds.

Removal of controls on overseas transactions, coupled with high domestic interest rates, saw New Zealand-based corporations seek out cheaper money offshore. Major firms, and subsequently SOEs, developed their own treasury operations. The Eurokiwi market emerged. Complex international transactions, some involving offshore tax havens, provided vehicles for tax avoidance and fraud, many of which were not discovered until the corporate entities collapsed. The 1994–95 inquiry into a Cook Islands tax scheme put the transactions of several leading New Zealand corporations under the microscope.[9]

Most finance sector expansion came through mergers and takeovers. Multi-divisional firms were created almost overnight. As competition increased, so did the pressure to cut costs. Large firms streamlined their operations, reducing staff and increasing productivity demands. Branches closed and unprofitable retail services were dispensed with, while new services to the corporate and wholesale sectors improved. As the number of firms was whittled down, foreign companies began to dominate. The theory of contestable market entry was used to justify increased concentration and overseas control. By 1995, fourteen of the country's sixteen registered banks were entirely or substantially foreign-owned. As a consequence of deregulating the finance markets first, spending was diverted from productive to speculative investment. This was fuelled by the reckless attitude of many local lenders. The new financial regime coincided with the world stock-market boom. The share price index rose by 140 percent from 1984 to 1987. Market capitalisation rose from $17.6 billion at the end of 1985 to $42.4 billion a year later and reached $42.8 billion by September 1987. By December that year it had collapsed to $24.2 billion.[10]

The lifting of financial controls also meant major changes to the capital ownership structure. Many major New Zealand companies listed offshore, initially in Australia but often elsewhere. The largest companies like Fletcher Challenge claimed they had to raise equity overseas because of the size of the New Zealand capital market and the prudential requirements on major investors and fund managers to spread their exposure. This was reinforced by the reduction in listed companies following the share-market crash which effectively limited demand and capped the companies' share price. Major manufacturers moved offshore too. Treasury saw this as 'quite sensible' if goods could be produced more efficiently elsewhere. The manufacturing sector had no constant or ideal size, and needed to respond to changing international conditions; in most OECD countries traditional manufacturing was being replaced by the rapidly expanding service sector.[11]

A profound shift in corporate ethos accompanied this transition. In 1990 Richard Carter, co-founder of the country's then third-largest company, Carter Holt Harvey (CHH), condemned the merchant bankers and property developers who abandoned traditional loyalties and embraced Rogernomics during New Zealand's boom times as 'traitors to the country. . . . During all the hype throughout 1985 to 1987 we hardly got a mention. We were not a property developer or a merchant banker. They were in all the greatest newspaper articles. We were simply the backbone of New Zealand industry.'[12] Another of the patriarchs of New Zealand business, Sir James Fletcher, lamented the erosion of long-term commitment to productive enterprise caused by the quest for quick returns:

> In my time you worked for the company. . . . But today . . . the first consideration of these chief executives is their own financial package and it seems to me that in many cases the company is there to make wealth for the executives rather than make wealth for the shareholders, or at

least the shareholders rank a pretty poor second . . . or to create jobs. I think they have done a tremendous disadvantage to business because they tended to make shareholders look for a quick return.[13]

Competition law

The New Zealand economy was now driven by finance, rather than productive, capital. The shift to market-driven commercial law was intended to complement that change. The Treasury argued that the purpose of competition law was to maximise efficiency, not to promote competition itself. They believed that vertical integration, restrictive trade practices and monopolies could be efficient responses in certain market conditions, and should not be impeded by unnecessary and costly regulation. Faced with tensions between competition and efficiency, Treasury insisted that *potential* for competition was enough. Monopolies that were inefficient or unresponsive to consumer demand, or whose products were overpriced, laid themselves open to 'hit and run' raids by new firms, provided these could enter the market freely. Removing legal entry barriers to potential competitors, coupled with the threat of regulation, would force monopolies to discipline themselves. Until that was achieved, competition law should focus on abuses of market power which worked to the consumers' detriment. Even then, intervention had to be weighed carefully so it would not impede efficiency.[14]

This approach was echoed by Commerce Commission member and Fletcher Challenge director Kerrin Vautier: 'Various collusive or contractual arrangements may be necessary to compete efficiently in a market, especially in view of information and transaction costs under conditions of uncertainty. The risk that such arrangements may diminish consumer welfare is minimised in reasonably accessible markets.'[15]

This 'contestability' model was denounced as 'unreal' in a 1988 seminar by US economist Douglas Greer. He argued that the conditions of cost-free entry and exit that underpin the hit and run approach almost never arise. Incumbent firms also erect informal barriers to potential competitors

through strategic behaviour, such as building excess capacity to fend off entry, engaging in exclusive dealing, proliferation of brands, hoarding scarce inputs to raise a rival's costs, granting loyalty rebates to customers, using pre-emptive patenting and so on. These strategic behaviours become more effective as concentration and firm market share rise (and they in turn foster the high concentration and market shares). Hence, a merger policy that liberally allows hefty increases in concentration and market shares on the presumption (or even solid proof) of imperfect contestability may be putting firms in a position to negate that partial contestability.[16]

Greer attributed the power of contestability theory to ideology and ignorance. It had gained influence in the US not on its merits but by riding on the coat-tails of compatible Chicago views embraced by Reagan's political and judicial appointees. 'Notwithstanding its inconsistencies, implausibilities, non-robustness, empirical immateriality, and impracticality of application, contestability theory has had a significant impact on competition policy in both the US and NZ.'[17]

From 1985 competition policy progressively embraced the economic efficiency and contestability arguments. The 1975 Commerce Act long title had read:

> An Act to assist in the orderly development of industry and commerce and to promote its efficiency, and the welfare of consumers, through the regulation, where desirable in the public interest, of trade practices, of monopolies, mergers and takeovers, and of prices of goods and services.

Its 1986 replacement was simply described as 'an Act to promote competition in markets'. Takeovers and mergers were subjected to a market dominance test, while restrictive trade practices were judged in terms of substantially lessening competition. Both could still be authorised if their public benefit to the public was shown to outweigh the absence of effective competition. Whereas the 1975 Act had defined 'public interest', 'benefit to the public' was now not defined.

Pressure on the Commerce Commission and the government to give priority to efficiency continued. Vautier argued that 'since the Commerce Act has been promoted as an integral and complementary part of the government's wider policy priorities of efficiency and economic growth, then its implementation should as far as possible be consistent with those priorities'.[18] The commission began relying heavily on argument and anecdotal evidence from proponents of mergers that competitive entry was possible, and its rulings tended to favour the contestability approach. Treasury's *Government Management* gave notice of a renewed attack in the forthcoming review of the Act. Following the review in 1988,[19] a specific instruction was inserted in the Commerce Act which required the Commerce Commission, from July 1990, to take efficiency into account as a measure of public benefit. Other elements of public benefit, and the weight to be given them, were still not defined.

A further Commerce Law Reform Bill in 1990 began as a simple amendment to reduce the statutory decision-making period. The legislation which emerged from the select committee repealed mandatory pre-notification and pre-clearance procedures for mergers or takeovers, in line with Australian competition law. Notification of moves which would create or strengthen a dominant market position was now a matter of voluntary compliance, or action initiated by private parties or the Commerce Commission through the courts. Yet another review in 1993 reinforced the contestability approach.[20] The tug of war over the application of the legislation continued in the courts as economists and judges disputed the meaning of efficiency. In a hard-fought case involving privatised Telecom, US economists William Baumol and Robert Willig were brought in to present an argument which justified the barriers placed by Telecom in the path of its competitor Clear Communications. One Court of Appeal judge created an alternative model which provided the basis on which the court decided that Telecom had abused its monopoly position.[21] On further appeal, however, the Privy Council adopted Baumol and Willig's 'tightly reasoned economic model'.[22] Despite intense pressures, by 1995 the implementation of the Commerce Act remained contested and unpredictable; the capture of competition law was not yet complete.

Securities law
An associated struggle took place over regulation of takeover activity. The corporate boom and bust of Labour's first four years had a devastating effect on the business sector, and fuelled demands for reform. The Securities Commission had begun reviewing the laws on nominee shareholding and takeovers soon after it was established in 1979. Their proposals required a formal offer once 20 percent of a company's capital had been acquired and equal treatment of all shareholders. These were effectively stymied by the Treasury, whose 1984 submission to the commission argued: 'Regulations which do not allow takeovers to take place with speed and secrecy will weaken the incentives to acquire this type of information in the first place. The gainers will be inefficient management, while society as a whole will be a loser.'[23]

The stalemate between investor protection and equity on the one hand and economic efficiency on the other continued until mid-1986. Concerns over the boom in share-market activity that followed financial and corporate deregulation, especially over insider trading and takeovers, saw the government ask the Securities Commission to continue working on these issues. The commission's report on insider trading was accepted by the government and actioned, despite opposition from the Treasury. Progress on take-overs moved more slowly. In October 1988, following a highly contested inquiry into a major corporate merger, the commission again recommended tightening the takeovers code.[24] Treasury argued strenuously against the move, backed by Harvard economist Professor John Pound, who had been imported to give evidence by investment bankers Fay Richwhite. Although the commission's report was accepted by the Cabinet, no legislation was introduced.

The Securities Commission was progressively sidelined from the takeovers debate. In 1989 a Ministerial Committee of Inquiry into the Sharemarket, with a broad mandate for law reform which referred to a 'fair and efficient' investment market, recommended a comprehensive system of financial sector self-regulation based on the guild model. Treasury reiterated its position that '[c]apital markets are not perfect, but it is clearly an area where there must be great doubt whether heavy-handed regulation will contribute to overall policy goals.'[25] The stand-off over takeovers continued. In its 1990 briefing papers, Treasury repeated the objection that tighter regulation would reduce incentives to carry out efficient takeovers. Capital markets necessarily involved an element of risk-taking and 'such failures generally result in the underlying productive assets of such firms being transferred to new owners. While there will be costs in this process, these assets are usually put to sound commercial use.'[26]

Writing in 1990, competition lawyer Jim Farmer regretted the deeply ideological nature of the company law debate and the pressure on government 'to be seen to be "doing something" about the unscrupulous and the incompetent (of whom there are certainly many)'.[27] Much of the debate

> has been fuelled by a concern, following the sharemarket crash, that the small shareholder has been savagely exploited by entrepreneurs motivated by greed and high flying company directors who have failed to observe fundamental notions of fiduciary obligation. This has contributed to an international view of New Zealand financial markets (and, increasingly, Australian markets) that they are completely lacking in

integrity and that regulatory controls are either non-existent or, at best, totally inadequate. Although there is considerable validity in those observations, it is perhaps unfortunate that in the last three years commercial law reform, and company takeover law in particular, has been considered in an atmosphere that has not been conducive to rational debate.[28]

Farmer warned against swinging too far in favour of shareholder equity at the expense of recognising the benefits to shareholders from takeover activity. Such fears proved unfounded. The National government set up a new body to consider securities law reform drawn equally from the private sector and bureaucracy. Membership included Treasury, but not the Securities Commission. Despite strong support from the commercial sector for a code, the Roundtable and others convinced the government that shareholders' rights should be addressed through the new Companies Act. This Act, passed in 1993, introduced a less prescriptive approach to company law that provided for a simplified and more flexible corporate structure, but imposed statutory restrictions on directors and increased disclosure requirements. The accompanying Takeovers Act merely enabled the Minister of Justice to appoint a panel to devise a takeovers code. The code would be brought into force only if and when the minister saw fit. According to the minister: 'The Government is attracted to the United Kingdom approach in which the market itself formulates the rules and takes responsibility for compliance with them.'[29]

This lack of action was blamed by one legal commentator on a deadlock between those who favoured regulation of takeovers and 'proponents of corporate raiding'. In this conflict 'it is the latter (mostly made up of institutional and other large investors) who have held sway, thereby facilitating for themselves freedom of reign [*sic*] in obtaining control of companies.'[30] In late 1994, a takeovers panel appointed by the minister produced a code very similar to earlier versions, accompanied by an explicit theoretical justification. The proposal met with vigorous resistance from within the Cabinet, the Treasury and the powerful private sector lobby, and in August 1995 implementation of a takeovers code was once more deferred.

Removing industry protections

Meanwhile, traditional productive sectors had been subjected to a scorched earth approach where only the most internationally competitive would survive. Treasury blamed industry assistance for producing a lower level of national income and welfare than would result if prices were determined by the market. While it acknowledged that withdrawing industry assistance would create adjustment costs as resources shifted from previously protected activities to expanding, more efficient ones, this was considered a temporary and inevitable price to pay. Treasury urged the government to move rapidly to minimise avoidable costs.[31]

Agricultural protection

Agriculture was the first target. New Zealand economic policies traditionally reflected farming's central role in the economy. In 1984 agriculture still contributed 60 percent of exports[32] and 7 percent of GDP,[33] and remained the major foreign-exchange earner. While other industries had received export incentives, farming had received both input subsidies, such as cheap finance and farm development incentives, and a supplementary minimum price (SMP) for output. Between 1984 and 1987 these were withdrawn. The 20 percent devaluation in 1984 was expected to help compensate for the phasing out of SMPs, but the dollar rapidly appreciated after it was floated in March 1985. Financial sector deregulation and the withdrawal of subsidised credit raised interest rates to market levels. User charges were imposed for most government research and, as a result of corporatisation, for utility services.

Many farmers who had invested at inflated land prices or expanded production during the SMP-driven boom were left over-exposed. As interest rates rose, farmers reduced on-farm expenditure on fertiliser and maintenance and cut stock numbers to service the debt. Farmer Robert Bremer and historian Tom Brooking note that, in the 1985/86 financial year, sheep farmers' terms of trade at the farm gate fell to as low as 56 percent of the base year of 1974/75, which itself was not a particularly good year. The decline was such that 'by 1985 a great number of influential policy-makers, including the Minister of Finance, were looking upon New Zealand's traditional agriculture as a "sunset industry", although most of the propounded alternative industries found their own sunset after the 1987 financial crash'.[34]

The agricultural sector survived, but underwent radical structural change. In 1987 economist Lewis Evans predicted the transition from the traditional family farm towards larger-scale farm companies. Fluctuations in foreign prices were expected to provide incentives for on- and off-farm diversification, with farmers devoting more effort to financial and marketing management.

Increased price uncertainty at the farm gate means that there are gains to diversification and that more financial management skills are required than has been the case in the past. Large firms will allow each of their different enterprises to be run at a large enough level to contribute significantly to profits. Furthermore large farms will generally be better able to hire the specialised skills required to handle well a diverse set of activities. It seems likely, therefore, that farm businesses which do react to these factors will become larger, and this is likely to entail a reduction in the importance of the owner-occupier family farm.[35]

Farms did become larger and fewer, run increasingly by entrepreneurial business people. Agribusinesses began to emerge. By 1995 the most prominent of these, 28 percent overseas-owned Apple Fields Ltd, held 660 acres of apple orchards and 33 dairy farms. The new breed of farmers, whether survivors of restructuring or new entrants, became stalwarts of the neo-liberal regime. At the same time, there was a 'growing awareness among farmers of rural deprivation arising from inexorable loss of rural services and amenities as economic restructuring has gradually depopulated the countryside'.[36]

Once agricultural production had been liberalised, processing and marketing through producer boards came under sustained attack. Most boards had begun as co-operatives to strengthen the position of domestic producers in their international markets. They were gradually incorporated into the state's regulatory machinery, and granted statutory monopoly powers. By the 1980s the boards controlled around 80 percent of all agricultural and horticultural exports.

Treasury's *Economic Management* argued that market competition between exporters should be positively encouraged. Lack of competition made it impossible to monitor the effectiveness of existing boards, and reduced their incentives to become cost efficient. Where firms could identify market opportunities, they should be able to test them against the prevailing alternatives.[37] Access by the boards to concessional finance was subsequently removed. Pressure continued to review the boards' ownership structures, lift their statutory monopoly, open them to competition and remove their power to make compulsory levies. The Business Roundtable made constant attacks on the boards. Renegade producers ran orchestrated campaigns, led by Roundtable company Apple Fields. Gradually the boards' powers were weakened and some fell. In 1995 many were still intact, but few were secure.

Industry assistance

Manufacturers began to feel the pressure in 1985 as the Labour government moved rapidly, and with minimal consultation, to dismantle trade protections. This had been signalled well before 1984. In return for promised benefits under the CER trade agreement with Australia, domestic manufacturers had agreed reluctantly to the progressive conversion of import licensing to tariffs and reduction of domestic protection. But they managed to stall its implementation. The US threatened, and subsequently imposed, countervailing sanctions and demanded more rapid progress.[38]

Economic Management attacked trade barriers and export incentives as inefficient in themselves. Their removal was considered integral to the trade liberalisation regime being pursued through CER and the GATT. By late 1986 the government had announced that most import licensing would be removed within two years and a programme of tariff reduction would be imposed. Export incentives would go before April 1990. Progress towards a free trade area with Australia would be stepped up.[39] Bollard described this process as 'multidimensional in its nature and radical in its impact, moving many industrial sectors from a high degree of external regulation to regulation by markets and other contractual arrangements within only three years'.[40]

Treasury was not satisfied. In 1987, 30 percent of manufactured goods output was still covered by industry plans that provided for the phase-out of protection. Import licensing and tariffs continued to provide some industry assistance, with most directed to motor vehicles, apparel and footwear. In *Government Management*, Treasury urged the government to speed up the pace of change: 'on the basis of experience to date we conclude that the reform programme for assistance to import substituting industries in particular could be significantly accelerated without imposing excessive adjustment costs on the economy, and that accelerating that programme would bring significant benefits.'[41] While Treasury conceded that there were 'potential problems with an excessively rapid programme for reduction of assistance', a 'period of notice would . . . allow people to search and if necessary to retrain for a new job. In short a reasonable period of adjustment will minimise the extent to which people are unemployed and production falls as a short term response to the new assistance regime.'[42] In this context, 'reasonable' was relative.

Treasury warned that a piecemeal approach would risk politicians capitulating to industry lobbies and encourage decisions based on particular industries' needs rather than economy-wide costs and gains. Ideally, all industry assistance levels should be reduced, with those on the highest levels cut by the largest amount. The onus would then fall on industries which claimed a greater degree of protection to prove how this would produce a superior outcome in terms of efficiency and liberty. Throughout, the benefits were assumed to be self-evident:

> A more even-handed policy will result in a more effective pattern of investment throughout the economy, leading to stronger economic growth and higher living standards. Faster progress towards those policy goals will bring those higher living standards more quickly.[43]

Transitional costs were swept aside in the discussion. The early devaluation had been expected to ease the adjustment process. But the rapidly appreciating exchange rate, due to the combination of tight monetary policy and financial deregulation, neutralised this. In 1987 an unrepentant Treasury blamed the situation facing exporters in part on the protection of inefficient sectors of the economy from competition, leading to an unfair burden on those export sectors which were exposed. The main problem, it said, was not the short-term effect of disinflation on the exchange rate, but the long-term distortions caused by regulatory control.[44]

Equity considerations were again marginalised—particularly in employment, a traditional justification for industry assistance. Treasury argued that industry protection merely shuffled jobs around the economy, thus protecting workers in one industry at the expense of those in another, and prevented labour from moving into new, more productive industries which would benefit all. Employment goals would best be met by ensuring that wages and labour responded to supply and demand in a vibrant, internationally competitive economy. That required deregulation of the productive, capital and labour markets.[45]

These arguments were based on theory—a statement of faith delivered largely in an empirical void. Treasury made no attempt in 1987 to examine the impact of deregulation since 1984, beyond a passing reference to an NZIER study on the impact of regulatory changes in six areas. That study found that increased market competition had tended to reduce prices to the consumer and increase product differentiation. It also reported that, as a result, some consumers, workers and firms were worse off.[46] A subsequent NZIER analysis commented on how little work had been done 'to establish the relative gains and costs borne by consumers and producers, and downstream distributional consequences. In fact the whole question of the magnitude of net benefits to the economy, and indeed whether they are positive, has been taken very much on faith.'[47]

The Labour government did largely as Treasury had urged. The effective rate of assistance for manufacturing fell from around 37 percent in 1985/86 to around 19 percent in 1989/90. The targets for deregulation with Australia were met by 1990, five years ahead of schedule. Most import licensing had been abolished, and the rest was to be eliminated by 1992. The tariff reduction programme ending in 1992 reduced levels to 14 percent, a very few exceptions aside. The next round of reductions set a maximum level of 10 percent by 1996, with higher protection continuing for textiles, shoes and cars. In the depths of the recession politics made a rare intervention. In June 1992 the Minister of Commerce, a former Manufacturers' Federation member, announced the deferral of tariff reductions for clothing 'as a safety net for the industry. I am not prepared to stand by and see the complete erosion of the industry's domestic base.'[48]

A further round of reductions was negotiated at the height of the 'recovery' in 1994, to begin in 1996. The targets set were described by government as 'tough but fair'. The differential between sectors was maintained, but tariffs in even the most protected industries were to be cut to 15 percent by 2000. With approximately 28,000 people still employed in those sectors, job losses were expected to be heavy, although the government predicted growth in efficient industries of 40,000 jobs a year over the following three years.[49] A further tariff review in 1998 would focus on reducing all remaining tariffs to zero.[50] This was the soft version of the policy. Treasury, trade and agriculture and fisheries officials had argued for much more.

Trade liberalisation

The dismantling of domestic protections was driven by the image of an internationally competitive New Zealand economy footing it with, and sometimes leading, the major trading nations of the world. Expositions of free trade theory took on an air of scientific truth, and drove New Zealand's zealous approach to trade negotiations with Australia and in the Asia–Pacific region, as well as the GATT.

The policy was quite divorced from the realities of international trade, where the US had a poor record of compliance with the GATT, and there was a history of resistance to reducing protections in both the European Community (later Union) and Japan.

Treasury dismissed claims that unilateral trade liberalisation would place New Zealand producers at an international disadvantage if other countries continued to protect their markets. It complained that this grudging and negative attitude had pervaded the GATT negotiations and ignored the major economic benefits which unilateral trade liberalisation could bring. Further, critics wrongly assumed that New Zealand could change the assistance policies of other countries.[51]

The New Zealand government was committed to a pure free-trade line that by the 1990s was being heavily contested overseas. Commentators from diverse ideological positions predicted a pragmatic combination of protectionism, regionalism and free trade over the next decade, and expressed doubts about the long-term prospects of the GATT.[52] International trade economist Paul Krugman observed the irony that

> in the early 1990s, when the political triumph of free-market economics is virtually complete, there is a growing trend in economic analysis towards models in which markets get it wrong. . . . If policy could be made without politics, the new trade theory and related developments elsewhere in economics would point quite clearly to a broad-based program of government intervention in the economy.[53]

Despite this, New Zealand governments held to the free-trade ideal with unshakeable resolve.

Closer Economic Relations

Removal of trade barriers in the 1980s was driven largely by the targets set in the Australia New Zealand Closer Economic Relations Trade Agreement (ANZCERTA or CER). The initial deal between the two countries was reached in January 1966 with the New Zealand Australia Free Trade Agreement. But its scope was limited, and a long list of exemptions covered almost all goods not already traded between the two. In March 1980 the countries' Prime Ministers endorsed the concept of closer economic relations in a joint communiqué. Negotiations moved quickly, with limited public debate, and a formal agreement was signed in 1983.

CER provided a valuable tool for supporters of internal deregulation in both countries. Under the initial CER agreement, export incentives affecting trade in goods with Australia were to be eliminated by 1987, tariffs by 1990, and import licensing by 1995. In late 1987 the target date for free trade in goods was brought forward by five years to 1990, and the parties agreed to extend CER by examining regulatory and restrictive trade practices. Their reasons were explicitly anti-protectionist, as both countries sought to improve their competitive trading position with third countries and take the lead in global liberalisation of trade. Australian Geoff Allen observed that 'the hard bilateral talk going on between the United States and Israel, the United States and Canada, and Australia and New Zealand became a laboratory for the trading world'.[54]

This leadership extended to trade in services. Service industries began pressing for inclusion in CER in the mid-1980s, bolstered by initiatives from the US, OECD and EC. The CER Trade in Services Agreement, which took effect on 1 January 1989, went further than the only other bilateral services agreement of the time, between the US and Canada. The agreement was described as 'full-blooded and comprehensive', even though it was explicitly subject to the 'foreign investment policies of the member states'.[55]

The two economies had become increasingly integrated through the private sector. The legal and regulatory environments were slower to change. Trans-Tasman application of competition law from July 1990 and the repeal of anti-dumping laws for trans-Tasman transactions signalled a major shift in emphasis. Traditional concerns about fairness in international trade gave way to the new efficiency focus of competition law operating within a single market. Competition lawyer Jim Farmer notes that the benefits of harmonisation were assumed throughout, without any clear assessment of the nature and extent of the barriers, or of the consequences of harmonisation for domestic and international trade with other partners.[56]

CER was always more important to New Zealand than Australia, and there were frequent arguments about who benefited most. Australia maintained a larger number of exemptions, but contended that these were far outweighed by the benefits to New Zealand of access to a market five times its size. Australia became progressively less enthusiastic about CER as its sights firmed on the growing markets of Asia. Deep-seated political tensions between the concept of a single economic market and independent national sovereignties also began to emerge. Ideologically driven New Zealand governments moved faster to deregulate than the Australians, who remained more attentive to domestic political considerations and structural adjustment costs.

These tensions came to a head in 1994, when Australia imposed visa requirements on New Zealanders, then informed the New Zealand government by fax that it was reneging on a deal to open its domestic aviation market to Air New Zealand, just days before the deal was to proceed. The New Zealand government chose not to seek arbitration under CER. Former Prime Minister David Lange condemned the government's attempt to play down the breach as a sign of weakness to Australia and other trading partners. Reflecting on the concurrent APEC leaders' summit, which had set a target of free trade by 2020, Lange observed, '17 of the 18 nations who were parties to the [APEC] accord know that they have more than 25 years to slap New Zealand in the face'.[57]

General Agreement on Tariffs and Trade

In the later 1980s the free traders focused further afield, on the Uruguay round of the GATT. In the negotiations, most governments based their offers on the realities of international trade—in particular, the record of major powers, who continued to protect their own interests first. New Zealand's Labour and National governments sought to bind future governments to everything they had already done, and more.

Both governments insisted that the future of agricultural exports, and hence of the economy, depended on a successful outcome to the Uruguay round. In return for a deal on agricultural subsidies, they were prepared to commit future governments to continued tariff reductions. They guaranteed foreign access to the New Zealand market for a wide range of services, including banking and finance, tourism and education. With this went an overall commitment to the movement of personnel engaged in services, and the continued openness of the overseas investment regime. No other country went so far. The same approach was adopted with trade-related intellectual property rights (TRIPS). According to the New Zealand Secretary of Commerce: 'We are relying on the United States in agriculture. It makes sense that we cannot ignore the United States when it comes to patent legislation in the GATT context.'[58]

Introducing the GATT (Uruguay Round) Bill in July 1994, the

Minister for Trade Negotiations proudly announced: 'While the outcome is significant for us, . . . the round will require us to do very little ourselves. . . . We have been ahead of the game. Our trading partners now have to open up their markets and cut back their subsidies to our benefit. What we have now achieved is, in effect, a bonus payment.' The only areas where the government had to move further than it had announced already were pharmaceuticals, pulp and paper, and beer, with some tidying up of the intellectual property laws.

> We have essentially agreed to maintain the status quo of current policy and present access to the New Zealand market by overseas suppliers of a broad range of goods and services. . . . The obligations assumed do not require legislative provisions because fulfilment of them is within the capacity of the Government to deliver—for example, through its existing regulatory administrative framework.[59]

The politicians, technocrats, corporate and farming lobbies, and economic commentators consistently talked up the benefits of the GATT. Yet the projected economic returns to New Zealand in the medium term were far from spectacular, and depended upon factors outside New Zealand's hands. Many of the case studies provided in the government's own assessment of the benefits, *Trading Ahead*, were extremely cautious. Even the much-heralded agreement on agriculture was acknowledged to be weak. The predicted returns from improved market access and export prices, particularly in agriculture, were an increased average annual income of $150 million to $230 million over the next ten years. A comprehensive World Bank study of the Uruguay round deal, released in April 1995, concluded that member governments had greatly exaggerated the extent of agricultural liberalisation which the deal would produce. The study lowered the estimated income gains for Australia and New Zealand from 0.6 percent of each country's GDP to less than 0.1 percent. The report suggested that farm protection might even increase under the deal.[60]

Other predicted gains were also suspect. The New Zealand government estimated that 20,000 to 30,000 new jobs *might* be created in the next decade as a result of the GATT.[61] Yet over 40,000 jobs *had* been lost in the manufacturing sector alone between 1988 and 1993,[62] many of which could be attributed, at least in part, to the tariff reduction programme. At the height of the recovery in 1994, the number of jobs in industry had returned to the 1988 level—but this was still 50,000 short of the 1986 high. The government's assessment also ignored the likely 'non-economic' impact of the new GATT/World Trade Organisation (WTO) regime on indigenous rights, cultural integrity, development planning, workers, the environment, and political and economic self-determination.

Under the Uruguay round agreement, future New Zealand governments were bound to maintain the deregulated free-trade regime. This would be almost impossible to reverse unless the new WTO fell apart. As the Law Commission noted, under such treaties 'New Zealand is bound by important undertakings, without any express power of withdrawal. The treaties are binding without limit of time. The undertakings limit in substance the power of the New Zealand Parliament.'[63] While there is provision in the GATT agreement (Article XII) to reimpose import controls for balance of payments reasons, that is a short-term measure which can be exercised only to forestall imminent threats of, or to stop, a serious decline in monetary reserves.[64] Its liberal use would invite threats of, or actual, sanctions from the WTO.

The commercially driven New Zealand media described the GATT as a 'ratings-killer',[65] so the official position was never subject to vigorous public debate. Nevertheless, the profoundly antidemocratic nature of the negotiations, the exclusion of potential critics from any consultations, and the excessive secrecy of the government's offer were strongly condemned by the Council for International Development, representing 30 aid agencies, the Environment and Conservation Organisations of New Zealand, the New Zealand Trade Union Federation (NZTUF) and the associations of university students and staff.

The National Maori Congress, which had consistently challenged the government's mandate to negotiate on its behalf and strenuously opposed the violation of cultural property rights in the agreement on TRIPS, served notice that it considered itself exempt from the WTO.

The Crown has not only neglected its Treaty of Waitangi responsibilities to the Iwi (tribal) Maori (indigenous) treaty partners, but it has violated the very principles of democracy by not adequately informing the public of the pros and cons of the GATT agreement and by not seeking the consent of New Zealanders before signing and ratifying an international agreement which has such widespread and direct consequences on the lives and livelihoods of individuals and communities.[66]

Asia Pacific Economic Co-operation Forum

Alongside the GATT negotiations, the government actively supported the development of APEC, a voluntary economic integration agreement covering the Asia–Pacific region. APEC has none of the institutional or bureaucratic structure of the European Union, nor even a set of binding agreements of the kind found in the North American Free Trade Agreement. It comprises an intangible process of meetings of leaders, ministers and officials, co-ordinated by a small secretariat, and relies for research on a tripartite business/academic/officials organisation known as the Pacific Economic Co-operation Council.

APEC was born in the frenzied atmosphere of the late 1980s, when the GATT negotiations constantly looked like breaking down. Europe and North America appeared to be retreating into defensive trading blocs. The countries in Asia and the Pacific rim—notably Japan, the Republic of Korea, the ASEAN countries, Australia and New Zealand—had strong if differing reasons for reaching a regional arrangement of their own. The US successfully insisted that it should not be left out.

The initial concept was of an outward-looking, non-institutionalised arrangement which would hasten liberalisation of the global economy, yet be tolerant of different levels of development and economic models. But the 1993 Eminent Persons' Group report represented APEC as a market-driven initiative which would work to 'ratchet up' the GATT process through co-operation at the regional level, and 'protect the forces of market-driven interdependence against governmental intrusion that could otherwise retard its natural evolution'.[67] In December 1994 the APEC leaders endorsed a programme for free trade and investment in the region to be completed by 2020, with staggered targets to reflect the different economic development of its members. But the future of APEC was uncertain. The aggressive liberalisation agenda pursued by the US, Australia, Canada and New Zealand was at odds with the more pragmatic approach of the ASEAN and most other Asian countries, publicly expressed by Malaysian Prime Minister Mahathir Mohamed.

Whether or not APEC survived, the realities of growing economic interdependence in the region meant that all its members had interests in one another's economies. All except the major powers were competing for the same pool of foreign investment in a potential 'race to the bottom', in which each sought to minimise costs and maximise opportunities for investors to exploit their natural and human resources. Some New Zealand-based trans-nationals had been quick to cash in on Asian countries' competitive advantage. Prime Minister Jim Bolger illustrated the benefits of APEC in 1994 by feting a horticultural plant operated in Thailand by Brierley Investments Ltd (BIL), where the workers earned 40 percent of the average Thai wage, or about NZ40 cents an hour. Bolger stated that New Zealand would trade with anyone, anywhere.[68] David Lange challenged the morality of such investments:

> The Government proposes that we shall be free trade partners with nations that have no minimum wage, no social security, safety standards in industry that have caused workers to be incinerated en masse, . . . limited press freedom and hardline right-wing governments. Worse, our Government has become an apologist for the inhumanity of some Asian labour market regimes.[69]

He might equally have held New Zealand's own TNCs culpable for profiteering from such regimes.

Deregulating foreign investment

The country's dependence on foreign capital and its exposure to foreign control had increased dramatically in a decade. By 1994 the top ten companies by turnover, excluding four co-operatives, statutory marketing boards and SOEs, had between 30 and 100 percent overseas ownership.[70] In 1995 around 40 percent of government stock, or $10 billion, was funded offshore, up 9 percent from one year before. Foreign investors owned half the share-market. Overseas ownership of companies (25 percent equity or more) increased 145 percent from $13.7 billion in the year ended March 1990 to $33.6 billion in the year to March 1994—in comparison, the assets of the Crown were valued at less than $30 billion. The three largest 'New Zealand' companies all had overseas companies holding well above 40 percent of their shares. Popular concerns about economic sovereignty were fuelled in 1995 by the US-owned International Paper's acquisition of a majority stake in forestry company CHH (a deal which also produced a windfall profit of $175 million to corporate raider BIL), and by yet another record profit to the US owners of the privatised Telecom, over 80 percent of which would be exported.

Since 1987, controls on foreign investment had been progressively weakened. The threshold for requiring approval for foreign investment from the Overseas Investment Commission (OIC) was raised from $500,000 to $2 million in 1987. In 1989 this was increased again to $10 million and approval requirements became perfunctory, except for broadcasting, commercial fishing within the exclusive economic zone, and rural land. Between 1987 and 1994, only four applications out of 7100 were declined, the last one in 1990.

Despite the raising of the threshold, the level of foreign investment fell, temporarily, after the 1987 crash. Net capital outflows in late 1987 through 1988 averaged 1.7 percent of GDP. Three-quarters of that went to Australia, where access to New Zealand's domestic market had been eased through tariff reductions and CER. From 1987 the focus of foreign investment shifted from servicing domestic production to resource-intensive exports and services. Through the privatisation programme some of New Zealand's largest companies came on the market: Telecom, Air New Zealand, State Insurance, Tourist Hotel Corporation, Bank of New Zealand, New Zealand Rail, alongside the sale of cutting rights to the state's plantation forests.

Most investment still came from Australia and the US, with increasing interest from Asia. The *Financial Times* reported in August 1993: 'US investment has risen sharply following publicity there about the success New Zealand has had in implementing policies favoured by the so-called Chicago monetarist school of economics.'[71] It pointed out that Bell Atlantic and Ameritech now controlled Telecom, International Paper managed (later owned) CHH, Wisconsin Central owned the national railway, and other US companies had substantial interests in plantation forestry and manufacturing. Asian investment centred on commercial property, with the bulk of it occurring from 1988. Some $2.5 billion was invested in the following five years, over $1 billion of which occurred in 1993 alone.[72] In the 1993/94 year, offshore purchasers secured over 71 percent of deals worth more than $5 million in the central business districts and 74.5 percent of their value. Buyers from Singapore and Hong Kong accounted for almost half of this.[73]

Approvals by the OIC in 1993 totalled $9.4 billion, a 37 percent increase on 1992. Main areas were manufacturing ($3 billion), communication and telecommunications ($1.9 billion) and commercial leasing ($1.8 billion). Approval for rural land sales into full foreign ownership increased from $44 million in 1992 to $138 million in 1993, reflecting an upsurge in purchases by US, Japanese and other Asian buyers, mainly for conversion to forestry. There was a noticeable shift to foreign-owned firms employing fewer than 50 people and a marked increase in the capital to labour ratio. Few invested in new business that created real jobs. The vast majority of approvals related to the takeover of existing companies or acquisition of assets.[74] How many of these approvals led to actual purchases is unknown, as neither the OIC nor the government keeps such figures.[75] However, it is known that net investment inflow in the year ending March 1994 was $NZ4.7 billion, more than twice that of the previous year.

Ultimately, foreign investment transferred control of the country's financial, energy, transport and communications infrastructure and much of its natural resource base (forestry and minerals, but not yet agricultural land) into foreign or trans-national hands. Approval for such investments was devoid of effective scrutiny or accountability, as the Ombudsman's 1993 report makes clear:

> The small number of staff in the [OIC] to handle applications has been explained by the Minister as not being a lack of adequate resources, but a reflection of the Commission's role in the wider context of government policy 'to foster the development of strong international linkages'. . . . The Minister continues, 'The Commission's operating procedures are consistent with the Government's intention that the regime facilitate positive investment. The Commission makes its decisions based on material supplied to it by applicants, and regards the information as having been provided in good faith.'[76]

As *Foreign Control Watchdog* observed, 'the OIC is designed not to care'.[77]

In 1995 the government moved to streamline the remaining restrictions on sale of rural land and offshore islands. Condemnation of this intensified when the revised version of the Overseas Investment Amendment Bill included draconian new secrecy powers. All information connected with an investment application to the OIC which was not otherwise in the public domain, including the fact of the application, could be deemed to be protected from public disclosure and remain so for ever. Publication would attract a maximum $30,000 fine or 12 months' imprisonment for individuals or a $100,000 fine for bodies corporate. Confidentiality powers under the Official Information Act had already been widely used by the OIC to prevent disclosure. The amendment would have made it virtually impossible for those who monitored foreign investment to continue doing so. Under pressure, the government agreed to delete the secrecy provisions and rely on the Official Information Act. When calls were made to tighten the existing rules on foreign investment, government officials claimed New Zealand's obligations under the GATT prevented the existing categories from being made more stringent.[78] However, criteria for consent to sales, which were previously administrative, were formally inserted in the Act. Investors in assets other than land who showed business experience and acumen, financial commitment to the investment and were of good character would be allowed to invest as of right. No criterion of national interest applied. For land, the 'national interest' was to be considered. In the final version of the Act the relevant ministers were required to consider whether the investment would, or was likely to, create new job opportunities or retention of existing jobs otherwise under threat; introduce new business skills or technology; develop new export markets or increase New Zealand's market access; increase market competition, efficiency or productivity; introduce additional investment for development; or increase the processing of primary products. Where land was being used for agricultural purposes they were also required to consider whether experimental research would be carried out, who controlled the company, and what use would be made of the land.

Foreign investment was portrayed as the key to New Zealand's future prosperity. Government was intolerant of criticism and debate, and the serious downsides of foreign investment were rarely addressed. *Foreign Control Watchdog* records that increased foreign ownership meant the export of profits, with significant balance of payments effects:

> Wisconsin Central picked up New Zealand Rail for next to nothing, after decades of the taxpayer shouldering its losses and promptly started reaping profits. The cutting rights to the publicly owned State forests were sold for a song to both local and international Big Business. Now New Zealand pinus radiata is flavour of the month and prices have rocketed. Carter Holt Harvey, New Zealand's biggest forest owner, is now American-owned. It announced a $325 million record profit for 1993/94. Seven TNCs between them reported a 1993/94 profit of $1 billion. Fletcher Challenge, which is over 40% foreign owned, set a NZ record with its 1993/94 $675 million profit (on which it paid all of $13 million in tax). . . . Telecom NZ is owned by Ameritech and Bell Atlantic. . . . It has announced a record profit every year. For 1993/94 it was

$528 million. . . . Those are examples of huge sums of money leaving New Zealand, money made from taking over productive New Zealand enterprises.[79]

Equally serious questions surrounded the sustainability of the current investment flow. In their pursuit of foreign capital the ideological purists eschewed active incentives to attract investors, claiming sound 'fundamentals' were enough. However, a handful of privatised businesses and resources aside, investment in New Zealand was not lucrative. Profit and dividend payments rose between 1991 and 1994, but this only returned them to historical levels following major losses in the finance sector between 1988 and 1990.

Despite international commitments to a liberalised investment regime, countries wanting or needing to attract foreign investment would continue to offer low wages, tax holidays and other incentives. Foreign investment therefore came at a price. New Zealand was competing in the investment market with poor countries offering lower labour, environmental and safety standards. The right to set independent product standards and impose consumer protections had already been compromised as pressure from trans-national food manufacturers saw New Zealand lower its requirements to Australia's level, in line with CER.[80]

Liberalisation of resource management

There were growing pressures from the tourism, mining and property development sectors, major corporations and the Business Roundtable for liberalisation of the resource management laws to reduce transaction costs and make foreign investment more attractive.[81] They had an ally in the Treasury, who in *Government Management* had argued that poorly designed environmental protection legislation was often costly and ineffective.[82] Throughout the review of the resource management laws, which ran from 1988 to 1993, Treasury argued for minimal regulation, backed by market-based mechanisms of tradeable pollution rights and taxes. After a hard-fought battle, the Resource Management Bill introduced in 1989 reflected a confusion of market, conservation and Maori perspectives within a formal regulatory regime. The legislation was still before the House at the time of the 1990 election.

Treasury's post-election briefing attacked the Bill's 'vaguely expressed values and aspirations', which would make resource management decisions unaccountable, and require costly and ineffective litigation. Treasury urged the incoming (National) government to leave areas like pollution to the market:

there is a world-wide move away from this [command approach] to the use of interventions such as transferable permits and emission charges where these are efficient. Because they can provide stronger incentives for those who can reduce pollution to do so, transferable permits and emission charges can often produce better environmental outcomes at a lower economic cost. By failing to encourage their use the Bill may lead to needless loss of both investment and environmental quality.[83]

Arguments in favour of unilateralism and providing a positive international example (which had been used to justify taking the lead in trade liberalisation) were not favoured when it came to the environment. Initiatives to improve environmental standards, such as reducing carbon dioxide emissions in response to global warming, were condemned as 'adversely affecting New Zealand's comparative advantage vis-a-vis trading competitors who have not yet taken action, with little effect on the overall world condition'.[84]

The Resource Management Act as passed in 1991 was still relatively proscriptive. But it contained significant concessions to the Treasury's arguments, with provision for transferable water abstraction permits, user charges for permit applications, performance bonds and environmental compensation. In 1995, when the Minister for the Environment made approval for building a gas-fired power station conditional on the energy company planting trees as a sink to absorb carbon dioxide emissions, he used existing powers under the Act.

The strong market-based prescription resurfaced in the National government's *Environment 2010 Strategy* in late 1994. The prevailing hands-off economic approach meant that government 'does not have direct control over environmental outcomes'. Desired outcomes should be pursued instead through 'least cost policy tools'— in effect, a system of taxes, user charges and performance bonds, alongside a market in tradeable pollution, extraction and ozone depletion rights. These would be administered through 'a regulatory framework which establishes property rights'. Voluntary industry codes would be preferred to national environmental standards. The latter should be used only where they were cost-effective in market terms. Direct environmental regulation should be a last resort, used where economic instruments, market mechanisms and voluntary measures were ineffective or cost too much.[85]

Deregulation of the media

The move to promote light-handed regulation and foreign investment had cultural implications, too. In 1989 deregulation spread to
the media. State broadcasting was divided into two SOEs—Radio
New Zealand and TVNZ—which were required to run as private
sector businesses and return a dividend to the government. Both
were opened to competition. The Radiocommunications Act 1989
saw radio frequencies put out to tender. TV3 was established as a
privately owned 'free to air' channel to compete with the two channels of TVNZ. Sky Television established three subscriber channels
and a regional channel was set up in Christchurch. Minister of
Broadcasting at the time, Richard Prebble, boasted of 'the most open
communications market in the world'.[86]

Removal of restrictions on overseas ownership and media cross-
ownership quickly followed. Ownership became concentrated in the
hands of an increasingly foreign few. Metropolitan daily newspapers
were effectively controlled by two companies—Independent News
Ltd, 40 percent owned by Rupert Murdoch, and Wilson and Horton
Ltd, a traditionally conservative 'family firm' which was now beyond the family's control. In 1991 these two companies controlled
90.5 percent of metropolitan newspaper circulation and around 65
percent in provincial areas. In 1994 asset-stripper BIL secured a
strategic 28.3 percent stake in Wilson and Horton, which it sold six
months later to Independent Newspapers Ltd, reaping a profit of
$70 million. BIL had previously bought, stripped and sold New
Zealand Newspapers, substantially reducing the number of titles,
coverage and independence as a result. Book publishing experienced
a similar trend of international mergers, takeovers and rationalisation. Local costs were reduced as the privatised Government Printing Office (known as GP) competed with overseas printers. But
access to distribution was jeopardised when GP's new owner, entrepreneur Graeme Hart, took control of the majority of retail book
outlets. TV3 also fell into foreign hands. Originally part-New Zealand owned, it was heavily undercut by TVNZ and forced into receivership. The Canadian part-owners bought out the remaining
shares. Sky Television was majority-owned by a US conglomerate of
Bell Atlantic, Ameritech, Time-Warner and Telecommunications Inc,
with TVNZ holding minority shares.

All branches of state media became profit-driven, with revenue
from the government-levied broadcasting fee providing only 15 per-

cent of TVNZ's revenue by 1989. Television advertising increased from five to seven days a week, and from a maximum of seven to twelve minutes an hour between 1975 and 1993, excluding programme advertisements, in-house promotions and 'advertainment' programmes.[87] Programmers and accountants assumed more importance than producers, programme makers and journalists.[88] Commercialisation devastated Radio New Zealand, which had to be bailed out in 1991. TVNZ substantially reduced its staff, with many redeployed in recently established subsidiaries.

Those promoting deregulation promised greater economic efficiency, flexibility, programme choice and diversity. Alan Cocker notes that, contrary to the assumption 'that increased choice and competition *ipso facto* leads to better quality broadcasting', abundance did not guarantee diversity; it meant more of the same. In a small competitive market, with limited audience elasticity and advertising growth, the media focused on the lowest common denominator. Cocker observed: 'Post-deregulation the programme range has narrowed with the genres of music; minority and special interest; arts, religion, education, public access and children's programming disappearing from the prime-time schedule.'[89]

The removal of quotas meant minimal protection for local content. The overseas influence was already putting pressure on local and 'minority' programming before deregulation, but this rapidly worsened. Media analyst Joe Atkinson reported that the proportional share of prime-time television for local programmes fell around 12 percent between 1978 and 1992.[90] Programmes called 'local' included foreign-formatted quiz shows and locally fronted foreign current affairs documentaries and cartoons. As a result, television became deluged with US soap operas, sit-coms and talk shows which bore little resemblance to the diversity of New Zealand life.

Niche options, especially Maori radio, offered more positive outcomes. Tribal radio stations provided invaluable conduits for the Maori language, music, news and political critique. But lengthy litigation failed to secure Maori a guaranteed share of the airwaves and programme funds, even though the courts and government conceded that access to broadcasting was vital for the Maori language to survive.[91] A minimal financial settlement locked Maori broadcasting into a government-constructed funding vehicle which was designed to boost their ability to operate in the commercial broadcasting market.

Winners and losers

Deregulation was carried out in the name of efficiency and consumer sovereignty. As the NZTUF pointed out to the post-1996 tariff review, the textbook justification that the 'consumer' was the ultimate beneficiary of the deregulated environment and cheaper imports was built on a deceit. Consumers were also workers, many of whom lost their jobs through deregulation or had their benefits cut in the cause of fiscal restraint. Communities (containing consumers) were often destroyed by economic policies which resulted in large-scale factory closures. Taxpayers (also consumers) had to pay the unemployment benefits for those who lost their jobs. The real beneficiaries of deregulation were abundantly clear: finance capital and trans-national enterprise now had the New Zealand economy firmly within their grasp. So deep was their infiltration that it would be extraordinarily difficult to wrest any effective control back, even if the pursuit of economic fundamentalism were to cease.

CHAPTER SIX

Limiting the State

ROLLING BACK THE STATE is a fundamental tenet of any structural adjustment programme. In New Zealand the desire to corporatise and privatise central and local government operations spread from overtly commercial enterprises and assets to include previously non-commercial activities of health, housing and government research, and ultimately embraced the policy, regulatory and service delivery roles of the state.

The corporatisation agenda

Treasury's 1984 briefing to the incoming government set the stage. In Treasury's eyes, government departments were dominated by in-ward-looking, institutionalised, empire-building bureaucrats, while ministers sought to accumulate and entrench their own power. Both were open to interest group capture and lacked incentives to perform. Commercial decisions, which should have reflected economic efficiency and optimal use of resources, were distorted by political considerations and by social objectives which sought to maintain services, increase employment and hold prices down.

The solution was to decouple political and economic control. Treasury's formula involved separating commercial state operations from non-commercial. Where possible, the former should be converted into state-owned trading enterprises (SOEs) functioning as private sector businesses in conditions of competitive neutrality. Permanent departmental heads would be replaced by entrepreneurial boards of directors and autonomous chief executives with incentives to perform. Profit should be the SOEs' overriding goal. Spending on non-commercial activities, such as subsidised utility and social services, could be made transparent through explicit contracts with

SOEs. Alternatively, income maintenance could be targeted to the deserving poor, who would then buy those services they desired. Where no compelling reason for state ownership existed, SOEs could be privatised, offering 'one way that the fiscal deficit can be financed in the short term'.[1] Any remaining regulatory and policy functions should be allocated to separate agencies or to streamlined, residual government ministries with managerial autonomy, performance targets and labour practices on private sector lines.

In *Government Management* Treasury's attack on the state intensified, with classic expositions of agency and public choice theories. The private firm provided the first, and only, point of reference: 'Although [the objectives of the government] may be more complex than the simple private sector analogy, the features of the management process which align the interests of those responsible for decisions with the interests of those setting objectives are common to both.'[2] The superiority of private over state ownership was simply asserted through what the Public Service Association (PSA) called 'universal generalisations drawn on the basis of a few empirical studies and impressionistic examples'.[3] Treasury claimed that,

> compared with private ownership, state ownership is likely to give directors and managers of SOEs inappropriate and inadequate incentives to act strictly commercially. This conclusion is generally supported by overseas studies on the efficiency of state enterprises vis-a-vis privately owned firms which suggest that private enterprises are probably more efficient although comparisons are difficult. There is general agreement internationally that when non-commercial functions have been separated from SOEs and the SOEs' regulatory environment reformed, governments should transfer the ownership of the state's commercial businesses and assets to private ownership. As there will be efficiency losses until this policy is fully implemented the policy should be implemented as soon as possible.[4]

Privatisation would offer fiscal benefits, too. Asset sales would 'increase productivity and growth in the economy and generate additional tax revenues without increasing average tax rates. . . . Since the price at which the assets are sold should reflect the higher value they will have under private sector control rather than their existing value, the transaction would increase the net worth of the public sector and reduce the future tax burden.'[5]

Local government was drawn into the analysis as Treasury targeted energy retailing, urban transport, sea ports, airports, refuse collection and abattoirs for sale.

> From an economy-wide perspective, as with SOEs, the contribution made to the economy by LATAs [Local Authority Trading Activities] is likely to be sub-optimal for two reasons. First, in many instances LATAs face little, if any, competition in the markets in which they sell their goods and services. Second, the existing organisational form places insufficient pressures on boards and managers to perform because of inadequate incentives, sanctions and accountability provisions. We conclude therefore that reform of both the regulatory environment and ownership form of LATAs is likely to be required in order to strengthen the incentives and disciplines for efficient resource use.[6]

As with the SOEs, Treasury's ultimate goal was privatisation. 'Moving to corporatisation of LATAs would be a significant step forward provided all statutory barriers to competition were removed. However, unless the move is made to full privatisation with transferable ownership it is likely that the maximum benefits possible from improved incentives and discipline on management would not be achieved.'[7] The optimal approach was to vest fully tradeable shares directly in the hands of citizens, free of charge. Former social policy functions would be met by central government through well-targeted social support packages.

The theory had an inexorable logic which was never opened to contest; it was implemented with the customary speed, lack of empirical support and determination to entrench the theoretical model against change.

Corporatisation[8]

The corporatisation policy was formulated during 1984 and broadly signalled in the 1985 budget. The details were worked out by officials in Treasury and the SSC. The technopols took control of steering the policy through the political process, with Richard Prebble later appointed as the first Minister for State-owned Enterprises. Those overseeing the policy were unwilling to trust existing bureaucrats to dismantle their departments and unable to do all the work themselves. So the responsibility for implementation was delegated to private sector establishment boards, led by corporate entrepreneurs and backed by consultants and technocrats.

Many of the framework issues were worked through in mid-1985 when the Forest Service was converted into Forestcorp, whose establishment board included prominent Business Roundtable members Alan Gibbs and John Fernyhough. The decision to create totally new corporations through a single piece of legislation set the overall framework for the SOEs, and was intended to minimise the scope for lobbying by individual departments. Starting with a clean slate also meant 'there was no obligation to take on all existing staff, previous hierarchies were irrelevant, the Corporation had no redundancy to pay, the old service pay and conditions did not apply, [and] unions would have to negotiate coverage from scratch'.[9] Chief executives, preferably recruited from the private sector, were expected to bring commercial experience and expertise and create a liberating, innovative corporate culture.

The State Owned Enterprises Act, passed in December 1986, established nine new government-owned corporations: Land, Forestry, Electricity, Telecommunications, Coal, Airways, Post Office Bank, New Zealand Post and Government Property Services (GPS). The overriding statutory objective of each SOE was to run a successful business. Within that, the SOE had to be as profitable and efficient as a comparable private sector business, be a good employer, and exhibit a sense of social responsibility to the community in which it operated 'when able to do so'.

The new corporations would become limited liability companies, with shares usually held by the Minister of Finance and the Minister for SOEs. The ministers would appoint the directors, give directions on dividends, and approve an annual statement of corporate intent. Operational decisions would be left to the board. The primary commercial objective and the hands-off structure were intended to eliminate cross-subsidies from profitable to unprofitable services and to insulate management from political control. The government could still meet its social objectives by contracting an SOE to provide specified unprofitable services. But this was at the shareholding ministers' discretion.

The SOEs would buy their assets from the government at a market price agreed through negotiation. Early valuations estimated total net book value at 31 March 1986 as $11.8 billion. With debt markets unable to absorb such a large immediate demand, the government acted as short-term banker. SOEs were to repay the debt over three years, at market interest rates. Overall, the government would receive payment for the assets, taxation, interest, and an annual dividend set by the shareholding ministers. The valuations of most assets were settled and the sales completed just in time for Douglas to deliver a promised budget 'surplus' for the 1987/88 year.

Over the next four years the Labour government applied the corporatisation formula to almost every state activity with a conceivably commercial function: works, railways, ports, government computing, government supply brokerage, radio, television, airport holdings and meteorological services.

The early corporatisation policy was implemented virtually without debate. The public service was widely perceived as inefficient, privileged and in need of a good shake-up, and no alternative models were being promoted. Few outside the state sector understood enough detail to challenge the logic of corporatisation or to foresee its impact. The restructuring of departments like lands and forests was linked to environmental reforms, turning potential critics into useful allies. The main private-sector criticism came from large companies for whom corporatisation meant a major new competitor and loss of preferential commercial arrangements. These self-interested corporations lobbied actively against certain SOEs, especially Forestcorp, and in favour of their sale to local buyers.

Critics within the state service were deliberately marginalised by the speed and secrecy of the reforms. The then head of the SSC was seen as an old-school bureaucrat protecting the vested interests of the public servants, and was consistently outmanoeuvred.[10] When he retired in March 1986, key technocrat Rod Deane, until then deputy governor of the Reserve Bank, took his place. The PSA was effectively excluded during the early phases of the project. By the time it became involved, its role was reduced to damage control within an intrinsically hostile environment.

The only effective opposition came from Maori. The government had promised to address long-standing Treaty of Waitangi grievances relating to natural resources such as land, forests and minerals. The government now proposed to transfer those resources to the SOEs. This gave rise to a stream of litigation aimed at stopping the corporatisation, and later privatisation, programme.[11] Maori secured promises, set down in legislation, that any SOE lands over which the Waitangi Tribunal upheld a claim would be returned to their tribal owners, if the tribunal so ordered.[12] But the tribes still did not own the land, and there was no guarantee they ever would. By 1995, the tribunal had never exercised that power.

Corporatising the welfare state

By the time National became the government there was little left to corporatise. Attention turned to areas previously designated 'non-commercial'. The SOE model was applied to such corner-stones of the welfare state as health and housing—firmly established in the popular psyche as basic social services, not commercial profit-making enterprises. These moves provoked controversy and resistance. But opposition was isolated and—a few minor concessions apart—proved largely ineffectual.

The 1991 budget announced that the Housing Corporation would be split into two: an SOE to run its housing stock as a commercial business at market rents, and a residual Housing Corporation which would retain the subsidised mortgages. Unsubsidised mortgages would be put up for sale. Policy functions would be transferred to the Department of Social Welfare (DSW). The social functions of state housing would be met through strictly targeted transfer payments.[13]

The move to replace subsidised state housing by a profit-driven housing company provoked an outcry in defence of the poor and the homeless. The government compromised by adapting the principal statutory objective of Housing New Zealand (HNZ) to operating 'as a successful business that will assist in meeting the Crown's social objectives by providing housing and related services'. The chair of the establishment board resigned, telling the Prime Minister that 'one entity trying to cover both commercialism and socialism does not enable either of them to be done properly'.[14] But the change was cosmetic. The actual social objectives were left to the statement of corporate intent or explicit contracts with government, not written into law. No such contracts were subsequently entered into. Treasury and housing officials reiterated at the time that 'the Government's intention is that the company should be primarily a business rather than a social delivery agency'.[15] After returning a loss in its first year, owing largely to restructuring and refurbishment costs, the government set HNZ a target of $39 million profit for the 1995/96 year, and $123 million for the year after.

National's 1991 budget also announced the corporatisation of the public hospitals. The major hospitals, along with clinics and diagnostic centres, were formed into 23 competitive Crown Health Enterprises (CHEs) along SOE lines. Smaller unprofitable hospitals were closed or transferred to local community trusts if their communities could raise the funds. The CHEs' principal objective was 'to operate as a successful business that provides health services, or disability services, or both, and that assists in meeting the Crown's social objectives . . . '. Each CHE was to be efficient and uphold the ethical standards generally expected of such providers, be a good employer and show a sense of social responsibility to the local community when able to do so. A central unit was established to monitor monthly performance indicators, and a separate minister made politically responsible. While the CHE would not return profits as such, the minister could withdraw all funds surplus to operating and investment needs, to be reinvested in health.

CHEs were administered by boards of directors appointed by the minister for their management skills. Health minister and technopol Simon Upton defended the shift from elected to appointed boards as an exercise in consumer sovereignty: 'You could choose every three years some of the board members by way of an election, but one vote every three years plus endless consultative committees and the potential for political paralysis doesn't add up to choice in my vocabulary.'[16] Each board appointed in 1993 had a minority of women and one Maori. Almost none had any professional experience of health and disability issues. Chief executives appointed to run the CHEs were likewise chosen for their managerial skills. This provided an on-going source of conflict with professional medical staff in many regions. The health corporations were established on schedule in July 1993. The crises that engulfed them, and the broader health restructuring, are discussed in Chapter 9.

National's other major corporatisation exercise involved state-funded research, science and technology. The former Department of Scientific and Industrial Research and parts of the Ministry of Agriculture and Fisheries were restructured into ten Crown Research Institutes (CRIs) required to carry out and promote research of excellence which would be of benefit to New Zealand. This hybrid tried to combine commercial structures with recognition that public-good research needed to serve long-term objectives in an 'experimental corporate form not closely based on any particular overseas model'.[17] The CRIs were funded partly from user-pays research, and partly by competing with private researchers for funding from the Public Good Science Fund, controlled by the government's new Foundation for Research, Science and Technology. The government determined the size of that funding pool and its priorities—and hence the type of research carried out or funded by the state.

Evaluating corporatisation

Whether corporatisation was considered a success depends on the criteria used. Non-commercial considerations were by definition excluded from official surveys. The most comprehensive study, by Ian Duncan and Alan Bollard in 1992, explicitly did 'not try to assess overall welfare effects of these reforms: the state-owned enterprises are principally judged by their commercial success'.[18]

Financially, most SOEs performed extremely well. Seven of the original corporations more than trebled their profits in the first four years of operation, from a total of $317 million in 1987/88 to $974 million in 1990/91. By far the most profitable were the monopoly providers of essential services, Electricorp and Telecom. In 1989/90, the government extracted $977.6 million from Telecom: a dividend of almost $200 million, taxes of $163.6 million, $48 million in interest, and repayment of a $568 million government loan to buy its assets. In 1992/93, despite extensive privatisations, the government still received a total of $384 million in dividends and $128 million in tax from the SOEs.[19]

Apart from a study of the social impact of forestry corporatisation on rural communities,[20] the government ignored the effect of decoupling commercial activities from non-commercial obligations on essential services, communities and jobs. The subsidisation provision, whereby government could contract SOEs to provide services it considered not commercially viable, appears to have been used only twice: to provide short-term relief for the closure of official post offices in 1988, which the government terminated before the period contracted for had expired; and a temporary subsidy to Postbank to provide mobile banking outlets.

Profitability came primarily from closing down services, removing cross-subsidisation and increasing charges, and from productivity gains through massive staffing cuts and a virtual wage freeze. Between 1987 and 1991 the number of post offices fell from 894 to 288 and three-quarters of postal agencies were closed, while the number of postal delivery centres and stamp retailers increased.[21] Telecom's average monthly access charge for business fell from $89.38 in May 1988 to $77.87 in January 1991; for residential users it rose from $18.23 to $28.96.[22] In the June 1993/94 year, household electricity prices went up an average 6.8 percent,[23] while the inflation rate was 1.3 percent and real incomes fell by 0.3 percent.

For workers, corporatisation generally spelt disaster. The employment base of entire towns and suburbs was destroyed almost overnight. The statutory 'good employer' clause in the SOEs Act had been intended by ministers to be 'quite harmless', but something with which the unions would agree.[24] They were right. The State Services Conditions of Employment Act 1988 gave SOEs private sector control over their workforce. Between 1987 and 1991 staff numbers were cut by half (see Table 6.1). Forestcorp eliminated almost all wage workers, re-engaging some on productivity-based contracts, in a move described by its then employee relations manager as the 'forerunner of the Employment Contracts Act'.[25] The ratio of after-tax profits to shareholder funds for Coalcorp, Electricorp, New Zealand Post and Telecom together rose from 5.7 percent in 1988 to 11.9 percent in 1991, while corresponding revenue per employee went from $93,000 to $153,000.[26]

TABLE 6.1 **After-tax profit ($m) and employment for selected SOEs 1987–92**

	1987	1988	1989	1990	1991
Coalcorp, after-tax profit		3.9	9.4	10.9	8.9
staff numbers	1861	892	806	715	675
Electricorp, after-tax profit	141.2	331.7	339.2	403.6	
staff numbers	5999	4424	4066	3690	3730
Forestcorp, after-tax profit		61	82	138	74.9
staff numbers	7070	2652	2547	2597	n/a
NZ Post, after-tax profit		72.1	31.2	53.1	30.0
staff numbers	12,000	9800	9500	8500	8200
Railways, after-tax profit		(148)	(333.1)	(38.2)	(155.2)
staff numbers	14,900	12,500	9900	8400	5900
Telecom, after-tax profit		64	235	257*	332
staff numbers	24,500	23,931	19,151	16,263	14,925

*sold in 1990

Sources: I. Duncan and A. Bollard, *Corporatization and Privatization: Lessons from New Zealand*, OUP, Auckland, 1992; Crown Companies Monitoring Advisory Unit.

Corporatisation could hardly be acclaimed a political success. Despite initial acquiescence, the model never enjoyed widespread public support. Growing opposition focused on three major concerns: that the social, environmental and cultural, as well as economic, needs of all New Zealanders be adequately protected, by government intervention if necessary; that SOEs and ministers be held to account for how that was done; and that corporatisation was a Trojan horse when the real agenda was to privatise.

In their quest for efficiency and profit, the attitude of some SOEs verged on contempt for their statutory social responsibilities and public image. Their agents seemed unwilling to be held to account. Electricorp epitomised the corporate pariah. With the Roundtable's John Fernyhough and Rod Deane as board chair and chief executive respectively, and Roger Kerr also on the board, Electricorp was uncompromising in pursuit of its goals. From a monopoly position, its profit rose from $196 million in 1988 to $404 million in the 1990/91 year, with a return on shareholders' funds of 12.2 percent—boosted by tax avoidance of $50 million through investments in loss-making companies. While the SOE lectured its workers and the public on the need for economic efficiencies, laying off almost 3000 staff in just five years, its managers seemed reluctant to apply the same constraint to their own salaries and perks.

Simmering discontent boiled over in late 1991 when Electricorp announced plans to increase bulk electricity prices by at least 20 percent over the next ten years. After a sustained outcry, and a parliamentary committee finding that the increase was not justified,[27] the government broke the corporatisation rules. Applying leverage to the Electricorp board, it secured a more moderate increase. Hostility to Electricorp was compounded by an electricity crisis in 1992 which the SOE blamed on a one-in-100-years drought, and critics attributed to lack of prudent planning, promotion of excessive consumption, preference for hydro-power over more expensive geothermal generation, and profit-linked bonuses for corporation executives.

Chief executive Rod Deane left the company in 1993, complaining of government meddling in its affairs and procrastination over privatisation. The *NBR* pointed to the irony that the government in the 1994 budget in effect bailed out Electricorp by $111 million for each of the next two years to remedy a blunder in financing arrangements made under Deane's management.[28] Fernyhough later declined reappointment to the board, citing similar concerns to Deane. Kerr left the board too. The Business Roundtable reiterated its call to privatise. But their accusations of political capture, coming from an organisation whose members had dominated the privatisation of SOEs, attracted little public support.

In terms of accountability, the corporatisation regime failed. The SOEs Act had promised accountability through annual statements of corporate intent (SCI), approved by their shareholding ministers, and half-yearly and annual reports tabled in Parliament. SOEs were also subject to the Official Information and Ombudsman Acts and scrutiny by the Auditor-General. This provided a source of on-going conflict between the official watchdogs and the Treasury, Roundtable and SOEs, who seized every opportunity to circumvent and undermine such restraints.[29]

The Chief Ombudsman's submission on the SOEs Bill in 1986 insisted that the corporatisation policy 'may well reflect the need for greater accountability in a commercial and economic sense, [but] it does not suggest as State owned or State majority enterprises, either monopolistic or in competition, they can avoid behavioural or constitutional accountability to the public whose organisations they are'.[30] SOEs could act just as unfairly or unreasonably as central government departments. Indeed, reduced ministerial control should have dictated greater, not less, public accountability.

The Auditor-General likewise argued that pressure to divest the audit function to the private sector ignored the government's own principal/agent responsibilities: 'taxpayers in particular, and the public in general, have a legitimate interest in both what is done by State enterprises on their behalf (the range and scale of operations) and how it is done (monopolistic pricing policies, customer services and relations, etc.) as well as in the financial results—the normal focus of business accountability in the private sector.'[31] A fundamental constitutional issue was at stake: 'the overriding right of Parliament, on behalf of the real owners, the public, to hold fully to account those responsible for the management and control of public assets'.[32]

The SOEs quickly found ways around these restraints. In 1988 the Auditor-General labelled the accountability provisions 'seriously deficient'. The SCIs 'certainly did not meet the accountability needs of Parliament'. The stated corporate objectives were very broad, difficult to assess, and provided little indication of the activity planned. Performance measures were generally inadequate and primarily financial. Many SCIs made no provision for regular reporting to the shareholding ministers.[33] Scrutiny of the SOEs before select committees and in Parliament was equally inadequate. Ministers continually refused to answer questions in the House relating to SOEs, citing commercial confidentiality, and tried to limit the information which management presented to select committees.

There was no formal regulatory restraint beyond those provided through civil law and judicial review. The courts adopted a hands-off approach to SOE activities, reflecting a strong neo-liberal line. The statutory obligations on SOEs to act as a good employer and exhibit a sense of social responsibility, and parallel clauses for CHEs and HNZ, were rendered impotent as the High Court deemed them subordinate to the duty to run a successful, profitable and efficient business.[34] The Court of Appeal considered the relevant section of the SOE Act merely stated a goal, not a duty whereby specific acts or transactions could be subject to judicial scrutiny. Accountability properly lay with the shareholding ministers and Parliament, not the courts. Contractual arrangements with SOEs were governed by the Companies Act, and best left to private law.[35]

Several decisions by the Privy Council suggested a less rigid approach. In assessing what amounted to a successful business, they implied that equal weighting could be given to the profitability and efficiency, good employer and social responsibility objectives.[36] The Privy Council also suggested that the decisions of SOEs were in principle amenable to judicial review.[37] But these were observations rather than binding precedent, and delivered by a court whose days as part of New Zealand's judicial hierarchy were numbered.

As public criticism of SOEs' unaccountability grew, the government reluctantly increased its centralised monitoring. A Crown Company Monitoring Advisory Unit was established in 1993. Its brief was to offer complementary and contestable advice to that from Treasury on the SOEs and similar agencies. This role was subsequently extended to provide additional analysis of Treasury's primary advice on financial issues. Treasury, predictably, fought for control of the unit, which was located in the Department of Prime Minister and Cabinet but funded from the Treasury budget vote. Treasury advised the government on appointing the CEO.[38]

A parliamentary select committee was also given power to scrutinise documents tabled by the SOEs in the House and to question the managers and ministers involved, within the bounds of commercial confidentiality. Some probing exchanges took place and some embarrassing information emerged. But most SOEs carried on undeterred.

These tensions were endemic to the corporatisation model. To the public these were *state*-owned enterprises where management should be required to 'put people before profits'. But the SOEs Act required them to be run as a profitable business—whether in trees, coal, research, housing or health services—free from government intervention and according to commercial objectives. Likewise, the public expected shareholding ministers to protect wider social interests and impose some restraint on rapacious SOEs. But the model was intended to prevent them doing precisely that. Attempts to devise hybrid corporations which sought to combine social and economic objectives and increased accountability within the neoliberal paradigm were destined to fail. Corporatisation was designed to maximise economic efficiency through private markets, and the 'decks were stacked' with management and directors to defend that goal. Social equity and democratic participation had no place. Attempting to impose social as well as economic functions within the commercial corporate structure only exacerbated the contradictions.

Rather than rethink the corporatisation model, the government seemed inclined to abandon its jurisdiction altogether. The response of the Minister of Energy to the problems with Electricorp typified the technopols' approach: 'Let us get some markets operating so that this matter does not become the responsibility of Government.'[39] The technocrats and fellow-travellers agreed. State involvement continued to undermine the market disciplines and incentives necessary for a profitable commercial enterprise and the efficient use of scarce resources. The government had to take corporatisation to its logical conclusion—all the SOEs should be privatised.

Privatisation[40]

Corporatisation eased the commercial path to privatisation. State businesses were repackaged into saleable entities—although it can be argued that they were sold too cheaply, before they had time to mature. Potential political opposition to privatisation was also defused. In 1986 it had been possible to gain acquiescence in the corporatisation of government trading operations on the grounds of improving efficiency, provided they were still able to deliver social services if contracted to do so, and were formally accountable to the government. But direct sale to private owners, whose driving force was profit, who had no social obligations and whose accountability was to their shareholders, would have placed the entire restructuring programme at risk. The strategy, for some of the policy's architects at least, became privatisation by stealth.

Off the record, Treasury officials acknowledged their ultimate goal was privatisation, having already foreshadowed the possibility in *Economic Management* in 1984. The logical progression was confirmed by Rod Deane in 1988, then chief executive of Electricorp: 'The SOE reforms should be seen as a consistent and integrated package of changes involving commercialisation, corporatisation, deregulation and privatisation. The ultimate effectiveness of the package depends on its completeness, and in this area the major part of the reform yet to come is that of privatisation.'[41]

All the technopols publicly denied plans to 'sell the family silver'. Prebble proclaimed during the passage of the SOEs Act in September 1986:

> The Government opposes the suggestion by the opposition members that they will sell off taxpayers' assets. The Government does not regard itself as the owner . . . of the State corporations affected. The Government is the guardian on behalf of the people. No Government has the right to sell off State trading enterprises to its cronies. Government members are willing to make it an election issue.[42]

How far Labour's technopols had a genuine change of heart over privatisation is difficult to tell. Initial moves were presented as one-off sales, and intended to be uncontroversial. Once the privatisation campaign was under way, it was breathtaking in its scope, speed and disregard for popular opinion. The 1987 budget announced plans to sell New Zealand Steel (already mooted in 1986), Petroleum Corporation, the Development Finance Corporation and the government's shares in Air New Zealand. The Health Computing Service, the Government Printing Office and Coal Corporation were soon added to the list.

Douglas's economic statement of 17 December 1987 announced a review of the rationale for ownership of all state-owned commercial assets. Treasury began a case-by-case assessment of the benefits of privatising each SOE. Predictably, Treasury argued that releasing government assets and businesses to private owners would increase efficiency, promote dynamic growth and ensure greater responsiveness to consumer needs. The receipts from sale, and relief from much-needed capital injections, would release funds for social spending and repayment of foreign debt.

In February 1988, SOEs Minister Richard Prebble asked the corporation boards to identify any impediments to sale. A steering committee on privatisation, chaired by Ron Trotter of the Business Roundtable and of FCL, later a major purchaser of state assets, was established to help co-ordinate the work and provide a sounding-board for Treasury. Three criteria for privatisation were determined:

- taxpayers must receive more from the sale than from continued ownership;
- the sale must make a positive contribution to the government's economic objectives; and
- the sale must contribute to the government's social objectives.

These proved little more than self-justifying rationalisations. Calculations that savings from repayment of debt would exceed future dividends from SOEs ignored both the residual value of the enterprises if they were not sold, and the vagaries of foreign exchange fluctuations. Debt repayment was, in itself, one of the government's economic objectives. The SOEs had already been stripped of social obligations, and the repayment of debt could be said to free up funding for social spending.

This exercise cleared the way for the 'garage sale' budget of 1988,[43] when Douglas predicted a $2 billion surplus for 1988/89. By 1990 Labour had sold eighteen government enterprises. Public unease mounted as the list grew. It seemed that before long control of the country's entire infrastructure would be in private, often foreign, hands. Despite political and public opposition, the programme continued apace. Labour's last controversial sale was Telecom—bought by telecommunications giants Ameritech and Bell Atlantic as a launching-pad into the Asia and Pacific rim markets where US firms were generally not welcome. Alan Gibbs's Freightways and merchant bankers Fay Richwhite also secured a share. In July 1990, four months before the election, Prebble announced that there would be no more asset sales to repay debt. But sales would continue under Labour if greater efficiency would result.[44]

The new National government, under siege for breaking election promises on superannuation and benefits, put privatisation of state assets on the back burner. However, it remained committed to selling remaining assets over time. Business interests locally and overseas expressed concern at National's lack of progress. The Business Roundtable complained in 1992:

> The government's privatisation programme has stalled over the last year. In addition, there is a widespread belief that political considerations are having a greater bearing on SOE operations. Experience with public enterprises around the world indicates that sooner or later political decision-making prevails and commercial failure ensues. *To capitalise on the progress achieved to date and to reduce the government's exposure to commercial risk, the privatisation programme should be revitalised.*[45]

The Roundtable's emphatic endorsement of privatisation, accompanied by a list of potential candidates, was hardly surprising. Privatisation offered new, potentially lucrative investment opportunities. Companies whose CEOs were members of the Roundtable had already bought billions of dollars' worth of assets.[46] The servicing of privatisation was also big business. Treasury alone paid out $120 million for sales, accountancy and legal advice on asset sales from April 1987 to December 1994.[47]

National moved more decisively to force the privatisation of local authority trading enterprises (LATEs), especially in Auckland. Labour had begun the process by making public funding for passenger transport and public works conditional on all such operations becoming LATEs by 1991 and opened to competition. In 1992 the Auckland Regional Council (ARC) was required to divest itself of all passenger transport, rubbish services, commercial forestry holdings and ports 'as soon as prudently possible', and to convert water works, bulk water supply, sewage treatment and disposal into LATEs. A proposal to require sale of the Auckland ports provoked a popular backlash, organised through private radio talkback. Deluged by letters and petitions, the government reluctantly rephrased the legislation. The decision to sell was left initially to the ARC, and subsequently to the Auckland Regional Services Trust (ARST), which was created by statute to oversee the Auckland sales.

Allowing the ARST to be elected rather than ministerially appointed was a serious miscalculation by the government. The Alliance party, standing on an anti-privatisation platform, secured a majority of seats on the new trust and a solid block on the ARC in the 1992 local body elections. By March 1995, the trust still owned all its core LATEs and had paid off almost all of its $159.3 million debt—an achievement in three years that had been calculated to take fifteen. Local government therefore proved a rare arena in which electoral politics could sometimes stall, though not reverse, the seemingly inexorable progression from public service to commercial corporation to private enterprise.

National went ahead with some relatively uncontroversial sales in 1993, including Housing Corporation mortgages, New Zealand Rail, the Export Guarantee Corporation and the Government Computing Service. But potential purchasers were much more interested in the possible sales of New Zealand Post, the residue of Forestcorp, Railcorp, Radio and Television New Zealand, and Electricorp.

Main attention focused on the lucrative electricity market. The plan was to separate generation, transmission and supply, and create competitive markets at all levels. This had begun in 1986 when the Electricity Department was converted into Electricorp. The SOE was divided into separate operational units, and the transmission network was commercially isolated through the subsidiary Transpower. In July 1994 Transpower and Electricorp were formally separated. Against the advice of several expert reports, Cabinet in 1995 decided to split Electricorp's generating monopoly into two competing SOEs. Critics feared that the widely predicted failure of the split would open the way to privatisation. Contestable generation was already on the cards, with FCL eager to play a major role. Despite numerous proposals, the method and ownership structure for Transpower's privatisation remained unresolved in 1995.

Historically, non-profit elected power boards had been responsible for electricity supply. In 1990 these were transformed into electric power companies with ministerially appointed boards of directors to oversee the transition to public companies. Most elected board members were relegated to shareholding trustees. National passed legislation in June 1992 to corporatise the 48 energy distribution companies, conservatively valued at $2.5 billion, on SOE lines. Their principal statutory objective was to operate as a successful business, having regard, 'among other things, to the desirability of ensuring the efficient use of energy'. The establishment plan and ownership structure were to be drawn up by the directors, sent to the trustees for comment, opened for public submissions and approved by the minister by 31 December 1992. The new power companies would be formed and registered by 1 April 1993. The Minister of Energy made it clear that he wanted privatisation, preferably with fully tradeable shares. Most power boards were reluctant parties to this venture, but they had no choice.

The power companies were intended to compete first for domestic, then for commercial customers throughout the country using existing distribution lines. Their names—Power New Zealand, EnergyDirect, Top Energy, Capital Power, Mercury Energy—encapsulated the entrepreneurial intent. Commercial pressures for economies of scale or spreading the geographical risk were expected to see around six large power companies emerge. A rash of hostile takeover bids and friendly mergers followed, with Canadian and US interests and local FCL playing a prominent role. The issue of shares to consumers turned into a lolly scramble as tents and booths appeared in main streets and shopping malls, and extensive television and newspaper advertising enticed the poor to cash in their windfall.[48] Supplying electricity seemed almost a sideline.

There was widespread public scepticism about the entire strategy. Even if privatisation produced greater efficiencies, the benefits were unlikely to trickle down, especially not to those who had cashed in their shares. A price war was predicted for the big accounts, meaning lower rates for the largest commercial consumers and increased charges for domestic use, as well as further cuts in staff. Profits would be skimmed off by the corporate and foreign owners, and often exported, while local consumers were left to pay the debt incurred by secretive takeovers, excessive expansion and subsidies to major corporate clients.[49] Promoting consumption would take precedence over conservation, with large- and small-scale dams congesting the waterways, while resource management regulations were attacked as barriers to investment.

Electricity privatisation had been captured by the ideologues. The less doctrinaire Minister of Conservation observed along the way: 'There is a feeling in some quarters that the Government is building a fascinating new tin budgie but nobody is really sure whether the damn thing will fly or whether we are placing too much on the sloping shoulders of the free market.'[50]

Evaluating privatisation

The privatisation of electricity distribution was not unique; controversy had enveloped virtually every one of the asset sales.

- New Zealand Steel was sold to Equiticorp, one of the 'boom and bust' corporate cowboys of the mid-1980s, in late 1987 for $327 million after the government had written off nearly $2 billion in debt. Equiticorp's offer was made the day before the share-market crash in October 1987 and the deal was completed the next month. Equiticorp was placed in receivership in January 1989. The preferential terms secured by the government in the unorthodox commercial transaction severely disadvantaged thousands of large and small creditors, and was the subject of complex litigation in 1994–95.

- An outcry against the sale of Petrocorp to British Gas in 1987 saw it sold to 'local' FCL instead. The deal included a put-and-call option which FCL invoked in March 1992, requiring the government to buy 104.5 million shares for $400 million. The government paid $3.83 per share when the market value was over $4. By 30 October 1992 FCL's shares had plummeted to $1.63 and the government faced a massive loss. In November 1993 it was estimated that the government would need to secure between $4.10 and $4.20 a share to cover the holding costs and avoid losing money.[51] Fortunately for the government, the price recovered and it sold the shares in December 1993 for $418 million.

- The Development Finance Corporation (DFC) was bought in 1988 by government-owned National Provident Fund (80 percent) and Salomon Brothers (20 percent) with an implicit guarantee of government support. This was withdrawn without the investment advisors, Fay Richwhite, and hence the mainly overseas investors, being informed. DFC was placed under statutory management in October 1989. Litigation regarding the government's liability to the investors, especially Japanese, continued in 1995.

- The Rural Bank's debts were written down by $1.1 billion before it was sold to FCL for $550 million in August 1989. It returned a profit of $133 million in the first year, $127 million in 1990/91 and $145 million in 1991/92. FCL sold the Rural Bank to National Australia Bank in December 1992 for $445 million. The government recouped $137.5 million in clawback for surplus loan loss provisions.

- The National Film Unit was sold for $2.5 million—only a quarter of its book value. The government had to pay the cost of redundancies.

- Officials valued the state forests variously between $1 billion and $7 billion. The price received from the sale of cutting rights over 61.8 percent of state forests to private buyers and 33.9 percent to SOEs by March 1995 was $1.393 billion.

- The Government Printing Office, initially valued by consultants at $70 million, was sold for $23 million with a further $10.6 million from property sales. A twelve-month delay in settlement cost the government an estimated $700,000 to $1 million in interest on debt. The government's main consultant for the sale, Fay Richwhite, complained that the process had taken much longer than anticipated. Treasury agreed to vary the terms of the written contract, and the government paid out $270,000 more than it was legally liable for. Fay Richwhite's fee was calculated on the expected sale price of $43 million, as valued by the merchant bank itself, rather than the actual return from the sale.[52] The purchase by Graeme Hart's Rank Group provided the launching-pad for his subsequent capture of the New Zealand retail book trade.[53]

- Telecom was sold to Bell Atlantic and Ameritech for $4.25 billion in 1990 with a requirement to on-sell within three years, when no foreign shareholder or consortium would be allowed to hold more than 49.9 percent of shares. Local corporates Fay Richwhite and Freightways would pick up 5 percent each. In 1993 the government gave Telecom an additional year to sell down its shares, the bulk of which were sold overseas. Telecom's profits rose from $257 million in March 1990 to $528 million in 1994 and $620 million for 1995 (a return on equity of 30 percent). Its dividends increased from $198 million in 1990 to $473 million in 1994, and from 14.75 cents a share (fully imputed) in 1994 to 16.5 cents in 1995. *Foreign Control Watchdog* complained that: '[m]ost companies pay out about 50% [in dividend]; Telecom has averaged 70% since it started and in 1994 announced that it was increasing that to about 90%' making it a 'major invisible export from New Zealand'.[54] Meanwhile staff had been cut from 16,263 in September 1989 to 9257 in 1994 and 8568 in 1995. The target was 7500 by April 1997. Loss of experienced staff was blamed for a rash of exchange problems and slipping service standards in 1995.[55]
- Half the Housing Corporation prime rate mortgages were sold in 1992 and 1993 to a private consortium arranged by Fay Richwhite, who had twice previously advised the corporation on possible sale of the mortgages. The deal was underwritten partly by the Bank of New Zealand, which Fay Richwhite previously co-owned with the government, and partly by the merchant bank itself. The scheme involved securitisation of the mortgages, for which Fay Richwhite received a commission. The Mortgage Corporation purported to be a charitable trust, with any cash remaining once the mortgages were repaid to be distributed to charities for women and children. But the funding structure required it to charge its primarily poor customers interest rates which were consistently above those charged by retail banks. This, along with a punitive exit fee, caused intense embarrassment to the government, but it remained unwilling or unable to act.
- In the mid-1980s the Bank of New Zealand (BNZ) helped fuel

the speculative frenzy which followed financial deregulation. The bank's heavy exposure to corporate failures in New Zealand and Australia prompted two government-led bail-outs. The first, under Labour in 1989, for $600 million included a cash injection from Fay Richwhite that gave them a 30 percent stake in the bank. The second, by National following the 1990 election, was for $720 million. Sale of the BNZ to National Australia Bank was concluded by the major shareholders in November 1992 for $850 million. The BNZ's after-tax profit trebled within the next two years. The negotiations had proved virtually impenetrable to minority shareholders who unsuccessfully campaigned for a better deal. Refusal by both Labour and National to support a public inquiry into the bank's dealings provoked allegations of collaboration with big business. The BNZ's role in facilitating Cook Islands tax avoidance schemes was central to the limited inquiry that was commissioned in 1994 to investigate those deals. Whatever the outcome, it was unlikely that the government-appointed directors, the ministers responsible and their advisors would ever be held to account.

Asset sales were promoted as a strategy to repay debt, producing returns which would exceed their capital value and income if retained. But the financial returns from privatisation were not spectacular. Total receipts from asset sales to December 1994 were $13 billion. Critics claimed that many were underpriced because the government was too eager to sell and there were few buyers. Sale by tender had been preferred to share floats to maximise the return. Since few locally based companies were large enough to tender, overseas control of key resources and industries became inevitable.

Initially, privatisation was justified to help retire debt. Labour set the goal of a one-third reduction in public debt by 1992. As journalist Simon Collins pointed out, however, 'all the revenue actually received from asset sales in 1988-9 was swept away again by the lottery of the foreign exchange markets.'[56] Treasury acknowledged in early 1990 that, while public debt had declined as a percentage of GDP, reduction targets had not been met. National repaid some overseas debt from asset sales, although the effect was again overshadowed by movements in the dollar. Meanwhile, total foreign debt increased. Corporatisation had initially moved the burden from 'official' to 'other government' debt. Subsequent sales to major New Zealand companies, funded primarily from overseas, shifted this again to private overseas debt.

Douglas admitted that the debt argument was a red herring: 'I am not sure we were right to use the argument that we should privatise to quit debt. We knew it was a poor argument but we probably felt it was the easiest to use politically.'[57] The primary purpose was ideological. As Douglas argued in the 1988 budget, by disengaging from the state, government businesses would 'be freed to realise their full potential' and the government enabled to concentrate its energy and resources on 'fulfilling its proper role'.[58] Indeed, former Forestcorp chair Alan Gibbs reportedly 'believed that public ownership should be liquidated at any cost and that the benefits to the country were much greater than any discount in price. He would have given the forests away to have got them out of public hands.'[59] Treasury too confirmed that debt reduction, 'which has tended to be identified in the public minds as the overriding aim of asset sales, is more of an intermediate goal—albeit an important one—in achieving broader economic objectives. . . . In particular, the Government has been driven by a wider concern about the quality of Government interventions in the economy as a whole.'[60]

Regulation

Strategic assets and natural monopolies, once privatised, remained largely uncontrolled. Any anti-competitive practices were dealt with under the weak, efficiency-oriented Commerce Act. Foreign investment was rubber-stamped by the OIC. Disciplines on overpriced and inadequate services were left to the market, aside from certain guarantees under the Fair Trading and Consumer Protection Acts. Attempts to scrutinise the government's performance in the sales process through the Official Information Act were commonly neutralised by invoking commercial confidentiality.

Specific controls were imposed in only two cases. In one, international aviation requirements obliged the government to retain a directive share in Air New Zealand. The other was the sale of Telecom. Concerns about private, and foreign, control of a key infrastructural service and guaranteed affordable access were deflected by the device of the 'kiwi share'—a variant on Thatcher's 'golden share'—which gave the government a strategic stake in the company's decisions. It was backed by three pledges:

* not to increase standard rentals for residential telephone lines faster than the rate of inflation, unless Telecom's regional operating profits were unreasonably affected;

- to ensure phone line rentals for rural residential customers were no higher than those in the cities, and all residential services remained as widely available as at present; and
- to maintain a free local calling option for residential users.

These were advertised on television as etched in stone, but the government refused to enshrine the pledges in legislation. Instead, they were included in the articles of association, and protected from breach or alteration by retention of the kiwi share. Enforcement remained in the shareholding ministers' hands. One public lawyer warned: 'Retention of a kiwi share recognises that some form of regulation is necessary and that questions of pricing in a strategic industry cannot be left safely to market forces. But the kiwi share is a very crude form of "regulation" which, by itself, is not certain to be effective.'[61]

Within a year Telecom's owners complained that cross-subsidising its domestic service to honour the pledges imposed an unreasonable and unfair burden at a time when competitor Clear Communications (part-owned by US multinational MCI and Bell Canada) was eroding its income from toll calls. Under public pressure, the Prime Minister confirmed that the pledges remained binding. When Telecom announced another record profit of $402.3 million for 1991/92, management claimed they had grounds for breaking free of the pledges, whether or not the government agreed.[62] They chose instead to raise charges for public telephone calls and equipment rentals which were not covered by the pledges, but which still affected domestic users most. The prospect remained, however, that Telecom would find new loopholes, unilaterally disregard the pledges and/or convince a future government to waive or amend them.

The philosophical purpose, and practical effect, of corporatisation and privatisation had been to transfer economic, and indirectly political, power into the hands of private corporations driven by economic efficiency to maximise profits. With no effective protection of consumer interests or guaranteed rights of access, private sector owners had become able to determine the quantity, quality and price of New Zealanders' access to basic goods and services, and hence their quality of life.

Public service restructuring[63]

What remained of the state sector was subjected to changes which the Logan review in 1991 described as 'the most far-reaching and ambitious of any of their kind in the world'.[64] According to former

Treasury head Graham Scott, briefings on them were later sought by the OECD, World Bank, the finance ministries of Canada, Australia, Germany, UK and Singapore, and the accounting office of the US Congress.[65]

The initial focus on what Scott called 'hygiene factors' attacked structures, systems, corporate planning, remuneration policies, information technology and financial management.[66] Once these had been dealt with, it was intended that attention would shift to 'soft' management techniques. These included motivational factors of leadership, values, personal responsibility, empowerment, team-work and strategic thinking. But the government was preoccupied with fiscal restraint. That, backed by the Employment Contracts Act (ECA), dictated an endless cycle of restructuring which featured budget cuts, job insecurity, a pay freeze and threats to privatise. For most of the state sector, phase two—reconstructing a positive work environment, building a coherent team and raising job satisfaction—never came.

State agencies were reorganised according to their functional role—commercial, policy, regulatory or operational. This produced a disaggregated three-tier hierarchy, described by public sector analyst John Martin as:

- core agencies responsible to ministers for policy advice, administrative, regulatory, contracting and control functions;
- Crown-owned agencies which provided goods and services funded by core agencies; and
- private sector organisations from which the previous two purchased goods and services.

Policy analyst Jonathan Boston records that, by August 1990, 'there were twenty new departments, ministries and offices in existence, fifteen of those operating in July 1984 had been abolished, corporatized or privatized, and most of the remainder had been extensively reorganized'.[67] The plethora of small ministries and agencies tended to encourage defensive positioning in the policy-making process, making policy co-ordination more difficult and isolating policy from operational realities.

The Logan committee review of the state sector reforms in 1991 identified tensions among the central agencies, which were dominated by Treasury, and tensions between the central agencies and other departments, who viewed the former's influence as excessive. Certain ministries had accumulated power through rationalisation and mergers, and their strategic role in the reforms; smaller departments, especially advocacy ministries, which were considered intrinsically 'captured' by their constituencies, tended to be marginalised and under-resourced. The review considered that these problems could be resolved through better dialogue, greater commitment and development of a shared vision. Others saw the tensions as endemic to the entrepreneurial limited-state model.

State Sector Act

The new state sector regime centred on two complementary measures. Under the State Sector Act 1988 CEOs were employed to run government departments on renewable performance-related contracts for up to five years. These contracts would be negotiated through the SSC. Originally the Prime Minister was to have direct control over CEO appointments.[68] That proposal was revised to require the SSC to recommend an appointee to the Cabinet, which could then approve the recommendation, or decline it and direct the appointment of another named person. Any such direction would be published in the *Gazette*. The power to decline a nomination was exercised only once, in 1990.[69] The Cabinet convinced the SSC to readvertise a position, avoiding the need publicly to impose a preferred alternative. Nevertheless, the need for caution when making politically unpalatable appointments was clear.

The new regime allowed considerable flexibility and range in CEOs' salary packages. While information on bands of executive salaries was released, arguments of commercial confidentiality were used to keep details of individual salaries secret. Appointment criteria stressed management and efficiency skills, and the number of CEOs with business qualifications significantly increased in the early years. Initial turnover was rapid. Eighteen months after the Act was passed two-thirds of departments had new CEOs. Three-quarters of those appointed since the Act had worked outside the core public sector.[70] Some were short-term change agents, moving from one agency to another: from transport to social welfare, from forestry to education, fisheries and social welfare, from commerce to justice, from Treasury to labour, health and prisons. Their lack of knowledge of the subject area seemed of little consequence to those making the appointments—the restructuring formula and managerial skills required were the same.

CEOs were expected to enter into separate annual performance agreements with their ministers, setting down the outputs to be supplied, financial performance to be achieved and management practices to be followed. These agreements were not, however, legally required, and their existence frequently depended on the minister's grasp of policy objectives and commitment to taking management responsibilities seriously. Performance incentives were linked to specific outputs and budgetary targets, prompting concerns that attention would focus on those elements at the expense of departmental operations overall. The agreements were not public documents, so such influences were difficult to assess.

Under the Act, CEOs and other senior management to a maximum of 500 formed a Senior Executive Service. This was intended to provide 'a unifying force at the most senior levels of the public sector' in an increasingly decentralised public service. Individual contracts with flexible pay and incentives were intended to attract high-calibre private-sector managers. But neither the terms of appointment nor the public sector environment proved particularly appealing.

CEOs were to have full autonomy to hire and fire staff. The tension between ministerial oversight, the political impartiality of government appointments, and managerial autonomy surfaced in late 1994 when a CEO resigned after his minister publicly condemned a controversial senior staff appointment. Commentators agreed that it was proper for chief executives to consult their ministers informally before such decisions, and prepare them for any political flak. But they differed as to the line between CEOs' autonomy and ministerial interference.[71] Former SSC chair Mervyn Probine spelt out what he saw as the risks to professional independence under the new regime:

> One wonders whether very senior public servants will now feel less free, where it is necessary to give unpalatable advice (albeit professionally sound) to ministers for fear that it might affect their prospects of future promotion to CEO level. Furthermore, one wonders whether CEOs approaching the end of their current contract will be as prepared to give ministers free and frank professional advice knowing that there will be political input into the re-appointment process, and that that input can be decisive.[72]

The Act retained some progressive elements of state-sector employment policy secured over the years, notably the equal employment opportunity provisions for women. The commitment to 'biculturalism' was of more doubtful provenance. Claims by various departments and the SSC to have embraced 'biculturalism' were seen by many Maori as another device to placate demands to share real power. The policy rarely went beyond the cosmetic co-option of Maori intellectual and cultural property by 'mainstream' government departments. Maori organisations were forced to compete for resources and programmes. Maori staff faced increasing conflicts of interests as employees of the Crown. Underlying these tensions was the unresolved issue of 'whether their Maori policies and programmes are conceptualised on the basis of Maori as a disadvantaged minority or as tangata whenua [first nation] with constitutional guarantees in terms of some autonomy and residual sovereignty'.[73]

The new legislation had drastic implications for state employment. The traditional centralised employment structure and the collective award, tenure and grievance procedures of the public service gave way to decentralised employment, enterprise bargaining, individual contracts and Employment Tribunal coverage, first under the Labour Relations Act 1987 and subsequently the ECA 1991.

The State Sector Act obliged the SSC and government departments to be a 'good employer'. But their practices were as ruthless as those of their private sector counterparts. Former leading unionists were recruited as consultants to advise the SSC and departments on their employment strategy. The government's policy of fiscal restraint and its industrial role as an employer became intertwined. In theory, CEOs had full authority over terms and conditions of appointment. But the SSC, backed by the Cabinet committee on state sector employment, played a highly directive role. The Cabinet's 'expectations' for the 1992–93 wage round included:

- fiscal restraint;
- no additional money for wages;
- outcomes should be fiscally neutral at minimum, and preferably fiscally positive (i.e. cuts);
- vigorous negotiations should seek to increase productivity;
- over-generous redundancy provisions should be reduced;
- transition costs in any restructuring should be minimised;
- flow-on effects to other departments should be taken into account; and
- CEOs should keep the SSC informed.

The SSC argued that the projected budget deficit for 1992/93 required fiscal savings to be made. Yet in 1994/95, when the budget was in surplus, the same expectations and demands to cut costs

applied.[74] The sinking lid on departmental budgets, and performance incentives for CEOs to meet expenditure targets, encouraged
nil or negative pay adjustments and reductions in redundancy,
overtime and penalty rates. Low morale and high turnover contributed to deprofessionalisation in some state agencies, which were
increasingly staffed by a de-skilled and casualised workforce.[75]

As one commentator concluded, public servants were 'being asked
to do more work with fewer resources, their personal accountability
has been increased, the security of their positions removed, and the
distance between the public and the Public Service widened'.[76] Quali-
ties of professionalism, loyalty, innovation, integrity and commitment to public well-being were being subordinated to the goals of
efficiency and managerialism under the corporate model. Meanwhile
politicians were further distancing themselves from responsibility for
the operation and inadequacies of the state sector.

Public Finance Act

The second element in restructuring the core state sector was the
Public Finance Act 1989 (PFA). The emphasis moved, in the jargon
of the times, from *inputs*, or the amount of money a department or
Crown agency could secure, to identification of and accountability
for *outputs*, or goods and services including policy advice. These
outputs would form the basis of the department or agency's corporate plan, and its annual budget. Ministers would buy outputs from
the state agency for a certain price to achieve the government's desired *outcomes*. An outcome was defined in the Act as 'the impacts on,
or the consequences for, the community of the outputs or activities
of the Government'.[77]

Funding was delivered through a contract between the minister as
purchaser and the agency as provider. Government accounts were
placed on a private business basis. The commercialised approach
required substantial changes to administrative arrangements:
* funding of outputs, not inputs;
* charging departments the full cost of their operations, including
  a capital charge;
* accrual accounting;
* improved reporting; and
* incentives and penalties.
While other countries had adopted some of these principles, it was
unusual to see them set down in an Act. June Pallot notes: 'Incorpo-

rating the main features of the changes in legislation, rather than relying on guidelines and instructions, has brought certainty into the environment and known parameters within which to manage, but runs the risk of being more difficult to change.'[78]

The PFA had two potentially conflicting goals: to improve the quality of service and responsiveness to changing client needs; and to increase efficient and accountable use of resources. While Treasury frequently talked of quality control and responsiveness, its prime concern was to keep operations and spending in line. Departments and staff became absorbed with constant restructuring, compliance with stringent financial targets and providing quantified outputs. Parallels were drawn between the growing obsession with management and the clamour by private firms to secure ISO 9000 accreditation. As ISO critics pointed out, an efficient management process could still produce a poor-quality product.

The policy was implemented at breakneck speed, being developed as it went along with no time to establish monitoring and evaluation procedures. The PFA provided new opportunities, in particular, for the burgeoning industry of consultants in change management, software and systems analysis, policy development and service delivery. Consultants had been used before by New Zealand government agencies, but never so many, for so much, so rapidly. The restructured ministries were already deluged with new responsibilities, including risk management, accrual accounting and managerial autonomy. There had simply been no time to put the necessary procedures and safeguards for contracting out in place.

A damning audit of government consultancies published by the Auditor-General in 1994 concluded that many departments failed to meet sound management standards in awarding, monitoring and evaluating contracts, while inadequate documentation made some contracts impossible to assess.[79] Too little thought was given to the choice between developing in-house skills or using private consultants. Some departments were reluctant to carry out formal evaluations which could prove contentious and delay completion of the assignment. Yet Boston noted in 1991 that some of the consultancy reports on departmental restructuring had 'proved difficult to implement and so far have borne little fruit'.[80] It was unclear whether these were teething problems or endemic to short-staffed departments focused on short-term goals. Whichever, the remedies suggested by the Auditor-General's report, and indeed the report itself, were concerned with the soundness of contracting procedures, not with the quality of the result. It seemed that neither the departments nor any other government agencies were responsible for that.

The assessment of quality outcomes was meant to be the responsibility of ministers. Yet outcomes were almost impossible to specify or measure with precision. That meant outputs, which commodified policy advice, regulation and service delivery, became the primary reference-point. Complex functions were reduced to easily measured targets irrespective of whether these were accurate or appropriate. Achieving the performance targets became an end in itself. The technical specifications and mass of documentation this entailed often proved incomprehensible to the professionals in departments or agencies who were required to perform, and to the ministers and MPs who were meant to hold them to account.

The failure to match accounting and reporting practices with quality appraisal of either policy advice or outcomes achieved was sharply criticised by economist Dennis Rose:

> Despite continuing attention to the format and content of government financial statements, there has been a disappointing lack of progress in developing publicly available official analysis of policy trade-offs and macro-economic outcomes of alternative policy packages. If growth in output and employment is to be given its proper weight in policy formation, decision makers and the community need to be informed by such analysis which should, ideally, be provided by the Treasury. Treasury's failure to provide adequate public analysis in this area suggests that there may be a case for commissioning such analyses through competitive tendering.[81]

Evaluating state sector restructuring

Some of the reasoning which lay behind the state sector restructuring was valid, and some of the changes genuinely increased efficiency and accountability. But there was a dearth of empirical data on which to assess the success of the regime, even where criteria could be clearly defined. The financial costs of initial and on-going state sector adjustment, redundancy payments, relocation costs, recruitment expenses, systems creation and management remained unknown. So did the social, human and employment impacts of the continual reorganisation of management, policy and service delivery through the state. The primary justifications for the change—reduction of capture, consistency of objectives, quality of advice and accountability for decision-making—were very difficult to assess.

The absence of any effective, on-going monitoring and evaluation in a programme whose *raison d'être* was to improve the efficiency of accountability showed how far the state sector restructuring had been ideologically driven.

In the new structure, power and responsibility were diffused, creating what Martin describes as a 'dangerous vacuum of responsibility'.[82] Accountability for specific policy decisions or events became almost impossible to tie down. Many senior officials and agency boards interpreted managerial autonomy to mean that their advice and operations should be immune from scrutiny. Ministers complained that CEOs did not always appreciate their needs for political, as well as financial, risk management. They wanted to be better informed, without being overwhelmed by a mass of information which they were ill equipped to analyse.[83] But ministers also hid behind managerial autonomy and commercial confidentiality so as to evade demands to explain the actions of a department or ministry. This confused the *managerial* functions of chief executives, for which they were responsible to the minister, with the minister's *political* accountability to the electorate. The public could not get at the chief executive; but it expected the minister to answer in Parliament, and to the media, not only for policy but for individual cases.

Many of these problems can be sourced to the theoretical paradigms of agency and public choice which equated government with the private firm, a distinction that ignored the diverse responsibilities of ministers and of a professional public service, and the ultimate coercive power of the state. In theory, the changes were concerned to ensure that CEOs had incentives to act in the interests of their ministers, who in turn represented the public interest, and that ministers could monitor and assess their outputs. This assumed a linear principal/agent relationship which in government did not exist. Boston describes the notion of 'a government of twenty autonomous Ministers serviced by thirty to forty separate businesses' as 'completely at odds with Westminster-style constitutional conventions'.[84] A complex set of relations was involved that required professionalism, not just managerial skills. As Martin observed: 'The exercise of discretion in dealing with the entitlement of citizens is a very different activity from serving customers at a supermarket.'[85]

The long title of the State Sector Act described it as 'An Act to ensure that employees in the State services are imbued with the spirit of service to the community.' This implied a professional detachment from the direct political interests of the minister and the government. Martin notes that reconciling 'conflicting duties—for example to the law, to the minister as client, to the public as customer, and to the public interest . . . requires a prior commitment to the learning of the craft and an allegiance to the continuity of government, irrespective of the nature of the governors temporarily in office'.[86] The elevation of efficiency over other values and priorities which in the public service were of equal or greater significance meant professionalism was replaced by managerialism as the dominant ethos.

The analogy with commercial contracting was equally flawed. If ministers were given only the advice they specifically contracted and paid for, there would be no room for full and frank advice, for proactivity or for expanding the minister's knowledge base to enable properly informed decisions to be made. Martin stressed the two-fold professional duty of the public servant: to offer neutral, high-quality advice, and then dutifully to execute whatever decision was made.

There were other contradictions. The assumption that all state employees (except the technocrats) were self-maximising bureaucrats intent on capturing the machinery of public power, and so needed to be held to account, sat uncomfortably with a model that stressed managerial autonomy and an arm's-length political relationship. Indeed, incentives to self-regarding behaviour would seem much stronger in contractual performance-based employment arrangements. The underlying premise of bureaucratic 'capture' was also ill defined. Boston points to the

> various forms of 'capture' [that] can occur in a bureaucratic context: ideological capture, client capture, producer capture, and capture by professionals or technical experts. The case for separating policy advice from policy implementation is concerned only with . . . producer capture. Yet it is by no means clear that this is the most widespread or pernicious form. Indeed, it can be argued that ideological capture and professional capture are of greater concern and that separating policy advice from delivery will do nothing to overcome such problems.[87]

The state sector/public finance regime could be seen as itself an exercise in the capture of the state bureaucracy by the technocrats, who then reshaped it according to their preferred ideological lines.

Privatisation of the public service

The restructuring process blurred the public/private sector distinction. Policy advice functions were increasingly contracted out. Private sector analysts were employed on short-term contracts and to participate in working groups, task forces and advisory committees. Ministers recruited their own advisors to vet departmental advice and oversee contracts with private sector agencies. Ministerial offices and their staff, although paid from the public purse, were exempt from PFA scrutiny, and their terms of employment were protected from public oversight by commercial confidentiality and privacy laws. Government sought further advice from task forces of selected officials and sympathetic outsiders. And select committees sought to employ their own expert advisors in place of the departmental officials who traditionally serviced them.

Predictably, the Business Roundtable advocated greater private control of core state functions. Private sector boards of directors could be appointed to oversee departmental operations along SOE lines, with ministers kept at arm's length. These boards could monitor efficiency and pre-empt any moves to reverse or corrupt the new regime.[88] Alternatively, the statutory function of the public service to provide policy advice could be made contestable. This option was examined by the SSC in 1991,[89] and endorsed in 1994 by the principal advisor to the Crown Company Monitoring Advisory Unit. He predicted:

> Cadres of private sector purchase advisers located in ministers' offices will develop, many with open political affiliations. Core public sector institutions will find their monopolies removed and themselves operating in a highly contested market for provision of public policy advice. The Government will gradually move away from ownership of public policy providers and focus on purchase, with an emphasis on minimising transaction costs and maximising quality.[90]

The accompanying requirement for competitive neutrality would see any remaining advantages enjoyed by the public service removed. State agencies would have to pay tax, profits and capital charges (already in place) and provide access to state information and databases. In turn, they would be freed to operate in both the public and private market-place. Ethical obligations would be specified in contracts, and PFA requirements replaced by contractual terms enforced through private contract law. Many existing staff would move into consultancies. Lowering transaction costs and the need to ensure continuous supply would favour contracts for entire terms of government. Advisors in ministers' offices would co-ordinate this process and provide the final ministerial advice. This was a logical extension of the new regime.

Boston pointed out that such a model would fail even on its own terms:

> any attempt to improve the purchase and supply of governmental policy advice needs to start from a recognition that the widespread reliance of governments on relatively permanent, in-house policy expertise and advice is not due wholly, or even primarily, to rent-seeking or slack-seeking behaviour on the part of career officials. Rather . . . such practices can be explained and justified on the basis of the very theories that have promoted the recent drive to contract out a wider range of governmental activities.[91]

The 'sunk costs' of expertise, trust between ministers and advisors, information systems and data bases would make entry unprofitable unless long-term contract commitments were made. Such contracts would reduce the incentives for others to build up similar resources and to compete, defeating the purpose of the exercise. Term contracts would create incentives for suppliers to advocate policies that increased demand for their services, and to pander to the ideological and policy preferences of the government to improve their chances of reappointment, instead of giving free and frank advice. It would be difficult to specify contractual requirements for policy functions in a way that would could be monitored and enforced. The tasks of contracting-out, co-ordination and monitoring would also require a strong central agency with its own costs. There would be regulatory concerns over handling and disclosure of information, controls on mergers and takeovers, employment policies and investment in staff training, and conflicts of interest that could not be left to private contract law. Responsibility would be further disaggregated across specific policy areas, and the competitive commercial environment would place inter-departmental co-operation at risk. Corporate memory could disappear. Boston concluded that 'it is in the public interest for governments to maintain an in-house advisory capacity across the full range of public policy issues'.[92]

Maintenance of a stable, centralised public service would become even more important with the onset of MMP. Martin argued that the potential for rapid turnover of government and coalition politics made 'the case for a "permanent" public service imbued with the ethos of "free and frank" advice and acting as trustees for the cumulative institutional memory [seem] even stronger than it does in the present state of the polity'.[93] With the state corporation model so pervasive and almost impossible to unwind, a positive role for the state needed to be publicly asserted and maintained.

The reality was anything but that. In a parody of public choice theory, strategically placed technocrats held the machinery of the state captive. The state sector reforms were designed to ensure their control was retained, or was divested to private enterprise. Any Cabinet intent on wresting control of the state machine back from the technocrats—which would by implication be neither Labour nor National, and would comprise new ministers with no experience of government—would face an exceedingly difficult task.

CHAPTER SEVEN

Monetary Policy

MONETARY POLICY, embracing money, credit, interest and exchange rates, played a dominant role in the early years of the structural adjustment programme. The Reserve Bank and the Treasury had internally espoused a monetarist theory since the mid-1970s, but the Muldoon government stood in their way. Following Labour's election in 1984, they moved rapidly to put the theorising into effect. By 1990 it formed the foundation of government economic policy.

The monetarist agenda
The Reserve Bank described the strategy of 'firm' monetary policy as 'an essential prerequisite for lower, more stable interest rates and inflation rates over the medium-term. It is also a complement to a range of other macroeconomic policies introduced or under consideration.'[1]

Treasury's *Economic Management* explained the technocrats' case against inflation. Rapid rises in inflation over short periods of time had

- made it difficult to distinguish price changes that were part of the inflation process from relative price changes. This obscured price signals which would ensure resources were directed to their most efficient use;
- produced incentives for governments to create inflation so they could reduce their interest bill and the public debt;
- played havoc with tax measures such as progressive tax rates, asset depreciation and interest rate deductions, and distorted investment decisions for tax purposes;
- arbitrarily redistributed wealth between savers and borrowers, and owners and users of assets.[2]

Treasury proposed a raft of monetary reforms to the new government. As its first priority government should remove regulations on mortgage interest rates, lending interest rates, financial services and interest on deposits. It should also withdraw lending growth instructions and the marginal government security ratio that applied to finance companies. Other 'pipeline' issues included operation of the reserve ratios system, the move to a tender system for Treasury bills, and more active short-term liquidity management by the Reserve Bank through open market operations.

Monetary policy was to be operated not by controlling interest rates or the reserve ratios of financial institutions, but by the Reserve Bank controlling the money base. This came to be defined as the settlement deposits of banks at the Reserve Bank, plus all securities which it agreed could be cashed in at a discount to obtain more reserves. Excess liquidity would be drawn away from the private sector to the government by Treasury bill tenders and open market operations in the short term, and in the medium term through an active public debt policy using sale of government securities. This last requirement involved fully funding the deficit by debt purchases, which would retrieve from circulation all the funds injected into the economy by the government. The Reserve Bank would monitor the various indicators of monetary conditions, including money and credit aggregates and interest and exchange rates. It had much less concern about controlling short-term influences like retail prices and wages, given the belief that these would come under control once the stabilisation mechanisms were in place.

Economist Paul Dalziel has identified two major theoretical influences on the technocrats' monetary policy.[3] Both focused on inflationary expectations. Variations on Friedmanite monetarism argued that, once inflationary expectations became built in, any short-term employment gains achieved by higher inflation were neutralised. People constantly adjusted their expectations to inflation, and unemployment always returned to some 'natural rate'. It was therefore better to target monetary policy at medium-term price stability.

The second 'rational expectations' hypothesis disputed the assumption that expectations were based on past experience, and argued that people would base their expectations on the future result of government policies as predicted by economic theory. They would not be fooled by governments' attempts to manipulate monetary policy in the short term. Securing and maintaining the credibility of price stability goals should therefore be the primary aim.

Rational expectations theory underpinned the more detailed theoretical discussion of monetary policy in 1987 in *Government Management*. The goals of consistency, credibility and transparency in turn required:

- a clear and unequivocal policy direction;
- consistent and mutually reinforcing policies;
- incentives to avoid policy reversal; and
- clear explanations of the benefits of change.[4]

Treasury acknowledged that there had been problems with monetary reform since 1984. Registered unemployment had more than doubled and inflation remained around 10 percent. But the longer-term benefits of stabilisation policy had to be balanced against its short-term impacts. Successful disinflation 'almost invariably entails costs in the form of temporarily lower output and higher unemployment'.[5] Employers, workers and investors were often slow to adjust their expectations to a lower inflation environment, and it took time for resources, especially labour, to shift from one use to another.

Treasury also acknowledged an 'unfortunate aspect of the disinflation process is that the burden of adjustment has been spread unevenly across the various regions and sectors of the community'.[6] Treasury considered it was probably inevitable that those most directly affected by changes in interest and exchange rates would feel the pressure first. This could be expected to flow through to the wider community as weaker demand spread to suppliers, and lower incomes led to reduced consumer demand. The unevenness would be ameliorated more quickly if price factors were free to adjust and sheltered parts of the economy—by implication in industry and labour—were fully exposed to the market.

Any moves to compensate those adversely affected were steadfastly opposed.[7] Treasury argued that people should carry the losses as well as gains from risk-taking behaviour in the market-place. Risks would be minimised by a clear and consistent policy direction. Compensation to specific groups would encourage others to resist change and overstate their costs, and incentives to limit their exposure to loss would be reduced. The additional tax revenue needed for compensation would divert funds from more efficient investment. Those affected would be hard to identify, especially as many of the benefits took time to seep through, so a short-term focus on winners and losers was likely to mislead. Ultimately, improved low-inflationary economic performance would secure both equity and efficiency goals by generating wealth and creating sustainable job growth. Its effectiveness would depend on the flexibility of the labour market to adjust. Any question of compensation should be left to the general programmes for social support—despite the fact that the bulk of *Government Management* sought to minimise the cost and scale of such support.

Treasury strongly defended a rapid disinflationary approach. Faster reform would mean that the full benefits could be enjoyed earlier. Gradual change increased the risk that resources would gravitate to poorly performing activities, and people would question the government's commitment to the price stability goal. Equally, however, too rapid a transition could cause political fall-out and put the policy at risk. 'A balance must therefore be struck between a policy that is so aggressive that reversal is thought highly probable and a policy that is judged so feeble that it lacks credibility.'[8] Again, Treasury's notion of balance was relative. 'While a concern exists that if a severe recession resulted from rapid disinflation political support for the entire restructuring programme would be undermined, the balance of considerations argues for accelerating the pace of disinflation. . . . If anything, the experience of reform to date suggests that the main dangers lie in moving too slowly.'[9] Treasury therefore urged the government to 'move forcefully and rapidly to complete the disinflation process notwithstanding the costs . . . '.[10]

In passing the Reserve Bank Act 1989, the Labour government intended to do precisely that. Monetary policy would be narrowed by law onto a single price-stability track.

Implementing monetary strategy
The Reserve Bank initially appeared to operate an orthodox monetarist programme. But the total stock of money proved difficult to control by sales of public debt in the highly deregulated financial environment. All recorded monetary and credit aggregates grew by at least 80 percent in the four years to December 1988.[11] The Reserve Bank increasingly relied on interest rates to limit the excess. That did not work well either. With the government offering high interest rates, other financial institutions sought to increase their borrowing at comparable rates. With money flooding into the country, and no effective constraints on financial sector behaviour, economist Jan Whitwell suggested this could be 'more appropriately described as a high interest rate policy than a tight monetary policy.

Price level increases set in train market forces which are free to generate a monetary expansion'.[12]

The exchange rate assumed a growing importance. Foreign exchange controls were lifted in December 1984. Prior to that the New Zealand dollar had been pegged to a basket of the currencies of its major trading partners. Regulations had limited the market exchange of foreign currencies and set rates for approved dealings. There were restrictions on portfolio investments abroad, on overseas borrowing by local financial institutions to boost their short-term liquidity, on private sector borrowing overseas and on foreign-owned companies raising funds on New Zealand capital markets.

These had been loosened gradually since the 1970s, as the globalisation of finance markets and innovative moves to circumvent the regulations made comprehensive supervision even more difficult. These deficiencies had been exposed in June 1984, as expectations of a devaluation saw money flow out of the country, almost exhausting the Reserve Bank's liquid foreign reserves. Immediately after the election, the bank closed the foreign exchange market. Intense debate over devaluation continued for several days until the out-going Muldoon government finally conceded, after which trading in the New Zealand dollar was resumed.

The entry restrictions on foreign exchange dealerships had been relaxed in 1983, with authorised exchange dealers required to submit regular information for Reserve Bank surveillance. The combined impact of this and the removal of foreign exchange controls in December 1984 was dramatic. Between 1983 and November 1986 the number of authorised dealers grew to eighteen, along with four foreign exchange brokers. The total monthly turnover on the New Zealand foreign exchange market rose from $12,763 million in September 1983 to $172,622 million in September 1986.[13]

The free float of the dollar was announced in March 1985. Between mid-June and mid-November 1985 the exchange rate appreciated about 22 percent, as foreign investors flooded in to take advantage of anticipated long-term high interest rates. The devaluation in July 1984 had been expected to compensate producers for the removal of subsidies and border protection. But the rapid appreciation saw competitiveness decline. Export returns, especially for farm produce, fell. As profitability declined, so did output in traded goods, while the non-traded sector grew. Unemployment in the manufacturing and agricultural sectors began spiralling upwards.

The Reserve Bank moved to ease liquidity in late 1985, and again in mid-1986, following requests from exporters for the Minister of Finance to intervene to protect the export base. Exchange rates and interest rates fell. But between September 1986 and June 1988 the trade-weighted exchange rate rose again by 20 percent, and the dollar appreciated 56 percent against its US counterpart.[14]

The implications for the disinflation policy were significant. The free float had been necessary before New Zealand's inflation trend could depart significantly from those of its trading partners to whose currencies the dollar was pegged. Whitwell argued that the float had also opened the way for monetary policy to be pursued via the exchange rate. 'Flexible exchange rates neatly accommodate official eclecticism for they allow the authorities to move imperceptibly from one control technique to another without destroying the overall credibility of the stated policy stance. . . . [T]here is a lot of informal evidence to suggest that the New Zealand monetary authorities have done precisely that.'[15]

Indeed, the Reserve Bank's 1984 post-election briefing had explicitly recognised that 'the exchange rate is primarily an instrument of monetary control'.[16] Changes in the exchange rate had a strong and rapid influence on prices. The higher the exchange rate, the lower the cost of imports. In theory, this should flow through to domestic prices, lowering input costs and forcing import-competing industry to become internationally competitive. Lower export prices also meant less spending power and lower demand. Domestic prices were expected to adjust to these changes in supply and demand.

As Whitwell repeatedly stressed, however, the price of most inputs, especially labour, remained administered, not market-driven, as Treasury's model required. Instead of reducing prices of products and wages, producers reduced their output. Workers were laid off. Factories closed. The economy descended into a recessionary spiral. Increases in real GDP averaged less than 1 percent a year between December 1984 and December 1988. Official unemployment almost trebled to 158,000. Investment in agriculture and manufacturing fell. Whitwell concluded:

> In spite of strenuous efforts by the Reserve Bank to make its new monetary policy appear consistent and credible, its base control programme has clearly proved to be a highly inefficient anti-inflationary strategy. . . . There is now little doubt that early in the transition period, perhaps even at the outset, the New Zealand authorities came to rely

primarily on interest rate control and that their day-to-day operations in the financial market were designed to influence the overall level of interest rates directly and hence the exchange rate indirectly, once the move to a flexible exchange rate regime had been accomplished in March 1985. Increasingly the real exchange rate came to be regarded as an important, if not the critical, link in the process by which monetary changes are transmitted to the inflation rate. Managed exchange rates thus became an integral part of the overall anti-inflationary strategy as the policy focus shifted from the monetary aggregates to interest rates.[17]

She went on to argue that managing the exchange rate directly by buying and selling foreign currency would have been preferable to manipulating it through high interest rates, with their flow-on effects to the productive sector. But such direct intervention 'would blatantly infringe the government's more market-oriented strategy',[18] and the credibility of the programme was at stake.

Evaluating monetary policy 1984–89

During Labour's first term, the inflation rate climbed to an all-time high. The consumer price index (CPI) rose from an artificially held 3.5 percent in the March 1983/84 year to 16.5 percent in March 1985, due partly to the lifting of the wage, price, rent and interest rates freeze. It fell back to 10.5 percent in June 1986 but rose again to peak at 19 percent in June 1987. Contributing factors were a high wage round, especially for public servants, and the one-off effects of the new expenditure tax, GST, and accompanying increases in income support. The rate fell dramatically from 16.9 percent in September 1987 to 9.6 percent three months later as the GST factor declined.

The Reserve Bank claimed relative success, and argued that, despite monetary growth, deregulation had brought fringe financing back onto the banks' balance sheets where greater control could be exerted over it.[19] But Treasury conceded in its 1987 post-election briefing that the induced slowdown had not been as sharp as expected, and there were problems holding liquidity management settings sufficiently tight.

The persistent underestimation of the strength of the economy appears to derive at least in part from the difficulty of incorporating the likely effect of liberalisation measures into assessments of the macroeconomic situation. In some areas the benefits of liberalisation have created favourable demand conditions (for example in financial services) despite the weak macroeconomic picture. In others, particularly where industries are exposed to international competition, rapid restructuring has enabled producers to maintain surprisingly high levels of output and activity despite the strengthening of the real exchange rate. Perhaps most important, deregulation of the financial sector has allowed households to maintain consumption levels by increasing their borrowing in a way that was not previously possible, and high inflation expectations have made them willing to do so despite high levels of retail interest rates.[20]

Rather perversely, the combination of deregulation and monetary policy worked to the Reserve Bank's advantage. The October 1987 share-market crash wiped almost 57 percent off the share index in four months. The collapse of the inflated property market followed. As the bubble burst, aggregate monetary and credit growth plummeted. Bad debts from ill-considered loans plagued the financial sector and helped keep real interest rates high. The worsening recession gave monetary policy a significant boost. None of this prompted the Reserve Bank to reconsider the soundness of its monetary approach: 'while it is true that monetary and credit control have become considerably easier since the sharp downturn in demand at the end of 1987, this . . . simply acknowledges the difficulties inherent to running monetary policy in a market economy.'[21]

The prolonged failure of the Reserve Bank's anti-inflation strategy raised important questions about the sequencing of reform. While no particular sequence enjoyed universal support, economist Robert Buckle observed there was a 'convergence of informed opinion, based on theoretical reasoning and empirical results' in favour of a number of 'useful rules': trade reforms in slow-moving goods and factor markets and gradual liberalisation of the financial system should be introduced early, with relaxation of international capital controls left until last.[22] Otherwise expectations of high interest rates and property values would increase demand for the dollar, raising its value at the expense of export- and import-competing producers and loosening money supply. The credibility of both the liberalisation and stabilisation programmes would then be undermined.

Buckle considered it likely that the technocrats were aware of these arguments.[23] But there were practical considerations that affected sequencing. Financial markets were sympathetic to the structural adjustment programme, eager to expand, and influential in the policy-making process. The July 1984 foreign exchange crisis had exposed the failings of the existing currency controls. Deregulating the exchange markets was one way to set the programme under way and provide tangible proof of the government's intent.

Harper and Karacaoglu agreed that Labour's advisors would have known the arguments. But Labour faced the prospect of only one three-year term in government. The change agents 'could not afford the luxury of carrying out the reform process in an "optimal" manner'. The more restrictions and regulations they removed, the more they could force the hand of an in-coming government to continue the process.

> In the present environment, deregulation (especially financial deregulation) would be almost impossible to reverse, while an economy with a deregulated financial sector but regulated non-financial sectors would be impossible to sustain. Thus the short run costs of following the 'wrong' sequencing would be far outweighed by the long run benefits of eventually restructuring the whole economy.[24]

Treasury was defensive on the question of sequencing: 'The experience of recent reform in New Zealand has not raised any particular sequencing problems which could have been easily avoided. Undertaking a simultaneous programme of stabilisation and liberalisation has, as expected, involved some tensions.'[25] The experimental nature of the programme had meant there was no overseas experience on which to draw.

The OECD also played down the sequencing argument. 'Success' depended on the credibility of the overall programme, and speed of adjustment as well as sequencing. It was 'probably inevitable' that the costs fell on the tradeable sector, and doubtful whether other sequencing would have lowered those costs. New Zealand, it claimed, had little choice about the initial timing. The exchange rate crisis required financial deregulation. Interest rates were freed to stem capital outflows. The OECD also noted the strategic benefits for the structural adjustment programme:

> Early liberalisation of capital markets provided an important discipline on policy makers, as any subsequent decisions regarded as inconsistent with the broader reform process would be quickly reflected in higher borrowing premiums in international financial markets. In addition, it provided a strong rationale for proceeding with other reforms—such as public sector restructuring, government expenditure reductions, and the liberalisation of the labour market—whose benefits were not immediately obvious to the general public.[26]

Reserve Bank Act 1989

In 1988, following the share-market crash and with unemployment on the rise, the benefits of monetarism were far from obvious to most. The architects of Rogernomics were striking obstacles within and beyond the Cabinet. An increasing number of ministers, caucus and party members, motivated by a mixture of genuine concern and electoral expediency, sought to slow, stop or even reverse the restructuring process. The monetarist goal to eliminate inflation, which accepted the side-effects of high interest and high unemployment rates as inevitable, was at particular risk from political intervention. There were strong demands for government to prime the economy and boost demand. So the agency responsible for implementing that policy, the Reserve Bank, was in effect quarantined from direct government control.

The 1988 budget announced reforms to the Reserve Bank Act to codify the overriding price stability goal which had been espoused, if not always practised, since 1984. Early rumours of its effect were exaggerated. *The Banker* in November 1987 reported that the New Zealand government was 'flirting with an idea that even the UK's privatising Conservatives have not yet dared to entertain—flogging off the central bank'.[27] The new approach was unprecedented nevertheless.

In one sense, the bank returned to the objectives of the 1930s. Dalziel records how the statutory objectives of the Reserve Bank had altered at least eight times from those first proposed by Sir Otto Niemeyer of the Bank of England in 1931. Niemeyer recommended that 'an independent Reserve Bank should be set up charged with the responsibility for the stability of the New Zealand currency, invested with the privilege of note-issue, and charged with holding the Government account and the banking reserves of New Zealand'.[28] The exchange rate would be tied with strict parity to the pound sterling.

The first Reserve Bank Act, passed in 1933, replaced Niemeyer's proposed requirement for currency stability with control over monetary circulation and credit to ensure 'generally that the economic welfare of the Dominion may be promoted and maintained'. Changes in 1936, 1950, 1960, 1964 and 1973 saw the bank nationalised and its goals progressively broadened:

> The first Labour Government added 'social welfare' to the 'economic welfare' objective of the initial legislation. The second Labour Government changed the order of the two major objectives to give priority to

promoting production, trade, and employment. The third Labour Government changed 'employment' to 'full employment' and added a clause reinforcing that priority in monetary policy.[29]

The fourth Labour government's 1989 amendment removed production, trade and employment from the objectives, leaving price stability as the Reserve Bank's sole objective. Dalziel observed: 'Monetary policy is again divorced from any role in maintaining short-term economic activity; the only difference from Niemeyer's 1931 proposals is that the [overt] measure of currency stabilization has switched from its external value (the exchange rate) to its internal value (the consumer price index).'[30] The new legislation represented price stability—in effect zero inflation—as the desired norm. Yet New Zealand's inflation rate had fallen within that range on only two brief occasions this century: in 1961 and immediately after the Second World War. During the longest period of sustained economic growth, in the 1950s and 1960s, inflation had averaged around 4 percent.

The Reserve Bank Act 1989 contained a number of distinctive elements:

- independence of the bank from direct government control;
- price stability as its sole objective;
- separation of economic policy from its implementation;
- transparency of government policy, with an explicit statement to be made when a government deviated temporarily from the price stability norm;
- performance appraisal and accountability measures for management under an independent board;
- distinct rules for exchange rate operations; and
- new financial prudence requirements.

As the long title to the Act stressed, the government had the right to determine economic policy, while the central bank was responsible for its implementation. The Minister of Finance would set a target range for inflation which was written into the Reserve Bank governor's five-year contract and published in the *Gazette*. The bank was to issue six-monthly policy statements setting out how it intended to achieve its immediate target and its proposals for monetary policy in the following five years. The government retained four powers in relation to the Act. It could

- substitute alternative economic objectives for six-month periods, transparently by an Order in Council laid on the table of the House;

- alter the target band for inflation, with any change to be publicly disclosed;
- sack the governor for failing to meet the terms of contract or not renew the contract when it expired; or
- amend or repeal the legislation.

All were considered exceptional powers. While section 169 of the Act made it an objective of the bank to 'exhibit a sense of social responsibility' in exercising its powers, this was subordinate to its primary function of achieving and maintaining price stability.

Debates among the technocrats in preparing the Bill highlighted differences between the Treasury and Reserve Bank agendas. The bank's primary concern was monetary policy and inflation. Treasury agreed with those policy goals, but sought to locate changes to the Reserve Bank's structure and functions within the broader framework of state sector reform. Both were adamant in their submissions to the Finance and Expenditure Select Committee that monetary policy could achieve only one objective, and that was price stability. Other gains would follow. According to the Reserve Bank:

> There is no serious questioning in orthodox macroeconomics that price stability is the appropriate long run objective for monetary policy— indeed, that it is the only long run objective monetary policy can successfully pursue. This issue is essentially a technical one, regarding the limitations of an instrument, not an ideological one. Simply put, over anything other than the very short-term, monetary policy cannot directly do anything to improve employment or output levels, or the competitiveness of the tradeable goods sector—such variables are determined at much more fundamental levels in their own markets in the real economy.[31]

Treasury likewise asserted a 'general consensus in respect of the technical argument that the lasting and predictable effects of monetary policy are largely confined to the price level'.[32] Strongly critical submissions on the Bill from some of the country's economists suggested a distinct lack of consensus. But these were peremptorily dismissed by the bank:

> the economists consulted by the [Manufacturers'] Federation are out-of-step with mainstream economic thinking, both in academe and in the wider world. We accept that the general approach to monetary policy being adopted in New Zealand does not enjoy wide support in the New Zealand academic economics community. However, given the broader international support received, we suggest that this lack of local aca-

demic support says more about the state of New Zealand academic economics than about the correctness of the Reserve Bank's and the Government's approach to monetary policy.[33]

The Reserve Bank correctly predicted two major points of attack: the exclusive focus on price stability and deletion of references to production, trade and employment; and the vesting of responsibility for implementing monetary policy in the hands of officials rather than elected representatives.[34]

Industry responses to the Bill varied. Federated Farmers insisted that the international competitiveness of the export sector in an open economy depended on price stability, despite the impact of a high exchange rate on their export returns. The Manufacturers' Federation strongly opposed the change in focus. Since 1984, it said, the government had abdicated responsibility for controlling credit or money supply, allowing unlimited funds for speculators who believed they could afford the price. Unable to pay the same price, the productive sector had been crowded out of the investment market. Manufacturers believed they would remain the most susceptible under the proposed regime. External influences, especially international inflation and interest rates and access to credit overseas, were beyond the bank's control. When inflationary shocks arose from other sectors or sources, the bank could still apply pressure only through the productive sectors. These would bear the brunt while other sectors, including those primarily responsible for the inflation, were affected much less.

Paul Dalziel's submission accepted that price stability and full employment were contradictory objectives, and price stability should take precedence—but not to the exclusion of employment. His concern was the 'hysteresis' effect of anti-inflation policy on employment.[35] Low inflation was achieved by inducing a recession which reduced income claims as firms and workers struggled to avoid bankruptcy and redundancy. A move back towards full employment would remove this restraining pressure on inflation, causing a rebound as workers and firms tried to recapture previous real wage rates and normal profit margins. To protect the price stability goal, output and employment would have to be kept low, and the 'natural rate' of unemployment permanently increased. The alternative of combining inflation and employment goals, Dalziel argued, involved co-ordinating monetary and incomes policies. This would require a compact negotiated with unions, and changes to the Reserve Bank's objectives by allowing it to take into account the effect on businesses forced to close and on workers who became unemployed if monetary conditions became too tight.

The Reserve Bank objected that these factors could still be considered under the Act. 'There seems to be a misunderstanding in many of the submissions that the state of the real economy is completely irrelevant to determining the target for monetary policy.' Ministers could take the real economy into account when setting the period within which price stability had to be achieved. 'However the overriding principle is that targets must be consistent with the primary function.' Future governments who believed some other objective was more important than price stability still had the power to substitute this for specified periods of time, without the legislation offering them the 'wish list' of the previous Act.[36]

But, as the BERL economic consultancy pointed out, policy statements to be issued by the bank would include no assessment of the real sector consequences which would result. Nor was there any group outside the bank to do so. 'We do not think it fitting that in the 20th century the bank should be charged with selecting a policy target in consultation with the Minister of Finance without at the same time being required to submit an empirically founded argument to show what the consequences of this choice are likely to be from a cost-benefit perspective. Similarly, we think it unreasonable that Parliament should not be entrusted with the duty of evaluating the Bank's recommendations.'

From the union side, the Council of Trade Unions (CTU) expressed concerns that a recessionary strategy of tight credit, sluggish sales and high interest rates would become the norm. It also condemned the shifts in objectives and control as

> a misguided and dangerous initiative that is likely to result in gross imbalances in the application of macroeconomic policy (to the detriment of employment and economic growth) and which is a direct challenge to democratic control over the machinery of government. . .
> It is time to modernise the regulatory mechanisms that apply in a vastly changed financial sector. However, it is important to use the law to establish administrative structures, not to enshrine a currently fashionable ideology in it and to build a wall around that ideology in order to protect it from democratic control. Unfortunately, the Bill diminishes the attempts to modernise by reflecting the hands of the ideologue.[37]

The PSA concurred, condemning the 'anti-democratic' Bill as 'an imposition of failed policies on governments of the future and an abdication of key political decisions and policy making to technocrats who have no democratic accountability or public mandate'. The Bill also introduced new rules for supervision of the banking system. In *Economic Management* Treasury had argued that financial institutions needed incentives to become responsible for managing their own portfolios and risks, without support from monetary authorities. While government had to ensure stability of the banking system '[i]ntervention in an institution-specific way should only occur if there are serious grounds for thinking that the collapse of a particular institution might cause a collapse of the banking system as a whole'.[38] Prudential oversight and liquidity management would ensure the system's stability. Contestability, defined as the potential for competition, could provide the necessary disciplines for an efficient financial market structure and sound internal management.

Under the new Bill, the Reserve Bank could no longer impose reserve requirements and conditions on the ability of financial institutions to over-issue in the face of demand. This would make it even more difficult to prevent another speculative upsurge and stop banks overreaching themselves, as prudential surveillance measures contained in the Act would record the consequences only after the fact, and were limited to registered banks. Economists D. J. Sheppard and Jan Whitwell argued that the surveillance should be extended to non-bank financial institutions, or the market-supporting measures such as lender of last resort and the clearing bank function should be restricted to registered banks. The CTU agreed, observing that the main recent financial failures (such as Registered Securities Ltd, Equiticorp and the Development Finance Corporation) had involved secondary institutions. The bank needed power to fetter the explosive growth in lending to fund speculative ventures by individuals and companies which threatened the financial system and wider economy.

The Reserve Bank justified the limited coverage, saying most of the large financial institutions were registered banks and they comprised the critical mass on which the system's stability depended. There were incentives to be supervised, including access to banking status, low risk weighting, and liquidity support arrangements from the central bank. So only small gaps would remain.

The procedural aspects of the Bill reflected Treasury's 'managerial' line. Fiscal deficits and inflation were blamed on weak institutional arrangements. The bank had several conflicting functions which affected the credibility of monetary policy. It

- was a major participant in financial markets;
- controlled the issue of base money;
- gave economic advice to the government;
- operated a stock registry;
- administered and implemented financial sector regulations, including prudential supervision;
- acted as the government's banker and the bankers' bank; and
- acted as lender of last resort.

Treasury urged a zero-based review in which these functions were 'unravelled, reassessed and then reassembled into a much stronger institutional form'.[39] Operation and implementation of policy had to be separated. The bank needed clear non-conflicting objectives, with performance accountability for each. Its financial reporting standards should bring the bank within the 'Crown agencies' provisions of the proposed Public Finance Act. Funding should relate to separate functions and outputs to ensure accountability and prevent cross-subsidisation. Non-core functions should be privatised or made contestable with the private sector.

Treasury argued that this would combine genuine autonomy in monetary policy with accountability in financial operations. Five-year commitments to senior appointments, resources and targets would place the bank outside the three-year election cycle. The bank successfully objected to those aspects which it saw as encroaching on its institutional autonomy, and secured an adaptation of the new public finance regime. In practice, that meant separate contracting for its core monetary policy functions and other public policy functions such as prudential supervision. Responsibility for agency services like the Overseas Investment Commission and management of the government debt programme would be opened to contest.

Treasury also wanted the Reserve Bank's role as retail banker to the government privatised, with the Reserve Bank competing for the business in a commercial, contestable way. The reliance on Treasury bills to control primary liquidity meant Treasury could not change its cash management practices to reduce costs and better manage its interest rate risk without considering the effects on monetary policy. Interventions for liquidity purposes needed to become more transparent and market-based.

The Business Roundtable's submission echoed the Treasury line, stressing certainty, consistency, and credibility of the price stability goal. This convergence was not surprising, as the submission was prepared by Bryce Wilkinson, an author of *Economic Management* in 1984. The Roundtable considered the Bill very timely. The disinflationary process was now 'well-advanced'. But the policy was coming under stress, with renewed inflation risks and pressure on the government to settle for the current inflation rate of 4 percent. Investors reportedly feared that the government would resort to inflationary financing of its deficit and interest rate costs, in place of government spending cuts. The build-up in unemployment could also see the government reverse tack, especially if it remained un-willing to tackle labour market rigidities directly.

The Roundtable urged a distinction between the disinflationary period, with its transitional costs, and the maintenance of price stability, where a slightly more flexible monetary policy might allow the economy and employment to grow. It also wanted any govern-ment that digressed from the price stability goal to provide a cost–benefit analysis of the effect. Foreign exchange dealings by the bank to affect the dollar's value should be limited to where the govern-ment had instructed it to act. Rules on insider trading should also be revised to ensure that highest-quality private sector analysts could be appointed to the bank's board. The Roundtable dismissed sug-gestions that democratic government was being eroded by the Bill. Government had responsibility for determining the objectives for monetary policy and could specify different objectives if it saw fit, while the imposition of monetary policy targets and objectives on the bank increased accountability and control.

Both Labour and National members of the select committee en-dorsed the technocrats' line: 'the clarity of this objective will assist public and private sector planning, help consolidate lower inflation-ary expectations and boost business confidence in the medium term by the adoption of a consistent approach to monetary policy'.[40]

The Reserve Bank Act was amended again in 1995. Prudential supervision was transferred to the market, relying on statutory pub-lic disclosure by financial institutions to monitor and censure their behaviour. Capital adequacy requirements were maintained, and registration requirements simplified. The bank would still be able to intervene in a crisis to require investigation, give directions and recommend statutory management. Otherwise monitoring by lend-ers and shareholders was expected to curb any excesses. With all but two of the country's registered banks foreign-owned, their parent entities were assumed to provide oversight anyway.

The changes to prudential supervision were intended to make it clear that the government, through the Reserve Bank, would not guarantee or prop up any bank that failed—a reality obscured by the existing prudential system and the government's debt write-offs for the Rural Bank and bail-outs of the BNZ. But the main factor, as explained by the OECD, 'was a belief that greater emphasis on market disciplines, as a means of reinforcing existing incentives for banks to maintain prudent banking practices, would enhance the overall soundness of the banking system and . . . afford banks greater flexibility to respond to customer needs'.[41] Again this was a world first. When governor Don Brash publicly floated the idea in 1993 the *Economist* observed that other countries were asking how best to supervise banks. Brash was asking why they needed supervision at all.[42] Whether the government or the banks had adequate resources to ensure effective oversight in a complex financial market remained to be seen.

Consolidation phase

The inflation target set down in March 1990 in the first Policy Targets Agreement (PTA) under the Act was to achieve an annual increase in inflation of between 0 and 2 percent by December 1992. Pre-election nerves and the oil price effect of the Gulf War meant inflation was slow to fall in 1990. But the weak economy, low expectations of growth and slower world economy created the climate for sustainable interest-rate falls.

National in opposition had severely criticised Labour's target and promised to slow the process down. There were rumours that Ruth Richardson, as finance minister, would sack Reserve Bank governor Don Brash. Doubts about the National government's commitment to the inflation goal were quickly settled by its December 1990 'economic and social initiative' whereby benefits and government expenditure were severely cut. However, concern about the impact of overseas inflation saw the target date extended to December 1993.

The deepening recession made that unnecessary. The combination of benefit cuts, continued strong interest and exchange rates, low demand and labour market deregulation saw inflation fall from 6.4 percent in the year to December 1990 to 2.6 percent in the following year. When it became apparent that the bank would overshoot both its 1991 and 1992 targets, monetary policy was eased. The resulting depreciation of the dollar helped boost an export-led recovery. By January 1992, the bank indicated there should be no further exchange rate decline.

The bank now focused on consolidating the monetary regime. The foundations for sustained price stability had been established. Cementing them in place, the Reserve Bank believed, would benefit 'the economy as a whole':

> These benefits include a more certain environment for longer-term investment planning, reduced cash flow constraints on investment because of lower nominal interest rates, increased incentives for business efficiency, the protection of recent international competitiveness gains, equity advantages for those on low or fixed incomes, and higher after-tax real returns for savers.[43]

The governor's five-year contract and the accompanying PTA were renegotiated in December 1992. This required inflation to be maintained within the 0 to 2 percent range. As the bank operated a 'comfort zone' of 0.5 percent at either end, in practice the range was 0.5 to 1.5 percent. Constant corrections were therefore required. Labour's finance spokesperson condemned the narrow range as rent-seeking by finance markets and a recipe for constant instability.[44] Labour's proposed band of -1 to 3 percent would mean less frequent intervention, but the midpoint of 1 percent would remain.

The highly exposed economy was still vulnerable to changes in offshore inflation, interest rates, capital movements, expectations and exchange rates. The bank could target only domestic interest and exchange rates, government spending and wages, when it perceived an inflationary trend. It did this by talking the markets (and government policy) up or down through its six-monthly policy pronouncements and public statements, in preference to intervening on the open market. The governor's first PTA had required him to consult with a party whose actions might affect the bank's ability to achieve its aims 'in an attempt to change that party's actions as necessary to reach the desired policy outcomes at minimum cost'.[45]

During 1992 and early 1993 the CPI remained stable, owing to the continued recession, low world inflation, falling unit labour costs, pressure on domestic prices from imports and a higher New Zealand dollar. The CPI rose slightly to 1.3 percent in 1993 as the country returned to positive economic growth. By early 1994 economic growth was over 5 percent and inflation was predicted to exceed the target range. The bank warned against letting the economy overheat, with threats to intervene if the market failed voluntarily to respond.

Interest rates went back up. At the same time the bank urged employers to hold the rein on wages and not jeopardise price stability or future growth.

The government and the Reserve Bank were now locked into a growth/recession merry-go-round. The post-1992 recovery saw annual GDP growth peak at 6.3 percent in June 1994. Manufacturing exporters reported a 16 percent increase in the year to March 1995. Inflation continued to rise, especially as the expansion of the property market, boosted by a large influx of wealthy immigrants from Asia and South Africa, flowed onto building costs. The bank aimed to talk growth back to between 3 and 4.5 percent a year.

A fall-off in the growth rate was likely anyway. Parts of the economy were at full capacity. Rising interest rates, which followed another Reserve Bank warning in November 1994 that the low interest rate was incompatible with price stability, pushed the value of the dollar up again, squeezing exporters and encouraging imports. The bank predicted that the trade-weighted index would rise another 2 percent a year until March 1998. The OECD argued that the rise in the value of the dollar in 1994, if maintained, would reduce the CPI by up to 2 percent on what it would have been otherwise.[46] But agricultural exporters were again feeling the pain. Beef prices from the US, for example, fell by 31 percent in the year to March 1995, and a large part of the fall was due to exchange rate gains. Higher interest rates also meant increased costs for households and business. Mortgage rates went from 7.4 percent in February 1994 to 11 percent in February 1995.

There were fears that tight monetary policy would produce another round of retrenchment and recession, and another speculative raid by foreign investors. Former British Labour MP Bryan Gould highlighted the unsustainable tension between the exchange rate as a counter-inflationary instrument and as a determinant of prices in international markets, which had been a constant theme of the policy's critics.[47] High interest rates and the overvalued dollar meant lower export earnings and reduced demand. As profit margins were cut, investment in new capacity and technology was likely to fall too. These concerns mounted in 1995. The June quarter figures showed the CPI had increased by 1 percent in the last quarter, to make an annual rise of 4.6 percent. The bank's own 'underlying' rate rose by 0.6 percent for the quarter, or 2.2 percent for the year, still exceeding the target range. Talking up interest rates was failing to work; the

Reserve Bank intervened to tighten monetary conditions again. CTU economist Peter Harris reflected: 'We were told that the reward of price stability was economic growth. But now economic growth has to be reined in because it threatens price stability.'[48] He reiterated the CTU's call for greater convergence with Australia's more flexible approach. The Labour opposition echoed concerns that, despite a strong budget surplus, an unemployment level which maintained competition, a fully flexible labour market, declining real wages and low inflation, real interest rates were again on the rise.

The low-wage, low-inflation economy
Having opted for the rational expectations approach, the Reserve Bank's credibility depended on achieving the inflation goal. As inflation rose, its definition assumed a new importance. The CPI was the commonly used reference-point. However, the governor's first PTA in 1990 provided flexibility 'to take account of deficiencies in the construction of the CPI'. As the inflation target came under pressure in 1994, the bank played up these deficiencies. 'Headline' inflation based on the CPI was distinguished from the bank's measure of the 'underlying' rate, from which 'one-off' influences, such as changes in government charges (like rising state house rents and tertiary education fee increases), indirect tax rates, oil prices and interest rates, were removed. These influences were deemed irrelevant to the bank's long-term price stability goal. The Government Statistician expressed considerable scepticism, noting 'a very high level of subjectivity about the underlying measure of inflation'.[49]

TABLE 7.1   **CPI increases in basic expenditure items 1994**
(percentage increase, year to December 1994)

Headline inflation (CPI)	2.8
'Underlying' inflation	1.5
Fruit and vegetables	7.1
Dwelling rentals	13.5
Home ownership	6.0
Energy	4.9
Public transport	3.6
Health care	3.0
Education and child care	9.5
Credit services	9.2

Source: Statistics New Zealand; Reserve Bank of New Zealand

The bank's measure of underlying inflation became increasingly divorced from the economic activities and expectations of investors, consumers and families, and from the impact of price rises on people's disposable incomes, especially the poor. The highest price increases in 1994 affected basic expenditure, not luxuries paid for by high earners out of discretionary income (see Table 7.1). The price of some basic items, including meat and fish, groceries, clothing, household supplies and services, and personal goods and services, also fell. But the overall impact was still serious. For many people and families, these price increases were accompanied by real income cuts and higher interest rates. As the ratio of wages to inflation showed, real wages fell, especially for the public sector workforce (see Table 7.2). Under a centralised wage system the shortage of skilled labour during the recovery would have flowed through in general wage relativities to the entire workforce. But the combination of the ECA and continued high unemployment (termed 'persistent labour-market slack') prevented such 'spillover' effects.

TABLE 7.2 **Wages to prices 1989–94 (annual percentage change)**

	1989	1990	1991	1992	1993	1994
Wages						
Average weekly earnings	6.4	5.9	4.3	3.0	0.9	1.8
Wages per full-time employee						
private sector	3.8	4.2	2.4	1.2	1.2	1.3
public sector	4.2	4.4	2.8	0.4	0.5	0.5
Consumer prices	5.7	6.1	2.6	1.0	1.3	1.3

Source: *OECD Economic Survey: New Zealand*, OECD, Paris,1994, Table 3

This was deliberate bank strategy. In June 1992 it reported:

> Unit labour costs are expected to continue to fall over most of the forecast period, as a result of productivity improvements combined with continued low wage growth. The forecasts also assume some moderate strengthening of profit margins and house prices as the recovery proceeds, together with some relatively slow growth in import and export prices.[50]

The bank reported again in June 1994: 'while our forecasts incorporate a gradual increase in wages through the forecast horizon, we have assumed that the new labour market environment will help prevent excessive wage pressures developing outside industries where genuine skill shortages are intensifying.'[51] The clear implication was that profits were allowed to rise, but wages were not. Price stability now meant a low-wage, low-inflation economy, assisted by the wage-deflating effects of the ECA. Threats of intervention from the Reserve Bank, in the context of continued high unemployment, a deregulated labour market and a state sector policy of fiscal restraint, helped justify the determination of state and private employers to hold real wage increases down. The real wage rate index showed a drop of 2.3 percent in the year to March 1995, as workers' incomes were unable to maintain parity with increases in the CPI. Alliance leader Jim Anderton warned: 'We are being told, in effect, that fairness in income distribution is incompatible with economic growth. This is totally unsatisfactory and cannot last forever. Sooner or later there will be a political and industrial reaction by those who are losing out.'[52]

The bank justified wage restraint by claiming that inflation was cyclical. Rational expectations should deter people, especially workers, from seeking compensation during times of rising inflation or higher interest rates in the knowledge that these would fall again. Yet, unless inflation became negative during the downside of the cycle, permanent income loss would result. Keeping inflation between 0 and 2 percent in practice meant virtually freezing the real incomes of most of the workforce. Anderton argued:

> If investment is only to be carried out by the private sector (out of operating surplus) and if real wages are effectively frozen, this implies an increasing inequality in the distribution of wealth. . . . In effect we are seeing New Zealand revert to a very old . . . economic model in which employees are seen as a resource to be exploited rather than as the cohabitants of the national home entitled to decent quality paid work and an equitable share of the national income.[53]

The stated aim of the Reserve Bank Act was to provide relative stability for those prices which were important to investment and free enterprise. In the process, monetary policy caused havoc with employment, interest rates, exchange rates and economic growth. This obsession with one economic indicator forced the economy into an abstract theoretical model which existed nowhere else, appealed to a norm of zero inflation which had never existed in the country's recent economic life, and benefited the rich, in particular finance capital, at the expense of wage labour, families and the poor.

CHAPTER EIGHT

Labour Market Deregulation

THE EMPLOYMENT CONTRACTS ACT 1991 was the jewel in the structural adjustment crown. Its traditional alliance with the trade union movement made deregulating the labour market and de-unionising the paid workforce impossible for a Labour government, although its economic policies significantly weakened the union base. National faced no such restraint.

Struggle for ascendancy

The Labour party went into the 1984 election with promises to restore compulsory unionism,[1] remove the wage freeze imposed by the Muldoon government, re-establish tripartite wage and incomes conferences, and consult on economic policy. The technocrats had a quite different agenda. Treasury's 1984 briefing papers, in addressing labour and unemployment, argued that workers needed to respond flexibly to changes in supply and demand. If wages could not move, employment levels would. Full employment was considered an unattainable and undesirable goal. In a dynamic, responsive economy some level of unemployment would always exist.

> The dynamics of unemployment . . . are that a large number of new jobs are being opened up all the time in response to changing economic conditions. At the same time many old jobs are being closed down. There will always be a queue of people searching for a new job. Some people would have left their jobs involuntarily or would have newly entered the labour force. Others would have intentionally become unemployed prior to obtaining a new job. . . . Because people enter and leave the queue at different points they experience varying durations of unemployment.[2]

This queue would move most quickly if there was employment-generating economic growth and the labour market was sufficiently flexible to adjust. Treasury therefore called for 'a reorientation of policies which are currently inhibiting our economic performance and the removal of impediments to a more flexible labour market'.³ The primary targets were the national award system, occupation-based bargaining, centralised arbitration, government wage-fixing and compulsory union membership.

Treasury's *Government Management* briefing in 1987 again laid the blame for rising unemployment and low productivity on a highly regulated labour market and national award rates that hindered, rather than promoted, the interests of the disadvantaged.⁴ Unions, too, were accused of increasing their bargaining power at the expense of the disadvantaged and being unresponsive to members' needs.⁵ Unions still had a role to play, provided they became contestable and enter-prise-based.⁶

Getting this policy implemented under a Labour government was always going to be difficult. Some significant changes were made. Compulsory arbitration was removed in 1984, sacrificing weaker unions who could not conciliate to an acceptable conclusion.⁷ The wage and price freeze was lifted in October 1984, although the Economic Stabilisation Act was not repealed until 1987. The Labour Relations Act 1987 forced the union structure to rationalise, while the State Sector Act 1988 helped break the grip of the strong public service unions and erode state employment conditions. Penal rates came under pressure with the introduction of weekend retail trading in 1989. Provision was made in 1990 for employer-initiated ballots to negotiate enterprise agreements at workplaces employing more than 50 people. All this occurred within the context of mounting unemployment and fears for job security. But the changes fell well short of the formal deregulation of the labour market which the technocrats and their private sector allies sought.

During its first year in office Labour relegated the labour market to the politically 'too hard' basket and concentrated on financial and industry deregulation. The Employers' Federation and the Business Roundtable forced the issue onto the agenda. Whereas a number of unions had exercised industrial muscle in the later 1970s, workers now found themselves under unprecedented attack. Some strong unions tried to fight back, but eventually they lost. Lockouts at Fletcher Challenge's Tasman pulp and paper mill and at New Zea-land Steel reflected a new employer determination to break the unions. These were portrayed as battles between today's economic realists and yesterday's union dinosaurs. The message was clear: big companies from the Business Roundtable were prepared to take the lead in forcing the labour market to change.

A green paper in late 1985 focused the debate on labour market reform. Advocates of deregulation insisted that a protected labour market posed a fundamental barrier to New Zealand's economic efficiency and international competitiveness. Without radical and rapid change the Rogernomics revolution would fail. As economic deregulation, state sector restructuring and the emerging recession began to bite, workers and unions struggled just to cope with the mounting redundancies in the public and private sector.

The unions may have lacked industrial muscle and militancy, but they were still in a unique political position to resist. Strategically placed allies within the Labour Party hierarchy, policy council, caucus and even Cabinet mustered all their resources to counter demands to deregulate. To a large degree they succeeded. Labour analyst Pat Walsh explained how

> an agenda for radical labour market deregulation was turned back. The key factors in that outcome were the political opposition to deregulation from the Minister of Labour, whose views coincided with the longstanding policy inclinations of key officials with whom he was able to form common cause. That coalition prevailed over the supporters of deregulation. They made effective use of their links with union officials and were backed by a majority in caucus, whose involvement was more significant than in other policy areas. They built upon the legacy of past relations and consensus and consolidated earlier decisions which favoured their cause. They operated effectively in political and policy infighting and at all times maintained control over the policy and legislative process.[8]

Labour Relations Act 1987

The result was the Labour Relations Act 1987. Its architects hoped to streamline and rationalise union organisation, not to destroy it. The Act retained some key features of the existing law. Registered unions kept their monopoly over categories of workers covered by their membership rules. The award would still provide blanket coverage, whether or not individual workers were represented by the union. Provision for compulsory unionism, reinstated by Labour in mid-1985, remained. But the unions were to be made organisationally and financially independent of government guarantees of membership, coverage or administrative support.

Registered unions were now required to have a minimum of 1000 members. This had mixed benefits. Few workplaces could meet the new membership requirements, so the advent of enterprise unions was slowed. Some of the larger unions emerged in a better position, but many smaller unions were forced to amalgamate. The average size of unions rose from 2198 members in December 1986 to 5793 in September 1989. By then, 66 percent of members were in unions of 10,000-plus, a 20 percent increase on 1986. Correspondingly, the combined number of state and private sector unions fell from 254 in 1986 to 112 in 1989.[9]

Many of those unions which remained became stronger and more efficient, although they were sometimes viewed as less accountable to their members. Centralised union power also increased. In an attempt to consolidate their resources, the majority of unions from the Federation of Labour and Combined State Sector Unions, along with some independent unions, agreed to join together under the banner of the Council of Trade Unions (CTU) in 1987. Such a move had long been mooted, but was resisted by both the old guard in the FOL and by the modernists in the public sector unions.

The CTU was established as a new organisation rather than a merger of the two old centres. Its creation changed the face of the trade union movement. The CTU's pragmatic centralised leadership adopted a submissive political stance, accepting the deregulated economy as a reality, and continued to rely on their 'special relationship' with the Labour government. They wanted an active role in future macro-economic decisions through a return to tripartite corporatism, with unions, employers and government all committed to a forward-thinking programme of growth and economic reconstruction.

According to CTU President Ken Douglas, this 'strategic response recognises that employers and unions may pursue their own interests, but with a common interest defined by the need to develop a flexible, innovative and efficient industrial relations system'.[10] In return, they would make concessions. Industrial-based unions might increase flexibility. Wage demands could be kept to levels that promoted investment and industrial development. Unions would support productivity gains that resulted from positive growth rather than recessionary squeeze. In the eyes of its critics, this required the CTU to compromise within a paradigm that was anathema to traditional unionism, destructive of the pay, conditions and job security of many workers, and careless of the unemployed. This co-operation—some say collaboration—did not get them far.

Immediately after the 1987 Labour Relations Act was passed, the Roundtable launched a major offensive. The revitalised Employers' Federation joined in. The new Act was pilloried ideologically as a denial of the workers' freedom to choose, and condemned on economic grounds as inefficient and inconsistent with the government's commitment to deregulation. Treasury's 1987 post-election briefing papers broadly supported this position, applauding Labour's move away from compulsory arbitration but arguing that there was still room for improvement—for the good of the workers themselves.

The advocates of labour market deregulation fixed their sights on the public sector workforce. In many ways this presented the easier task. The corporatisation programme had allowed some state employees to be declared redundant. Workers who were transferred to the new SOEs were deemed private sector employees, covered by the Labour Relations Act. The relative ease of this transition encouraged its extension to the 'core' public service. The State Sector Act 1988 effectively imposed private sector labour laws on public servants. Security of tenure was suddenly swept away, along with their superior conditions of employment. The way was cleared for large-scale redundancies, short-term contracts and the decline of the state sector unions.

The State Sector Bill was introduced on 10 December 1987—the day after settlement in a complex negotiation on restructuring had been reached—without any consultation or warning. It took effect on 1 April 1988. The whole exercise was non-negotiable. Walsh notes 'some considerable irony, in view of the subsequent breakneck speed at which the Government enacted the State Sector Act, that its introduction was delayed by the extensive process of consultation and search for consensus that accompanied the passage of the Labour Relations Act'.[11] Public service unions and workers mobilised against the Bill, but their protests made no difference. Their arguments and concerns were treated as the special pleadings of a protected workforce who were afraid of being held to account for their performance.

Emboldened by their own rhetoric and the novelty of support from lobby groups and from within government, employers became more militant. Some refused to renegotiate awards. Others used the deepening recession and mounting unemployment to force low wage settlements, or roll back conditions and penal provisions. Further concessions were secured from the unions in 1990: an amendment to the Labour Relations Act allowed employers of at least 50 employees at a workplace to initiate an employee ballot for the right to negotiate an enterprise agreement at that workplace. Securing a simple majority was enough.

All this was achievable under the existing regime. But a fully deregulated labour market would offer employers even greater gains. Flexibility would ease the 'shedding' of workers from one dying enterprise, and encourage them to re-skill and relocate in a new growth industry. Enterprise bargaining through individual contracts would ensure that agreements reflected the unique condition of each firm and maximise the choice of its workers. By refusing to implement such changes, the Labour government was blamed for prolonging the recession, and preventing the liberalisation programme from achieving its full potential.

The compact
The political opponents of labour market deregulation were determined to hold the line. The idea of a 'compact' between the unions, government and employers—similar to the 'accord' reached between unions and the Labor government in Australia in 1983—had been raised in 1984 but deferred. It was revived publicly by some in the Labour leadership in July 1988 and endorsed by the CTU hierarchy. The technocrats and technopols, however, saw no need for conciliation. Real wages were falling without intervention, and a compact might allow the unions to capture economic and social policy.

Predictably, the employers refused to take part in the compact negotiations. Many workers also remained sceptical. The Labour government had continued privatising state assets and restructuring the state sector, despite having promised to consult the Labour Party. During protracted negotiations, the CTU 'was caught between the pincers of a vacillating government displaying increasing disunity and little political commitment to the compact, and a sceptical union movement highly distrustful of the Labour Government'.[12]

The compact was formally signed in December 1989. A tripartite council was to be established with representatives of government, unions and employers. It would facilitate consultation and the effective co-ordination of policies across economic and social spheres, and encourage worker participation at enterprise and workplace levels. The council failed to get off the ground when the employers again declined to take part. Minister of Labour Helen Clark then offered unions a compromise—a bipartite consultative body, with possible tripartite consultation on specific matters. The proposal was overwhelmingly endorsed at a special CTU conference in April 1990. But they gained nothing more than a promise of consultation with a government that had shown arrant disregard for participatory decision-making, and which was driven by forces much more powerful than a struggling trade union movement.

By the end of Labour's term, the union movement was in a seriously weakened state. Total union membership had fallen from 63 percent of all wage and salary earners in 1987 to around 54 percent in 1990.[13] State and private sector unions had been equally hard hit. Labour analyst John Deeks reached 'the inevitable and paradoxical conclusion . . . that the interest group that was the major supporter of the government's election in 1984 was, in the ensuing six years, most weakened as a result of the policies of that government'.[14]

Employment policy under Labour had another unique twist. Pressure from women within the Labour Party for legislation ensuring equal pay for work of equal value confronted head-on the trend to market forces and deregulation. Women were over-represented in small workplaces and service occupations that were distinguished by low status and low pay. They were particularly vulnerable in the increasingly deregulated labour market. For years women at all levels of the Labour Party had lobbied for legislation drawn up by women, for women, to address pay equity. In 1987 the Labour Cabinet agreed.

The Employment Equity Bill did not appear until 1989. In the intervening period it encountered the same sorts of obstacles and intrigues as the Labour Relations Act.[15] The result was a highly compromised measure. It provided machinery to compare predominantly female occupations with better-paid jobs that demanded similar skills, effort and responsibility and where men were at least 60 percent of that workforce. But these 'pay equity assessments' were not enforceable. They merely provided a bargaining chip in direct negotiations with the employer. The Employment Equity Act was passed in the dying stages of the fourth Labour government, and came into force on 1 October 1990. There was barely time to appoint its administrators before Labour lost the election. This was one of the first Acts repealed by the new National government. Gender equity was then left to the market-place.

As Labour neared the end of its second term and a predicted landslide defeat, the union hierarchy, the Labour Party and the government became desperate. In a last-ditch attempt to change course and reclaim traditional Labour Party ground, the government announced a wages accord with the CTU. The unions would accept wage increases centred on 2 percent plus productivity payments, despite an inflation rate nearer 5 percent. In return, the Reserve Bank would be asked not to impede the lowering of interest rates or the exchange rate, and the government would consult the CTU on macro-economic decisions, including strategies for reducing the internal deficit. The Growth Agreement was in vain. Labour suffered a humiliating defeat.

Employment Contracts Act
Labour had opened the door to labour market deregulation—more by the effect of its economic policies than by its industrial legislation. The incoming National government was eager to complete the task. Unions were the natural enemies of a traditionally conservative National Party that was committed in theory, if often not in practice, to free enterprise. They were also the main political, and financial, supporters of the Labour Party. The introduction of voluntary unionism in December 1983 had enjoyed the support of the National Party, and almost all its MPs, and weakened the union base. In 1990 National had the opportunity to go further, and had openly committed itself to radical labour market reform.

Treasury's 1990 briefing papers urged the incoming government to act. Achieving the policy goal of sustainable higher living standards meant 'giving greater freedom to workers and firms to enter into mutually beneficial employment arrangements with minimal external interference. Such reforms would facilitate enterprise bargaining, reward productivity and training, and would encourage more efficient and responsive trade unions.' While this 'may put downward pressure on real wages for some workers' in the short term, increasing levels of skills and higher productivity would produce rising living standards and higher participation in the workforce in the medium term.[16]

The National government moved quickly. The Employment Contracts Bill was introduced in December 1990 and came into effect on 15 May 1991.[17] National award coverage and compulsory unionism were abandoned in favour of individual employment contracts. The new employment game was to be played out on the 'level playing-field' of the labour market between the individual employer and the individual worker. Each could represent themselves, or choose their own negotiating agent. That might be a union, a private sector consultant, a lawyer or almost anyone else. One worker or their agent had no right to know what another had negotiated. A contract needed to be filed with the Registrar of the Labour Court only when it covered 20 or more people, and even then it was not a public document. Contracts with state employers were excluded from the Official Information Act. Collective contracts were still allowed, but not encouraged. Even where an individual worker had authorised such negotiation, employers could not by law be compelled to negotiate a collective contract. Multi-employer contracts were even more difficult to achieve as strike action in support was illegal at any time.

Under the Employment Contracts Act (ECA) unions had no special privileges, and they lost their tax-exempt status. Indeed, except for a transitional clause, the legislation no longer referred to them as trade unions. They were now 'employees organisations' with the narrow role of 'advancing collective employment interests'. No employment contract could require workers to join, or not to join, a union. Instead, unions were compelled to compete with one another and with outside consultants who were touting their services, sometimes with employer support, to potential worker clients.

The machinery was, in market jargon, competitively neutral. But the Act was stacked against workers and unions in favour of the employer. All authorised agents had the right to enter the workplace at any reasonable time to discuss negotiations with those they had authority to represent. But there was no guaranteed access for unions or anyone else *seeking* the authority to represent workers on that site. This enabled employers to determine which potential bargaining agents could gain access to their workplace and workforce. Once they were authorised, the employer could still refuse to negotiate.

Transitional provisions allowed existing collective contracts to roll over once they expired. The new individual contract was presumed to be based on the same terms until a replacement was negotiated. As Walsh pointed out, however, workers whose employer was determined to change the terms of their contract unilaterally had two choices. They could accede to the employer's demands. Or they could lose their job, face an extended stand-down period before receiving the unemployment benefit, and pay a lawyer to take the case to enforce their legal right in the labour courts.[18]

Rules relating to industrial action also changed. Strikes were legal only in connection with negotiations for a collective contract, and after the existing contract had expired. So employers could let the contract lapse, and play off market conditions against the threat of industrial action. Strikes aimed at multi-employer coverage were prohibited, even where firms fell under the same corporate umbrella. The ECA imposed some restrictions on harsh and oppressive tactics and agreements, but they were of minimal practical value. The courts were prevented from applying common law remedies relating to unfair or unconscionable bargains, and the concept of contributory fault was introduced in personal grievance claims.

Impact of the ECA

Walsh describes the ECA's overriding goal as economic efficiency, with government seeking industrial stability 'coerced through economic adversity'.[19] With official unemployment at over 11 percent the impact was immediate and dramatic.

> The broad parameters of life under the Employment Contracts Act were already apparent in the first six months of operation—a substantial, perhaps irreversible fall in trade union membership and collective bargaining coverage, the continued erosion of employment conditions and employment security, a growing sense of employer strength and (in some quarters) militancy, and a more conflictual and antagonistic approach to industrial relations rather than the idealized picture of harmonious co-operation sketched by its advocates. Additionally, a more legalistic approach to industrial relations has emerged, accompanied by a new group of private bargaining agents, who may be an important force resisting future proposals for changes to the present bargaining structures.[20]

The ECA had two goals: to force wages down, and to break the unions. Penal rates and special allowances were the entry point for the first. Sometimes cuts were linked to small wage increases, although these were often limited to existing workers. Other companies offered lump-sum cash incentives. Some offered no compensation at all. Between the May and August quarters of 1992 average weekly earnings fell by almost $15, due mainly to reductions in weekly overtime earnings.[21] Walsh cites the example of Wellington transport workers, whose loss of penal rates and allowances meant a pay cut for some of $7000 a year from an annual income, including penal rates, of $28,000.[22]

Perhaps the most poignant case saw Presbyterian, Methodist and Salvation Army social service institutions offer their workers a flat rate, 10 percent wage increase, in return for abolishing weekend rates and other allowances—at the same time as the Council of Christian Social Services was condemning the inhumanity of the government's welfare cutbacks. While the agencies argued that the changes were cost neutral, the unions claimed that the employers would save 13 percent on wages. A hospital domestic worker on $451 before tax for a five-day week, including weekends, would now receive $382 gross. The union was prepared to negotiate the abolition of penal rates, but it wanted them phased out. The workers went on hunger strike in support of their position. Their union predicted that some of its members 'would be forced to seek charitable assistance from the very agencies for which they worked'.[23]

The attack on union coverage focused on negotiating rights and collective agreements. The statute required unions to secure specific authority to negotiate. This made enormous financial and administrative demands on the declining union base. Some employers required unions to seek written consent from every member to negotiate on their behalf, and prove this at every stage of the negotiations. In turn, some unions argued that being a member in itself implied authority, and waited to be put to the test. Even with proof of authorisation, employers could refuse to negotiate. A market survey in October 1992 showed that 64 percent of senior managers thought their organisation did not always respect the employee's choice of representative, while 37 percent of employees said they did not feel free to choose the type of employment contract covering them.[24]

With the government as its employer, the PSA came under heaviest attack. Many SOEs and departments, backed by the SSC, campaigned to de-unionise the workforce. In 1992, for example, the Department of Social Welfare (DSW) insisted that the PSA produce authorisation from the entire 6259 employees it claimed to represent. When it did so, the DSW refused to negotiate until the award had expired and workers had moved to individual contracts.[25]

Because the government ceased collecting detailed information after the Act was passed, figures on collectives vary. Ray Harbridge and Anthony Honeybone estimate that in the 1989/90 bargaining round, the last normal round under the old system, some 721,000 employees were covered by awards and collective agreements. Statistics New Zealand suggests that in February 1993 428,000 workers were still covered by collectives. Harbridge and Honeybone believe the figure may be lower, somewhere between 340,000 and 370,000. 'Regardless of which surveys are considered, there is no doubt that collective bargaining has collapsed by somewhere between 40 and 50 percent of the levels of coverage achieved in 1989/90.'

The shift to enterprise agreements and individual contracts increased the workload of unions dramatically. The PSA reported that collective contract coverage fell from 97.5 percent in 1991 to 70 percent in March 1994. In the insurance industry, 139 employers were covered by collective contracts in 1991, but only 21 in 1994. Stock and station industry collective coverage had reduced from 20 employers to two.[26] Negotiations by the National Distribution Union had increased from 55 to 700 in the transport, energy, storage, retail, textile and food sectors. By 1994 Harbridge and Honeybone concluded, on current data,

> that collective bargaining coverage has reached its nadir and will in all likelihood recover (albeit slightly) in the next year. Certainly there is (admittedly anecdotal) evidence that employers who had promoted (predominantly for ideological reasons) individual contracting amongst their employees have found the transaction costs of this type of employment contract too high for the limited gains, and a reversion to collective bargaining seems likely for some employers.[27]

But for many unions the damage had already been done. The number of private and state sector unions had already fallen from 254 in 1986 to 80 when the Act came into effect in May 1991. By 1993 '[m]any of New Zealand's best known unions had folded or otherwise disappeared through mergers with other unions. The overall number of unions fell to around sixty and union membership fell accordingly. Unions lost over a quarter of a million members in the decade.'[28] Total union membership as a percentage of the total employed workforce declined from a high of 45 percent in 1989 to 41.5 percent in May 1991 and 23.4 percent in December 1994. The construction, trade, agriculture and mining sectors lost over 60 percent of their membership in just three years (see Table 8.1).[29]

By 1995, the number of small unions had increased, with enterprise bargaining fragmenting the existing unions and new workers' associations being formed. The emergence of workplace unions, employer-sponsored workers' associations, ad hoc worker groups and private sector bargaining agents led the CTU to define its legitimate membership with greater care. Where bargaining agents were used, however, trade unions were still preferred. Use of staff associations and employer-sponsored 'unions' was relatively rare.

TABLE 8.1: Union membership by industry 1991–94

Industry	Membership		Decline 1991–94
	1991	1994	%
Agriculture & related	14,234	5,110	64
Mining & related	4,730	1,223	74
Manufacturing	114,564	86,654	24
Energy	11,129	12,791	(15)
Construction	14,596	5,338	63
Trade	64,335	19,778	69
Transport, communications	52,592	41,738	22
Finance	32,219	24,107	25
Public services	205,925	179,167	13
TOTALS	514,324	375,906	27

December years.
Source: R. Harbridge, K. Hince and A. Honeybone, *Unions and Union Membership in New Zealand: Annual Review for 1994*, Working Paper 2/95, Industrial Relations Centre, Victoria University of Wellington, 1995, Table 3.

The gender ratio of union membership remained stable. But this disguised the under-representation of unionised women in small workplaces, and the highly unionised women-dominated public sector. Union coverage now replicated the deeply gendered duality of the labour market. Some unions reportedly stopped servicing workplaces with fewer than ten employees, which was where women, especially clerical workers and shop employees, predominated. The occupationally based Clerical Workers' Union collapsed and its mainly women members were left to join male-dominated industrial unions. In larger workplaces incorporation into enterprise negotiations strengthened women's general bargaining position, but issues like pay equity became a low priority.

Labour market politics

In the new adversarial environment, both sides employed tactics which CTU president Ken Douglas labelled 'the start of American-like industrial terrorism here'. In an extended and acrimonious dispute at the CHH Kinleith mill, unions used scanners to intercept the cell-phone communications between company executives. In turn, the company hired private investigators and security firms to monitor union activities and protect their sites against sabotage.[30] The New Zealand Dairy Company paid low-level officials to campaign against their own union.[31] Alliance Textiles established an employer-subsidised incorporated society at Mosgiel, called the Mosgiel Independent Thought Society, to represent workers' interests as a rival to the union. Air New Zealand, NZ Rail and several hospitals recruited strike breakers from overseas.

Industrial disputes stretched across many sectors: factory workers, nurses, teachers, hospital interns, pulp and paper workers, shop employees, bus drivers. But these were isolated actions of individual unions and workplaces, not mass resistance by a labour movement asserting its strength and reclaiming its role. To some, this reflected the climate of rampant unemployment and on-going recession. But it also exposed the trade union movement as divided, dispirited and de-radicalised. There was strong evidence of rank and file support for a general strike to oppose the ECA. A narrow majority of the CTU executive had determined otherwise, believing—many would argue wrongly—that there was insufficient support to sustain effective nationwide action. The ECA became law by default.

The CTU came under stinging attack for its unwillingness to ally with those fighting against the accompanying benefit cuts in 1991. Sue Bradford of the Unemployed Workers Rights Centre told Canadian radio:

> one of the saddest things was that when they brought the Employment Contracts Act in at the same time as the massive benefit cuts, a lot of trade union people and unemployed people wanted to fight a general strike-type fight, really serious fight, to stop all that happening, but the Council of Trade Unions put the kybosh on that struggle. I think the CTU bears a huge guilt for having not allowed the people to do what they wanted to do. It's very hard to understand, I don't understand it, how anyone who calls themselves a workers' representative wouldn't have fought harder to stop the Employment Contracts Act and the benefit cuts coming in. Groups like ours were having massive demonstrations at that time, there was tremendous public opposition. So it wasn't that the people didn't want to fight.[32]

According to Ken Douglas the era of confrontational industrial relations was past and unions had to face the realities of global competition.[33] While he claimed there was still a place for mass campaigns, strikes, pickets and work-ins, the CTU had effectively shed that traditional role. Its failure to campaign actively against the ECA in 1991 was strongly criticised,[34] with accusations that some major unions were acquiescing in the hope of earning recognition from management.

The number of unions affiliated to the CTU dropped from 43 in December 1991 to 33 in 1993 and 27 by December 1994. The number of union members they represented fell from 445,116 to 321,119, then to 296,959 over the same period. Union affiliation with the Labour Party also declined, from eleven unions with 125,372 members in December 1991 to eight unions with 82,968 members in December 1993, and five with 71,625 members a year later.[35]

On 1 May 1993 twelve mainly small 'blue collar' unions joined together to form the New Zealand Trade Union Federation (NZTUF). Most of these unions had been hit by the economic deregulation policies of both National and Labour, particularly in tariff reduction, as well as the ECA. The unions were highly critical of the CTU's passive response to the introduction of the Act and its support for rapid trade liberalisation under the GATT. NZTUF launched major campaigns promoting tariff protection and opposing the Uruguay round agreement, as well as a wage push entitled 'Just Jobs, Just Wages', a type of activity not engaged in by the CTU since it was formed. But by 1995 NZTUF still covered only twelve unions with around 25,000 members. Its grip was marginal, and survival depended on other unions defecting from the CTU.

Some unions embraced the post-ECA environment. One of the most publicised was the Engineers' Union. Led by Rex Jones, a former president of the Labour Party, the Engineers' was feted by the mainstream media as a modernist union. It made a strategic decision to use the ECA to grow its business rather than campaign against its repressive measures, and restructured part of itself into a limited liability company. While losing many of its own members, it was accused of augmenting its numbers either through 'body-snatching' already organised workers from other unions,[36] or through amalgamations with unions which had no relationship to the traditional Engineers' coverage. It promoted workplace reform and other management techniques among its members, and publicly stated that it would serve employee and employer clients. Although it consistently poached the membership of other CTU affiliates, the Engineers' continued to enjoy CTU support.

It was Maori workers for whom the ECA provided most opportunities to be innovative. Traditional trade unions had rarely promoted Maori interests, preferring the ideological position that race and gender concerns diverted and divided the workers' struggle against the capitalist class. In the late 1980s some unions had developed Maori structures, but their influence was limited. In 1991 political activist and long-time unionist Syd Jackson formed Nga Kaimahi o Aotearoa, a union of Maori workers across all industries and workplaces. Pakeha who accepted the base line of Maori sovereignty were free to join. Nga Kaimahi was not afraid to challenge traditional unions, as shown by its support for Aotearoa Stevedoring Union's unsuccessful attempt to break the monopoly of the Waterfront Workers' Union in Auckland in 1992. A number of successful personal grievance and contract negotiations were concluded using Maori procedures on Maori terms for the first time.

Some would argue that the demise of traditional workplace practices and hierarchical, white, male-dominated unions was no tragedy. New workplace practices were potentially more congenial to many women, Maori and Pacific Islanders by utilising skills of teamwork, organisation and facilitation, provided they had an equal say in the operation of the reformed workplace. Yet mass production and exploitative contracting-out still affected those workers most. The ECA further undermined the potential for workers to exercise power in the workplace by reducing the leverage of unions. For this the union leadership, notably the CTU, shared a large part of the blame.

Judicial interpretations of the ECA

Where industrial relations broke down, disputes quickly became adversarial. In the past, unions would have helped resolve many conflicts by negotiation, and pruned out marginal cases before they went to court. The new regime encouraged a litigious approach from the start. With neither side prepared to make concessions, disputes headed straight for the Employment Tribunal and Employment Court. More lawyers became involved, many of whom were unused or ill disposed to informal resolution. This legalisation of disputes tended to produce excessive settlements which employers could ill afford, and compensation was often consumed by legal fees.

The number of industrial cases pending increased by 19 percent between June 1991 and June 1992. The Employment Tribunal was not established until August 1992, and faced a serious backlog from the start. In its first nine months it received 1245 applications for hearings. After that, they arrived at the rate of around 200 a month. Two-thirds of the claims related to personal grievances. These most frequently involved unfair dismissal, but 16 percent involved wage arrears and 10 percent were for compliance orders.[37] The upsurge in personal grievance disputes was predictable—in part because of the new environment, and in part because the unions were no longer acting as intermediaries and vetting the strength of workers' claims before they were lodged. An increased number of claims were from middle and upper management who had the superior knowledge and resources to take advantage of the new laws. Despite provision of more resources, the tribunal remained in overload, with approximately 2000 cases pending in July 1995. Delays for mediation ranged between two and five months, and for adjudication up to six months, although this was beginning to improve.[38] The enormous backlog effectively removed reinstatement as a remedy. In 1995 the Court of Appeal responded to this by upholding an interim injunction reinstating a worker made redundant, pending the full hearing of a personal grievance claim.[39]

The courts were delicately placed. Deregulation substantially changed the nature of the legal game. Economic relations, especially employment, were now governed primarily by the common law, especially the law of contract. The courts were responsible for creating and enforcing that law. But they also had a pool of precedent based on the old Act which they were reluctant to abandon. And they had to maintain a semblance of legitimacy with both sides.

The earliest cases suggested that the Employment Court might be sympathetic to workers under the Act. In *Grant* v *Superstrike Bowling Centres Ltd* the court agreed that the roll-over provisions of the Act meant existing terms and conditions of employment should continue until a new contract was mutually agreed, and could not be altered unilaterally by the employer.[40] But the court soon changed tack. In *Paul* v *New Zealand Society for the Intellectually Handicapped* the employer engaged in a partial lockout by cutting workers' allowances unilaterally, to force them to accept a new employment contract. The Employment Court agreed this was a breach of contract, but denied them relief because strikes and lockouts were permitted in pursuit of a collective employment contract.[41]

In the *DesignPower* case, a subsidiary of the SOE Electricorp sought to escape redundancy provisions in the existing collective agreement by negotiating new employment contracts. Initially it proposed new individual contracts. But the company changed this to a collective contract, and claimed it wanted to negotiate. Staff who refused were locked out. The court found the dispute related to negotiation of a collective contract, and the lockout fell within the terms of the Act.[42] These lockout provisions were not new: they had been carried over from the 1987 Labour Relations Act.[43] But their use had previously been unthinkable. Times had changed.

The test of the ECA's provisions to protect against 'harsh and oppressive' tactics came in the *Alliance Textiles* case.[44] The company vigorously sought workers' signatures on the new contract. They were warned against authorising the union to represent them, urged to revoke any such authority, and encouraged to appoint the employer-funded Mosgiel Independent Thought Society as their representative. After a bitter dispute, almost all the workers signed; the rest remained permanently locked out. The Employment Court decided that nothing in the Act required an employer to 'remain neutral while its vital interests are affected', and the court would not become 'some kind of censor of employer/employee communications'. Proof of undue influence would require 'more than non-co-operation, obstruction or even vituperation' on the part of the employer:

> The behaviour complained of must strike the court as reprehensible, as morally blameworthy and as meting out intolerable treatment. It will normally have elements of deliberation and of unwarranted severity. Deceptive or misleading statements of the kind alleged and aggressive marketing by strong personalities do not strike me as amounting to the behaviour described in the subsection.[45]

While a lockout could be considered as part of an overall climate which created economic duress, this had not been 'a prolonged lockout finally bringing employees to their knees by virtually starving them into submission'.[46]

On the question of authorisation to negotiate, the courts confirmed that positive proof of specific authorisation was required. A list of current members was insufficient, and employers could insist on production of written evidence for each individual covered.[47]

Aggressive employers did not have it all their own way. In a case involving the procedures for promotion, transfer and filling of vacancies, the Employment Court rejected the suggestion that compelling commercial reasons could justify breaching an employment contract.[48] In another case, the Employment Court fined a company for refusing to comply with an order to continue providing union access, deduct union fees, and pay for workers' attendance at union meetings in line with the roll-over of the award.[49]

In 1992 labour lawyer Bill Hodge reflected that the limits of the ECA were 'being explored in a market-place with downgraded labour value, and exalted managerial prerogative'.[50] He concluded that, 'although employers lost a few initial skirmishes in the opening rounds . . . they are winning more major battles in the bargaining war. . . . It remains to be seen whether we will next see "sympathy lockouts" to aid other employers to compel that employer's employees to accept terms offered by that employer.'[51] Some argued that this was simply market forces at work. Workers and unions in the past had been able to pressure employers when labour was in short supply and the economy was buoyant. Their time would come again when the economy recovered and labour was once more in demand.[52] Hodge observed that this depended 'on the sanguine assumption that unemployment in New Zealand is not now systemic and structural, and that inflationary times of full employment will return'.[53] Even if they did, the trade union movement might be so debilitated by the combined ravages of recession and the ECA that it was unable to fight back.

ECA review

The ECA repeatedly suffered a bad press. This probably overstated its impact, in that positive experiences were rarely related. But the degree of abuse that was exposed forced the government into damage control. In 1992 a select committee was authorised to inquire into the effects of the Act. Labour MPs on the committee pre-empted the final report by releasing their own minority report in September 1993—one month before the election. They claimed the evidence disclosed 'a pattern of abuse for illegitimate ends which are either without remedy under the Act or which cannot be enforced because of the overloading of the institutions and inspectors'.[54] The Act had failed to provide:

* fair and equitable working conditions;
* a bargaining system that protected the choice of parties about representation and conditions;
* improved living standards for working people; and

- protections for collective bargaining.

The Act's legal institutions were badly designed and stretched to breaking-point. Labour's minority report argued for minimum standards legislation and a code of basic employment rights, legislative recognition of collective representation by unions, the right to strike for multi-employer documents, and improvements to the institutional base.

The official select committee report spoke for the government majority only. Its chair, Max Bradford, had been influential in designing and passing the Act. Predictably, the majority found evidence in support of the legislation. The new system addressed the needs of individual employers and employees in a more constructive, less adversarial way. Unions had been forced to become more responsive to members' needs, although where they continued to be involved industrial relations had often deteriorated. The majority of workers had not seen their take-home pay drop, although some had lost pay or worked longer hours for the same amount. Productivity had increased through more flexible working hours, reorganisation of shift work, and better training and management. Overall, the Act had improved the financial position of business through increased productivity and competitiveness. This was expected to flow through to job growth as companies expanded.

Four important caveats, aside from partisan politics, cast doubt on the majority's findings. First, the methodology relied primarily on 'impressions, together with opinions and facts', rather than formal submissions, research or statistical data. It therefore provided a weak foundation on which to base arguments for law reform.

Second, the study centred on workplaces with more than 25 staff, despite the predominance of small businesses in New Zealand industry. In 1993 New Zealand had 174,700 separate enterprises which employed 1,170,000 full-time equivalent (FTE) workers, an average of seven workers for each enterprise. Only 1123 enterprises employed more than 100 workers, although they comprised 42 percent of the FTE workforce.[55] Almost a quarter of workers were in enterprises with five or fewer employees. In particular, the choice of methodology excluded consideration of the pressures faced by isolated workers, often women, from their usually male employer. As the Working Women's Resource Centre explained:

> women tend to be employed in small businesses on a part-time or casual basis, and are often low paid. Frequently women are sole employees, and

are forced into a confrontational situation with their (frequently male) employer when considering conditions of employment. This leads to women often accepting a contract without negotiation, or not receiving a contract at all and being too intimidated to ask for one.[56]

Third, seven of the 40 companies approached by the select committee declined to co-operate. These were unlikely to be employers proud of their employment records, so the sample was biased.

Finally, the evidence from almost all staff and management was solicited at joint meetings, introducing the obvious risk that workers would feel inhibited from freely expressing their views.

The evidence showed:

- The streamlined enterprise bargaining system provided benefits for many employers, while unions faced more onerous demands to secure worker authorisation and then negotiate in a multitude of individual workplaces. Greater efficiency for business therefore meant increased inefficiencies for union representation.

- Most examples of conflict given by the committee involved negotiations through unions. The employers generally blamed this on union intransigence and adversarial tactics. Unions blamed bad management, lack of statutory protections and employers abusing the Act. Most conflict occurred in industries where hardnosed unions and employers tended to coincide.

- Many workers who had negotiated direct with their employers reported improved communication, access to information and a sense of empowerment. Where trust between workers and employers was given as the reason for agreeing to a contract, however, workers frequently acknowledged they would be vulnerable if the relationship broke down or new management took over.

- Not all employers viewed union involvement as a bad thing. Some saw knowledge of the industry, a single transaction with skilled negotiators and building on an established union relationship as efficient and constructive. Nor were all management out to exploit their power under the Act. But when bad employers exploited the Act, good employers felt pressured to reduce their workers' entitlements so they could compete. Unions argued that a ratcheting-down process was under way, with adverse consequences for workers' pay and conditions, positive employer–union relations and harmony in the workplace.

Other elements of the structural adjustment package had reinforced these pressures. Removal of import licences and tariff cuts had lowered the price of overseas goods, meaning that labour costs had to be reduced or production moved offshore. Corporatisation of the ports imposed competitive pressures which required operators to undercut one another constantly. Pressure on SOEs to return a profit, compete and prepare for privatisation meant employment practices frequently fell short of their statutory 'good employer' requirement. Similar problems, combined with uncertainty, in the health restructuring caused on-going conflict in the public and private sector over both working conditions and the quality of health care that staff felt ethically obliged to provide. School boards had neither the negotiating skills nor the knowledge of the ECA to ensure that employment practice maintained educational standards. Unstable economic conditions generally made employers reluctant to take on full-time workers because of redundancy and service costs. The qualifying rules for unemployment benefit meant some workers were lodging personal grievance claims to avoid the 26-week stand-down period, thus adding to the backlog of cases before the tribunal.

There was also an important message for unions. Too often they had been driven by their own agenda, failed to involve their members in negotiations or taken them for granted. Now that their resources were stretched to the limit, many unions were unable to do the remedial work required to convince members to stay or new workers to join.

The recommendations made to the select committee by most workers and some employers sought: a minimum code to protect vulnerable employees, in particular reintroduction of a minimum youth rate; accessible information on the rights and responsibilities of employers and workers; more resources to enable labour inspectors to investigate abuse; a 'good faith' bargaining requirement; and a balancing of power in strikes and lockouts. The majority's response was weak. The only recommendations of substance were to review the eligibility criteria for unemployment benefit and the impact of the 26-week benefit stand-down period, monitor the delays in the processing of Employment Tribunal cases, and review government intentions on further ratification of International Labour Organisation (ILO) conventions. Evidence of serious exploitation of youth workers was dismissed as mere anecdote. As a concession to public concern, however, the committee proposed a Labour Department free-phone hotline to advise young people on their rights.

The pressure to protect youth workers against exploitation continued after the report. The Roundtable objected that minimum statutory wages caused joblessness. The Employers' Federation likewise deemed it 'unwise and unfair' to introduce further barriers for people wanting to take up new job opportunities created by strong economic growth, and argued for 'non-wage' transfers for the poor. The government finally agreed to introduce a minimum wage for youth at 60 percent of the adult rate, which had been frozen at $6.125 an hour since 1990. Faced with demands from the CTU for a rise of $1 per hour in the adult rate, and from the corporate lobby to extend the freeze, the government announced a 2 percent or $5 per week raise for adults in 1994—which amounted to a cut in the real wage of around 7 percent over the preceding four years.[57]

ILO complaint

When the union bureaucracy finally responded to the ECA it opted for the politics of embarrassment. In February 1993 the CTU laid a complaint with the ILO that the Act breached Convention 87 (freedom of association) and Convention 98 (collective bargaining and right to organise). These conventions had never been ratified by the New Zealand government, ironically because of the compulsory unionism provision in previous labour laws. Before the ECA was passed the Department of Labour had advised the government that the Act probably breached the conventions. In September 1991 the government had asked the central workers' and employers' organisations for advice on ratification. The unions heard nothing more.

The National government gave its formal response to the CTU complaint in September 1993. The ILO's tentative working paper criticising the Act was leaked just before the November election, causing a predictable furore. Formal consideration of the complaint by the ILO committee was deferred until March 1994. At that meeting they adopted the 1993 working paper, and delivered a long list of interim recommendations. Key among these were to:
* underline the principle of consultation and co-operation between public authorities and employers' and workers' organisations at industrial and national levels;
* note the absence of express provisions in the Act which recognised unions for the purposes of collective bargaining;
* note that moves by employers to bypass union representatives in negotiations had been held to be consistent with the Act;
* draw government's attention to the ILO principles that collective

bargaining and negotiations between employers' representatives and unions should be encouraged and promoted;

• note that the law allowed employers to pressure workers to withdraw authorisation to unions, making it more difficult to bargain collectively;

• note that protection against interference and discrimination on the basis of trade union membership or activities was ineffective in practice;

• ask government to ensure that the legislation prohibited negotiations on behalf of employees by representatives appointed or dominated by the employer;

• indicate that obligations on unions to establish their authority to represent all their members were excessive and impeded the unions' right to act on their members' behalf;

• indicate that the prohibition on strikes for multi-employer collective contracts was contrary to the freedom of association and right to strike; and

• reiterate the principle that unions ought to have the possibility of recourse to protest strikes, in particular to criticise government economic and social policy.[58]

However, the ILO committee did approve the restrictions on strikes in an essential industry, and found that the right of access to workplaces was sufficiently guaranteed.

The government, Employers' Federation and Business Roundtable launched a concerted counter-attack on the ILO. In a speech to the ILO's plenary session in June 1994, the Minister of Labour reiterated the government's view that trade unions should not have any special status.

> Amongst the great treasures of New Zealand is our inheritance of the common law of England. It gives precedence to the rights of the individual. . . . For the ILO to appear to support a special, legal status for unions, as opposed to the rights of the individual, suggests a different underlying philosophy. . . . The ILO appears to view the world according to a Europeanised notion that only collectivism will work. In New Zealand, collective bargaining is accepted, union representation is accepted, but these are only two of many options.

The minister claimed that it was the ILO, not the Act, that needed reform: 'The ILO can and must be a force for good. To remain relevant, it must continue to adapt, not only in reviewing the type of standards it promotes but also in its working methods. The New Zealand Government believes that constant adaptation to the real world is the path to providing social and economic justice to New Zealanders. We commend the same practical approach to the ILO as it plans for its future.'

The Business Roundtable commissioned an Australian lawyer to write a critique of the ILO's interim report. He concluded that the ILO had difficulty understanding a labour relations system that provided no special place for unions. 'Confronted with legislation like the act, the initial ILO reaction is likely to be to see it more as an attack on trade unions, and therefore on workers' entitlements, than as a new approach to achieving precisely the peace and social justice aims for which the ILO exists.' The ILO had been philosophically in tune with the CTU, but out of its depth with the government's submission.[59]

In similar vein, Employers' Federation chief executive Steve Marshall claimed: 'The ILO, in its 75th year struggling to retain its former relevance has, in criticising the ECA, found a method of reasserting itself.' The Act was, he said, one of the foundation stones of the future, as international organisations more credible than the ILO had confirmed: 'This is no empty, vested-interest, ideological rhetoric. Authorities worldwide, most recently the OECD, have commended the ECA.'[60] Speaking to the commercial community, an *NBR* editorial applauded the government's steadfast position:

> The government should not be tempted to dilute the Employment Contracts Act to satisfy the prejudices of the antiquated International Labour Organisation. . . . The ILO, located in a European timewarp of central planning, overblown state spending and poor productivity, should sweep its own doorstep first. Far too much time is spent in this country kowtowing to foreign 'experts' whose opinions are better ignored. What can the ILO do other than smack New Zealand on the wrist? In world competitiveness terms, New Zealand is ahead of many OECD countries and that's been without the help or support of the Geneva-based public servants.[61]

In its formal response to the interim report, the government defended the Act as an important element of its strategy for growth, employment and social cohesion. 'The approach of successive governments since the early 1980s to economic reform has been the implementation of orthodox economic policies based on international best practice, which is best articulated by agencies such as the

OECD, the World Bank and the IMF.'[62] As one of its fundamental building blocks, the ECA had been instrumental in the resumption of sustainable high economic growth which had translated quickly into improving labour market outcomes. 'As economic growth continues and productivity improves, wage growth is expected to pick up and wage dispersion may increase before it reduces. The latter will depend on how quickly and successfully individuals invest in training in order to take advantage of new opportunities.'[63]

The government also claimed that judicial interpretations of the Act since 1993 had put paid to most of the CTU's complaints. On 5 November 1993—the same month as the ILO was due to consider New Zealand's case—in its decision on *Alliance Textiles*, the Court of Appeal dramatically altered its stance. According to the President, the employer was free, short of undue influence, to try to persuade an employee to leave or not to join a union, and was still not bound to negotiate. But employers were obliged to recognise the union's authority once this had been established for so long as negotiations were under way. 'To go behind the union's back does not seem consistent with recognising its authority.'[64] The comment of Justice Gault is particularly significant, given the timing of the judgment: 'The right to elect and pursue collective bargaining . . . is conferred by Part II of the Employment Contracts Act and that right should be fully accorded bearing in mind ILO Convention No 98 concerning the right to organise and bargain collectively.'[65]

The Employment Court later adopted the Court of Appeal's dicta. In *Dunollie Coal Mines* it issued an injunction against an employer who went behind the authorised union to negotiate a new collective contract direct with workers and locked them out when they refused.[66] In *Capital Coast Health* negotiations with the authorised union for a collective contract had broken down and the employer contacted the workers direct. The court held that the CHE had unlawfully bypassed the union. This breached both its statutory obligation to be a 'good employer' and the mutual obligations of trust and confidence between employer and employee.[67]

The government relied on these revised interpretations to show that the Act provided adequate protection. The CTU disagreed. The decisions

> did not set clear guidelines, were often ambiguous, were sometimes the product of a divided tribunal or court, and were uncertain case-law which could easily be overturned on appeal or in subsequent cases.

Moreover, to seek judicial enforcement of basic rights . . . was terribly costly, time-consuming and required efforts on the part of the trade union that were sometimes beyond its capabilities. . . . [B]y the time the judicial process was completed and the law clarified . . . even if the union (or employee) prevailed, the damage had been done (perhaps the destruction of the union organizing effort in the enterprise concerned) and . . . no compliance order or award could afford an adequate remedy.[68]

The ILO's final report, released in November 1994, generally sided with the CTU. While conceding that 'the line of jurisprudence . . . indicates at least a trend more favourable to workers' organizations than was initially the case', it was 'not clear whether and to what extent the reasoning of the courts applies to other issues raised in the complaint e.g. employers' interference and domination'. Nor had the existence and extent of a duty to bargain collectively been addressed. Ultimately, the employer was free not to negotiate at all.[69]

Irrespective of judicial interpretation, 'examples indicate, on a prima facie basis, that a significant number of collective bargaining problems have arisen and continue to arise in practice'.[70] While it appeared that the drop in union membership and collective agreement coverage had bottomed out (which subsequently proved not to be the case), and collective bargaining continued to occur, there was a risk that this was limited to large workplaces where unions were active and employees had more freedom of choice. The large proportion of the workforce in small enterprises may be more vulnerable.

On multi-employer bargaining, the government had argued that such contracts were an option, but the Act balanced employees' rights to strike with employers' rights not to be forced to associate with potential competitors to the possible detriment of their legitimate business interests. It was also unreasonable to subject employers to industrial sanctions for actions by other employers over whom they had no control.[71] The ILO agreed that employers did not have to accept multi-employer bargaining but 'the parties should be left free to decide for themselves on the means (including industrial action) to achieve particular bargaining objectives'.[72] As for the central issue of collective bargaining, the ILO committee concluded:

> On the whole . . . problems of incompatibility between ILO principles on collective bargaining and the Act stem in large part from the latter's underlying philosophy, which puts on the same footing (a) individual and collective employment contracts, and (b) individual and collective representation. . . . [T]he Committee finds it difficult to reconcile the

equal status given in the Act to individual and collective contracts with the ILO principles on collective bargaining. . . . [T]he Act *allows* collective bargaining . . . ̄ rather than *promoting* and *encouraging* it.[73]

These clear conclusions having been spelt out, the long list of concerns in the interim report was reduced to four. These basically reasserted the tripartite foundations of industrial relations and recommended on-going monitoring by the government and the ILO of the Act's operation. Within an hour of receiving the faxed report the government had seized the initiative, ingenuously claiming that the ILO had recanted its interim criticisms and issued a virtually clear bill of health. The only critical recommendation, it said, had been to legalise strikes for multi-employer agreements, and the government had no intention of complying with that: 'We are not going back to collective tyranny and terrorism. It's anti-consumer, anti-competitive and it's a total breach of any concept of people's rights to choose with whom they contract.'[74]

On the basis of research in Geneva, Nigel Haworth and Stephen Hughes reported in early 1995

> that the NZCTU position in the Final Report is in accord with the views held in the ILO. Senior ILO officials, when interviewed, expressed both surprise and concern at the misrepresentation of the Committee's findings and the wilful dismissal of its recommendations by senior members of the New Zealand Government. . . . [I]n ILO circles in Geneva it is widely accepted that the public interpretation of the Final Report offered by the New Zealand government is seriously and embarrassingly at odds with the report's contents and intentions.[75]

Haworth and Hughes suggested that, given the government's position, there was some merit in arguments that New Zealand should withdraw from the ILO, thus 'unshackl[ing] New Zealand from the burden of an international labour code domestic critics accuse of being outmoded and out of date, and an ILO it finds bureaucratic, eurocentric and irrelevant'. But they noted also that the ILO was 'the oldest agency of the UN with 169 member states covering 98 percent of the population of the world and whose activities have had a profound and lasting influence on the supervisory processes of other UN agencies'. While the 'efficacy and significance of the ILO in the world of the 1990s' was a broad issue of debate, the New Zealand government's response reflected more directly the 'clash of orthodoxies—on the one side the consensus management of tripartism; on the other, the maximisation of individual choice and competitive outcome'. They predicted that the impasse between the ILO and the New Zealand government was likely to continue. This might carry a fair share of international criticism. But 'in the current political circumstances facing New Zealand, internal posturing will take precedence over international commitments'.

Moderation of the ILO's critique had not been caused by a better understanding of the ECA or New Zealand conditions, but was attributable almost solely to an abrupt and timely about-face in judicial interpretation of the Act.[76] The intervention of the judiciary was fortuitous for the National government, and helped defuse demands for amendments to the more extreme and politically damaging parts of the Act. Whether that reflected a desire by the court to protect the judicial and legislative regime from critical international review, or a recognition that the blatant pro-employer bias of earlier legal decisions placed the courts' own credibility at risk, remained a moot point. So, too, was the potential for this new position in turn to be reversed.

Indeed, the courts themselves came under attack. In July 1995 the director of the Business Roundtable condemned the judicial activist approach of the Court of Appeal and Employment Court, accusing the judges of 'economic illiteracy'. Kerr observed that 'the idea that there is any systematic inequality in bargaining power between employers and employees is a basic fallacy in labour law which was rightly set aside in the Employment Contracts Act'.[77] Recent decisions[78] amounted to a 'deliberate and conscious snub to parliament's intentions in passing the Employment Contracts Act' and usurped 'a policy making role which should be the preserve of democratically elected and accountable institutions'.

Workplace health and safety

The ECA had proved a powerful economic tool to incapacitate the unions, abolish national awards, minimise the role of collective agreements, and drive down wages and conditions of employment. The Act gained further strength from the deregulation of health and safety in the workplace.

In 1987 Treasury had claimed that health and safety regulations often imposed 'substantial costs on business while not necessarily improving the desired outcomes'.[79] It wanted them replaced by private insurance and price-based incentives. Instead, the Occupational Safety and Health Bill, introduced in 1990, combined statutory provisions, codes of practice and regulations. These would operate through elected workplace representatives and committees, and consultation with employees.

The Bill was carried over after the election, and substantially revised by National as part of its strategy to rid the country of its 'Stalinist' industrial relations framework.[80] The Health and Safety in Employment Act 1992 removed any enforceable right for employees or unions to be involved in safety issues, and left management to decide whether to consult. It also removed the statutory right to refuse dangerous work. Employees would have a common law right to refuse, and a right to strike lawfully under section 71 of the ECA if they believed that was justified on health and safety grounds—a claim which by 1995 had yet to succeed in court. Direct government control of workplace standards gave way to a system of incentives and penalties to encourage employer compliance. Employers' accident compensation premiums would receive a loading or discount, with their 'experience rating' based on the cost of claims by individual employees.

Technical health and safety standards were to be set down in regulations. By July 1994 no regulations were in place. The Minister of Labour indicated that 'it has become clear to me that the Act does not require massive regulatory underpinning for its successful operation. Instead, a minimum number of regulations should be sufficient.'[81] These would set minimum standards for high-hazard industries and work practices. Guidelines and codes of practice for other areas would be developed in consultation with industry. The CTU objected that downgrading legislation to unenforceable guidelines implied a lower status and less obligation to conform. Critics also pointed to the poor compliance record of New Zealand employers with the existing Voluntary Code of Practice for Health and Safety Representatives, even when unions had been strong. The worst noncompliance was expected in small enterprises, where accident risks were seen as highest and union action least likely to occur.

The select committee review of the ECA was warned that employees were trading off health and safety aspects of their employment to keep their jobs, and felt unable to ask for protective clothing, challenge unsafe conditions or take time off work sick. Productivity demands meant that employees had to maintain standards while doing more in a shorter time. Stress levels increased, with more accidents blamed on pressure to complete jobs.[82]

Only official inspectors could enforce the Act, again as a means to keep unions out. Departmental policy treated enforcement as a last resort. Field staff focused on 'auditing management systems and work processes rather than looking for breaches of legislation.' In theory, prevention was better than punishment. But the CTU complained that prosecutions were rare, and that 90 percent of those lodged concerned accidents after serious injury had occurred, not failure to maintain standards. All cases by 1994 had involved injury, not occupational disease or illness.[83] Cases which reached the courts drew a limited response.[84] While workers' advocates criticised enforcement and penalties as too lax, employers and their allies accused the courts of going too far and using penalties as an alternative source of lump-sum compensation for workers which was no longer available under the accident compensation scheme.

Accident compensation

The CTU also laid complaints with the ILO that the government had breached conventions 12 (workers compensation for agricultural workers), 17 (replacement of artificial limbs and medical aids) and 42 (occupational diseases) in the way it restructured New Zealand's accident compensation system. The internationally acclaimed no-fault scheme had been introduced in April 1974 to replace the expensive, arbitrary and adversarial system of remedies at common law and the Workers Compensation Act 1956. In return for losing the right to sue, all New Zealand residents became entitled to a compensation package covering lost earnings, a lump sum for non-economic loss, and costs incurred. Employers were relieved of their common law liabilities and workers compensation insurance. As a *quid pro quo,* they were expected to fund all injuries to earners wherever they occurred. Motor vehicle accidents were funded from vehicle registration fees and part of the tax on petrol. Lump-sum compensation for non-earners' injuries was funded by the government.

Until 1984 the Accident Compensation Corporation (ACC) had maintained its income above expenditure with substantial reserves to cover the growing 'tail' of longer-term compensation payouts. Under pressure from employers, who cited adverse economic conditions and international competition, the commitment to maintain a fully funded scheme was abandoned. By 1987 the ACC had used most of its reserves and was virtually bankrupt. Employer levies had to be increased to return reserves to a prudent level by 1990.[85] This 'crisis' in ACC was blamed on the inefficiencies and extravagance of a scheme designed in the days of a protected, high-income, high-employment economy. But it was a crisis compounded, if not created, by the decision to abandon full funding of the scheme.

In 1990, Treasury and the National government resumed the assault. Their goal, consistent with their broader approach to social security, was to squeeze costs down, remove universal coverage, and shift responsibility to private insurance, backed by a minimal safety net. Treasury promoted a 'needs-based' approach, with parity to other income-tested benefits, and increased incentives for employer and worker responsibility.[86] The Employers' Federation agreed. Employers objected to funding the part of the scheme which dealt with non-work, off-road accidents without having a say in administration and the rehabilitation processes, or any ability to control such injuries. They also complained that ACC had become 'an unaccountable gravy train for many claimants and health professionals—at the employers' expense'.[87] The Business Roundtable advocated privatisation of ACC and open competition with insurance companies for its business.[88]

A working party set up just after the 1990 election concluded that the principles of community responsibility for compensation 'do not necessarily sit comfortably with reforms based on principles of individual responsibility, a uniform welfare floor and the least possible government intervention (and taxpayer cost)'.[89] Their initial recommendations were for a four-stage legislative process which would ultimately deregulate and privatise injury compensation insurance cover. This proved too politically controversial. Less obvious transitional measures which could clear the way for competing private insurance providers were introduced.

Drastic cuts to ACC eligibility and entitlements were effected through the Accident Rehabilitation and Compensation Insurance Act 1992, as foreshadowed in Richardson's 1991 budget.[90] Employers' liability was limited to workplace accidents, with premiums loaded or discounted according to their experience rating. Employees were levied to cover injuries outside work. Earnings-related payments for the first week reverted from ACC to employers, with no machinery to enforce payment. Lump-sum payments for non-economic loss, including permanent disability, pain and suffering and loss of enjoyment of life, were abolished in what the New Zealand Law Society's submission on the Bill labelled 'the clearest possible breach of the social contract'.

Rehabilitation to get people back to work was replaced by a punitive incentive scheme: a work capacity test was legislated (though not yet introduced) whereby earnings-related payments would terminate once the injured worker was considered 85 percent fit for any kind of work, irrespective of whether they could find a job. Numerous other cuts, including costs for medical treatment, transport and on-going support, had drastic effects. But the right to sue was not restored. Nor was compensation for victims of sexual abuse and other crime formerly provided by the Criminal Injuries Compensation Board. A pilot exempt-employer scheme, which enabled large employers to opt out and self-insure for the first twelve months after injury, was introduced.

These changes were implemented through detailed regulations from which all administrative discretion had been removed.[91] New problems of bureaucracy, complexity, delay, expense and adversarial process soon emerged. Successive inquiries catalogued deficiencies of the new regime which could not be laid at its predecessor's door.[92] The ACC's own 1993 report concluded 'the legislation has not delivered the intended outcomes', 'the results have been undesirable for the Scheme and the Corporation', 'the expected outcome has been thwarted by administrative difficulties in applying the legislation as drafted' and 'public perceptions regarding the Scheme's fairness may well pose the greatest threat to its long term survival'.[93]

The government-induced funding crisis continued. The new 'pay as you go' approach could not cope with the 'tail' of long-term claims. National had set levies below what the corporation recommended. By June 1993, reserves had fallen below levels of financial prudence, and the government once more had to raise employer levies to replenish them. Predictions for 1995 showed a deficit in the employers' account of $100 million, requiring further rises in levies—proving, the government's critics said, that 'ill-conceived legislation rushed through Parliament for the benefit of employers does not necessarily benefit employers' or anyone else.[94] They insisted that the problems facing ACC could be addressed within the basic principles of a fully funded scheme.

The rigid regulatory regime and the pilot exempt-employer scheme were seen by critics as precursors to privatisation. 'Because private insurers cannot be relied upon to exercise discretions in favour of the injured claimant, a system had to be devised to comprehensively prescribe entitlements, which would then be administered by competing insurers or (in the case of some large employers) self insuring.[95] This would open up a lucrative new market for the insurance industry, and opportunities for investment. Despite added costs of product development, marketing and delivering a dividend, the superiority of private insurance was simply assumed. Compulsory workplace accident insurance would become part of a package included in each worker's employment contract. Former ACC official Grant Duncan observed the 'kind of coverage and treatment . . . would then be dependent on managerial goodwill and commitment to good industrial relations. This may or may not be better than having to deal with a bureaucracy like ACC. Employees would just have to take their chances.'[96] Alternatively, government could continue reducing the coverage provided by ACC and leave individuals to top this up with private insurance as people increasingly did with health care. ACC would become another component of the state's minimal safety net.

Future prospects

In its early days, the structural adjustment rhetoric had talked of a high-employment, high-productivity, high-income economy. But international competitiveness required low wages, minimal regulatory restraints and legal obligations, and a 'natural' rate of unemployment, with rich and poor, educated and unskilled, competing for the available jobs within the private sector market-place.

The fundamentalist lobby was delighted by the success of the new labour market regime. According to Business Roundtable chair and Lion Breweries head Douglas Myers in 1992, even Charles Dickens and the Pope would praise the ECA as the embodiment of individual freedom.[97] Employers' Federation chief executive Steve Marshall went further. The Act could be seen as a 'transitional evolutionary link' between the interventionist labour laws of the past and a future where there was no specialist labour legislation at all. Employment contracts could then be treated like all other contracts, and left to the common law.[98]

Historically, the courts had proved a fickle source of protection for unions and workers. Any move to abandon the labour market completely to contract law in the civil courts, light-handed regulation of health and safety through market incentives, and private provision for accident compensation posed a frightening prospect indeed.

CHAPTER NINE

Fiscal Restraint

FISCAL POLICY, or the use of government expenditure and revenue collection to distribute resources and redistribute income, has always been more than an accounting exercise. Under the interventionist welfare state, it was driven by the assumption that citizens had basic entitlements that were determined and delivered by a benevolent central government. As the primacy of the welfare state gave way, the market was left to reconcile competing efficiency and equity outcomes, and the state retreated towards providing a minimal safety net.

The fiscal policy agenda progressed through three overlapping phases. Treasury's 1984 briefing focused on cutting the budget deficit, especially in social services, and the efficiency gains to be made from a move to indirect taxation. In 1987, the emphasis shifted to the 'devolution' of key social policy areas, coupled with the partial transfer of responsibility for funding these services to the consumer. By 1990, the focus had returned to reducing government expenditure and debt through cuts to services, core departmental operations, transfer payments and income support.

Phase 1: Adjusting revenue and expenditure

Just as the Labour government had political problems implementing labour market deregulation, a direct attack on government spending would have meant recanting the party's historical commitment to the welfare state. That, in turn, would have risked an organised and even militant challenge to the whole structural adjustment programme. But there was no real urgency. Restructuring the economy would eventually dictate the nature of fiscal and social policy change, while taxation reform and state sector restructuring would erode the principle of a comprehensive, state-centred welfare base.

Again, the conceptual groundwork was laid in Treasury's *Economic Management*. 'Social welfare' rested on the ability and opportunity for workers, or those on whom people depended, to earn an income. Achieving social policy objectives therefore required 'the promotion of a more efficient economy and a stable macroeconomic environment which is conducive to improved living standards and full employment'.[1] Actions to reduce inequalities in the community often entailed efficiency costs by weakening the incentives for individuals to undertake productive and otherwise profitable activities. Government expenditure posed impediments to economic performance and community welfare. There were direct costs involved in administering government's social support programmes. Many beneficiaries also incurred costs in complying with the requirements to obtain assistance.[2]

In Treasury's view, the existing taxation system neither delivered enough revenue nor met basic efficiency and equity criteria. Taxation deprived people of choice and stifled incentives, imposed administrative and compliance costs, diverted resources and crowded out investment opportunities. Progressive tax scales, in particular, adversely affected incentives and achieved limited redistribution of wealth. The proportion of personal income tax being paid under the progressive tax scheme was considered excessive, even though total personal income taxes ranked only twelfth of 23 OECD countries as a percentage of GDP.[3] Inflation had pushed increasing numbers of earners to the top end of the scale. Exemptions and rebates had been introduced to mitigate this effect. But tax avoidance and evasion among higher income earners and companies had become widespread.

Treasury wanted a new system that was economically efficient, equitable, simple and certain. It argued that broadening the income tax base and introducing a comprehensive goods and services tax would improve equity across all people earning a similar income. Efficiency would be improved by using a 'relatively flat scale on a comprehensive base', rather than a steeply progressive scale on the existing base. Concerns about redistribution could be addressed through targeted rebates or negative tax. 'Under the latter, much existing welfare support could be delivered through the tax system on the basis of need, formulated to take account of family composition, incomes and other relevant factors.'[4]

Labour made only limited attempts to contain government expenditure in the first couple of years. Subsidies and other industry supports were removed. User charges, including a small one on prescriptions, were imposed. On the other hand, a 'family care' scheme was introduced in December 1984 for low income earners in fulltime employment. Douglas's primary concern at this stage was to broaden the tax base. A move to indirect taxation had been proposed, unsuccessfully, in 1967 and again in 1982. In his 1984 budget Douglas foreshadowed a comprehensive 'goods and services' expenditure tax or GST. The details were set out in the 1985 Statement on Taxation and Benefit Reform and the tax, set at 10 percent, was in place by October 1986. Only certain financial services, life insurance, rental accommodation, some second-hand goods, exports and very small traders were exempt. Sales tax was abolished. Income tax rates were reduced from five steps to three, set at 15, 30 and 48 percent from April 1987. Tax loopholes were closed and personal income exemptions removed. Between 1985/86 and 1987/88 the proportion of indirect tax increased from 22.5 percent to 33.2 percent of government income.

The impact of GST was predicted to fall more heavily on low income earners and large families. Rather than exempting essentials like food and clothing, compensation came through a one-off increase in benefits and revisions to the income support scheme. Family care and other family rebates to earners were merged into 'family support', and the scheme was broadened to cover beneficiaries. Beneficiaries also received an early 5 percent benefit increase, although this amount was excluded from the subsequent CPI adjustment in April 1987. In that year economist Bob Stephens observed:

> The tax reform so far has been consistent with the general market liberalisation, with improvements in economic efficiency resulting from the neutrality of the tax system in economic decisions. But the lack of indexation of personal tax scales and family assistance parameters will mean that the switch to indirect taxation and poverty relief for large families will be only temporary. A further problem is the effect on work incentives of a marginal tax rate of 48 percent for most family groups.[5]

By 1987 the fiscal position was not looking good. Although the financial deficit had declined as a proportion of GDP from 6.9 percent in 1983/84 to 3.1 percent in 1985/86, it slipped again in 1986/87. The lifting of the wage, price and interest rate freezes had released rampant inflation, driven partly by large increases in public sector wages. The package to compensate for GST involved a net fiscal cost of $737 million, and boosted inflation further. Higher overseas interest rates added to the deficit, although inflation reduced the capital value of the government's debt. The deficit had been expected to fall to 2.2 percent of GDP in 1987/88, but the worsening economic climate prevented that.

Behind the scenes, a struggle was brewing within the Labour Cabinet between the technopols and social democrats over where to draw the structural adjustment line. In March 1986 Prime Minister David Lange announced a Royal Commission on Social Policy. The terms of reference listed the 'social and economic foundations of New Zealand' as:

- democracy based on freedom and equal rights;
- adherence to the rule of law;
- collective responsibility of New Zealand society for its members with continuing roles for individuals, families, voluntary social groups, ethnic and tribal affiliations and other communities as well as local and central government;
- the principles of the Treaty of Waitangi;
- the operation of a mixed economy with private, co-operative and public activity;
- the responsibility which all people have to be independent and self-reliant to the best of their ability and to contribute to society;
- a commitment to the children of New Zealand and regard for the future generations of New Zealand; and
- the equality of men and women, and the equality of all races.[6]

Labour went into the August 1987 election with promises to balance three years of hard-line economic policy with social policy reform. Many voters must have assumed this would be based on the royal commission's findings. But a very different agenda was soon revealed. In the wake of the October share-market crash, Douglas and his advisors prepared a radical new package. Its centre-piece was the proposal for a flat income tax of 23 percent and a company tax of 28 percent, with a rise in GST to 12.5 percent. Comprehensive welfare provision would give way to a new Guaranteed Minimum Family Income (GMFI). This would operate as a top-up for families of full-time earners who fell below a certain income base, to ensure a margin of $70 between the incomes of working families and those on benefits. Income-tested health care payments would require better-off families to pay for their own health care up to 4 percent of their income. Housing assistance was to be devolved to local bodies. All except the GMFI had already been proposed in Treasury's 1987 *Government Management* brief.

The package provoked intense controversy within the Cabinet,[7] fuelling the Lange–Douglas feud. The technopols lost this battle. A modified version of the package was made public on December 17. Missing were the proposals on health and housing (and others on labour market reform), and the flat tax level was unspecified. In late January 1988, Lange renounced the Douglas package. More moderate tax changes were introduced. Income tax was set at two statutory rates of 24 and 33 percent from October 1988, although a low-earner rebate made the rates 15, 28 and 33 percent in practice. The top company tax rate was reduced to 28 percent from April 1988 (later increased to 33 percent) while foreign-domiciled companies paid 38 percent. In return, almost all personal exemptions, rebates, deductions and, in theory, opportunities for avoidance were removed. GST went up to 12.5 percent in July 1989.

The flattening of tax rates was largely a transfer from middle to high income families, while the regressive nature of the universal GST redistributed the tax burden to the poor. According to Stephens, changes in tax structures between 1982 and 1988 meant that effective average tax rates including GST for couples on average earnings with two dependants increased from 18.7 percent to 24.1 percent. Average tax rates for similar couples on three times the average income declined from 40.3 percent to 34.9 percent.[8]

The zealots had lost the battle, but they won the war. The combination of *Government Management* and Douglas's post-election economic statement undermined the Royal Commission on Social Policy. Under pressure, it reported early in April 1988. After eighteen months of extensive consultation, the commission's message was clear: the majority of people wanted a return to priorities of full employment, and improved state-funded education, housing, health and other social services. But the commission's five-volume report was very large, very confused, and hence very ineffectual. It was successfully ridiculed by free-marketeers as a monument to the inefficiency, intellectual woolliness and political ineptitude that typified the welfare state.

Lange's strategy to hold the line on social policy had failed. Even though Douglas and Prebble were removed from the Cabinet in late 1988, and Treasury's dominance temporarily waned, the paradigm shift had already taken place. Reductions in marginal income tax rates and the introduction of GST had made important inroads into the traditional redistributive philosophy of the welfare state.

Phase 2: Rethinking the welfare state

The early period of fiscal policy focused largely on the revenue side. Reducing government expenditure, in particular the cost of state services and administration, was the next major phase. This centred on the decentralisation and 'devolution' of central government activities to local communities and private markets, and the targeting of state support for people using those services. This was more than just a cost-cutting exercise; it was justified in *Government Management* as liberating individuals from the oppressive power of the central state. Individual freedom depended on people's ability to calculate costs and benefits rationally, free from the tyranny of decisions made by, or for, the majority. If the true cost of specific programmes was known, people would withdraw support from those which they valued least. And if the state's monopoly was removed, competition for supply of goods and services would ensure efficient use of resources and responsiveness to consumers' needs.

Methods of delivery also had to change. The devolution of social responsibilities currently carried out by centralised government departments to elected or appointed bodies, or to private enterprise, would ensure that they responded to individual personal preference. The precise model would vary between agencies. But consistent features needed to include clearly drawn parameters, contractual arrangements for delivery, accountability for taxpayer resources, and sanctions through the withdrawal of funds.

People had to be convinced that '[i]nstead of empowering the poor, [state-provided entitlements] are disabling of taxpayers, restrict the choice of users of social services and empower the public servants involved in their delivery'.[9] This meant the assumption of universal entitlement to social services and support also had to be broken. Equity concerns could then be dealt with through targeting, tax credits and rebates or vouchers to provide a minimum income floor.

Public policy analyst John Martin notes how the ambiguity of the term 'devolution' speaks to widely shared concerns, while enabling radically different prescriptions for change. The policy was couched in the rhetoric of community empowerment, responsiveness, accountability and consumer control. Yet '[e]fficiency and effectiveness as organizational goals require a strong sense of direction set from the top and the ability to control behaviour so that it is aligned with the preferences of those who hold power.'[10]

A task group advising the SSC in 1987 warned that a 'client-centred view of devolution would demand that those exercising devolved power have a high level of autonomy to control "micro" policy but this creates tension with macro (government) policy and with formal accountability requirements—notably compliance with financial reporting standards'. It stressed the need for clear limits on the degree of authority to be devolved: 'the ultimate transfer of policy responsibility lies beyond the scope of any power sharing process because it implies the possibility of Parliament's powers to appropriate money being effectively abrogated'.[11]

While the government talked about *devolution,* described by Martin as 'the *transfer* of power, authority and responsibility from a national to a sub-national level', what it practised was *decentralisation,* or 'the *delegation* of power and authority to lower levels, with ultimate responsibility remaining at the national level'.[12] The policy was progressively applied to the gamut of departments involved in social service delivery, including education, health, labour, social welfare, justice and Maori affairs. Most government departments were expected to view these changes with suspicion, if not hostility. So a series of external reviews was commissioned to report on key social policy areas, chaired by private sector sympathisers and usually serviced by the Treasury. These reports set the terms of debate, and forced their critics onto the defensive. Even the most extreme, Alan Gibbs's blueprint for *Unshackling the Hospitals,* created the space for less radical, but incremental, changes—which ultimately led towards the outcome Gibbs had proposed. Local government devolution followed suit. To ease its path, Labour did away with voter polls and surveys, public consultation, and the right to appeal over forced local body mergers. National empowered the Local Government Commission to recommend a further reorganisation, to be implemented by Order in Council. Again, the right of legal challenge was removed.

Many of those who believed the devolution sales pitch were quickly disappointed. Once the formal agencies of the state had been dismantled, communities were thrown back onto their own skills and resources. Ministers were able to determine who secured funds, in what amount and on what terms, and disclaimed responsibility for the quality of the result. If consumers were dissatisfied, they could take it up with the providers. There was nothing the government could, or would, do. Those who had the greatest ability to survive prospered, and those who were in a structurally weak economic, cultural and gender position, or had personal disabilities, suffered most.

Health

Proposals to 'devolve' health funding were not new. A system of regional health authorities to co-ordinate private and voluntary providers, including general practitioners, and funded by a centralised national authority was proposed in a white paper back in 1974. Sustained resistance from hospital boards and general practitioners saw a softer scheme for the voluntary amalgamation of existing health bodies into area health boards introduced in 1983.

Health remained a politically sensitive issue, subject to an effective lobby. In 1987 the technopols established a Taskforce on Hospital and Related Services under Alan Gibbs. Its report condemned wide regional variations and poor integration of primary and secondary health services. Management lacked accountability and incentives to minimise costs, and their information systems were poor. Many of these criticisms were justified. The Gibbs solution was to devolve health funding to six regional bodies which would purchase primary and secondary health services from public and private providers through competitive contracts. Parallel ideas emerged in Treasury's *Government Management* around the same time.[13] The Gibbs report was widely dismissed as extreme. Labour ministers focused instead on governance problems with the area health boards, and became locked in battle with general practitioners over a contract funding scheme.

The new National government, with technopol Simon Upton as Minister of Health, had no such reservations. The health service was in a fragile state. Real public spending on primary health care had increased by 42 percent between 1980 and 1991, but overall health spending had risen by less than 9 percent. Most of the increase had occurred in the mid-1980s. Per capita government spending on health had declined by 7 percent since 1989. Waiting lists for surgery had lengthened by 61 percent since 1981.[14] Hospital buildings were deteriorating. Equipment was ageing and poorly maintained. Funding from public sources as a proportion of total health spending had fallen from 88 percent in 1980 to 81.7 percent in 1991.[15]

Within three months National had established a task force to advise on options for redefining the roles of government, private sector and individuals in the funding, provision and regulation of health services. The details, which broadly mirrored the Gibbs report, were released alongside the July 1991 budget and were to be implemented by July 1993.[16]

The fourteen two-thirds-elected area health boards were replaced overnight by ministerially appointed commissioners. Four regional health authorities (RHAs) were then established for the whole country. The ministerially appointed RHAs received bulk funding, calculated on a population basis, to buy health services from public and private providers. Responsibility to identify core services and terms of access was delegated to a National Advisory Committee. A Public Health Commission was established in response to objections that commodification of health would marginalise public health and education programmes. Policy was left to a streamlined Ministry of Health. Public hospitals were converted into commercial Crown Health Enterprises (CHEs). According to the Health and Disability Services Act, the purpose of the new entities was, *inter alia*, to 'Secure for the people of New Zealand . . . [t]he best health . . . . that is reasonably achievable within the amount of funding provided'.

The restructuring was overseen by a National Interim Provider Board, chaired by Fletcher Challenge's Ron Trotter, and a Policy, Regulatory and Implementation Unit, headed by a Treasury technocrat located in the Department of the Prime Minister and Cabinet. The proposals attracted concerted opposition, especially from nurses and the medical profession. The Medical Council challenged the primacy of profit and business success over ethics and access, while the Wellington Area Health Board predicted that 'co-operative medicine as we know it will disappear'.[17] Their objections were dismissed as special pleading.

To complement the structural changes, entitlement to publicly funded health care became rigidly targeted. The population was initially divided into three categories of income earner, entitled to different levels of subsidy for doctor's visits, prescriptions and hospital services. Category one and two users would carry a 'community services card', colloquially called the 'poor card', to prove their eligibility. These two levels were later condensed into one. A 'high income' meant any family that was ineligible for family support, most of the elderly with any private income, and most single people earning over $17,500 a year.

When implementation of the new charging regime began in February 1992, the administrative details had not been finalised. As with many aspects of the experiment, these were made up along the way. Estimates of the economic costs and benefits were wildly inaccurate. The government initially predicted revenue gains from user part-charges of $95 million a year. By July 1992 these were revised down to just $14.4 million. The abolition of charges for in-patient hospital services in April 1993 as a result of a public outcry reduced this again. The minister admitted that the Treasury figures 'had always been somewhat speculative' and that the charges were not intended to raise money—'so in a way the numbers are really beside the point'.[18]

The establishment cost for the elaborate scheme was considerable. The budget for the first year, originally estimated at $15.7 million, had escalated to $82 million by December 1992.[19] Efficiency gains were expected to cover the future cost of directors' fees, new layers of management, accounting procedures, public relations and debt recovery without eroding the resources available to provide actual health services. With chief executives receiving output and efficiency-linked incentives, the quality of health care risked becoming subordinate to cost cutting and preventing 'waste'.

The government's share of total health spending declined from 82 percent in 1991 to 76 percent in 1993, although it increased by 1 percent in 1994. The surge in private health insurance coverage—according to the Consumers' Institute, from around 40 percent of the population in 1991 to 46 percent in 1993 and 55 percent by 1995[20]—confirmed a deepening lack of confidence in the public health services.

By 1995 the impact of the devolved health system was difficult to assess. Innovation and improved flexibility and efficiency were evident in some areas. Competitive tendering was still in its infancy. Existing funding arrangements had been rolled over in 1993 while information systems were being established. Many contracts continued until March 1995. Several technical problems with contracting had emerged, especially with hospital services; it was unclear whether output should be defined by facilities, bed days, number of cases or quality outcomes. High transaction costs and capital sunk in equipment and trained staff also dictated that contracts should be long-term; yet that would inhibit the emergence of a competitive market.

The experiment of turning public hospitals into CHEs, however, appeared to have failed dismally. In the first year, CHE expenditure exceeded revenue by 11 percent. The government was forced to write off $300 million in debts and inject another $100 million in the 1994 budget. Another $534 million was allocated to the CHEs later in the year. Information on their operations was difficult to secure. Despite coverage by the Official Information Act, in the competitive commercial climate almost all data was deemed confidential. Certain trends were apparent, however. As local hospitals were closed and services centralised, the number of public hospital beds declined. While the number of surgical procedures increased, so did waiting lists, although that may have been part of a long-term trend. Capped funding forced CHEs to set priorities for certain services and categories of patient, including age and severity of illness. The cost factor increasingly affected clinical decisions. Individual inequities received extensive publicity, and doctors objected to being forced to 'play god'. Demoralisation, stress, underfunding and new opportunities in the private sector created critical shortages of key medical staff.

Public confidence in the scheme was further eroded by payment of performance bonuses to CEOs of controversial CHEs, at a time when surgical operations and services had been suspended for lack of funds and operating theatres and wards remained idle. Board members and CEOs who were not prepared to work within the government's constraints resigned or were sacked. The international reputation of the health system also began to decline. In 1994 the Australian Medical Council reported risks of 'a climate in which the essential elements of collegiality, quality health care and education are impossible to maintain' and warned that New Zealand graduates faced losing their favoured status in Australia.[21]

With the RHAs and CHEs focused on reactive services and profits, critics expressed concern that preventive health issues would fall through the cracks. This was reinforced when the Public Health Commission was disestablished and reintegrated into the core health ministry in mid-1995, having incurred the displeasure of corporate interests with its campaigns against tobacco and alcohol. Reports of diseases associated with poverty—tuberculosis, scurvy and rickets—also reappeared. On the other hand, the new regime allowed the development of innovative primary health care programmes, especially by Maori, whom institutionalised Pakeha health services had failed.

There were strong suspicions that privatisation was the real agenda behind the health restructuring process. The original proposals in the 1991 budget discussion paper had included a controversial option for consumers to transfer their health care entitlement to private health care plans. Critics warned that, once those in the top strata of society lost their involvement in the public health system, service to the rest would be undermined too. Private health insurers would benefit from increased patronage and the sale of under-used state assets, including run-down public hospitals earning less than they were 'worth'. The logical destination was a privatised health and hospital system based on the American system of vouchers, redeemable through public and private health care providers—an outcome urged in a report prepared for the Business Roundtable by CS First Boston, who were also consultants to the Interim Provider Board which set the new system in place.[22]

The Roundtable argued that private health plans should take over many of the RHA's functions, with income tax 'scaled back as consumers accept responsibility for their health costs directly and via compulsory insurance premiums'. Government would remain responsible for public health and regulatory functions which it was best equipped to undertake. The CHEs should also be privatised to improve efficiency and promote competition. In the Roundtable's eyes, health was simply another commodity to be bought and sold on the level playing-field of its particular market-place.

> Recent criticism of modest moves to increase health charges ignores the information which is conveyed by the pricing mechanism and the value of this in deciding what goods and services should be produced and consumed. A centralised agency cannot hope to make decisions which accurately reflect the interests and preferences of a diverse population. It is vital that the price mechanism be employed in the health sector so that better value is obtained for the consumer's dollar.[23]

The government's health care entitlement plan was set aside in 1992 owing to concerns that the RHAs would be left with the high-risk patients, along with logistical problems of assessing individual entitlement and overall health needs, and planning integrated services. But increased private control of the health care system remained on the agenda. The new regime increasingly resembled the health maintenance organisations of the United States, where providers were contracted or subcontracted to cover the primary and secondary health requirements of those on their register. A bulk funding scheme for general practitioners was seen as the first step.

Private health insurance had already increased dramatically and was providing a significant new source of capital for the insurance companies. In 1994 investment corporation and asset-stripper Brierley Investments (BIL) bought half of Aetna Health (NZ) from its US owners. A company run by BIL's founder Ron Brierley bought MedicAid, New Zealand's second-largest health insurer, and sold it seven months later to Aetna at a handsome profit,[24] giving BIL access to an even larger pool of cash.

Health policy analyst Geoff Fougere predicted that an increasing reliance on private insurance would leave the state directly responsible only for those unable to insure themselves. 'Caught between continuing fiscal pressure and the disproportionate rise in health-care costs, the state defines downwards the core it guarantees to everyone. Meanwhile its own regulatory role is increasingly compromised.' Government's motivation to intervene would be reduced because it had less fiscal stake in the system, while new pressure groups would lobby to protect and enhance their opportunities for profit within the privatised framework. 'Overall the system evolves toward a high-cost, low-efficiency outcome with wide differences in health-care entitlement. New Zealand again becomes an international showcase, but of a different kind.'[25]

Education

There was no groundswell of dissatisfaction with the education system to justify reform. In 1982 the OECD review of New Zealand education policy found 'to an extent greater than in some other OECD countries the parents, citizens, employees and workers of New Zealand appear to be reasonably well pleased with what is done for them in schools, colleges and universities.'[26]

Treasury thought otherwise, and dedicated the entire second volume of *Government Management* to education restructuring. Its 'devolutionary' goals were to rationalise the costly and inefficient educational bureaucracy, eliminate the 'provider capture' of the teacher unions over education policy and practice, and increase parental choice and voice. This meant opening education to the competitive market-place. The groundwork was done by the Picot review of education administration in 1987,[27] which reported to the ministers of finance and state services as well as education—an early indication that the restructuring of education would be driven primarily by the Treasury and SSC.

The new regime known as Tomorrow's Schools was introduced in the Education Act 1989. The funder/regulator/provider split saw several new agencies created, all reporting independently to the minister:

- a streamlined Ministry of Education to oversee policy development and funding;
- an Education Review Office to audit schools, including curriculum implementation;
- a Teacher Registration Board to register professional standards of teachers;
- a Parent Advocacy Council to convey community views to the minister (abolished in 1991); and
- the New Zealand Qualifications Authority (NZQA) to monitor post-compulsory education qualifications.

The restructuring was underpinned by three contradictory goals: a deregulated, artificially constructed education market, where education was a commodity subjected to the rigours of supply and demand; the development of a highly skilled and technologically literate population, which required a centralised, skills-based approach; and community participation, diversity and accountability, which demanded effective democratic input into decisions on policy, operations and resources.[28]

At the primary and secondary school levels responsibility to administer fixed annual budgets was devolved to local elected school boards. The boards would operate within ministerially approved charters. These began as contracts between the community and the institution, and the institution and the state, who together formed a 'partnership'. But the standard charter required highly directive and non-negotiable commitments from the boards, so the community was effectively cut out. The government made no guarantee of funds in return. Regional educational service functions were privatised. Schools were required to contract with private providers for curriculum advice and support, special education services and teacher development and training. What the boards could not afford from their shrinking annual budgets they would seek to raise from 'voluntary' student fees.

National's revised education policy combined decentralisation and choice with fiscal restraint. The school-leaving age was raised to sixteen, but budgets did not expand to compensate. Zoning was abolished. School boards were allowed to limit enrolments in certain conditions. Compulsory teacher registration was removed as an attempt to cut administration costs and allow hard-up schools to employ cheaper, untrained staff. Funding to private schools was doubled. Neither school trustees nor the teachers' unions were consulted on the changes.

Removal of zoning was meant to reallocate students to available places according to supply and demand, with high-achieving schools expanding as failures closed. The government's reluctance to fund new schools in growth areas produced overcrowding and shortages. There was no legal right to attend the nearest school, meaning that some children either fell outside all their local schools' self-defined enrolment zones or found that all available places had been filled. Parents in wealthy suburbs complained there was no guarantee that their children could attend the prestige local state school, with consequences for both education and property values. The influx of wealthy Asian migrants with minimal English skills, and the lack of any government assistance programmes, saw moves to introduce residence and language tests. In poor suburbs, the realities of transport costs, after-school care and commitment to community condemned many children to local schools, which became increasingly run-down. A two-tier system of rich and poor schools emerged. Schools increasingly relied on fees 'donations' from parents. These varied from over $100 down to around $15 per student in different parts of the country.[29] Many schools looked to other innovative, and in some cases dubious, sources of funds.

National was determined to introduce full bulk funding, whereby school boards would receive a single grant to spend on operational expenses, including salaries, as they saw fit. The teachers' unions attacked this as a device to break down their collective awards and cut costs. Schools in wealthy areas could draw on parent and community resources to top up their grants, while poorer schools would face larger classes, less qualified teachers, and decisions on which educational essentials to go without. The scheme was aggressively promoted by the Business Roundtable and its ally, the Education Forum:[30]

> full budgetary self-management and devolution of the employment role would enable schools to reward performance and to adjust remuneration to reflect supply and demand in the relevant locality. The education union-led opposition to bulk funding is indicative of the extent to which the interests of parents and students have been subordinate to those employed within the system. The abolition of zoning and compulsory

teacher registration is also consistent with the desired direction of policy.[31]

Strenuous opposition from teachers, school boards and teachers' unions saw the scheme deferred. But it re-surfaced in stages. In July 1992, legislation to allow bulk funding for salaries of senior staff with administrative responsibilities was introduced without consultation. A trial of 70 volunteer schools showed that the views of management, parents and teachers were still deeply polarised after three years.[32] Despite this, in early 1995 the minister announced plans to give all boards a choice between full bulk funding and the existing system in the coming year. This was confirmed in the 1995 budget.

In the name of devolution, the state had divested itself of responsibility and accountability for the delivery of educational services. Failure to meet parent, student and community expectations became the problem of the school boards. Some had the skills and private funding to take full advantage of the competitive liberated environment. Others found it impossible to cope, and had difficulty attracting enough nominations for the second round of elections in 1995. There were frequent complaints that effective educational planning was being undermined by the lack of an educational bureaucracy and the fragmented, unco-ordinated structure of administration and schools. Continued budget restraints compounded the problems.

Again, Maori gained some advantages from the decentralised approach. By 1995 a vertically integrated system of Maori language immersion teaching, which had been designed and nurtured by tribes and urban communities, operated at pre-school, primary, secondary and tertiary levels. But tensions remained as the government insisted on the right to determine qualification standards and administrative structures, and retained ultimate control in return for providing educational funds.

The tensions between market-driven education and the government's need to ensure an appropriately skilled future workforce remained. Once the education bureaucracy had been dismantled and decentralised, central state control progressively re-emerged. The government's blueprint for a new curriculum and educational framework was set out in *Education for the 21st Century* in 1994. A 'seamless education' system would operate through a 'qualifications framework' which allowed people to build up credentials throughout their lives. NZQA would develop a system of 'unit standards' for each level, to be provided by approved delivery agents. Under the new framework, the boundaries between different levels of educational institutions would become flexible, with senior schools able to offer courses previously available only at universities and polytechnics, and an increasing emphasis on on- and off-work trade training. The framework was to be in place by 1996.

The new curriculum was refocused to meet the future needs of an internationally competitive economy, with specifications to be developed by users (students and industry) and funders (the government). Teachers were excluded. Educationalist Joce Jesson records: 'Curriculum direction was now dependent on politicians, and backroom networks of influence. There are increased professional requirements for teachers at the classroom level, but teachers have lost their professional voice at the national level.'[33] Teachers' unions were reduced from being professional partners in educational development to bargaining agents seeking to protect the wages and conditions of their members in negotiations with the fiscally driven SSC. The curriculum framework raised another paradox. 'Picking winners' was anathema to advocates of non-interventionism. The government's targeted curriculum highlighted the failure of the artificial education market, and the increasingly selective exercise of government control disguised as increasing student choice.

Polytechnics and industry training organisations were incorporated into the qualifications framework administered by NZQA. The universities insisted on maintaining academic freedom and excellence and resisted attempts to impose central government control over accreditation of their degrees. Proposals to locate on the framework all tertiary qualifications offered by accredited providers, and to remove requirements that students undertake a course of study at a particular institution, threatened to replace university degrees with a mix-and-match of unit standards taken across a range of institutions.[34] Government proposals to replace university councils with ministerially appointed boards, to impose capital charging for university assets and to introduce flexible funding (vouchers) for tertiary students were fought equally hard.

Tertiary institutions were forced to become more commercial and competitive.[35] Government funding per funded tertiary student fell by 6.7 percent between 1990 and 1995, with the greatest cuts for colleges of education.[36] Institutions carried significant numbers of unfunded students. The shortfall was met by student fees. Labour imposed a uniform fee on tertiary students in 1989. National replaced this with a 'Study Right' fees subsidy directed primarily at young students taking their first degree. Tertiary institutions were left to decide whether or not to cross-subsidise more expensive courses and older students not in receipt of the full Study Right grant (which most did), and what level of fees to charge. Following a controversial review of tertiary education funding in 1994,[37] National announced government contributions to fees of funded students would be reduced to 75 percent of government-estimated costs by 2000.

Universal allowances for students aged 20 or over were replaced in 1991 by strict targeting. For unmarried students under 25, eligibility was based on joint parental income, whether or not they were living at home or came from a non-university town. Students over 25 would receive the equivalent of the adult unemployment benefit, income-tested on their own and any spouse's income.[38]

An income-contingent loan scheme for students operated at near-market rates, and imposed onerous repayment conditions. Repayments started when the former student was earning less than half the average wage, compared with around the average wage in Australia. The repayment rate was set at 10 percent of income above the threshold, compared with 1, 2 or 4 percent in Australia. Economist Susan St John explained the regressive effect of the scheme: 'Lower income earners will repay for longer and will pay a higher proportion of their lifetime income than will high income earners. The poor will also face high marginal tax rates for longer, and perhaps for ever. Some women may never pay any of their loans back if they marry and have children. They may well be discouraged from part-time work of any significance by the high marginal tax rates they face.'[39]

Housing

Housing, unlike education and health, was not viewed as a universal social entitlement. Around 70 percent of New Zealanders (along with their banks) traditionally owned their homes, although the rate was much lower among single-parent and Maori families. Nevertheless, the state house was a revered symbol of the welfare state.

Labour's early housing policy was a mixed affair. The accommodation benefit was increased in 1985 and broadened to cover low income earners as well as beneficiaries. The Residential Tenancies Act in 1986 provided new guarantees to tenants, although it also required a four-week bond to be lodged with a government agency which increased the cost of entry. However, funding for the Housing Corporation, which funded the purchase and construction of houses, declined from 1984 to 1987.

In 1988, under a new minister, the policy became more progressive. Labour made a commitment to house an increased proportion of clients who had serious housing need. The target rose from under 50 percent in 1987/88 to 80 percent in 1989/90 and was slightly higher by July 1991.[40] Labour also boosted the state housing stock and restricted sales. Low interest loans for low income families were increased, although they were sharply targeted to the very poor and tax rebates for mortgage interest were removed. Equity sharing and sweat equity schemes were floated. The Housing Corporation began to address issues of concern to Maori and Pacific Island tenants.

Labour's economic policies undercut these advances. Financial deregulation and monetary policy meant high interest rates, a speculative boom and bust in the property market, and removal of lending subsidies available through state banks. Recession and unemployment forced many home-owners into debt and mortgagee sales. Corporatisation destroyed employment and slashed property values in many small towns and rural communities; yet many of those affected could not afford to sell and move. All this deepened dependency on state support and compounded the housing problem.

National's solution was to transfer responsibility for housing to the private market, either directly or through a fully commercialised SOE. Historically, state house rentals had been pegged at 25 percent of the tenant's income. The 1991 budget announced that rents would be raised to their full market value in three annual increments. The increase would be partly compensated for by a cash accommodation supplement for low income families. This could be used for private or state housing rents, or mortgages from the Housing Corporation or commercial lenders. The supplement would replace all other forms of government housing assistance and be administered by the DSW. A report prepared for the government by the Infometrics consultancy in 1991 warned of the tension between commercial and social housing objectives and suggested softening plans for full market rents. The government not only refused, but later added a tough assets test to limit the cost of the new supplement. In return, it agreed to limit yearly rent increases to $20 a week, although this appears to have been exceeded in the final round.

The market-driven strategy was not unexpected. The state had progressively reduced its role in lending, from half of all new home lending in the 1970s to under 4 percent in 1991. The Housing Corporation's budget had already been cut by $110 million in the December 1990 economic statement. The housing minister, another of National's technopols, was sympathetic to a privatised housing market. Treasury had been promoting a local version of the US housing coupon system for several years.

The uncompromising approach of the restructured Housing New Zealand (HNZ)[41] attracted constant bad publicity. In late 1992, for example, it sought to evict a sole-parent mother who had lived in her state house for almost twelve years, and who was one week behind in repayment of rent arrears. The DSW had suspended her benefit pending production of a birth certificate. Ruling in the woman's favour, the court observed: 'This case is brought against a background of grinding poverty, a case of a woman with young children being sought to be evicted from her home for what I consider a venial breach. . . . I consider it unduly harsh if the appellant was to lose her home because of some misunderstanding with the Social Welfare department which was her only source of income.'[42]

HNZ's 1994 annual report showed its tenants paid 54 percent more in rent in 1994 than in 1993, while social welfare figures in October 1994 showed a ten-fold increase in numbers receiving the accommodation supplement.[43] Market forces of supply and demand were meant to ensure sufficient accommodation at acceptable standards. In practice, the accommodation supplement proved inadequate as housing shortages in areas of high demand forced rentals to rise. Yet the relocation costs of removals, supply connections, Telecom, rental and power bonds and school uniforms meant that poor families could not afford to move to another part of the country. An estimated 7000 state tenants were expected to quit their state houses with the onset of full market rentals in 1995. The 1994 budget announced that more state rental houses would be sold to existing tenants, potentially reducing the government's stock, although the onerous terms of sale meant that very few deals went through.

A damning Ministry of Housing report in March 1994 calculated that between 20,000 and 30,000 households were in serious housing need, the overwhelming majority of which were single people.[44] Half the total were living in inadequate conditions and half in unaffordable housing (defined as housing which consumed more than half the income of a low income household, including the accommodation supplement). Those paying rent in the private sector faced the greatest affordability problems.

The Treasury portrayed the strategies of devolution, targeting and competition as liberating the individual from the oppression of the central state; the Salvation Army condemned a housing policy which forced people with no discretionary income to cut back on essentials as 'taking from the poor to give to the poor'.[45]

Phase 3: Fiscal responsibility

Labour had failed to cut spending effectively. While the budget deficit as a proportion of GDP fell from over 5 percent in 1984/85 to just over 1 percent in 1989/90, that was due to increased revenue, not reduced expenditure. The demand-based nature of government spending, especially on social services, made it difficult to control without changing levels of benefits and eligibility. The best Labour could do was to moderate the increase by greater administrative controls on expenditure. This meant net government expenditure as a percentage of GDP (both adjusted for one-off items) rose from 35.9 percent in 1984/85 to 39.2 percent in 1989/90.[46]

The proportion spent on social benefits increased each year, reaching over 61 percent of adjusted total government expenditure in 1989/90, although some of this was recouped in tax. Education and health experienced real increases too. This reflected greater demand rather than government profligacy. The number of over-60 year olds had increased 10 percent between 1970 and 1990, with a serious impact on superannuation and health care costs. Unemployment beneficiaries rose from 20,850 in 1979/80 to 139,625 in 1989/90. Numbers on domestic purposes and sickness benefits also increased. Greater demand saw average annual increases in university funding from 1984/85 to 1988/89 of 5.8 percent, yet funding per student fell 1.9 percent. By contrast, the Housing Corporation budget fell quite dramatically during Labour's first four years, being less even in nominal terms in 1987/88 than in 1984/85.[47]

Labour faced continued deficit problems as the economy continued to stagnate. Falling profits and income tax receipts, generous tax credits to purchasers of several state assets, and creative accounting in the deregulated financial environment saw the tax take fall. The shortfall was funded by debt. Net public debt rose from $21,879 million in 1984 to $39,721 million in 1989. Privatisation offered one source of cash and debt repayment, but the depreciating exchange rate largely neutralised that. Raising income taxes was ideologically out of the question. The alternative promoted by Treasury and the Roundtable was a rigorous round of spending cuts, with social welfare the main target. The Labour government's approach was much more piecemeal, explained as economic necessity and never on ideological grounds.

A progressive income-related surcharge on universal superannuation had been imposed in 1985 to claw back from those on higher incomes. In 1989 superannuation was renamed the Guaranteed Retirement Income (GRI) and indexed to wages and prices. The eligibility age was to increase gradually from 60 to 65. Prescription charges were increased and health subsidies cut. State house rentals were gradually raised and houses provided to government employees in railways, works, forestry and education were put up for sale. Social security benefits were taxed, although the real level remained the same. The unemployment benefit was abolished for those under eighteen. A flat fee was imposed on students at tertiary institutions.

Labour's Minister of Social Welfare boasted in March 1990 that they had cut benefits by at least $800 million a year, with $150 million from changes to indexation, $300 million from the superannuation surcharge, $58 million from accommodation benefit changes, $25 million from benefit control units, $57 million from superannuation changes for those whose spouses did not qualify, $23 million from changes to youth unemployment, $7 million from school-leaver stand-down and $200 million from other measures.[48] A comprehensive review of social spending in 1990 culminated in proposals to base social security eligibility on the single adult as the norm. This would have reduced the income levels of many beneficiaries, particularly single parents and Maori, although others would have been better off. Labour lost the election before the policy came into effect.

In its 1990 briefing, Treasury acknowledged: 'after two years of a faltering recovery New Zealand still faces the prospect of slow growth. The outlook is for rising unemployment, increased debt, and more people becoming dependent on the state or limited in their opportunities. To become a high-income, high-employment economy is a massive challenge. We are off target.' Far from taking responsibility for the policy failures of the preceding years, Treasury laid the blame in part on adverse events and trends in the world economy. 'Much of it, however, is the consequence of domestic economic and social policies that lack harmony.'[49] In other words, social policies and government spending had to be brought into line with the prevailing market model.

Government's primary goal, Treasury argued, should be to improve its net worth—its total assets minus total liabilities—and avoid increasing debt unless assets increased too. Once inflation came under control and stopped depreciating debt, the government would need to spend less just to maintain the same net worth. Positively improving its net position would require significant fiscal cuts. This would allow the government to reduce debt and the future tax burden, and free investment for private activities with higher return. It would also enhance inter-generational equity.

While budget balance had improved since 1984, the deficit was still too high. Treasury urged a comprehensive reappraisal of government spending on existing institutions and policies, especially health, education and social welfare. Inefficiencies, it argued, worked against the poor and unemployed by depriving them of the benefits of economic recovery. Meanwhile, a lack of incentives prevented people from achieving dignity, security and participation in society. The solutions lay in redesigned benefit policies, incentives to reduce state dependency, and targeted assistance to the deserving poor.

Immediately after the 1990 election, National set about ruthlessly cutting the benefit base. An inflation adjustment which Labour had promised to beneficiaries, including superannuitants, was withdrawn, making the real effect of the cuts even more severe. Ruth Richardson's December 1990 economic statement announced that the single adult rate for the dole would be reduced by almost $14 a week. Against departmental advice, the stand-down for the 'voluntarily' unemployed—including those who refused two job offers, or failed to attend an arranged job interview—was increased from six weeks to six months. The age for youth rate benefits was raised from 20 to 25, meaning an income drop from $143 to $108 a week for those affected, or 24.7 percent. Social Welfare Minister Jenny Shipley explained: 'generally younger single people are competing for jobs which attract lower wages and they generally have more ability to change their circumstances'.[50] Widows and domestic purposes beneficiaries suffered cuts of 9 to 16 percent as an 'incentive' to become self-supporting. The universal family benefit was abolished, removing many women's only independent source of family income. Targeted family support was increased by an equal amount to compensate low income families, the first rise since October 1986. Subsidies for doctors visits were cut, and prescription charges trebled.

Economist Dennis Rose expressed the common belief that the 'deficit reducing measures introduced in the 1990 post-election package impacted through reductions in consumer demand, upon output, market incomes and, ultimately, on tax revenues in ways which worsened rather than improved the fiscal balance'.[51] The severity of the recession and the rising demand for income support, coupled with the tailing-off of asset sales, made it hard to hold the fiscal line. But National's zealots were determined to reduce government spending as a proportion of GDP and repay overseas debt. Spending cuts continued to corrode the welfare base. Some of the harshest rules were blunted, but only after desperate cases had provoked a public outcry.

Prime Minister Jim Bolger described the cuts as 'necessary short-term sacrifices'. Richardson claimed they 'would increase the "rewards" for moving from welfare to work'.[52] This concept of incentives was perverse. Lower tax rates for the rich had been justified as increasing incentives to earn. That rationale was ignored when it came to the high equivalent marginal tax rate (EMTR) which rigid targeting and abatement imposed on the poor. There were explicit warnings of more to come—in particular, user charges for health and education for the top third of all income earners. These, alongside the radical restructuring of health, housing, accident compensation and social welfare policy and further cuts to departmental votes, emerged in Richardson's 'mother of all budgets' in 1991.

The 1992/93 fiscal deficit showed the effects of such dramatic cuts. Spending had been held below budgeted levels, removing the need for supplementary estimates. Debt servicing was lower than expected. However, tax receipts also continued to fall relative to GDP. The 1993 budget further constrained government spending, with a projected deficit of $2.3 billion or 2.8 per cent of GDP. Just before the 1993 election this prediction was lowered to 1.8 percent. The June 1994 budget announced that a surplus of $527 million had been achieved. Faster economic and income growth had meant higher tax receipts, with accumulated tax losses from the later 1980s almost exhausted. Renewed spending had increased the GST take. Government spending cuts and lower social welfare costs, notably for the unemployment benefit, reduced expenditure. Debt servicing costs also fell as declining domestic and international interest rates re-

duced government borrowing and the New Zealand dollar strengthened. The government predicted a budget surplus for 1994/95 of
$730 million.

This budget surplus could have been used in four ways:

- to compensate those who had suffered disproportionately in the
  structural adjustment process;
- to cut taxes as incentives to earn, save and invest;
- to repay debt; and/or
- to invest in assets and infrastructure.

Many expected that increased economic growth and any budget
surplus would flow through to more generous support for those who
had paid the greatest price. In the 1994 budget, finance minister Bill
Birch declared that a 'social dividend' would be allocated between
health, education, welfare, housing and employment to help restore
the social infrastructure and compensate for the years of pain. But
the Treasury successfully argued that fiscal policy was a vital part of
monetary policy and required a continued tight rein. A generous
social dividend was ruled out. In what *NBR* commentator Colin James
called 'surely one of the most cynical of the public relations ruses
dreamt up for Bolger over the past four years',[53] the 'dividend'
amounted in total to $375 million. For a single mother with two
children whose domestic purposes benefit had been cut in 1991 by
$26 a week, it meant an extra $3 a week.[54]

The option of lowering taxes was rejected by the purists as fuelling economic growth and inflation, despite the technocrats' earlier
enthusiasm for flattening the tax rate. But the tax option had considerable political appeal. Despite strong opposition from some in caucus, the government offered the tantalising prospect of tax cuts in
1996/97, coinciding with the next scheduled election, provided the
fiscal reins were held tight.

Investment in assets by a government committed to privatisation
was never an option. Nor was any serious attention paid to rebuilding
the neglected and under-funded parts of the country's physical infrastructure. Neo-liberal orthodoxy dictated that a budget surplus
should be used to reduce the level of net debt to GDP, and decrease
the vulnerability to international trends in interest rates, terms of
trade and exchange rates to which New Zealand had been increasingly exposed. Ironically, exchange rate appreciation wiped $2.3 bil-
lion off the debt in the December quarter of 1994.

As income from the recovery continued to flow, the predicted surplus was revised upwards from $1.3 billion (now calculated in accrual terms) to $2.3 billion. National promised an extra $200 million for priority areas like education and welfare. Much of that, it turned out, was assistance already announced. Other concessions were minimal. Families that were accepted by DSW as being $20 short on basic weekly income had been able to apply for a special benefit, but perversely were required to meet the first $20 shortfall between their income and expenditure themselves. The government now reduced that contribution from $20 to $10, with entitlement to be reviewed every three months.

At the same time, the government announced that 16- and 17-year-olds would lose access to the student allowance, sickness benefit, job search allowance and training benefits from January 1996. More than 8000 youths currently received those benefits. To compensate, family support would increase by $13 a week for each affected child. The government promised more money for schools which had to cope with more students, but gave no guarantees. Some were prepared to accept the government's justification of improving educational skills, but worried about the pressure on schools already under stress. Others saw it as a cynical device to absorb unemployed youth, reduce official unemployment rates and cut the costs of benefit support.

Fiscal Responsibility Act 1994

National's technopols were intent on locking in their policy of fiscal restraint. In the 1993 budget, finance minister Ruth Richardson announced 'a new initiative for honest and open government' which would require governments to report on their long-term fiscal objectives and progress towards achieving them.[55] In theory, the move dated back to the Labour government's refusal at the 1990 election to disclose the imminent need for a bail-out of the BNZ. In response to a complaint from the new National government, the Chief Ombudsman recommended that an authenticated non-political survey of the state of the economy should be prepared jointly by the Secretary to the Treasury, the Government Statistician and one independent person, and published prior to each election.

In reality, the Fiscal Responsibility Act (FRA) was designed to embed the current fiscal strategy of budget surpluses, repayment of debt, privatisation and low taxation in law. The measure emerged in two stages. The original version introduced in September 1993 adopted the 'New Zealand Inc' model. This treated government as a private sector business, subject to the 'neutral' constraints of market measures and commercial accountability, with financial accounts to match. By the time the Act was passed in July 1994 it had imposed a positive requirement to maintain a surplus-driven, low debt regime.

The detailed work by Treasury and Richardson began during preparation for the 1993 budget. Treasury argued that short-term fiscal thinking, driven by influential groups and electoral politics, was biased against sound economic principles. This led to increased borrowing, debt risks, inter-generational inequity and inefficient allocation of resources. Longer-term fiscal stability would ensure sustainable economic growth, increase certainty for investors and build confidence in the economy. The onus should therefore shift onto those wishing to depart from sound fiscal principles to justify their case.

Relying on Cabinet procedures and commitments was too weak to achieve this. While the Cabinet Economic Committee had improved fiscal discipline, and coalition agreements under MMP would probably have a constraining effect, compliance would still depend on political will. Richardson wanted legislated targets for expenditure and debt. Treasury disagreed. Targets risked becoming ends in themselves and invited deceptive reporting. They lost credibility when they were not achieved, and tended to be effective at times of fiscal crisis but weak in times of growth. They could also be reversed, although again this might become more difficult under MMP. Even specifying fiscal objectives or dimensions of credible fiscal policy would be hard.

Treasury preferred requirements to disclose fiscal information, targets and results along the lines of the Reserve Bank Act. Fixing them in legislation would raise their symbolic importance. This approach also had a greater chance of surviving electoral change and MMP, and would be difficult for any party to argue against. 'A broad legislative framework for reporting fiscal objectives could encourage the bi-partisan evolution of reporting practice that might prove more "entrenched" than if it were to be unilaterally imposed by highly specific legislation.'[56]

The legislation would aim to 'increase the constituency for fiscal discipline'. Treasury argued that effective constraints on future governments would depend on convincing those who influenced electoral opinion—political parties, media, business and union leaders—of the economic costs and social implications of loosening fiscal restraint. The 'fundamental force underlying the success or failure of any particular mechanism is electoral preferences. In the long term, public and political awareness of the implications of fiscal imbalance and expenditure patterns is likely to underlie any effective "entrenchment" of sound principles of consistent fiscal policy in New Zealand.'[57]

Treasury saw the proposed Act as part of a package deal.

> The last few years have seen a number of steps taken to improve the quality of fiscal management. These include the reforms to SOEs, the State Sector Act, the Public Finance Act, and the Reserve Bank Act. These reforms have been supported by better budget processes, greater fiscal transparency, more frequent fiscal updates and the development of the Crown Balance Sheet.[58]

The Public Finance Act already required departments to produce corporate plans, provide a range of purchase and ownership information to select committees, account for outputs and, most recently, to prepare purchase agreements. But politicians complained the financial information they received was not user-friendly. The mass of information already being produced could be revamped to provide high-quality documentation under the new Act.

The Fiscal Responsibility Bill formalised a number of reporting requirements, most of which had recently become common practice:

- monthly expenditure and revenue out-turns for the year to date;
- a fiscal update for the current fiscal year, tabled with the supplementary estimates;
- economic and fiscal updates and three-year forecasts prepared by the Treasury, and published with the budget and in December of each year. As a minimum, economic forecasts would cover movements in GDP, including consumer price, unemployment and employment, and the balance of payments' current account position. Fiscal forecasts would cover at least the end-of-year financial position, forecast revenue and expenses, cashflows, borrowings and other statements deemed necessary to reflect fairly the financial position;
- a report on the government's ten-year fiscal strategy outlined along with the budget. This would include annual fiscal objectives for expenditure, revenue, budget balance and government debt, and the general policy by which they would be achieved;
- a fiscal and economic update, produced by the Treasury and published between 42 and 28 days before an election along the lines of that prepared for the budget.

Technical changes to the preparation and presentation of Crown financial statements, including the introduction of accrual accounting, were also proposed. The new requirements were anticipated by National in the 1994 budget.

The Auditor-General questioned the relative costs and benefits of so many reports, especially the monthly financial statement. Treasury responded that: 'The financial markets and economic analysts advise that they make heavy use for their own forecasting purposes of the information provided monthly. . . . Many of the benefits of regular reporting, e.g. a better informed electorate, are however intangible and unquantifiable.'[59] If one assumes the latter would be well enough served by quarterly reports, the provision of detailed financial information at taxpayer expense was basically a subsidy to the financial service sector. While this was anathema to the philosophy of user-pays, in the market-driven economy financial analysts had become an indispensable adjunct to government.

The Bill was introduced unopposed. Early political response was subdued. Labour said it merely legislated current practice, and required no commitments to a balanced budget, on-going macro-economic policy settings or a specific revenue strategy. The Alliance welcomed the measure in general, but took exception to the Treasury's role. Leader Jim Anderton observed:

> In recent years Treasury has adopted an ideological and highly politicised stance in financial and economic matters, and in my view it has monopolised, in an unbalanced way, the advice that has been given to successive Labour Governments and National Governments. If the Government really wanted to have a genuine opening-of-the-books exercise, it would have been prepared to invite the participation of independent analysts who were independent of Treasury and/or the Reserve Bank . . .[60]

Before the powerful Finance and Expenditure Select Committee (FEC) could hear submissions, the 1993 election intervened. Richardson was deposed as Minister of Finance after the election. But she was made chair of the FEC and tightened the reins on the Bill. She still wanted specific debt targets, a formula which tied future governments to a budget surplus, and new principles of fiscal responsibility set down in law. The Business Roundtable's submission was almost identical. Sympathetic economists invited to give evidence before the committee gave enthusiastic support to Richardson's proposals. Treasury reported that 'a number' of select committee members also expressed concern that 'the present neutral language . . . was too permissive'. They supported a tightening of objectives, and the automatic referral of all reports to the FEC, as the Reserve Bank Act required.[61] New finance minister Bill Birch played his part, asking Treasury to report on strengthening the fiscal objectives. Treasury set its earlier reservations aside, and advised that more explicit fiscal objectives would increase fiscal credibility and investor confidence with the advent of MMP. But it was still opposed to legislated targets.

Three new provisions emerged: a more directive clause set out the principles of fiscal responsibility; a budget policy statement would be required prior to the budget itself, enabling debate on overall fiscal policy to be separated from detailed budget allocations; and the major reports tabled under the Act would be referred to the FEC for review and report-back prior to completion of the budget debate. The changes, approved by Cabinet and caucus, were conveyed to the select committee as a statement of government policy.

The Bill as reported back, and subsequently passed, required compliance with five stated principles of 'fiscal responsibility':

- reducing public debt to 'prudent' levels by running budget surpluses;
- maintaining 'prudent' levels of public debt by achieving a budget surplus on average over a 'reasonable' period of time;
- achieving and maintaining the Crown's net worth at a level that would provide a buffer against adverse conditions;
- prudent management of the fiscal risks of the Crown; and
- pursuit of policies which would provide reasonable predictability about the level and stability of tax rates.

Governments could depart temporarily from these criteria, but they had to explain why, how they would return to the stated principles, and when. Prudence was not defined, but was expected take account of numerous factors: the structure of the economy, its degree of vulnerability, the strength of the Crown's balance sheet, the credit rating of sovereign debt, the financial strength of the country's competitors and demographic factors. The Crown Law Office advised that compliance with the five principles was likely to be seen as 'high policy' and not subject to judicial review.

The criteria for select committee review were to be set out in new sessional orders, not in the Act, making them less visible and shielding them, too, from judicial review.[62] The sessional orders which the government subsequently introduced, however, simply provided for consideration and reporting on the various documents with the opportunity for debate on their report back to the House; no criteria for review were specified.

The government played down the radical amendments as 'good housekeeping' provisions which had been endorsed by independent experts before the select committee. Labour had a different perspective. Finance speaker Michael Cullen complained that the Bill had been hijacked in the select committee by Richardson, some major business interests and one or two 'right-wing economists', including former Secretary to the Treasury Graham Scott.

> If we are to have a consensus about those principles, those changes themselves have to be the subject of public consultation and public submission. They have not been. . . . [A] small group of people were invited to make submissions on what was originally a rather narrow technical Bill. Even then some of them disagreed with the contents of the Bill, notably the two economists nominated by the Labour Opposition.[63]

The SOP setting out the details had been released before the select committee could consider any change. Cullen unsuccessfully moved an amendment which defined the objectives of fiscal policy as: sustainable economic growth; a more fair and equal society; full employment; and (somewhat contradictorily) an AAA credit rating. Moves to refer the Bill back to the select committee also failed. The government's controversial new clauses passed into law by a single vote.

An element of party politicking lay behind the Bill. National was determined to present itself as the natural party of government, especially as the electoral rules were about to change. It had built its credibility on reduced deficits and debt. With this established as the norm, National's opponents would have to endorse its strategy or justify their deviation. According to finance minister Bill Birch: 'Either way we gain.'[64]

Despite the provision in the Act for select committee review, critics foresaw political temptations to manipulate the forecasts. Over-ambitious targets and seriously inaccurate forecasts could be used to justify further spending cuts or asset sales, allowing governments to shift the blame. Given Treasury's role over the past decade, and its gravely inaccurate costings of the Labour opposition's manifesto proposals prior to the 1993 election,[65] the potential for Treasury to facilitate such outcomes caused genuine concern. The potential political benefits were already apparent from National's 1994 budget. The government had predicted sustained budget surpluses and unprecedented economic growth, and floated the prospect of tax cuts in the (safely distant) future. As one journalist observed, 'Mr Birch presented a joyous picture of wealth and happiness, a bit like those romantic landscapes in which the sun always shines on sturdy folk bringing in the bountiful harvest.'[66]

There were technical problems as well. Treasury's recent forecasting record was highly erratic. In the 1990 Budget it had forecast GDP growth for the coming year at 2.4 percent, but growth was less than 1 percent. In the 1991 budget Treasury predicted 0.8 percent growth. By December 1991 this had become an output decline of 1.3 percent. The predictions in the 1994 budget of 4.6 percent growth for 1995/96 and 3.5 percent the following year were highly speculative, and were subject to international developments, exchange rate levels, climatic conditions and moves by the Reserve Bank to dampen what it saw as excessive growth.

Treasury's deficit predictions were no better. For the 1992/93 year its estimates of the deficit were variously $1.6 billion (1990 budget), $4.5 billion (1990 post-election briefing papers), $686 million (1991 budget), back to $2.3 billion (1991 December economic statement), and $3.3 billion (1992 budget). The 1993 budget estimate of the actual deficit was $2.3 billion. For 1993/94 Treasury predicted deficits of $2.2 billion (1990 December economic statement), $528 million (1991 budget), up to $2.25 billion (1991 December statement) and still around $2.3 billion in the 1993 budget. The actual result was a surplus in 1993/94 of $527 million.[67] The 1994/95 figure, predicted as a deficit of $2 billion in the 1993 budget, became a surplus of $730 million in the 1994 budget, and was up to $2.3 billion by the end of year. These extreme fluctuations over very short time periods reinforced concerns about the amount of weight being placed on Treasury forecasts, and the need to involve genuinely independent analysts in the process.

Looking to the future

The subtext behind the FRA was the advent of MMP. In theory, a government could still pursue any set of social and economic outcomes it chose in a transparent, fiscally responsible way. It just had to persuade the politicians, economic and media commentators and electorate of its case. But Treasury argued: 'Whatever was in legislation would effectively become the minimum standards governments would have to observe.'[68] Government MPs were equally explicit about its effect: 'We all know that a Parliament cannot bind its successor. . . . Although any succeeding parliament can change legislation, I doubt whether any Government, with this Bill in place, would seek to do so.'[69] Credit rating agency Moody's agreed: 'The Fiscal Responsibility Act, which guarantees not only far greater fiscal transparency, but which also provides fiscal and economic benchmarks, will limit the actions of future governments regarding possible policy shifts.'[70]

Labour argued that binding future governments to a specific fiscal policy was 'constitutional nonsense', especially when done by a dying system of government to provide 'a form of legislative contraceptive for the MMP parliamentary system'.[71] The Employers' Federation chief executive countered such concerns with arguments of inter-generational equity: 'While some people may feel that it would be undemocratic to restrict the ability of political parties to introduce policies which lead to an expanded deficit, this fails to consider the costs to future generations of the failure to achieve and maintain budget balances.'[72]

The Fiscal Responsibility Act was passed three days before Richardson announced her resignation from Parliament. It had not legislated the fiscal targets as she had sought. But she could leave knowing that the policy mix she had helped put in place was now embedded in law. No future New Zealand government, without a major political struggle to repeal or amend the legislation, or defending its 'fiscal irresponsibility' against the powerful forces of the market, could deviate from that 'norm'.

PART THREE

THE DEFICIT

CHAPTER TEN

The Economic Deficit

By 1995 NEW ZEALAND'S 'turnaround economy' was being feted on the international stage. The short-term trends certainly looked impressive. The longer-term ones were much less so. This chapter puts the claims to 'economic success' since 1993 in perspective. It measures the impact of the structural adjustment programme on the domestic economy in terms of its key performance indicators, and examines the state of the economy after a decade of turbulent, radical change.

Key economic indicators

A balanced view of the economy should take into account a number of key indicators: economic growth, inflation, public debt, balance of payments, income distribution, employment and unemployment. New Zealand governments since 1984 have focused selectively on inflation and public debt and, less successfully, on employment. They have taken credit for rising growth and balance of payments improvements when those occurred, despite pursuing policies designed to dampen growth and to encourage foreign investment which, if successful, necessarily lead to rising balance of payments deficits. The issue of income distribution has simply been ignored.

Economic growth

New Zealand spent almost seven years of the experiment in stagnation and recession (see Figure 10.1). The average growth across OECD countries in the period 1985–92 was 20 percent. New Zealand's economy shrank by 1 percent over the same period.[1] The OECD calculates that New Zealand's real GDP in 1992 was still about 5 percent below its 1985/86 level. Although real GDP grew by nearly 5 percent in 1993, with an even higher rate for 1994,

OECD figures indicate that this recovery only brought GDP back in line with the long-term trend.[2] As a result of the economy's limited capacity and the Reserve Bank's recessionary policies, GDP growth was widely predicted to fall back to between 2 and 3 percent in the year to March 1996.[3]

FIGURE 10.1 Annual percentage changes in GDP 1984–94
Production indexes; December year, constant to 1982–83 prices

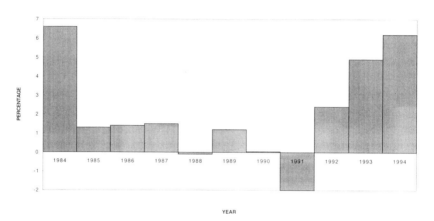

Source: Statistics New Zealand

This hiatus in growth will have long-term consequences. From 1955 to 1966 the New Zealand economy grew at about the OECD average rate. In the next decade growth was perceptibly slower, owing to falling terms of trade as export prices fell. The response was to diversify the economy from its pastoral base. From 1977 it again began to grow at around the OECD average rate; but the economy was now operating significantly below its level in 1966. In 1986 the growth paths diverged again. While OECD countries continued to grow, New Zealand stagnated, even though there was no fall in terms of trade. Economist Brian Easton questions the frequent attempts to blame this on the Muldoon government's Think Big projects. Although there were many deficiencies in Muldoon's policies, he nurtured the growth-generating external sector. The economic policies of Rogernomics seriously damaged the productive ability of the external sector, and slowed economic growth. Even if New Zealand were to grow again at the OECD rate the losses of 1986–93 would not be recovered—according to Easton, the economy would grow at a level 12 percent below that which prevailed when Labour came to power in 1984.[4]

Inflation

Contrary to monetarist expectations, the inflation rate had continued to climb as the Reserve Bank put the squeeze on interest rates after 1984 (see Figure 10.2). The CPI annual increases peaked at 19 percent in the June 1987 quarter following the introduction of GST and were still at 16.9 percent in September. Benchmark nominal 90-day bond interest rates rose to a high of 20.4 percent in June 1987, pushed up by a combination of factors: the high interest and exchange rate policy, deregulation of the financial markets and removal of constraint on capital flows, the speculative boom in equity and property markets, cavalier lending practices and continued high inflation. The contribution of the finance and business services sector to producer price inflation at this time was significantly greater than the impact of other sectors.

Inflation had plummeted to 9.6 percent by December 1987 as the effects of state sector salary increases and the introduction of GST wore off, and the stock-market crash dampened speculative investment. The recessionary environment of the late 1980s saw a continued decline in the CPI rate of increase, with some fluctuations, to a quarterly low of 0.8 percent in March 1992. The price of this was a high exchange rate, which lowered import and export prices and drove the country deeper into recession in 1991. The return to positive economic growth in 1993, due largely to the depreciated exchange rate, in turn increased inflationary pressures. But the Employment Contracts Act (ECA) and continued high unemployment helped keep wage increases well below increases in the CPI, and so the inflation rate remained below 2 percent in 1994.

As inflationary expectations began to rise, the Reserve Bank increasingly emphasised its measure of 'underlying' inflation. This enabled it to remain within the target range and continue to proclaim the monetary policy's success. In June 1995, however, the CPI increase hit an annual rate of 4.6 percent while the bank's 'underlying' rate of 2.2 percent for the year exceeded the permitted level. The strategy of 'talking to the markets' was no longer keeping interest rates as high as the Reserve Bank required. The bank was forced to intervene by cutting the settlement cash target several times in an attempt to raise interest and exchange rates and force inflation back down.

FIGURE 10.2 Inflation 1984–95 (annual percentage change)

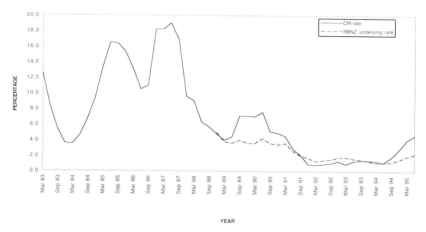

Sources: Statistics New Zealand; Reserve Bank of New Zealand

Debt

New Zealand's net public debt—gross debt offset by similar financial assets—was among the lowest in the OECD in the early 1970s. It grew dramatically during the Muldoon years and continued to increase at a rate well beyond the OECD average after his departure, peaking at 51 percent of GDP in 1992. In 1993 the lower deficit, strong exchange rate and asset sales reduced that to 42 percent, close to the OECD average. The 1995 budget reported net public debt had continued to fall to an estimated 38 percent of GDP. The government predicted further reductions to 33.6 percent at the end of the 1995/96 year, and below 30 percent of GDP by 1996/97.

The government had targeted overseas debt, with varying degrees of success, by asset sales and over-funding of domestic debt[5] since 1987. Net foreign currency debt had reduced from 44 percent of total public debt at June 1991 to an estimated 22.7 percent at June 1995 (see Figure 10.3). The government planned to have repaid all net foreign currency debt by June 1997. In the process of reducing overseas debt, however, the state's asset base, with the accompanying earnings flow and potential for hands-on control of the country's essential financial, transport, communications and natural resource infrastructure, had dissipated too.

New Zealand's total foreign debt rose from around $12 billion to over $67 billion in the decade to 1994 (see Figure 10.4). The private

FIGURE 10.3 **Foreign and domestic public debt 1984–94 (as at 31 March)**

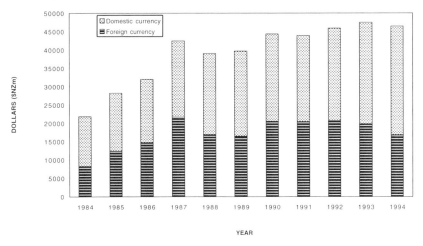

Source: *New Zealand Yearbook 1994*, Table 26.11

FIGURE 10.4 **Overseas debt 1989–94**
1989–93 as at 30 September; 1994 as at 30 June

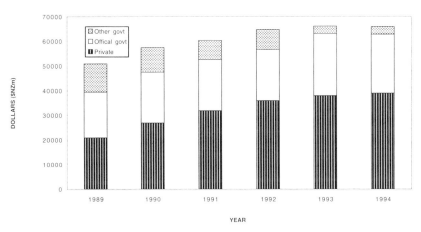

Source: *New Zealand Yearbook 1994*, Table 27.19; *1995*, 17.17

sector component of this (including debt from companies, financial institutions and producer boards, and foreign ownership of New Zealand companies which appeared as a liability because their profits were exported) increased significantly from 41 percent in 1989 to 59 percent in 1993, as an inevitable consequence of the structural adjustment programme. In the December quarter of 1994 total overseas debt fell by $1.4 billion to $65.8 billion. Official government overseas debt was $24.1 billion, with $2.4 billion in other government debt. Exchange rate gains of $2.3 billion had offset new borrowing by the private sector and increased overseas investment in New Zealand-issued securities.

Balance of payments

By 1994 New Zealand had run a current account deficit in 27 of the last 30 years (see Table 10.1). The level of the deficit fell substantially from 9 percent of GDP in 1985 to under 2 percent by 1993. Between 1987 and 1989 terms of trade improved.[6] Export volumes surged in the early 1990s, but slowed in 1992 and early 1993, due partly to a drought and an electricity crisis, and the effects of the world recession.

While the ratio of imports and exports to GDP had risen strongly since 1984, it was still several percent below the average for other small OECD countries in 1993–94. New Zealand's share of world trade dropped from around 1 percent in 1950 to 0.3 percent in 1993, although it held a major share of the world's sheepmeat and dairy markets.[7] Services (especially tourism), niche manufactures and forest products began to challenge agricultural and horticultural commodities as the country's dominant export-earners. Export markets were also diversified, with the UK's share of export revenues reduced from 53 percent in 1960 to 14.2 percent in 1980 and 6.4 percent in 1993. Exports to Australia increased from 12.6 percent of total exports in 1980 to almost 20 percent by 1993 as part of general economic integration. Asian countries accounted for 34.7 percent of export revenues in 1993, 40 percent of which went to Japan. The Asian share was up from 2.9 percent of export revenues in 1960 and 15.6 percent in 1970, but had not increased a great deal since the level of 31.1 percent reached in 1980—hence the government's enthusiasm to establish stronger links with Asia.[8]

As the economy emerged from recession after 1992 and the Reserve Bank forced interest and exchange rates to rise, the position of exporters continued to decline. Meanwhile, the recovery and high exchange rates saw imports grow rapidly. The external trade deficit for June 1995 was $409 million. Even after adjustment for a major aircraft purchase, the trade surplus was $414 million compared with

$1341 the previous year. By mid-1995 the balance of payments account had deteriorated significantly to a deficit of $3.3 billion. Exports were virtually static, while imports continued to grow, although at a slower rate. Whereas in the 1980s balance of payments deficits had been covered by overseas borrowing, they were now being met by overseas purchases of government stock and sale of New Zealand resources to foreign buyers, few of which added to the productive base of the economy—and the profits from which mostly went offshore.

Budget balance

Accompanying the belief that government could be run like any other business came an increasing obsession with balancing the books, irrespective of the economic and social consequences. Again, for most of the structural adjustment decade this policy failed. Labour ran persistent budget deficits as a percentage of GDP from 1984 to 1990, reflecting increased pressure on government expenditure, although asset sales provided an illusion of improvement from 1987/88 to 1989/90. The deficit to GDP ratio rose rapidly under National, again underpinned by recession, until the dramatic reversal in 1993–95.

Central government expenditure figures show that the cost of government administration more than trebled between 1984 and 1990, but fell as state sector cuts came in under National (see Table 10.2). Commitment to industry development almost halved, with the largest cuts under Labour. Foreign relations spending was cut back slightly after 1990, with New Zealand's proportion of overseas aid only 0.18 percent of GDP, compared with the international community's minimum standard of 0.7 percent. Increases in expenditure on health, education and social services during Labour's term reflected large public-sector pay rises in 1985/86, increased demand for educational and social services, unemployment benefits and other forms of income support, and inflation adjustments. These categories remained almost static under National. Debt servicing costs grew sharply after 1984. Reductions in Labour's later years reflected the short-term effect of asset sales, but costs blew out again from 1991 to 1993; yet government could no longer call on the revenue earned by the assets which had been sold.

On the revenue side, personal and corporate income tax rates were reduced and receipts fluctuated with the state of the economy. GST played an increasingly significant role, rising from 7 percent of all tax receipts in 1987 to 25 percent by 1994. Revenue from interest,

TABLE 10.1 Balance of payments 1987–94 (NZ$m)

	1987	1988	1989	1990	1991	1992	1993	1994
Exports	12,234	13,475	14,778	15,408	16,564	18,207	19,352	20,187
Imports	11,237	10,189	13,186	13,883	12,976	15,101	16,151	17,881
Trade balance	996	3286	1592	1524	3588	3105	3202	2306
Non-factor services, net	-776	-919	-1310	-1393	-1541	-1883	-1317	-650
Investment income, net	-3418	-3269	-3249	-2767	-4408	-4133	-4528	-4916
Transfers, net	235	409	779	1012	1188	1276	989	1520
Invisibles, net	-3961	-3782	-3780	-3148	-4761	-4739	-4856	-5565
Current balance	-2965	-496	-2189	-1623	-1172	-1632	-1654	-1738

Source: OECD 1994, Table 5

Table 10.2 Government expenditure, selected items, 1984–94 (NZ$m)

	1984	1985	1986	1987	1988	1989	1990	1991	1992	1993	1994
Administration	816	851	1043	1171	1953	2280	2897	3026	2751	3039	2978
Foreign relations	804	887	928	1056	1329	1466	1617	1582	1638	1505	1586
Industry development	1826	1614	1046	1181	1185	1117	1117	1327	916	1073	1019
Education	1624	1629	1729	2066	2738	3248	3917	4251	4800	4418	4575
Social Services	3928	4199	4686	5157	6841	8302	9938	9966	10,694	10,494	10,398
Health	1751	1801	1986	2354	2975	3311	3642	3850	3882	3800	4027
Transport & communications	521	512	745	827	576	612	855	798	822	704	794
Debt services & misc. investmt.	2173	2558	2835	3248	3275	2011	700	4467	4176	3825	3495
Total net expenditure	13,443	14,051	14,998	17,060	20,872	22,347	24,683	29,267	29,679	28,858	28,872

Sources: 1984–93: OECD, 1994, p.143, Table F; 1994: Treasury estimated actual, *Fiscal Outlook* 1994. Deflator: Table 10.10, PC INFOS, *Key Statistics*.

profits and miscellaneous receipts grew significantly in the later 1980s, but declined with asset sales and refinancing of SOE debt. In 1993/94 total central government tax revenue was 33 percent of GDP, personal income tax was 16.6 percent and corporate tax 3.8 percent of GDP.

The National government's budget surpluses in 1994 and 1995 came primarily from forcing government expenditure down through cutbacks to social services, income support and the state sector. The June 1995 budget made it clear that the future held more of the same. The forecast $3.3 billion surplus (on an accrual basis) would be used primarily to retire debt. This was a budget for the financial markets. First priority was the confidence of the local and international money markets and analysts, then the corporate sector, Business Roundtable, employers, some of the manufacturers and media partisans.

Critics agreed that debt levels were important. But reducing debt seemed to have become an obsession. There was no significant social dividend. Benefit eligibility was to be tightened yet again. The only social expenditure item to show a significant increase, education, involved controversial measures such as the introduction of bulk-funded and performance-based salaries for teachers. In a provocative move, government funding for private schools was doubled. The promise of income tax cuts once the ratio of net public debt to GDP was reduced to below 30 percent was repeated; this was expected to be achieved by 1996/97. The extent of the tax cuts, and their real beneficiaries, remained undisclosed, while the timing of an announcement no later than mid-1996 appeared strategically designed for electoral appeal.

The National government was treating the country as if it was a private sector business. But it did so without prudent business practices such as managing debt in a predictable counter-cyclical way, assessing the benefits as well as the costs. There was no appeal to the hearts and minds of its citizens, nor any recognition that legitimacy and stability required more than balancing the books. In the 'turnaround economy' everyone had to keep running just to stay still, while structural unemployment and income inequality were cemented in.

Investment

Overall investment fell dramatically, with the proportion of GDP in investments in 1993 only 70 percent of that in 1984. By 1994 nonresidential fixed investment as a proportion of GDP was 73 percent of its level a decade before. Manufacturing investment had just regained its 1989 level, and farm investment its 1986 level, both of which were about half that of 1984.[9]

Infrastructural investment suffered badly as the sinking lid on government spending and commercialisation of public goods and utilities promoted short-term cost-cutting. Financial pressures on local government and Transit New Zealand (the former National Roads Board) meant that maintenance was deferred. In December 1994 the Auditor-General warned of the imminent collapse of some basic services. 'I am aware of several major timebombs around New Zealand . . . instances where councils will be up for many millions of dollars to prevent the collapse of their infrastructure.'[10]

Research and development expenditure declined as a proportion of GDP from the OECD average of 1.4 percent in 1984 to 0.9 percent a decade later. Meanwhile the OECD average rose to 1.7 percent.[11] Falling private-sector investment reflected the recessionary squeeze and the government's refusal to provide incentives. While government spending on research and development increased slightly, the increase was never enough to offset the shortfall. The division of the Department of Scientific and Industrial Research into Crown Research Institutes, funded from the government's contestable fund, private contract research and user charges, seriously reduced the pool of publicly accessible information and limited access for those who did not have the up-front ability to pay.

Savings were expected to grow during the 1990s as a result of reduced unemployment, more cautious debt-gearing among households and improved corporate profitability. Private provision of health care, education, superannuation and other social services increased the funds held by insurance companies. The number of new members of registered superannuation schemes in 1994 was almost double that of 1990, with a decline in the proportion of employer-funded schemes and an increase in individual policies. Funds under management increased from $11 billion before the 1991 budget to $14 billion in 1994. As superannuation funds increased, however, the rate of private savings fell.

Fixed capital investment surged in response to the post-1992 recovery, driven by high confidence, rising capacity utilisation, profitability and the lower cost of labour and capital. Much of this investment was upgrading of plant and machinery that had been deferred during the recession. Housing sales revived to pre-recession levels, as mortgage costs fell, new migrants arrived and consumer confidence revived, especially among higher income earners. How long this would be sustained as the economic growth rate fell, and how far the investment was productive rather than speculative, was unclear.

Business activity
Agriculture, manufacturing and services sectors all responded to the new environment differently. The services sector was the major beneficiary. Deregulation created lucrative new opportunities in public relations, economic and management consultancy, legal work and investment advice. Financial services expanded. Telecommunications, transport and energy recorded mounting profits. By 1994 services comprised 25 percent of exports. Employment loss varied accordingly (see Table 10.3). The net outflow from manufacturing towards services reinforced a growing differential between the skilled and unskilled labour forces.

In the industrial sector, there was very little evidence of new 'efficient' industries arising from the ashes of the old, despite the economic recovery and the growth of niche market providers. Many workers who had been laid off found great difficulty in obtaining further employment, and the retraining packages promised by the government after the previous tariff reduction rounds did not eventuate. In its submission to the post-1996 tariff review the New Zealand Trade Union Federation, together with the Textile, Clothing and Footwear Union Council, made it clear that workers had borne the brunt of the deregulation:

> New Zealand has come through an all round programme of deregulation and 'liberalisation' with tariffs only one aspect of this process. The substance of this deregulation has been a reconstruction of the market relationship between labour and capital, with the bargaining power (and therefore the share of national income) of capital substantially increased. The pressures unleashed by lowered tariffs have been shifted (by surviving businesses) onto the shoulders of labour. The lowering of tariffs plus other deregulation policies have contributed to the growing inequalities in New Zealand society.

Successive governments had eschewed any responsibility to nurture business through the restructuring, leaving many ill equipped to handle the hostile and unstable economic conditions. An NZIER

TABLE 10.3 Labour market composition 1985–94 (thousands)

	1985	1986	1987	1988	1989	1990	1991	1992	1993	1994
Total civilian employment	1329	1544	1557	1508	1468	1481	1461	1467	1496	1559
Agriculture	148	167	164	157	152	157	157	159	158	162
Industry	430	444	425	393	373	364	343	331	351	390
Other (services)	751	933	968	958	943	960	961	977	987	1008
Registered unemployment	51	65	86	118	150	159	193	216	211	185
Unemployment rate as % of civilian labour force	4.1	4.0	4.0	5.6	7.1	7.8	10.3	10.3	9.5	8.2

Source: OECD 1994, Table C; Treasury; thousand persons 1985 and 1986 April; rest yearly average based on Household Labour Force Survey

study of business dynamics in New Zealand from 1987 to 1991 noted far greater turbulence in the late 1980s than earlier in the decade. Survival rates for business fell markedly. The old pattern of firms adjusting to change by internal restructuring was replaced by a pattern of shedding old firms and spawning new ones. This revealed greater flexibility in response to the changing operating environment, but it also created instability well above international standards. Three-year business survival rates fell from an internationally high level of 88 percent in the early 1980s to only 57 percent in 1988, well below the rates of countries traditionally considered as having business populations with high turnover.[12]

The study saw lower survival rates as a probably inevitable consequence of increased dynamism. This was positive in 'clearing away inefficient firms, and potentially bringing in new industries and technologies more quickly'.[13] But the impact of adjustment costs was far from neutral.

> Such a business population can adjust faster to change, but it is likely to place its labour force under more stress as they are required to change jobs more frequently. Whether such flexible adjustment at the firm level minimises overall adjustment costs and results in a more flexible and successful macroeconomy remains an open question.[14]

Business failures remained historically high even during the recovery. The dramatic collapse in 1994 of the Fortex meat-processing business symbolised the fragility of the success stories. In 1988 Fortex had concluded an innovative agreement for a double-shift and profit-sharing in the meat works which was hailed as a break-through in workplace democracy and co-operative industrial relations. With a new high-tech plant, Fortex was voted business of the year in 1992. Two years later it went into liquidation, owing to a combination of over-capacity, over-extension and mismanagement.

Income distribution
Under the structural adjustment formula, income inequality was bound to increase. Monetary policy, operating through high interest rates, meant that incomes for those who owned property or capital rose more rapidly than for wage earners or net debtors. In times of recession, lower-skilled workers in the flexible labour market tended to be laid off sooner than executives. In a recovering economy, rising export income based on improved terms of trade increased demand and wages for more highly qualified staff, while residual unemploy-

ment kept increases for lower-skilled workers down. International competitiveness in a deregulated labour market also required employers to keep labour costs down, while international investment was lured by promises of high profitability. State sector restructuring created a core of highly paid executives and a rump of lower-level staff increasingly on short-term flexible contracts. Continued retrenchment of benefit levels in the name of fiscal restraint was calculated to maintain a significant income gap between beneficiaries and full-time earners.

Differentials between quintiles of wage and salary earners increased significantly under the Labour government, even before the ECA was introduced (see Tables 10.4, 10.5).

TABLE 10.4 Average gross income, full-time wage and salary earners 1984–90

	first quintile	third quintile	fifth quintile
June 1984	1450	1443	1439
June 1990	2549	2573	2623
% change	75.79	78.31	82.28

TABLE 10.5 Real disposable incomes, full-time wage and salary earners 1984–90

June 1984	973	974	1052
June 1990	937	952	1081
% change	-3.69	-2.26	+2.76

Base: March 1981=1000
Source: Adapted from M. O'Brien, 'New Wine in Old Bottles: Social Security in New Bottles', *Reports and Proceedings*, 108, Social Policy Research Centre, Sydney, 1993, pp.92-93.

When National deregulated the labour market in conditions of unprecedented unemployment, labour productivity appeared to rise without any real increase in wage workers' incomes. Economist Keith Rankin points out that, while each person of working age was producing more on average, this came mainly through an increase in hours worked—up 7.4 percent in 1995 from 1990, and up 4.8 percent from 1993. Increased labour supply, rather than increased productivity, was driving economic growth.[15] Pressure on wages through the ECA and unemployment was reinforced by tighter eligibility for the dole through work tests, longer periods without work, removal of benefit entitlements for 16- and 17-year olds, and cuts in benefit levels.

Average real disposable income increased after 1992, but that reflected rises in the non-wage incomes of entrepreneurs and the self-employed, in the number of people in employment and in hours worked. Real wages hardly moved, especially in the state sector, and remained below the rate of inflation. Any new earnings came primarily from increases in labour supplied. Take-home pay fell for about 5 percent of employees.[16]

The government's Social Policy Agency in its post-election briefing papers in 1993 drew attention to the widening gap between rich and poor. The extent of income inequality depends on the data and methodology used, but different approaches showed similar trends. The Infometrics agency in September 1993 reported that the top 20 percent of households currently received 45 percent of all gross income, up from 35 percent in the late 1970s. It predicted that their share would increase to 50 percent by 1997/98. This left 3 percent of the total income for the poorest 20 percent of households in 1993. The real spending power of those in employment between 1987 and 1992 rose by 7 percent for the wealthiest 20 percent and fell by 2.9 percent for the poorest quintile.[17]

Using annual tax returns from 1980 to 1991, Integrated Economic Services (IES) reached a similar conclusion. Compensation of employees for labour as a percentage of GDP, adjusted for changes to employment in the working age population, fell from 50 percent in 1986 to 47 percent in 1993. During the 1991–92 recession the combination of the ECA, a $1 billion reduction in benefit payouts and high unemployment had forced benefit and wage incomes down; but because profits were down too, the differential between profits and wages narrowed. The gap widened again during the recovery of 1992–93, leading IES to suggest that swings in income during the course of a business cycle were becoming more pronounced.[18]

Easton also points to major changes in the top and bottom deciles. Between the early 1980s and early 1990s, the income share of the top 10 percent increased about 4 percent (to almost 20 percent), due largely to the tax cuts of 1988. Middle income earners each lost half a percentage point. The ninth (or second bottom) decile, while experiencing a smaller 0.3 percent cut in income share, suffered a proportional cut of around 5 percent. Incomes of the bottom tenth fluctuated through the vagaries of self-employment.[19]

This was seen as an inevitable, and for its supporters acceptable, product of the new regime. In late 1994 neo-liberal economist Girol Karacaoglu predicted: 'While the good majority of New Zealand people will share in future economic prosperity, the gap between the top and bottom groups of income earners will continue to widen', owing to market rewards for the higher skilled, the declining welfare state and 'the power of technology and international capital flows to make unskilled labour . . . substitutable around the world'.[20]

Unemployment

The most important test of economic success for the mass of New Zealanders was its effect on jobs. There is a risk that over-emphasising the value of paid work to the economy devalues unpaid productive labour, especially by women in the home. Yet paid employment has traditionally provided not just an income, but a source of self-esteem, identity, human contact, training and community for many New Zealanders, especially men. In the words of former Anglican Social Responsibility Commissioner Richard Randerson: 'Without employment, life withers. Employment is the most critical socio-economic factor that any country could aim for, providing not only income but satisfaction in life.'[21]

Full employment had been the cornerstone of economic and social well-being since 1935—a goal reflected in the obligations of the Reserve Bank, trade practices law, market regulation, state commercial activity and industrial relations. It was driven in part by a sense of reciprocal obligation. Employers had acknowledged full employment as a primary social and economic objective, and workers moderated their demands to promote economic growth and social well-being. After 1984, the goal of full paid employment, as traditionally understood, was treated by policy-makers as unattainable, unaffordable and undesirable. The rhetoric of the market redefined workers as 'human resources', as mere commodities to be purchased by capital for the lowest market price in the quest to maximise profit, and shed when profitability declined. Mounting unemployment cast a pall over the lives of hundreds of thousands of people, their families, their marae,[22] their communities. One resource worker with the unemployed reflected on the devastating result: 'No matter how hard you try, some of the people who are suffering will slip through the cracks. We will have some suicides. There will be marriage break-ups, we will have the domestics. We will have the children who slip behind, and are lost.'[23]

Under the Labour government, the household labour force survey showed unemployment rising from 3.8 percent in December 1985 (when the survey began) to 7.7 percent in October 1990. Labour force participation rates fell from 67.6 percent to 63.2 percent over the same period. National pledged in its 1990 election campaign to halve unemployment in three years. It quickly abandoned that goal. By March 1991 the official unemployment rate had risen to 9.9 percent. A year later it peaked at 11.1 percent, or 215,000 people. By March 1993 the figure had declined to 10.2 percent, falling further in March 1994 to 9.5 percent.

In December 1994, after two years of economic recovery, official unemployment had only just dropped below the level when National came to power. The seasonally adjusted number of registered un-employed was 128,000, or 7.5 percent, comparable to the situation under Labour in June 1990. The last two quarters were the first time New Zealand had fallen below the OECD average unemployment level (7.9 percent in September 1994) since 1988, although the two rates were not directly comparable. Seasonally adjusted workforce participation was at its highest level since 1988. Youth unemploy-ment had also declined. How far this reflected young people remain-ing at school was difficult to tell, as decentralisation of education meant there was no national school roll. The higher school-leaving age, high youth unemployment and removal of eligibility for the dole clearly contributed. Long-term unemployment dropped too, but 45.5 percent of the registered unemployed had still been without a job for six months or more and 11 percent for more than two years. By June 1995 the official unemployment rate had continued its decline to 6.3 percent, the lowest level since December 1988—but this was still three times higher than in 1985 when the Labour government had called an Employment Promotion Conference to discuss the unemployment 'crisis'.

The pliant nature of official statistics meant that the true level of unemployment for people wanting paid work was far worse. Falls in official unemployment reflected reduced benefit levels and eligibility, withdrawal from the workforce and increased numbers on the sickness and invalid benefits, as well as the positive indicators of job growth. The official number of jobless (those without a job and wanting one, but not actively seeking work owing to lack of skills, the wrong age, the right work unavailable in their area, looking only in newspaper, discouraged) rose from 112,900 in March 1987 to peak at 270,000 in December 1991. By December 1994 the figure was still 209,700, almost exactly what it had been when National was elected in October 1990. While the official unemployment rate was now 7.5 percent, official jobless stood at 11.6 percent.[24] Even though official unemployment had fallen to 6.3 percent by June 1995, the official jobless figure still stood at 9.7 percent (see Figure 10.5).

FIGURE 10.5 **Unemployment, jobless and workless* rates 1984–95**

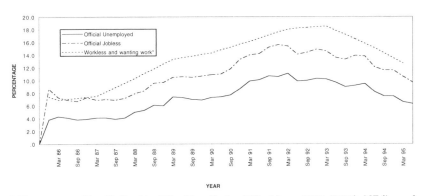

* Terms as used by K. Rankin, 'The New Zealand Workforce 1950–2000', *NZ Journal of Industrial Relations*, 1993, p.235
Sources: Statistics New Zealand, HLFS; K. Rankin, Department of Economics, University of Auckland

Even the jobless figures were misleading. People working one hour a week or without pay in a family business, or beneficiaries allowed to work a small number of hours, were all defined as employed. The survey on which the jobless statistics were based canvassed approximately 16,000 households. Non-return rates were around 10 percent. These, plus itinerants, were likely to represent a disproportionate number of the unemployed.

Keith Rankin has taken the unemployment statistics further, to the measure of 'inactivity' (see Figure 10.5). This includes those who are neither employed, nor students, nor caregivers for children. In 1995 almost half of the inactive of working age were men. A disproportionate number of these were Maori and Pacific Islanders. Given that numbers on the unemployment benefit were consistently 50 to 55 percent of the inactive, it appeared that a significant number of working-age men had withdrawn from the paid job market altogether.[25]

The burden of unemployment was unevenly spread (see Figure 10.6). For the year ended March 1987 the official unemployment rate among Maori was 10.8 percent, Pacific Islanders 6.1 percent and 3.2 percent for Pakeha. As unemployment grew, the disparities got worse. By March 1992 the rate for Maori, who comprised 8 percent of the country's labour force, had reached 25.8 percent. The Pakeha rate was 8.1 percent, while that for Pacific Islanders had reached a massive 28.8 percent. In the quarter to June 1995, the figures were still 16.1 percent for Maori and 17 percent for Pacific Islanders, and down to 4.4 percent for Pakeha. Other sources suggest the disparities were even worse. According to 1991 census figures, 40 percent of Maori and of Pacific Islands men aged between 20 and 59 were not employed, and Maori and Pacific Islands unemployment had continued to rise until 1994.

FIGURE 10.6 **Unemployment 1987–95, by race (1995 June quarter only)**

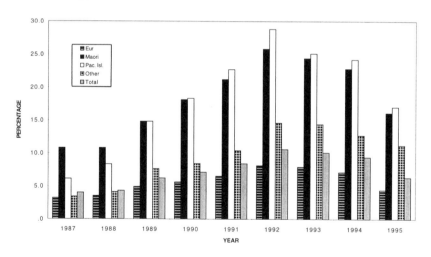

Source: Statistics New Zealand, *Labour Market 1994*, Table 5.5

Unemployment task force

In the 1993 election, predictions that high unemployment would continue into the next century became a political embarrassment. The strategy of victim-blaming no longer worked.[26] Most people of whatever class knew someone who had been laid off and become involuntarily unemployed. Unemployment could not be dismissed as transitory, a short-term cost on the way to a prosperous future of full employment for all. It had become a structural feature of the growing, but increasingly polarised, economy.

Public pressure by the churches and some unions, and militancy by unemployed rights groups and other unions, kept the issue to the fore. The Alliance proposed an all-party task force on unemployment. The government eventually agreed, establishing a committee of three parliamentary parties: National, Labour and the Alliance. New Zealand First was sceptical, and declined to take part. This committee set up a multi-sectoral task force which reported at the end of 1994. The political parties were then required to reach a common position. Their response, and subsequent government action, would prove whether the task force was a genuine response to unemployment or an elaborate public relations exercise.

Submissions from the corporate sector demanded further sacrifices from the unemployed to sustain economic growth. The Employers' Federation wanted the system of taxpayer-funded benefits replaced by an insurance-based system. Workers would buy unemployment insurance with premiums based on employment records, earnings and level of redundancy coverage desired. The dole would be replaced by vouchers to cover costs of food and health care. School leavers would be granted a job search allowance for the first six months of unemployment, and vouchers to spend at any training institution. Wage rates and benefit levels would be closely monitored to ensure that people without jobs had 'incentives' to seek work. The only concession to interventionism was greater assistance for small businesses to foster their potential for growth.

The task force was dominated by government nominees and officials. It included the CTU and Employers' Federation, but contained no representation from the unemployed. The final report contained a broad range of proposals to promote and co-ordinate employment initiatives and restore a skilled workforce. It suggested moderate adjustments to the benefit system. Contrary to the expectations of many, the minimum wage was endorsed. Priority was placed on reversing unemployment among Maori and youth. There was minimal reference to employment creation, beyond expanding infrastructural investment and enterprise support. The terms of reference ensured that broader economic issues were excluded from the start.

There was a positive sectoral and community response to many of the task force's specific proposals. Yet critical commentators insisted that the major issue of redirecting the structure of the economy had not been addressed—specifically, acceptance of full employment as a policy goal; widening fiscal and monetary policy goals to balance the economy; responding to the economic and social costs of unemployment; and providing positive encouragement for students into education and training, rather than threatening them with poverty. Economics professor Tim Hazledine laid the problem on the line:

> the Taskforce report is nearly all about honing and polishing the 'pegs'—the workers—so they fit better into the existing 'holes'—jobs. But what if the real problem is that there just isn't enough holes to go around? And, if pegs and holes are different shapes, why not explore the exciting idea of reshaping the jobs, rather than always assuming it is the workers who have the wrong skills or attitudes or wage expectations and who must adjust to fit in.[27]

Six months after the report was released the parties produced a joint response. Almost all the task force recommendations were endorsed, but there was no commitment to a timetable or to the resources essential for the proposals to work. These, the parties considered, were matters of policy best left to the government of the day. The Minister of Labour praised the accord as an example of how consensus politics would work under MMP—reinforcing the belief of some that electoral reform would consolidate rather than reverse the policies of the past decade, and their consequences.

Employment
Contrary to the political promises, increased productivity did not guarantee new jobs. 'Rationalising labour costs' or 'downsizing' was justified equally in good times and bad. In many enterprises higher profits were accompanied by further cuts. Extensive layoffs in the banking industry, for instance, fed profitability in boom time, were used to cut costs when banks faced the consequences of lending

disasters in the later 1980s, and continued when competition squeezed their new high profit levels in the 1990s.[28]

The same pattern emerged with corporatisation and state sector restructuring. In the 1986/87 financial year alone, one quarter of staff were affected, with 11 percent moved into SOEs, 8 percent into new departments and another 6 percent taking redundancy or early retirement.[29] The nine new SOEs created in 1986 had employed around 70,000 people. Five years later only half the original SOE workforce still had their jobs, as a result of redundancies, contracting out and the privatisation programme. Profitability of the SOEs and privatised businesses was sustained largely by continued cuts to their workforce; in four years, for example, Telecom more than doubled its profits and almost halved its staff.[30]

The long-awaited economic recovery during 1993–95 produced the paradox of an apparent skill shortage and continued low wages and high unemployment. Lucrative new opportunities for the well-educated emerged in the entrepreneurial economy. Experienced trade workers were in high demand in growth areas, especially construction. New jobs for wage earners came primarily from ratcheting down wages and conditions under the pressures of residual unemployment, reinforced by the ECA.

Behind job growth figures lay important questions about the quality of new work. Between 1990 and 1994, 57,000 jobs were reportedly created. But many of these were part-time. In the year ended March 1992, an average of 92,400 people employed part-time wanted to work additional hours. Yet part-time work increased 11.1 per cent in the year to February 1994, compared with 5.6 per cent for 30 hours a week or more. Of a near-record 1,390,600 filled jobs in the New Zealand economy in August 1994, 28 percent were still part-time, although the trend in 1995 showed an increase in the proportion of full-time work.

The uneven distribution of new work reinforced labour market inequalities. Falling real wages placed pressure on all adult members of households to join the workforce, especially part-time. Employment tended to cluster around households that already had jobs, with skilled workers more likely to secure jobs during the recovery, irrespective of the level of skill required. Rankin reported 'the emergence of a society with many households having multiple income earners, co-existing with a growing underclass of households earning less than a minimum full-time wage'.[31]

Job security was also a problem. The instability of business meant that work created one month could disappear the next. Individual companies made decisions in response to short-term prices. Increasing use of sub-contractors, frequently former employees, offered employers the flexibility to shape their workforce to meet current demands but left workers with no security of income. There was no long-term industry planning, and forecasts of massive job opportunities in growth areas warranted scepticism. In late 1991 the Minister of Forestry predicted 350,000 new forestry jobs by 2020. A study by the Forestry Industry Council the next year reported that even 12,500 new jobs by 2001 was optimistic, and these would be offset by losses from new technology elsewhere in the industry.[32]

According to the OECD, about only half the job losses since the 1980s had been recovered by early 1994.[33] The workforce participation rate was still 2 percent down on the mid-1980s, despite new jobs, the negative incentives of benefit cuts and a higher pension age.[34] The participation rate for adult men was even lower, creating significant social flow-on effects for their families and themselves.

In June 1995 the number of jobs had reached its highest level since the household labour survey began in March 1986. But the labour force participation rate was static. The number of new jobs had also significantly slowed. Only 5000 jobs had been created in the preceding three months, compared with 12,000 in the quarter before. The building and construction and manufacturing sectors had lost jobs. Almost all commentators predicted the downward trend would continue as the economy slowed. Yet employment growth even at the higher levels of 1994 was likely only to keep pace with the population. Easton calculated then that seriously to reduce unemployment would require a growth rate of 4 to 5 percent for the next seven years.[35] That was well beyond the rate which the Reserve Bank was likely to countenance as non-inflationary.

Education and training

The short-sighted nature of the government's withdrawal from planning and investment in training was exposed as soon as economic growth returned. A severe shortage of engineers, builders, printers, fitters and turners, machinists, electricians, sheet metal workers, quantity surveyors and architects was attributed to emigration and a lack of investment in training. By November 1994 only half as many people were taking apprenticeships as ten years before,[36] although in

1995 that trend had reversed. Numbers had dropped dramatically after National repealed the Apprenticeship Act in 1991 and employers thought the entire system was about to be scrapped. Polytechnics were cutting back on training courses owing to lack of funds. Government training schemes involving wage subsidies and training programmes were poorly publicised, and participation rates low.[37] A survey of one programme in 1994 showed that 90 percent of employers would have taken the young people on without the subsidy, and three-quarters of the employers did not know of the scheme until the worker was hired.[38]

Education and training policy was unco-ordinated. Piecemeal reforms and adjustments in response to market failure created continual contradictions. The government believed that too many polytechnic students were opting for social science, liberal arts and business studies, rather than science and trades—an inevitable consequence of setting up polytechnics to drive down costs in the universities by allowing them to offer degrees. Polytechnics were required to restructure as business units and funds were cut by 3 percent for most courses in 1994. Future funding would be directed more towards job training programmes, with polytechnics tendering competitively with the private sector for industrial training funds.

The vision of 'seamless' education through the national curriculum and qualifications framework proved cumbersome to design and implement. On- and off-work training was to be provided by new industrial training organisations. Employers warned of the dangers of fragmenting training into narrow vocational areas when generic qualifications could apply across several fields. The OECD's 1994 report likewise urged a flexible approach, in preference to detailed prescriptions which had high transition costs and limited adaptability. It also urged the government to play a greater role in co-ordinating industry-led training, given the lack of collective organisation within business—although measures to reduce unemployment or raise skill levels should not compromise 'the adaptability and flexibility of the economy, or undermine the policies necessary to raise long-term growth potential'.[39] It seemed that the government would struggle to reconcile its market model of training designed and funded by 'stakeholders' (the employing industry and trainees) with the planning that was required to ensure broad-based skill development for a dynamic, constantly adjusting economy.

An economic success story?

Successive governments tended to ignore these hard economic indicators in favour of extraneous, subjective and self-serving sources of praise such as credit ratings and international competitiveness scales. The National government and its media supporters proudly acclaimed New Zealand's rating in the Swiss-based IMD/World Economic Forum *World Competitiveness Report,* a neo-liberal checklist for free market economies. That report ranks countries in eight categories according to performance on nearly 300 measures. Criteria include hard indicators, such as government debt and tax rates, and softer, more judgemental information on the impact of legislation and social stability. In the September 1994 report, New Zealand dropped one place overall to ninth of the 41 countries surveyed, and seventh in the OECD. But it topped the 'government policy most conducive to competitiveness' category. New Zealand also scored highly for its monetary and fiscal policies, legislative and regulatory environment, and for the absence of price controls on goods and services. It did less well on research and development spending, and was considered to need more qualified engineers as well as foreign trade, partnerships with foreign firms and foreign direct investment.[40]

The US-based credit rating agencies (CRAs) Moody's and Standard and Poor's provided similar support. Credit raters used to concern themselves with whether a country could repay its debts and interest on time, irrespective of the economic policies employed to do so. In the 1980s they became aggressive advocates in the neo-liberal cause, passing judgement on the soundness of a government's economic policy. Speculation on the mere possibility of a rating review became a potent tool in the political armoury of structural adjustment. This was not unique to New Zealand. Australian sociologists David Hayward and Michael Salvaris have observed the 'crucial part [the CRAs] now play in actually shaping the public and social policy agenda' there.[41]

Despite enthusiastic endorsement of the New Zealand experiment from the CRAs, New Zealand's sovereign credit rating did not fare well. Standard and Poor's downgraded the rating from AAA to AA+ in April 1983, to AA in December 1986, and AA- in January 1991. Moody's lowered its rating for New Zealand to Aa1 in 1984 and Aa3 in 1986. In December 1994 Standard and Poor's announced a revision from AA- to AA, following Moody's one-step upgrade earlier in the year. Citing fiscal progress in budget surplus and debt repayment, it remained critical of the overall level of external debt, both public and private. The paradox of the CRAs' demands was that structural adjustment programmes made an increase in private external debt inevitable.

The cheerleaders of New Zealand's experiment glossed over the harsh reality that, for most of the decade, those policies had deepened the crisis in the New Zealand economy. The extremity of measures taken to address inflation, debt, government spending, benefit dependency and unemployment was largely an attempt to retrieve the damage caused by the policies themselves. Time and again these failures were excused by claiming that not all elements of the programme were yet in place, and that those who were holding up completion of the process were to blame. Others argued that the sequencing had been wrong but, given time, market equilibrium would be restored. Both highlighted the delay in deregulating the labour market, and that the 'recovery' occurred as soon as labour markets and wage levels were 'freed'. Historian Tony Simpson observes: 'You see the same sort of thing in weird religious sects . . . who in fact build a totally coherent structure of reality around themselves in terms of which they interpret every single thing that's happened.'[42]

The supporters of the programme claimed that the long-awaited recovery in 1993 was qualitatively different from any before. It came early in the world cycle. It was backed by competitiveness gains, and built largely on labour market flexibility. It was business-led, reflecting high levels of business confidence. It was export-driven, with entry of non-commodity manufactures into new markets. It was fuelled at home by increased spending of domestic business and households.[43]

Others were less sanguine. The chief executive of the Auckland Chamber of Commerce talked in December 1994 of a partial recovery which was not yet locked in, and where prospects for full participation and rising living standards were grim. He called for reduced compliance costs on business, strategic investment policies to encourage smaller and medium-sized businesses, replacement of producer boards with contestable development grants, a blitz on education and training through increased government support, and lower real interest rates.[44] Federated Farmers warned that the 1994 drought would cause the economy to contract, and Reserve Bank pressure would over-correct any perceived inflationary pressures and push the exchange rate dangerously high.[45]

The Auckland Manufacturers' Association in May 1995 expressed concern that the tightening economy and rising exchange rate were starting seriously to affect manufacturing confidence and performance. Its March survey had revealed a sharp turn-around in business confidence in the preceding three months, and performance was down on a year before. Reduced profitability was anticipated by around 35 percent of those responding, with an expected adverse impact on future investment in plant and employment.

> The record growth and booming economy indicated in 1994 has evaporated quickly in the first quarter of 1995. Manufacturers now face the tough challenge of retaining competitiveness on both domestic and export markets. . . . There is a close correlation between reduced confidence and the belief that the recovery has been killed off completely, which in turn is forcing many manufacturers to consider returning to strategies for survival at the expense of growth. If New Zealand's economy is booming, not all of the manufacturing sector is sharing the excitement.[46]

CHAPTER ELEVEN

The Social Deficit

IN 1994 THE *Economist* OBSERVED:

> It is no coincidence that the biggest increases in income inequalities
> have occurred in economies such as those of America, Britain and New
> Zealand, where free-market economic policies have been pursued most
> zealously.[1]

While there were weaknesses in how the *Economist* arrived at its figures, there was no argument with the overall finding that economic
inequality had increased. The New Zealand government not only
agreed—it believed this was an acceptable result. Finance minister
Bill Birch was reported in March 1995 as saying that income disparities 'are widening and they will widen much more. That doesn't worry
me.'[2]

The result of a decade of radical structural adjustment was a
deeply divided society. The traditionally marginalised had been
joined by growing numbers of newly poor. The social structure was
severely stressed. Hundreds of thousands of individuals, their families and communities had endured a decade of unrelenting hardship. The burden fell most heavily on those who already had least.
This was neither coincidence nor bad luck. It was the calculated
outcome of a theory which many New Zealanders viewed as mor-
ally and ethically bankrupt.

The goal of New Zealand's social security system, according to
the 1972 Royal Commission on Social Security, had been 'to ensure,
within limitations which may be imposed by physical or other disabilities, that everyone is able to enjoy a standard of living much like
that of the rest of the community, and thus is able to feel a sense of
participation in and belonging to the community'.[3] The warrant of the

Royal Commission on Social Policy in 1987 prescribed similar standards for a fair society:

- dignity and self-determination for individuals, families, and communities:
- maintenance of a standard of living sufficient to ensure that everybody can participate in and have a sense of belonging to the community:
- genuine opportunity for all people, of whatever age, race, gender, social and economic position or abilities, to develop their own potential:
- a fair distribution of the wealth and resources of New Zealand including access to the resources which contribute to social wellbeing:
- acceptance of the identity and cultures of different peoples within the community, and understanding and respect for cultural diversity.[4]

This brand of ethical values, social responsibility and moral leadership could not survive the structural adjustment programme. While Labour had begun the slide, the National government presided over a fundamental realignment of the state's obligations to its citizens. The universal welfare state gave way to a limited safety net founded on the 'fundamental principles' of:

- *fairness* (ensuring those in genuine need have adequate access to government assistance);
- *self-reliance* (policies should increase the incentive for people to take care of themselves);
- *efficiency* (highest possible value from each dollar);
- *greater personal choice* (encouraging alternative providers of health, education, housing and welfare services);
- *realism* (a level of state-provided social security and social services that is economically sustainable in future years); and
- *change management* (changes to be carefully managed 'without haste and with sensitivity' so needs of users and recipients are paramount).[5]

The transition was encapsulated in the statement of goals for the Department of Social Welfare (DSW). In 1991 DSW was mandated to ensure that 'All people in New Zealand are able to participate within the communities to which they belong'. In 1992 this was reduced to ensuring that 'policies for social welfare contribute to a fair and just society and promote self-sufficiency and responsibility of individuals and their families/whanau'.[6] Treasury's key architect of social policy confirmed: 'The important shift is away from a commitment to income support at a level so that recipients could "belong and participate" in society (in the words of the 1972 Royal Commission) to a "modest safety net" to "maintain individuals in the daily essentials of food, clothing, power and housing at a decent level".[7] By the mid-1990s, as the government and markets proclaimed the long-awaited economic recovery, the state was failing to provide even that for some of its citizens. The growing level of social dis-ease, polarisation and alienation risked becoming a permanent feature of New Zealand's social landscape.

Poverty

While New Zealand has no official poverty line, evidence of widespread and growing poverty was clear. Reports from agencies throughout the country provided extensive anecdotal evidence that poor people were going without adequate food, clothing, heating, health care and education opportunities.[8] Economists confirmed the deepening and widening of poverty in relative and absolute terms.

The two main sources of income were wages and benefits. Both fell relative to prices for the poor. Real wages and conditions for lower income earners were forced down throughout the recession and locked in by the ECA, despite the return to economic growth. Benefits were constantly being cut to maintain relativity to paid work, to provide 'incentives' for reduced dependency, and to lower the fiscal deficit.

National's 1991 budget formalised the stratification of New Zealand society which Labour had begun. The rich had to pay more for basic services. But they were also paying less tax and could afford to top up their state-provided entitlement or buy private insurance. Middle income earners also faced increased costs for social services. Combined with lower pay, uncertain job security, higher indirect taxes and increased insurance premiums, their standard of living was significantly reduced. But it was the purported beneficiaries of this new streamlined system of targeted state support—Maori, the poor, the sick, women and the unemployed—who bore the brunt of the change. Faced with a daunting combination of unemployment, benefit cuts, enforced dependence and user part-charges, their freedom of choice was whether to use their scarce resources to buy housing, health, education or other essentials like food—and which of these essentials to go without.

An international academic study of how welfare states guaranteed their people's standards of living was published in 1992. New Zealand was ranked fifteenth out of eighteen.[9] In 1993 New Zealand dropped from sixteenth place to eighteenth among industrial countries on the United Nations Human Development Index, which rates longevity (life expectancy), knowledge (adult literacy and mean years of schooling) and standard of living (purchasing power based on GDP per capita measured in the same prices).[10]

Given its emotive and political impact, the existence and extent of poverty became a matter for contest. Since at least the report of the 1972 Royal Commission on Social Security, the central concept for analysis of poverty in New Zealand has been relative poverty. Rather than ameliorating absolute poverty only, sufficient to maintain life and health, it is argued that an individual should have sufficient means to be able to function as part of society or, in the words of the royal commission, 'to be able to participate in and belong to the community'.

There have been two general approaches to studying relative poverty. One involves asking a group of people to what extent they are able to function properly, and to participate, and whether they feel they belong. Typically these questions are not asked directly because they are too general; instead, questions are asked about practical aspects of people's lives. A common question is: what do these people have to go without? A characteristic of the poor, for example, is that they will give up going to a doctor because of cost. Although such surveys indicate the hardship that people face, it is difficult to aggregate these individual experiences into some overview of the total severity of poverty.

In a more sophisticated version of this approach, researchers can examine material gathered from asking such questions of people to identify a point where hardship appears to become sharper. The measure most commonly used for this in New Zealand is the Benefit Datum Line (BDL), which was proposed by the 1972 royal commission as a suitable level for a married couple on a benefit, and which is adjusted for inflation over the years. In 1994 Brian Easton noted that average household incomes had hardly risen over the last two decades, and that most of the surveys seemed to suggest that hardship became poverty-like at a level near the BDL (although he admitted that a better figure might be 10 percent higher or lower). This approach was subject to certain methodological problems, but it gave some feel for the magnitude of relative poverty in New Zealand.

Using this method, Easton traced the numbers in poverty as defined by the BDL (and six other levels) between the March year

1982 and March year 1993. The estimates suggest that there was a mild increase from 11.6 percent in 1981/82 to 12.9 percent in 1989/90. However in 1991, following the benefit cuts, the proportion jumped, and by 1992/93 16.3 percent of the population were below the BDL, or almost 600,000 people—one in six of the country's population.[11] The profile of the poor met all the predictable specifications: sole mothers with children, families affected by long-term unemployment, the elderly, the single unemployed, those on stand-down with no income for up to six months, and low wage earners. So did the profile of the rich. Easton reports:

> the largest group of the poor remain children and their parents. Almost 29 percent of all children are in the bottom quintile (in contrast to a fifth of the population). The relative proportion in the lowest decile is even higher. In contrast the rich are adults only households, who make up 76 percent of those in the topmost quintile, despite being only 41 percent of the population.[12]

A second approach is to examine the total incomes of families and assess those who are below some poverty line. That line may be chosen by the researcher's judgement. One such study by Treasury set the poverty line by using food entitlement, derived from an estimate of minimum nutritional requirements, multiplied by four to cover other costs. No rationale was offered for the method or the multiplier, nor was there any clear definition of 'poverty'.[13] In a more sophisticated study, economist Bob Stephens adopted the common international measure of median household disposable income,[14] although the choice of a 60 percent poverty level, rather than the usual 50 percent, invites criticism of arbitrariness too. Combining statistical and empirical data, Stephens showed a decline in median income between 1982 and 1991 of 19.2 percent, with the income share of middle income households falling relative to top income earners. This measure placed 17.8 per cent of New Zealanders, or 611,000 people, below the poverty line in 1991.

Both these approaches give no indication of the number of people in absolute poverty, which some surveys suggested was occurring. Moreover they concentrated on the income of the family. Other factors might also reduce people's ability to participate and belong. A society which was intolerant of the specific cultural needs of, say, Maori would compound income deficiency with other pressures generating social deprivation.

Benefit cuts

Full employment had been the foundation for the welfare state. Welfare benefits and social services provided only second-tier support. Social policy professor Ian Shirley explained, 'we have never had a lavish welfare state when compared with the expansive systems operating in other countries. . . . When full employment was set aside it exposed the deficiencies of a selective benefit system and inevitably led to a substantial increase in social casualties.'[15]

Labour began the erosion of the universal benefit base by:
* shifting the emphasis from progressive income tax to consumption tax, which had a regressive effect;
* a surcharge on the universal superannuation payment to the elderly, affecting those who had other income, and changes for those whose spouses did not qualify;
* taxation of social security benefits, with an adjustment to benefit rates to compensate;
* abolition of unemployment benefit for those under 18 years;
* a flat fee on students at polytechnics and university;
* changes to benefit indexation and accommodation benefit levels;
* a further review of social security which based eligibility on the single adult (Labour's election loss in 1990 meant this policy was not implemented).

TABLE 11.1 Benefit cuts of 1 April 1991 (selected benefits only)

Benefit type	Rate as at 31/3/91($)	Rate as at 1/4/91($)	Change %
Unemployment			
Single unemployed			
18–19	114.86	108.17	-5.8
20–24	143.57	108.17	-24.7
>25	143.57	129.81	-9.6
Married couple	223.22	216.34	-3.1
Single, 2 children	292.87	266.83	-8.9
Sickness			
Single, 18–24	162.26	129.81	-20.0
Married couple	270.44	245.86	-9.1
Single, 2 children	292.87	266.83	-8.9
Domestic purposes			
Single	162.26	135.22	-16.7
Single, 2 children	292.87	266.83	-8.9

Source: M. O'Brien, 'New Wine in Old Bottles: Social Security in New Bottles', *Reports and Proceedings*, 108, Social Policy Research Centre, Sydney, p.45

National's December 1990 economic statement and the 1991 budget imposed draconian benefit cuts across the board (see Table 11.1). The promised adjustment for consumer inflation of 4.9 percent was also abandoned, which made the cuts even more savage than they at first appeared.

A review of changes in income between 1990 and 1993 showed that household income of beneficiaries fell from 72 percent of the mean equivalent disposable household income before the benefit cuts to 58 percent in 1993.[16] Families on the lowest incomes made the largest dollar contribution to budget savings. No families in the top 20 percent had to pay the same amounts. In every family category, the beneficiary family made the largest contribution. Beneficiaries in the bottom 20 percent experienced a reduction of between 13 and 30 percent in disposable income. For the top quintile no group lost more than 4.6 percent. The impact on single-parent families, primarily women, was the most serious, deepening the feminisation of poverty. Many elderly people in the lowest 40 percent also experienced severe income cuts. Again, Maori and Pacific Island people were found predominantly in the bottom two quintiles.[17]

Budgetary restraint was now the driving force behind income support. The potent combination of ideological and fiscal objectives was reflected in the statement of 'major outcomes desired by the government' for the DSW in the fiscal 1995 year.

> The services provided by the Department of Social Welfare will contribute to Government's goal of a fair and just welfare system taking into account other demands on national resources. The services are to be delivered in strict conformity with legislation and in a manner which might reasonably be expected of an efficiently run organisation.

As reinforcement, National introduced a Social Welfare Reform Bill that replaced all discretionary powers to grant emergency benefits with rigid formal regulations. Similar moves with the ACC had proved disastrous, where deserving cases had not been anticipated but officials had no room to move. The amendment was a response to a succession of rulings that DSW officials had acted unreasonably or unfairly in exercising their discretion. Beneficiary groups objected that the answer was 'for the Government to tell Income Support to exercise its discretion properly—not to remove the discretion altogether'.[18]

Decisions on funding cuts and eligibility levels were based on either ideology or arbitrary ceilings on government funding. For example, the age until which students were deemed dependent on their parents for means-tested student allowances was set at 25 years by calculating backwards from the amount government was prepared to allocate. The level of benefit cuts in 1991, supposedly designed to increase incentives, was pure guesswork by the Treasury. The Minister of Social Welfare admitted that decisions on benefit levels were based on instinct and expediency, not empirical research. 'Quite frankly, the research I rely on is the marketplace. If the marketplace cannot pay, there is no such thing as an arbitrary, isolated, adequacy level. . . . We had to make judgements on the whole package as to where we would pitch the levels.'[19]

The lack of a sound statistical base for decisions was severely criticised by the New Zealand Statistical Association in late 1994. Important decisions, such as setting levels for benefits, were being made with inadequate data and no monitoring of their impact.[20] The Government Statistician confirmed that economic and social indicators were often inaccurate and late because Statistics New Zealand was underfunded.[21] The government, presumably aware that such deficiencies undermined its claims to sound financial management, promptly allocated the agency more funds.[22] Even when research was done, it was generally too little, too late. For example, in October 1994 DSW announced plans to spend $225,000 on research as to whether beneficiaries receive enough money to live on. But the results were unlikely to be available until early 1996, five years after the major cuts were announced.[23]

Cuts to benefits were accompanied by increasingly tight targeting and heavy abatements. 'Efficiency' of government expenditure meant that the availability of state assistance for health, housing and education, as well as most social security benefits, including family support, became strictly targeted. This in turn required extensive and intrusive assessment of the financial position of individuals and families to establish their eligibility. The major exception was the provision of national superannuation for the aged, but this was subject to a severe rebate. A study by Susan St John and Anne Heynes of the effects of targeting across a range of services showed:
- inconsistencies in definitions of income used in targeting;
- differences in abatement ranges; and
- differences in groups—low income families, superannuitants, beneficiaries, students, low income working people.[24]

Abatement of benefits and supplementary allowances (family support, accommodation supplement, student support and community service cards), plus tax, left very little gain from part-time work or initial re-entry into the full-time workforce; some beneficiaries would lose income. Poverty traps worsened. It was possible for effective marginal tax rates (EMTR) to reach 98 percent, depending on income, and above 100 percent in some situations. The Report of the Employment Taskforce confirmed that the poverty trap was a major issue facing the unemployed as they explored options for paid work.

Cost-cutting by reducing payments, narrowing eligibility and sharpening abatements was justified as fostering self-reliance and reducing dependency. Under Labour the number of people on welfare benefits excluding superannuation had almost doubled, from 179,964 in 1984 to 318,651 in 1990. Benefit demand continued to grow under National as unemployment rose and economic growth declined. Despite the cuts, between 1989 and 1993 expenditure on social welfare benefits increased from 20.2 percent to 23.9 percent of GDP.[25] In March 1993, one dollar in every three received by lower income households came from a government benefit, compared with one in seven a decade earlier.[26]

The assault on the domestic purposes benefit (DPB) halted the growth in number of recipients of that benefit from 1991 to 1993. But feminist research contradicted the government's rationale: only 17 percent of those moving off the DPB in 1992/93 were placed in work—the majority either changed their marital status, transferred to another benefit, or no longer had dependent children. Stigmatisation, invasions of privacy and cuts to eligibility and benefit levels forced others off the benefit, and pressured women to remain in abusive and dysfunctional relationships. The costs of support then fell to voluntary agencies run predominantly by women, to their families, and indirectly to the government.[27] Despite the cuts and 'incentives', the number on the DPB rose again by 2.5 percent in the second half of 1994. By this time a quarter of families had only one parent, and 102,400 families depended on the DPB. Perversely, because benefit eligibility reflected individual circumstances, and benefit rates and means testing were based on family income, many families were better off financially to separate. The numbers on sickness and invalid benefits also grew, while official unemployment figures fell.[28]

There was no government research to explain these trends, or assess how many transfers reflected the tighter conditions for the dole, withdrawal from the potential job market, or increased family breakdown. Nor was the goal of immediate savings in the government's welfare budget balanced with assessments of the risk that the cuts might create longer-term problems that placed burdens on less visible parts of the government accounts.

Rationalising the cuts

Three main arguments were used to justify the benefit cuts: 'incentives' to enter the paid workforce, inter-generational equity, and moral responsibility.

'Incentives' were double-speak for punishing people not in paid work. Treasury's *Government Management* claimed: 'The likelihood of undertaking paid employment is inevitably reduced by the offer of income support for those without paid employment.'[29] The 1990 briefing also recognised the disincentive effect of the high EMTR. Treasury's solution was to cut benefit levels, not to ease the abatement rate. National's Minister of Social Welfare agreed:

> we consider that current rates are too high in relation to what can be earned in the workforce, and that they act as a barrier to self-help. For too many there is too little financial reward for their efforts to support themselves. It is critical that the incentives be improved. It is therefore important to set benefit rates, especially for those who have the best chance of finding work, at a level which encourages them to compete for work opportunities.[30]

The Change Team on Targeting Social Assistance, otherwise known as the 'razor gang', designed a new 'seamless, global system of abatement of all social assistance' based on a single family income and a single phase-out rate. This was to be facilitated by the development of 'family accounts' which would gradually be extended to include family support, tertiary allowances, child subsidies and health care subsidies. The family account idea proved unworkable, and gave way to piecemeal changes with increasingly tight targeting on a widely varying basis. St John and Heynes note that, rather than solving the problem, 'the disincentives that arise from a set of arbitrary effective marginal tax rates caused by overlapping income tests have been exacerbated'.[31]

St John argued that lowering the levels of benefit abatement would provide more incentive to seek paid work than lowering the benefits themselves, a point reinforced by the Employment Taskforce. The government's argument assumed, without any evidence, that beneficiaries preferred not to be in paid work. Feminist economist Prue Hyman pointed out: 'Sole parents . . . may find considerable difficulty in rejoining the paid workforce through a shortage of vacancies, a lack of suitable training, the unavailability or unaffordability of childcare and discrimination against women with dependants. They might then be justifiably cynical about the need for an incentive for them to rejoin the paid workforce in the form of a lower benefit.'[32] Supporters of the flat tax and tax cuts for the rich had no problem arguing that lower taxes provided an incentive for the wealthy to work, even when the cuts made them better off for doing nothing more. Yet the bigger incentive of cutting abatement rates and the EMTR was ruled out for the poor.

Cuts to benefit spending and repayment of debt were also justified by the technocrats in the name of inter-generational equity—not burdening future generations with debt incurred to pay the excesses of the present. This applied particularly to the imposition of the hefty superannuation surcharge. Yet, as Hyman pointed out, each cohort benefited from inter-generational transfer and provided for others at different stages of life. Many of the old, especially women, still provided unpaid care and made a productive input to community life. Effectively, the surcharge meant that one generation was being cut out of the life cycle to meet fiscal and ideological demands.[33]

The moral responsibility argument was aimed mainly at the domestic purposes beneficiary. The prevailing image was of a young woman who had deliberately got pregnant knowing she could bludge off the state for the next fifteen years. She was never the victim of rape and incest, or the beaten wife who had escaped with her life but had no means to support herself or her children on her own, or a mother who had been deserted and left to fend for herself. She was frequently assumed to be cheating not only the state, but those of her fellow citizens who were prepared to make sacrifices, pay their taxes and obey the rules.

Ruth Richardson had already made it clear that young single parents were the responsibility of their parents, and if that failed the child should be adopted out:

> If the 16 year old engages in sexual adventure and there's an unintended pregnancy, she has to make choices. If she chooses to have and keep the child that must be a family decision. A 16 year old is a dependent child,

not an independent adult. If her family doesn't want her and if she is not able to get her partner (who is liable to be the same age) to support her economically, she must look at other choices, which is adoption. That is not a forced choice, it's the choice young women made before the domestic purposes benefit was available as of right.[34]

Richardson failed to mention that few of those on the DPB were 16-year-old single parents. Such misleading generalisations provided a politically convenient justification for broader benefit cuts and the assault on the welfare state.

The DPB was the economic lifeline for many sole mothers. National's changes to eligibility, benefit levels and liability of the non-custodial parent had a clear punitive element. Moves to tighten the accountability of (primarily) fathers for on-going maintenance of their children through the liable parent contribution scheme were prompted by a desire to cut costs and punish recalcitrant fathers, not to improve the quality of life for the custodial parent and her children. The money went to reimburse the state, not to supplement the family's income.

The DPB cuts were intended to convey a market message to existing and potential parents. As expressed by the Business Roundtable, the benefit 'weakens the incentives of individuals to consider the implications of family responsibilities in advance and to individuals to provide for caregivers and their children'.[35] Apparently pregnancy was as amenable to market forces and consumer choice as any other of life's decisions—just as leaving a violent relationship, or being left to cope alone, could apparently become a market decision based on the price mechanism of the DPB. Those who made the wrong 'choices' would have to pay for their own mistakes.

The fundamentalist rhetoric bore no relation to reality. In their study of women on the DPB feminist researchers Christine Dann and Rosemary du Plessis reported:

> The people we interviewed are imaginative, resourceful and innovative managers—they budget, they barter, exchange, garden, bottle, freeze, collect driftwood for their fires and research the cheapest places to shop each week. . . . The analysis of how income is allocated in these households reveals the extent to which those interviewed are going without essentials in order to survive. Of particular concern are the very low amounts spent on food, and the lack of spending on health care for themselves.[36]

The overall picture from the study was 'of normal people in abnormal circumstances, using all sorts of strategies to survive'. They went on to ask: 'Why are parents who show so much ingenuity, effort and care for their children often treated as moral pariahs by others? Why are they blamed for the material and moral poverty of Aotearoa/New Zealand when they consume so much less than many others?'[37]

Other techniques used against beneficiaries included stigmatisation and harassment. Petty obstructions heightened the stress beneficiaries faced and further eroded their dignity. The media was replete with such stories. Families received demands to repay the fortnightly benefit for a loved one who died hours before the benefit payout. Benefits were terminated wrongly after social welfare staff read death notices for someone of that name in the newspaper and failed to carry out independent checks. A full-time adult student with children successfully appealed against being denied the accommodation and special benefit, which denial had forced him to abandon study in favour of the dole. The tradition of paying out benefits just before Christmas was stopped in 1994, purportedly in the interests of beneficiaries who were unable to budget, but actually to limit the number who would then seek emergency grants when their money ran out. DSW finally agreed to pay out early, but only so that banks could process the payments before their holiday break. Beneficiaries with automatic money cards could access their money before Christmas. Those without could not.

The poor
The impact of structural adjustment was never arbitrary. The fictional level playing-field was premised on the structural poverty of race, gender and age. As Rev. Charles Waldegrave observed, after the 1990 and 1991 benefit cuts: 'The post-war welfare state never adequately addressed the racial and gender inequalities inherent in its system. . . . [P]ast social policy failures are further aggravated by this current policy. The social implications for New Zealand's future are grave indeed.'[38]

Maori
Maori were the most marginal of the marginalised. Having been systematically stripped of the resources that guaranteed their economic, cultural and spiritual well-being, Maori were reduced to an underclass in their own land. As predominantly unskilled wage labour they depended heavily on employment by the state. In the 1950s and 1960s

a number of tribes transferred resources to the Crown in return for jobs and the protection of sacred sites, on the understanding these would be returned when no longer required. Through corporatisation and privatisation successive governments sold those resources, cut the jobs and cast many rural Maori communities adrift. Maori were made more dependent on state handouts than ever before.

In the paid labour force, Maori were traditionally over-represented in the production, transport, equipment and labouring sectors, which suffered the greatest job losses. While the total number employed in these sectors declined by 20 percent between 1986 and 1990, the number of Maori employed fell by almost 37 percent. Young people suffered heavily too—30.8 percent of Maori aged between 15 and 19 years were unemployed in 1991, compared with 23 percent of non-Maori. In December 1994, one in three young Maori was still unemployed. Maori remained under-represented in professional, managerial and sales occupations, where the majority of new jobs were predicted to arise.

The children suffered heavily. Almost two-fifths of Maori children were members of households in the lowest 20 percent of incomes. There were some positive developments, mainly as a result of Maori initiatives. Participation in early childhood education increased, with more than half of Maori children attending kohanga reo (Maori-language kindergartens). But the figure was still well below non-Maori pre-school participation rates. By 1992, 318 schools were offering varying degrees of Maori-language immersion education, six times higher than in 1987. There were 13 kura kaupapa or complete immersion schools operating; but these catered for only 510 students. While increasing numbers of Maori were staying at school, and participation rates at tertiary level, especially in polytechnics, had increased, the rates were again well below those of non-Maori. Maori were still more likely to leave school with no formal qualifications—40 percent of Maori compared with only 10 percent of non-Maori.

Maori women, especially those under 30, had the highest rates of unemployment, were more likely to be sole parents and had lower incomes than either Pakeha women or Maori men. Maori girls were most likely to leave school without formal qualifications, and the qualifications gap between Maori and non-Maori students was growing. This carried through to unemployment statistics, and other negative indicators such as teenage pregnancy and suicide.

The combined effects of benefit dependency and low-wage, low-skilled labour meant that in 1990 the average Maori household received only 79.2 percent of the average income of all households. The 1991 census showed that median income for Maori women had actually risen, from 68 percent in 1981 to 88 percent of that earned by non-Maori women; but for Maori men the median income had fallen, from 82 percent of the non-Maori rate in 1981 to 65 percent by 1991.[39] Again, families with children were hit harder. The median income of non-Maori households with children was a third higher than for Maori, as was that for sole-parent households. Only couples with no children came out about equal. Single-parent families suffered most. In 1991 only 12 percent of Maori sole parents were in full-time paid employment, 78 percent had received an income of less than $15,000 in the previous year, two-thirds had no school qualifications, and over half lived in rental accommodation. The vast majority of these were women.[40]

Levels of benefit dependency remained high. In the twelve months before the 1991 census, 49 percent of Maori men and 58 percent of Maori women received some income support other than the family benefit, compared with 38 percent and 45 percent of non-Maori. Most of these were sole-parent families, headed by women. Very few (6 percent) of those mothers were teenagers. Benefit cuts therefore hit Maori beneficiaries disproportionately hard. Officials warned Labour's social welfare minister that its proposed 1990 benefit cuts would affect almost a quarter of all Maori families, compared with 9 percent of Pakeha. They observed that 'any policy which redistributes money away from the Maori and Pacific Islands populations seems hard to justify'. The minister dismissed their advice as 'reverse racism', saying it was inevitable some would be better, and some worse, off in any reform.[41]

The evidence was clear that, with the onset of structural adjustment, the colonial legacy of poverty, dispossession and alienation that had operated since 1840 had taken another, equally pernicious, form.

Women

The unequal burden was shared by women generally. Before the 1980s recession, a quarter of non-Maori women and almost half of Maori women were totally dependent on social security benefits as their source of income, compared with only 11 percent of Maori men and 6 percent of non-Maori men. Women were forced to rely on all public services—from benefits to transport—far more than men. And they were the most dependent on the state sector for income and employment in 'women's work' of teaching, nursing, clerical and social services.

Among the major concerns expressed in a 1994 community survey by the West Auckland Women's Centre were:

- the negative impact on women's health of their diverse roles and increasing responsibilities;
- lack of recognition for unpaid work;
- the extreme difficulty of combining paid and unpaid work;
- women's marginalisation in part-time work;
- inflexibility in the workplace with regard to family responsibilities;
- lack of financial independence;
- increased levels of debt and the feminisation of poverty;
- the escalating cost of education and the increasing inaccessibility of further education for women and their children; and
- lack of representation and voice.[42]

Provisional census figures from 1991 showed fewer women than men in all income groups over $20,000 a year. Fewer than one in seven workers earning $70,000 or more was a woman, while women made up 60 percent of all those earning under $20,000.[43] National had repealed the legislation on equal pay for work of equal value before it was in operation. In the highly deregulated labour market the variation in workplaces, regions, firms and individual workers, secrecy surrounding contracts and the priorities of male-dominated unions militated against its reintroduction. As Hyman pointed out, the philosophy of individual freedom of contract sits uncomfortably with third-party enforcement of equal opportunity or gender-neutral comparison.[44] Similar concerns applied to generic rights for parental leave and childcare funding and facilities.

Women appeared to be affected less badly than men in the overall numbers of employed and unemployed, fostering claims that flexibility worked to women's advantage. That disguised women's overrepresentation in the part-time, temporary and low-wage workforce. Women's part-time income had traditionally relied on now rapidly vanishing penal rates. Wage increases were concentrated in male-dominated occupations. Maori and Pacific Islands women in particular were clustered in the lower-paid, secondary labour market and substantially under-represented in professional, administrative and managerial occupations.

A 1993 survey by the Service Workers Union showed that 40 percent of women members had suffered a drop in household income since 1991. Thirty percent had lower take-home pay, 47 percent the same and only 20 percent higher, mainly through working longer hours.[45] Women often needed several income sources to survive. Part-time, casualised or home workers on contracts for service or defined as self-employed often fell outside the coverage of labour legislation, including the Equal Pay Act. Non-unionised small workplaces left women more vulnerable. Union membership declined seriously in women-dominated and low-paid work: clerical workers lost 45 percent of membership before disbanding, cleaners about 20 percent each, and service workers around a third.[46]

Women's economic role had traditionally been marginalised, as orthodox economics refused to recognise the productivity of unpaid household work, undervalued their participation in the paid workforce, took them for granted as community workers and volunteers, and penalised them for being dependent on men and/or the state. Structural adjustment deepened the feminisation of poverty from which many women had no escape.

The elderly

The elderly suffered as much from uncertainty as from poverty. The relatively generous superannuation scheme introduced by National in 1976 had, despite some cutbacks, reduced poverty among the aged. There was some justification for revisiting aspects of the scheme. This could have been achieved through consultation, sensitivity and realism. Instead, the Labour government in 1985 imposed a special tax of 20 percent on all other income above a low exemption until all net superannuation had been clawed back. National promised to remove this surtax. But its replacement, announced in the 1991 budget, was more draconian. A new, harsh income test, assessed for couples on joint rather than individual income, would have meant an EMTR of 92.8 percent above a low threshold. Full withdrawal of the state pension had previously occurred at $71,000 of other income for a married couple and $43,000 for a single person. This would reduce to $23,700 and $16,200 respectively. Abatement would have made working virtually pointless. Yet there was no assets test. The level of the Guaranteed Retirement Income (GRI) would remain frozen from 1990 to 1993. The age of eligibility would rise rapidly from 60 to 65, although universal base entitlement would begin at 70.

The extremity and brutality of the government's 1991 proposals provoked the elderly to mobilise nationwide. Fuelling their anger was a fear of poverty reminiscent of the 1930s Depression, and indignation at the government's contempt for their contribution to society in the present and the past. Their activism forced a rare backdown. Under a revised system, from 1 April 1992 the tax surcharge would see the GRI fully clawed back at the less draconian rate of $54,940 for a married couple and $35,908 for single people. The age of eligibility would still increase, but the proposals for universal base entitlement and joint-income testing were dropped. More generous transitional provisions for those affected by the higher age were introduced on 1 April 1994, along with inflation indexing of pensions, as a result of the three-party accord between Labour, National and the Alliance on most superannuation issues.

Again, it was older Maori and women who were most directly affected by these changes. Given the substantially lower life expectancy of Maori, less discretionary income to save and extended family obligations, the effects on Maori of changes to age entitlement, eligibility and income levels were severe. Women comprised 55.8 percent of those over 60 and 66.4 percent of the over-80s. With relatively few savings or assets and little outside income, and being much more likely to live alone, women depended more heavily on the basic pension than men.

The furore over superannuation was followed by similar outrage and protests over a new system introduced in 1993 for asset and income testing of older people in residential care. The rationale was to equalise treatment of those in rest homes and in private or public geriatric hospitals by subjecting them all to the same test. As a result people in geriatric hospitals faced an asset test for the first time in a generation. Intense pressure forced the government to introduce a cap on the weekly charge levied on the elderly for some long-stay geriatric care and some changes to the asset threshold. But a single person without dependants was still entitled to retain only $6500 with no exemption for the family home. A married couple both in care were effectively treated as two single people, with a joint exemption of only $13,000.[47]

The three-party superannuation accord deferred the risk of further cuts and compulsory private retirement schemes which would have disproportionately penalised elderly women, Maori, the peripheral workforce and other poor. But the interest of the finance sector in such lucrative business meant that these proposals were bound to recur.

Children and families

The ultimate indictment of the structural adjustment programme was its effect on New Zealand's youth. The 1991 census figures showed that a quarter of all children belonged to families where the parent or parents did not have paid work. The fathers of only 61 percent of Pacific Islands children and 66 percent of Maori children in two-parent families were in full-time paid work in 1991, compared with 88 percent of fathers of European children.[48] The number of parents a child lived with correlated strongly with their family income. Sixty percent of children living with one parent were in the lowest 20 percent income group. Yet the proportion of children living in sole-parent families had increased from 12 to 22 percent of all children between 1981 and 1993; the figure for Maori in 1993 was 40 percent.[49] The majority of these households depended on state support, especially the DPB.

In December 1994 St John documented how seriously direct family assistance had been eroded since the introduction of 'family support' in 1986. Real purchasing power had declined, along with incomes. Reliance on benefits had increased. So had costs, with user-pays for education, health and housing, and high real interest rates. Families also faced additional responsibilities for older unemployed teenagers and adult children up to age 25. St John estimated the percentage loss in the annual value of family support since 1986 (in 1994/95 dollar terms) was 46 percent for a one-child family on three-quarters of the average weekly earnings (AWE), 51 percent for a three-child family on the AWE, and 100 percent for a three-child middle income family on one and a half times the AWE. She concluded that 'cumulative losses for low income families have been large, contributing, no doubt, to a deterioration in the net wealth of many families from which it will be difficult to recover'.[50]

Families in poverty faced charges for health care and education which once were free. Staff in schools reported having to deal with poverty-related problems before they were able to teach. In a study, *Poverty and Hardship,* in Manukau city in 1992 about half the schools surveyed said that over 50 percent of their families were facing moderate to severe hardship. In one school, almost none of its pupils' families had been able to pay the school fees. Fourteen schools had waived fees or arranged for them to be paid by instalment, and ten had provided their children with food. This had a flow-on effect on the ability of the schools to meet the shortfalls of decreased government funding. The burden was falling on those parts of the city with the highest non-European populations.[51]

The Special Education Service warned in October 1994 that one in five secondary students was at risk of failing school because of poverty, severe behavioural problems, truancy or abuse.[52] But monitoring truancy had become extremely difficult: there were no centralised rolls, and students who left a school simply disappeared unless or until they enrolled elsewhere.

This short-sighted, cost-cutting mentality undermined the educational opportunities, health and emotional well-being of the next generation. A prosperous, healthy economy would require a future adult population that would be skilled, confident, well-adjusted and employed. As economist Keith Rankin observed:

> The young are easily the worst affected, suggesting a much greater dependence than ever before by people in their twenties on parental accommodation and income support. The social implications of prolonged economic dependence within a generation should be an urgent topic of public debate . . .[53]

Privacy[54]

The neo-liberal rhetoric was replete with talk of individual freedom and getting the state out of people's lives. But not for everyone. The price for retaining a targeted safety net was data-matching, information-sharing and the increased surveillance of beneficiaries. Information exchange, it was reasoned, was not an invasion of individual privacy as the state had the right to verify data which formed the basis of benefit entitlement, and only people with something to hide had anything to fear. The main targets were accident victims, single parents and the unemployed. The bogey of welfare fraud was used to justify the harsh new approach. No figures were produced in support. It was enough to claim that the state and fellow taxpayers were suffering from the greed and dishonesty of beneficiaries.

In return for increased surveillance 'protective' legislation was put in place. The Privacy Commissioner Act 1991 originally provided for an information-matching regime between several state agencies. But there was nothing to prevent information-sharing by other govern-

ment departments outside the Act. Any information-matching programme had to be covered by a written agreement between the agencies involved which had to reflect the rules in the Schedule to the Act.
That meant very little because the rules were vague. This initial legislation was later incorporated into the Privacy Act 1993. Heralded
as conferring rights to privacy in non-governmental spheres, the Act
tended to provide greater protection for those in power than those
without, and was commonly used to withhold information about
individuals placed in positions of authority by the state.

Targeting also required proof of entitlement. Community service
cards, known as the 'poor card', were issued as proof of eligibility for
health care subsidies, thereby categorising the population according
to income. People reported being ranked by social agencies according to the sort of card they carried. Stories of the system's fallibility
soon emerged. Some of those who were sent the cards were not
entitled to them. Others who had major assets but low cash incomes
received cards they did not want.[55] Serious penalties attached to
misuse of the cards. Over time, the poor card became a resented but
integral feature of economic life.

The Treasury's original plan was for a 'smart card' which would
store personal information on magnetic tape and provide the basis
for the integrated family accounts. The community service cards
when issued contained a magnetic strip which card-holders could
not read, but which apparently remained blank. The Privacy Foundation warned: 'The mass issue of these cards provides the nucleus
of a possible national identity card system which has serious implications for personal rights.'[56] By 1995 the smart card had still proved
practically too difficult to implement.

Privatisation of dependency
While the restructuring failed to reduce dependence on the state, it
created new forms of dependency. Policy analyst Jonathan Boston
observed that, by 'self-reliance the government appears to mean not
that individuals should be able to care for themselves, but that they
should become dependent on their immediate families and voluntary
agencies rather than on the state'.[57] Charity was compatible with the
neo-liberal ethos, enabling the rich to choose for themselves how
much benevolence to bestow, and on whom. Decentralisation, deinstitutionalisation and devolution were all sold as 'empowering the
community'. When not properly funded—and they never were—this

double-speak meant shifting the burden from the state to primarily women 'volunteers' who were assumed to have a limitless capacity for unpaid labour in 'the community' or the home. The public symbol of charity was the rise of the foodbank. Social welfare minister Jenny Shipley accused the foodbanks of creating the demand. But New Zealanders had not become a nation of bludgers overnight. Tim Hazledine has argued that unemployment benefits in the 1970s were reasonably generous in international terms, but then few people were on the dole. 'People cared about each other enough not to abuse a system which works well for all of them.'[58] They had been made dependent by the disabling policies of structural reform.

A 1994 report on foodbanks nationwide showed that the government Income Support Service was commonly referring people to foodbanks without formally assessing their right to government help. Many of those denied support were not told of their right to appeal.[59] Benefit cuts and housing rentals were the main causes of their poverty. Rent now took more than half of the income of most families on benefits. Emergency grants, in the form of loans, were deducted from benefits at source. Next came essentials with fixed costs, such as electricity, water, and in rare cases a phone, to avoid hefty reconnection fees. Spending on food, clothing, medical care and school fees inevitably got cut back. The deficit in the household budget was made up by charity and high-interest debt.

Salvation Army food parcel assistance increased 76 percent in the first three months of 1991, 432 percent in 1992, and 30 percent in 1993, or a more than tenfold increase (1117 percent) over three years. Recipients were mainly under 35 years old with children, and disproportionately Maori and Samoan. One third were single mothers. In 1994, 120 foodbanks in Auckland distributed 5000 to 6000 food parcels a month. The Auckland City Mission alone distributed 7000 food parcels in 1994, compared with 600 four years before.

Activists for the poor criticised the foodbanks for becoming a new arm of social policy implementation, thereby relieving the onus on government to address poverty at its roots. The first conference of Auckland foodbanks in September 1994 warned the government that it would not continue to prop up policies which created poverty. It called for benefits to be restored to pre-1991 levels, abandoning of market housing rentals, better benefit administration, easing of benefit stand-downs, and more support for psychiatric patients in the community. A formal complaint was laid with the Human Rights

Commission that the government was contravening human rights guarantees to food, clothing, housing and medical care for all. Even the government's Social Policy Agency concluded that the 'explosion of demand' in the early 1990s was linked to the 1991 benefit cuts, increased state housing rentals, and tighter eligibility for income support such as longer stand-down periods. Based on 1993 figures, it estimated that more than 40,000 food parcels were being distributed to New Zealand households each month, with around $25 million worth of assistance provided in the year. Whereas foodbanks had initially been viewed as a temporary stop-gap, continued demand suggested that 'the needs they are meeting may be deeper and more enduring than anticipated'.[60] The report warned the government that 'it is likely that foodbanks will become entrenched as a more enduring component of the welfare system unless action is taken to reduce demand for their services by some form of public provision'.[61]

At the same time, voluntary agencies suffered major cuts in government support and private sources suffered donor fatigue. Citizens Advice Bureaux reported growing demands on their dwindling resources, as other state and community services closed their doors. Reported domestic violence and child abuse increased dramatically. Yet cuts to the DPB and women's refuge funding left many women with no economic choice but to return to their violent partners.

The functional reorganisation of state agencies created a bureaucratic nightmare for community organisations, who were required to contract separately with different agencies for each aspect of their service and report in detail on every 'output'. Community organisations whose grants were refused and budgets cut expressed outrage that the Community Funding Agency had underspent its budget by $3 million in 1994. Already marginal community organisations had been pushed to the brink.

Many larger, well-resourced voluntary organisations and charities became quasi-state agencies accountable to and dependent on approval by centralised funding providers. When arch-technocrat Rod Deane, in his capacity as chair of the Society for the Intellectually Handicapped, condemned the health contracting system he attracted considerable support. The 39-page contract the Regional Health Authority (RHA) wanted the society to sign said that the authority could not be criticised publicly, was immune from liability, could alter the contract on eight weeks' notice, could cancel the agreement but require services to continue for six months, could insist on complex records and statistics and compliance with statutory requirements irrespective of their relevance, and could require open access to records despite only partial funding. Deane's solution, to cut out the RHAs and further streamline the funding process, was consistent with the Business Roundtable's desire to hasten the shifting of government's social responsibility onto the private charity industry—not to revest the obligation of caring for its citizens in the state.

Social dis-ease

Since 1984 people had been forced to operate within a paradigm whose values most of them did not share. The citizen became a customer, buying a range of services from a public or private provider which were once their entitlements under the (albeit fictional and often dysfunctional) social contract with the state. Responsibility for social well-being was individualised, privatised, neutralised. The wealthy were relieved of the burden of social responsibility and ethical human behaviour by imposing greater hardships on those who already had less.

Responsibility for the fall-out was likewise individualised and privatised. With many, sometimes most, adults in some communities unemployed and young people ineligible for the dole, the underground economy of drugs and crime thrived.[62] Instrumental crime, such as burglaries, armed robberies and fraud, increased, alongside the crimes of despair—violence in the home and on the street, arson and vandalism. The sex industry became a positive alternative for an increasing number of women.

The 'crime wave' was popularly blamed on growing moral decay, a lack of community standards, bad parenting and the failure of schools to maintain discipline. A 50 percent increase in violent crime in ten years[63] produced a self-fulfilling cycle of raised penalties, new offences and more police, and more criminals serving longer sentences. Legal aid was cut and penal services were to be privatised to minimise the cost. Police claims that civil rights were fettering their power at a time of mounting lawlessness produced recommendations that restrictions on police powers in the New Zealand Bill of Rights Act[64] and the Children, Young Persons and Their Families Act be reduced.[65] A five-year police strategy to fight crime even saw police in some districts circulating photographs and personal details of 'known criminals' within local communities, including those whom the police admitted they had insufficient evidence to put on trial.[66] In October 1994 the Ministry of Justice conceded that the reasons for rising crime had yet to be fully researched.[67] Those studies which had been done, notably one which identified colonisation and alienation as the major cause of Maori crime,[68] were ignored.

So were the causes of stress within the home. Marriage Guidance, now called MG Relationship Services, reported a dramatic increase in family violence towards children and between couples in recent years, with some correlation between rising unemployment and the reports of violence in the 12,000 cases handled during 1991. At the same time the group's national director cautioned that this 'should not be used as an excuse. If we keep blaming it on redundancy and unemployment or society generally, it takes away from what the real issue is and that is men's violence towards women.'[69] A report in 1993 damning the failure of the legislature, police and courts to provide protection for battered women,[70] followed by several tragic murders, forced the government to take a public stand. While the changes to domestic violence laws and police practice, and limited new funding for support services, were welcomed, many women's support groups were sceptical of the government's commitment and viewed it as too little, too late. The key issues of economic stress, male violence and gender inequality remained unaddressed.

One of the most telling indicators of social distress was the increase in suicide. Between 1974 and 1990 the rate of male suicide had risen by 288 percent, with the greatest increase in the late 1980s. In 1990 New Zealand had the highest rate of suicide for 15- to 24-year-old women in the OECD, and the third-highest rate for young men.

Conclusion

The structural adjustment rhetoric talked constantly of the need for stability—but always in terms of the economy, never of people's lives. The strain of constant change fostered uncertainty and insecurity, and made it impossible for people to plan ahead. 'Labour market flexibility' meant going to bed not knowing if there would still be a job the next day. 'Price stability' meant sudden hikes in interest on mortgages and loans, and risks of induced recession. 'Fiscal responsibility' meant continual cuts in income support, benefits and social services. Privatised state services meant having to choose which essential service to keep on, with no one being held to account. Constant policy failure meant revisions and reversals as new versions of the experiment tried to remedy the disasters of the old.

In this decade of greed, talk of 'short-term pain for long-term gain' had meant pain for the poor to achieve gain for the rich. Poverty, alienation and stratification along the lines of class, gender and race were intrinsic, and apparently acceptable, features of the new order. The repercussions went well beyond those who were its immediate victims. Ian Shirley observed

> Within our dual society we have established an underclass which no longer has a vested interest in democracy or in democratic institutions and as a consequence we should not be surprised if those ostracised from the mainstream of New Zealand life willingly promote its destruction. The social deficit we have incurred will condition our development options as we enter the 21st century and there seems to be little appreciation on the part of Government or Governmental advisors either of the extent of the deficit or the forces which produced it.[71]

The deepening social deficit was counter-productive in the neo-liberals' own terms. As Alliance leader Jim Anderton observed: 'you can't go on developing an underclass of larger and larger numbers and always going to sit there happily being poverty stricken. Sooner or later they're going to start smashing the place to pieces and we've seen that in other countries so why would we think we're sacrosanct here? And then my point is to them, how secure is your investment then?'[72] Even National Party president John Collinge warned the party's 1992 annual conference that: 'We cannot risk being two nations, employed and unemployed. We cannot expect those with no jobs and no hope to embrace a society which has failed them.'[73] Yet those responsible seemed complacent in the belief that the poor, the alienated, the disempowered and the oppressed would not fight back.

CHAPTER TWELVE

The Democratic Deficit

IN LESS THAN A DECADE NEW ZEALAND had gone from a bastion of welfare interventionism to a neo-liberal's paradise. Real economic and political power shifted outside the realms of the central state. In this process of what might be termed the 'privatisation of power', citizens were reduced to consumers in the economic, rather than the political, market-place. Jonathan Boston observes how people's preferences as purchasers of goods and services seemed to assume more importance than their preference as to the kind of society in which they wanted to live. 'I think it would be fair to say that many of the advocates of the reforms have generally wanted to reduce the importance of, or if not delegitimise, preferences that are expressed through the political arena.'[1] The legacy was a deep-seated scepticism about electoral politics and parliamentary democracy.

Popular Pakeha politics

In a country where welfare ideology was so deeply ingrained, radical and unpopular change by undemocratic governments might have been expected to provoke disobedience and disorder. This did not occur. Most Pakeha were paralysed by the pace and content of change, confused by the role of the Labour government, and trapped in nostalgia for a centralised welfare state which was disappearing before their eyes. While they felt uneasy about what was taking place, people generally remained isolated, insecure, defensive, unorganised and politically inert. Tony Simpson explains:

> New Zealand is not a society well organized for political action outside the terms of the consensus, so although the consensus was still there, there was no machinery for dealing with the situation in which political élites had moved entirely outside that frame of reference and were doing things of another sort absolutely.[2]

Dissent became more visible under National as left and issue-focused groups which were traditionally aligned with Labour felt freer to criticise. But they had been left seriously weakened by Labour's term. The most notable feature of sectoral politics was the lack of resistance from organised labour. In its early years, the Labour government had kept the unions on-side by reinstating compulsory unionism and tripartite wage talks as promised at the 1984 election. As the economic policy ground shifted, the central union bureaucracy was at first outmanoeuvred, and then adapted to the new environment. The more they attempted to play the new game, the weaker they became, until they were unable, indeed unwilling, to resist the introduction of the ECA.

Limited popular dissent focused on specific issues and policies. Church leaders spoke out, using the politics of embarrassment to good effect.[3] Pensioners protested throughout the country at National's broken promise to remove Labour's surcharge, and again at asset-testing for long-term hospital care. Communities mobilised to defend their local hospitals against closure. Students rallied against the loan scheme and increased fees. Isolated groups of workers took industrial action to defend their jobs. The blockade of a bankrupt northern freezing works in 1994 even saw the traditional adversaries of workers and farmers, and their respective organisations, unite.

Most of those who were prepared to protest on the streets and in the pulpit wanted adjustments to economic policy to produce jobs, restore a decent standard of living, and provide basic social services at an affordable price—a return to the security of the past, not a radical redistribution of economic and political power. They retained an overriding loyalty to the social, political, economic and institutional structure of the New Zealand state, even when that state was not delivering what they sought.

There was a persistent element of militant action among small groups of Pakeha. Unemployed workers and poverty action groups held protests and occupations at Business Roundtable headquarters, the World Bank and Asian Development Bank meetings, and the Reserve Bank. A shanty town was built on merchant banker Michael Fay's front lawn to protest against a government grant of $1 million from lottery funds for his America's Cup challenge when lottery grants to community groups were being cut. Foodbanks were picketed by groups insisting that responsibility for poverty and unemployment be placed back on the government. Their message, if not their tactics, enjoyed considerable support. Yet the number who were prepared to take risks to get the message across remained small.

Electoral support 1984–93

In the absence of organised civil resistance the main point for Pakeha protest remained the ballot box. But political choice proved increasingly sterile. The traditionally dominant parties of Labour and National were deeply implicated in the restructuring process. Apart from labour market deregulation and overt attacks on the welfare state, the programme was a continuum of policies implemented, and embedded through legislation, by one or other party when in power.

Rival explanations have been given for voter behaviour during this time. Supporters of the programme argue that Labour was elected in 1984 because people had lost faith in the interventionism of Muldoon and wanted a radical change. Douglas was widely expected to be Minister of Finance and had made no secret of his views. Labour was voted back in 1987 because the majority of people supported the direction of Rogernomics. A post-election survey showed 65 percent of Labour voters were satisfied with the direction and speed of Labour's economic policy, while another 21 percent said the direction was right but the speed was too fast.[4]

Labour lost the 1990 election because, due largely to Lange, it had lost its way. In the process the economy was severely damaged, as was the programme's short-term success. National was elected because people believed they would complete the job and produce the promised results. People knew what Richardson was proposing to do. They were naive if they expected otherwise. Overall, the continued voter support for Labour in 1984 and 1987 and for National in 1990 and 1993 showed that a majority of New Zealand voters supported the direction and speed of policy change.[5]

Critics of the programme argue, on the other hand, that the election results reflected the duplicity of the parties and a deepening mistrust of party politics. Labour was elected in 1984 on manifesto promises that gave no indication of what would happen next. The blitzkrieg approach left people with little idea of what was going on, and no time to assess the implications of one major change before they were confronted by the next. Difficulties of access to information, resources and outlets limited the amount of independent research available to examine and expose the defects. The media largely abandoned their traditional role in favour of uncritical hype. Had the share-market crash occurred before the 1987 election, rather than two months later, critics claim that the deficiencies of the experiment would have been exposed and the election result may have been different.

In 1987 Labour won 57 of the 97 seats, but only 41.5 percent of the eligible vote. National won 40 seats. Minor party votes almost completely slipped away. According to the critics, Labour had retained the loyalty of its traditional constituency by default, while capitalising on support from the corporate sector and the *nouveaux riches*. It secured an exceptionally high share of the provincial as well as the urban wealthy and business vote, with several of National's safest and richest Auckland seats becoming marginal.[6] Some $3 million in donations poured in, largely from big business. Bob Jones, founder of the New Zealand Party (NZP) in 1983, came out enthusiastically in support of Rogernomics. Most NZP voters appeared to follow Jones's advice.

At the same time the working class did not take their votes elsewhere. Traditional Labour voters could not bring themselves to support National, believing that had to be worse. Labour's vote did fall in some safe seats as traditional voters stayed at home, but without jeopardising its hold. Others felt an obligation to exercise the hard-won right to vote, and took on board Labour's promises to balance the first three years of economic reform by attending to the social costs. There were some grounds for believing that promise. Labour had not yet attacked the welfare state or seriously cut government spending. It had established the royal commissions on social policy and on the electoral system. State servants had received generous pay rises. And Labour had reinstated compulsory unionism and tripartite wage talks.

In 1990 the configuration changed. National secured 48 percent of the popular vote and 67 seats, regaining lost ground in the provincials and in metropolitan Auckland. Big business abandoned Labour, as did the deflated *nouveaux riches*. National's support among farmers revived to 64 percent after falling to 54 percent in 1987. Labour's traditional support dropped away too. The rising vote for third parties indicated that Labour voters who were not prepared to support National were now prepared to look elsewhere. Others took seriously National's promises to halve unemployment and adopt a more pragmatic economic approach, and changed sides. Yet others stayed at home. Political scientist Peter Aimer notes that 'Labour's normal lead over National among manual voters had wasted away to nothing. Thirty per cent of the manual group supported each party.' Aimer attributes this to a large increase (to 25 percent) in non-voting by manual workers.[7]

The defeat in 1990, critics say, showed a resounding condemnation of Labour's duplicity. It had turned its back on the Royal Commission on Social Policy and extended the Rogernomics agenda into the welfare state. The effects of the share-market crash, the recession and rising unemployment had exposed the failures of the free market model and the damage it would do. The vote for National was clearly not a vote for more of the same. Survey results in 1990 showed 'opinion on economic policy had shifted markedly between the two elections. By 1990 a large majority of the population thought that it was either going too fast or headed the wrong way. Most strikingly, 60 percent of National voters in 1990 disapproved of the direction of economic policy under Labour.'[8]

The 1993 knife-edge election result in turn reflected unhappiness with National and continued distrust of Labour. Both governments had been equally guilty of breaking election promises and shown contempt for democratic process and the electorate. Both were seen as captives of the Treasury, the Business Roundtable and their clones. Some people continued voting for either Labour or National out of loyalty, long-term familiarity, or scepticism that third parties could offer a credible governing alternative. Increased support for these third parties, especially the Alliance, showed that others wanted to break the two-party monopoly on power. The vote in favour of electoral reform in 1992 and for MMP in 1993, despite a concerted big-business campaign, confirmed that a majority trusted neither party and wanted the electoral system itself changed.

American political scientist Jack Nagel has argued for a third 'coalitional' explanation. The Labour government elected in 1984 was quite different from the Labour governments of old. It was driven by young educated professionals concerned either with single-issue non-economic causes or by the emerging economic programme. During Labour's first term, two major policies worked in tandem: neo-liberal economic reforms and a left-wing defence policy. The law to ban nuclear ship visits was passed in June 1987, just months before the election. Nagel observes:

> The majority of respondents who *switched* to Labour in 1987 agreed with the party on both economic and defense policies; but among those who

stayed with Labour in both 1984 and 1987 despite agreeing with the party on only one of the two issues, anti-nuclear/anti-Rogernomics voters were more than twice as numerous as the pro-ANZUS/pro-Rogernomics group.[9]

Jack Vowles, on whose surveys Nagel draws, concluded that 'the two policies were at least of equal importance. If one was of greater significance, it was probably defence and nuclear weapons. But only with the combination of the two could the government have so easily survived the test of re-election in 1987.'[10] Some degree of voter support for both policies was not surprising given the strong anti-nuclear and independent defence policy theme of the NZP in 1984. Other sectors, according to Nagel, also contributed to the 1987 outcome:

> Labour differed significantly from National in four distinct dimensions: economic management, defense, industrial relations, and social policy. Its stands on each of these issues appealed disproportionately to a different element in its 1987 electoral coalition: market liberalization to a segment of affluent business and professional people, anti-nuclearism to the post-materialist middle-class who were especially numerous among party activists, compulsory unionism and relative liberality on wages to the trade unions and the blue-collar workers they represented, and welfare state policies to service providers and poor beneficiaries. The last three were already part of Labour's coalition in 1984, and the party could not win in 1987 unless they remained predominantly loyal despite Rogernomics, which . . . won over the pivotal first group.[11]

The battle between Lange and Douglas, which became public after the 1987 election, reflected the collision 'between the contradictory elements of Labour's unstable coalition'. National finally embraced free market policies and resecured solid support from big business and the farming sector. While it pragmatically shifted ground to support the anti-nuclear legislation just before the election, National had no need to concern itself with labour or social welfare issues and their accompanying votes. (National successfully played up the anti-nuclear factor again in 1995, emulating Labour's strategy of opposing French nuclear testing in the Pacific by seeking an interim injunction from the World Court.)

Nagel's thesis supports the view that Labour's re-election in 1987 was not a vote of confidence in Rogernomics. Only a minority of voters was motivated by active support for the programme. But neither was the majority opposed. That did not occur until Labour's second term. It seems clear that the anti-nuclear policy in particular ensured the Labour government re-election and offered a valuable diversion from economic issues. That, and the deferral of action on labour market and social policy until after 1987, effectively gave its technopols a second term. Likewise, the dumping of Labour in favour of National in 1990, strong support for the Alliance in the Tamaki (1992) and Selwyn (1994) by-elections, and the marginal 1993 election result, demonstrated no groundswell of support for the structural adjustment programme.

Electoral reform

Alternating between Labour and National provided different versions of the same paradigm. Deprived of real political choice in 1992 and 1993, the majority of people voted the whole electoral system down.

Demands for electoral reform had been simmering since the late 1970s. First-past-the-post (FPP) had been consistently criticised for allowing parties to govern with only minority voter support, while substantial numbers of those who voted for minor parties were effectively disenfranchised. The Electoral Reform Commission, appointed by Labour, reported in December 1986 in favour of a German-style system of MMP. Half the MPs would represent constituencies with the other half drawn from party lists. Electors would have separate votes for each. During the 1987 election campaign Labour promised a referendum on the proposal in 1989, but later reneged.

A small number of MPs from both Labour and National continued to press for reform. At the 1990 election both parties felt obliged to give qualified support to change, and committed themselves to a referendum on proportional representation. National went further, referring to a second chamber and citizens-initiated referenda as well. After some manoeuvring with private members' Bills, the National government held an indicative referendum in 1992. Voters were asked whether they wanted change and, if so, which of four options they preferred. Despite considerable uncertainty about the details of each option, there was an overwhelming vote for change. Only 15.5 percent said they wanted to retain the existing system. Of the almost 85 percent of those who wanted change, a huge majority (64.6 percent) supported MMP.

Politicians from both major parties were candid about their reasons. Labour's then deputy leader, Helen Clark, acknowledged that calls for change were 'closely linked to the extent of disillusionment with both Governments of recent times. In a number of respects both parties in government have departed from the manifestos on which they sought office and, more generally, from their traditions. In such circumstances the public no longer knows what to expect from those elected by a majority of seats to govern.'[12] National technopol Simon Upton conceded that: 'In retrospect, the past 20 years in New Zealand politics look like a battlefield in which traditional allegiances have been seriously frayed and a large number of voters cast up as casualties on the sidelines.'[13] Both insisted, however, that the answer lay not in electoral reform, but in reform of parliamentary process.

NewLabour leader Jim Anderton countered that both Labour and National could have introduced such changes but had not, and asked why electoral and parliamentary reforms could not both take place. Introducing MMP, he insisted, would ensure equitable minor party representation in Parliament and provide for more real challenges and debates. Government moves could be defeated by coalitions formed to defend areas of common interest.[14]

The National government reluctantly ran a binding referendum on the issue alongside the 1993 election. An intensive, well-funded anti-MMP campaign was led by members of the business élite in the name of the Coalition for Better Government. Campaign leader and chair of privatised Telecom, Peter Shirtcliffe, and other corporate supporters warned that MMP could destabilise economic policy-making and trigger a credit rating downgrade. FPP had enabled strong leadership to implement unpopular but necessary change. Such responsible government would be jeopardised by MMP.[15] Their stance reflected a (presumably calculated) trade-off between the desire to retain absolute power through the existing approach and the longer-term gains from restoring legitimacy to a discredited political system. The Roundtable's Roger Kerr justified their initial opposition to electoral reform as consistent with accountability and responsible government:

The opening up of the economy, the open financial markets, things like our Official Information Act, the Reserve Bank Act, changes in respect of government departments and financial management have very substantially placed checks and balances on political decision making in New Zealand. So the old idea that politicians had unbridled power to do what they want was no longer valid. To the contrary, we felt that the relatively simple first past the post system that we had enabled New Zealand as a small economy to adjust in the way that we will need to adapt to changes in the international environment and a more complicated electoral system might make that more difficult.[16]

In the binding referendum a small but significant majority (nearly 54 percent) of voters supported change. However, there was no guarantee that electoral reform would produce the politics of compromise, consensus and accountability that its supporters seemed to expect.

The new political arena

More fluid philosophies and allegiances infected not just voters, but officials and MPs during the decade as well.[17] Growing disaffection within traditional party ranks and the emergence of new political forces produced a number of genuine oppositional parties. Former Labour Party president and Sydenham MP Jim Anderton narrowly failed to resecure the party presidency in 1988. He was exiled from the caucus in December 1988 for opposing government plans to privatise the BNZ and to sell Postbank without consulting the party as promised. He quit Labour in April 1989 and formed the NewLabour Party, based on old Labour principles and with many of its former activists. In 1990 NewLabour attracted 5.2 percent support. In 1990 and 1993 Anderton retained the Sydenham seat he formerly held for Labour.

The Maori nationalist party Mana Motuhake was the survivor of an earlier breakaway. Former Cabinet minister Matiu Rata quit the Labour Party in 1979, citing the party's inability to grapple with issues raised by Maori within its ranks. Mana Motuhake faced serious philosophical problems in working for Maori self-determination within a colonial structure of majority rule. As a numerical minority, Maori were electorally insignificant to mainstream politics. Despite the Treaty of Waitangi's recognition of tribal authority, Maori were recognised only as individual citizens holding around 10 percent of the adult vote. This was concentrated in four Maori seats which had been captured by Labour since 1935. Despite creditable showings at the polls, Mana Motuhake never managed to displace any of the incumbent Labour Maori MPs.

Alongside these dissident MPs came the phenomenon of the Greens. Filling the void left by the Values Party, their brand of decentralised participatory decision-making and ecologically driven economic policies also sat uncomfortably with mainstream politics.

The Greens' electoral appeal was largely sentimental. There was no clearly explained policy or realistic strategy for traditional-style government. But they represented a set of values which rejected the traditionally adversarial and egoistic approach of New Zealand politics, and the market-centred policies that had dominated since 1984. In 1990 the Greens secured 6.9 percent of the vote but failed to win a seat. In 1993 they still had no MP.

These parties, along with a residue of the old Social Credit Political League of the 1970s renamed the Democratic Party, formed a federal arrangement known as the Alliance in 1992. This unlikely mix of deep ecologists, democratic socialists, Maori nationalists and small business conservatives was united more by opposition to the structural adjustment programme than by a set of coherent policies. As the vehicle for protest votes it had considerable appeal. In February 1992 the Alliance ran National close in a by-election caused by Muldoon's resignation in the blue-ribbon seat of Tamaki. Standing together at the 1993 election, the Alliance captured over 18 percent of the vote but still had only two seats.

National had its dissidents too. In 1992, two traditional Tory backbenchers rebelled against National's broken electoral promises and destruction of the welfare state, and left to form the low-profile Liberal Party. Both lost their seats in 1993.

A more successful newcomer was New Zealand First (NZF). Winston Peters, an outspoken populist National MP and one-time aspirant to the party leadership, was forced out of first the Cabinet, then the caucus, in 1993. He formed NZF, combining the popular nationalism and interventionist policies of Muldoon. In the October 1993 election NZF secured 8.4 percent of the vote and two seats: Northern Maori was taken off Labour by a young Maori candidate, Tau Henare, who enjoyed strong tribal support, and Peters (also Maori) was re-elected in his strong Tauranga base.

The election saw Labour and National initially deadlocked. For the next ten days, the Alliance and NZF, who were firmly opposed to the new order and who represented a quarter of voters, held the slender balance of power. Had that continued, the extent to which the fundamentals were embedded against change might have been put to the test. The subsequent confirmation of a one-seat majority for National reduced that leverage considerably, and the limited resources and parliamentary voice of the minor parties muted their effect. Their potential to disrupt the comfortable two-party monopoly

TABLE 12.1 Electoral results by party, 1984–93

Party	1984 % vote	1984 seats	1987 % vote	1987 seats	1990 % vote	1990 seats	1993 % vote	1993 seats
Labour	43.0	56	48.0	58	35.1	28	34.7	45
National	35.9	37	44.0	39	47.8	68	35.1	50
Social Credit	7.6	2						
NZ Party	12.3	0						
Democrats			5.7	0				
Greens					6.9	0		
NewLabour					5.2	1		
Alliance							18.2	2
NZ First							8.4	2

Source: Adapted from J. Nagel, 'Market Liberalization in New Zealand: The interaction of economic reform and political institutions in a pluritarian democracy', paper delivered to the 1994 Political Science Association annual meeting, New York, September 1994, Appendix D, p.64.

increased, however, as the country moved towards MMP. The electoral appeal of the Alliance continued to grow. In the Selwyn by-election to replace technopol Ruth Richardson in August 1984, the Alliance candidate came within 500 votes of taking the seat from National. Labour secured only 12 percent of the vote. The Alliance shadowed National in the monthly opinion polls. The markets, which had ridiculed the new-Keynesian economic policies of NewLabour, now began to take note. When leader Jim Anderton publicly said the markets could 'go to hell' a major panic hit the finance markets at home and overseas.

Anderton's unexpected resignation as leader for personal reasons in November 1994 temporarily defused that threat. The Alliance fell sharply in the polls, despite the elevation of a strong and articulate Maori woman, Sandra Lee, to take his place. The markets were relieved. Standard and Poor's commented that the change in Alliance leadership had greatly reduced the political risk to the debt reduction programme. Labour redirected its attack from the Alliance to National and began to position itself as leader of a coalition government in 1996. In May 1995 Anderton reconsidered his decision to stand down. The party re-elected him leader, and the Alliance recovered in the polls. Within a month its share of the party vote had doubled to 27 percent, overtaking Labour at 26 percent, and its constituency vote was 20 percent, compared with Labour's 35. It was the list (or party) vote which would ultimately determine the number of each party's MPs.

FIGURE 12.1 Support for major political parties, opinion polls 1984–95

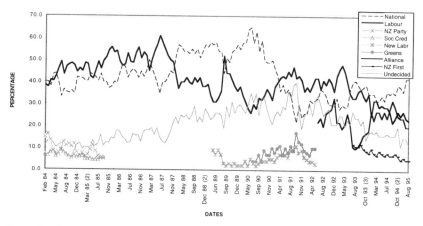

From October 1991 undecided = voter could not answer which party they were most likely to vote for. 1995 refers to party vote.
Sources: 1984–Nov. 1994, One Network News/Heylen Poll; 1995 One Network News/ Colmar Brunton Poll

These 'third' parties had been formed by existing political players out of genuine dissatisfaction with the behaviour and policies of their traditional party base. From mid-1994 the onset of MMP spawned a perplexing array of new parties as Labour and National began to fragment. MPs who saw little chance of securing reselection or election in the reduced number of constituency seats, or of a place on their party list, created vehicles of their own. Most were opportunists who seemed prepared to ally with either National or Labour in a coalition deal. While several individuals had a chance of winning their local constituency, none of their parties on its own was likely to meet the 5 percent threshold for a seat from the party list.

After several defections National lost its formal majority in late 1994, and faced a period of relative paralysis on policies opposed by both its former MPs and Labour. Gradually these fragments consolidated into new coalitions, united more by their position on the political spectrum—generally centre-right—than by coherent policy programmes. The defection of several Labour MPs to these minor parties in mid-1995 helped consolidate National's majority again on most policy issues.

Repositioning the parties

Politics had changed enormously in a decade. So, too, had the degree of autonomy which future governments would be able to exercise over economic, social, environmental and other policies. This created particular problems for parties whose history, constituency and visions were firmly located in the past, and especially for those with a tradition of social democracy and economic intervention.

Labour Party

By 1995 Labour had moved to reposition itself. Following its resounding defeat in 1990 the party spent several years in disarray, unable to restore its credibility and establish a clear political line. Labour lost the 1993 election, which many in the party believed it should have won. Populist Mike Moore, who had been made leader just before the 1990 election, was replaced by his deputy Helen Clark in a messy coup. Clark was subjected to continued sniping from within. Some of this related to the perceived feminist takeover of the party machine. But it also showed an on-going distrust of a leadership which had been prominent in the Labour Cabinet during the Rogernomics years.

Labour revisionists set about sanitising the party's image and selectively distancing it from the past. The economic liberalisation programme of the 1980s was confirmed as basically sound. Douglas and his cohorts had taken it to an unacceptable extreme, but they were now gone. The Labour government's social policy had been progressive and supported its traditional constituency, who then suffered tragically at National's hands. The rehabilitated Labour Party promised to build on the good of the past and leave the bad behind. With the economy now showing sustainable growth, Labour would redistribute the benefits to those who had suffered along the way.

Labour's new economic platform promised a middle line between 'a return to a closed, fortress economy or the rigid regulations of the past' and 'blind worship of the so-called "market"'. Its stated objectives were a pragmatic mix of full employment, higher real incomes, more equitable distribution of income, and sustainable economic development.[18] The style of government would also be different.

Labour promised a return to the negotiated economy based on tripartite representation from Cabinet, business and unions.

The ECA would be replaced with a 'fair industrial relations system' which would promote collective bargaining and a fair process for negotiations, and eliminate 'destructive wages competition'. It would set a minimum code for wages and conditions. A fair accident compensation system would be restored. While unions would regain legal recognition, voluntary unionism and the framework of individual contracts would remain.

The role of Treasury was to be reviewed, along with the State Sector Act, to ensure an efficient, impartial and strong public service. Objectives of fiscal policy would be broadened to include sustainable economic growth, full employment and social equity, and the principles of the Fiscal Responsibility Act reframed to meet 'sound economic and constitutional principles'. Labour would still aim for a budget surplus, funded partly by a small increase in income tax for the rich and reintroduction of estate tax. Social welfare benefits would be restored to around their level before the 1991 cuts and rationalised to remove anomalies. Family support for low income families with children would be raised substantially. Other areas of social spending would receive smaller increases, along with investment in 'sustainable growth'.

Other fundamentals of structural adjustment would be retained, including the Reserve Bank Act's exclusive price stability goal and the median of 1 percent, with target range for inflation broadened to -1 to 3 percent. Net debt would be reduced below 30 percent of GDP. Trade liberalisation and deregulation would continue apace, with active participation in APEC and other world trade forums. Environmental and social concerns would be pursued within the WTO.

Three questions hung over Labour's new image. First, could it be trusted to do as it said? Labour was intent on distancing itself from the arrogance and broken promises of the past. But some habits died hard. Accusing the National government of incompetence in April 1995, former associate finance minister and likely Minister of Finance under a new Labour government Michael Cullen claimed: 'At least we were competent when we broke our promises. One thing about the Fourth Labour Government, we broke our promises with style—competently and with a clear sense of direction.'[19] While sceptics believed they could do so again, there would be little need for that. The initiation phase of structural adjustment was over. Changes of the past decade would be consolidated more effectively if Labour re-established stability and secured compliance from the left within the new paradigm.

Second, who would benefit from Labour's policies and would they satisfy its traditional supporters who were seeking significant political, economic and social change? The tripartite approach was meant to re-establish the historical compromise—old-school, boys-together corporatism. Women, community and environmental interests would be accommodated but within the labour/capital/government framework. Despite a gesture in the direction of the treaty, there was no place for Maori to exercise constitutional power. The conditions under which corporatism once operated had also changed. As became obvious in the late 1980s, reinstating tripartite government would depend largely on the willingness of the corporate sector and employers to co-operate.

The final question was the effect of Labour's policy on the structural adjustment programme. It was clear that Labour was prepared to knock off the rough edges of the new regime and resecure a limited degree of domestic control. But it was not about to challenge the fundamental premises of the open market economy or reduce the economic power which now lay in international hands, nor to debate the costs and compromises its strategy involved.

The Alliance

The Alliance had survived when many predicted it would fail. It worked hard to build an organisational and policy base. Yet Anderton's resignation exposed the thinness of the party. Few of its key spokespeople were known. Without him it was doubtful whether the Alliance could present itself as a credible alternative government at the polls.

Despite this, Alliance policy enjoyed considerable popular appeal. Its central platform was full employment, defined in traditional terms as 'full participation in, and belonging to, society by all its members with an adequate income and a rising standard of social well-being for all'. The driving force behind its economic policy came from NewLabour. This reflected the concerns which many social democrats had raised since 1984: the narrow focus of monetary policy, the unaccountability of government and big business, the lack of regulatory control over strategic assets that had been privatised, the damaging effect of the high exchange and interest rates on manufacturers and farmers, the excessive commitment to free trade, the regressive changes to the tax system, the narrow definition of economic growth, and so on.

The Alliance's solutions, however, lay in nostalgic appeals to democratic pluralism, the welfare state and Keynesian interventionism. Anderton's telling the markets to 'go to hell' had a cathartic effect, with enormous political appeal; but it rested on an illusion that New Zealand could again—assuming it once did—chart its own destiny relatively free from the dictates of global capital. An Alliance-led government could certainly attempt to follow such a path, and there would be considerable popular support for it. But there was a worrying reluctance to explain specifically how the new reality of a highly exposed, deregulated, export-based and foreign-controlled economy could be dismantled and rebuilt, or even effectively contained—and at what cost to whom.

In late 1994 the Alliance announced a list of twelve 'non-negotiable' policies which it guaranteed would not be bargained away after the election. These were to provide the basis for any coalition, which the Alliance insisted had to be formed prior to an election to ensure transparency of the political process and accountability to both voters and Parliament. The base lines were:

- to recognise the Treaty of Waitangi as New Zealand's founding document and honour and implement its provisions;
- full funding of the public health and education systems;
- active measures to achieve full employment, including government and private sector investment in the infrastructure and environment, regional development funding and low interest local body loans;
- sustainable management of all natural resources;
- universal entitlement to all social security provisions, including reversal of benefit cuts;
- identification and removal of all barriers to equal opportunity;
- commitment in international forums to support social justice, self-determination and rights of oppressed people, and support ecologically sound global agreements;
- a fairer distribution of income and wealth through a broad-based, progressive tax system and removal of GST and tax surcharges;
- modified national accounts, including natural resource accounts, recognition of unpaid work, and environmental and social indi-

cators to assess effects of economic activity;
* no more sales of strategic public assets and services with restrictions on purchase of rural land;
* a minimum code of wages and conditions, pay equity, replacement of the ECA with legislation promoting industry-wide collective bargaining through democratic trade unions;
* amending the Reserve Bank Act to broaden its focus to include sustainable economic well-being and full employment.

Not surprisingly, in the political climate and economic conditions of 1995 no other political parties were prepared to negotiate with the Alliance on these principles, even when it offered to be more flexible. Unless they performed an embarrassing about-face and accepted a post-election coalition, Alliance parties seemed destined to spend three further years in opposition. Some saw this as a deliberate political strategy. If Labour won a significant share of the vote and attempted to form a coalition without the Alliance, it might be forced into bed with parties of the centre and centre-right, including National. That could destroy the Labour Party for ever—which had been the avowed purpose of some NewLabour activists when their party was formed in 1989. Any such strategy would, however, be an enormous political gamble for themselves, their supporters and the people of the country, who would be subjected to a further period of unstable and market-driven government.

Association of Consumers and Taxpayers

At the other end of the spectrum was Roger Douglas's new political vehicle, the Association of Consumers and Taxpayers (ACT). Following his retirement from Parliament in 1990, Douglas had aggressively promoted his ideological and personal interests within the country and abroad. ACT advocated a Hayekian form of limited government and the completion of the 'unfinished business' of the Rogernomics programme.[20] Widely seen as the political wing of the Business Roundtable, ACT incorporated many key technopols from previous Labour and National governments, as well as zealots from Federated Farmers, the financial sector, the commercial community and the Roundtable, and a once-prominent Maori radical.

ACT was estimated to have resources equivalent to all the major parties combined with which to fight the 1996 election. In a major publicity blitz in 1995, it took the credit for the economic recovery and promised more:

ACT is a new political party founded by Derek Quigley [a free market Cabinet minister sacked by Muldoon in 1983] and Roger Douglas, the architect of New Zealand's burgeoning prosperity. In 1984 Roger Douglas had the courage to make the hard decisions, taking a knife to one of the most regulated, out-dated economies in the world and turning it around. The process made him—to put it mildly—one of the less popular politicians on the scene, but he always did what he said he was going to do and his policies have proved resoundingly correct. Unfortunately he was never allowed to finish what he started, to bring the fruits of New Zealand's success into every home. ACT is the instrument of that vision.[21]

Like Labour, ACT faced the difficulty that many people still remembered the Douglas years as an overwhelmingly negative experience. The party sought vainly to shake off the label 'right-wing' which locked it into the conservative/social democratic discourse of the past. It aimed beyond the market players and ideological converts whose support it could expect, and sought to attract Maori, workers and the poor by offering to liberate them from the economic and cultural strait-jacket of the welfare state.

ACT's glossy manifesto was released in March 1995. Its simplicity had some appeal. All income and company tax would be abolished immediately. The resulting flood of capital into the country would create economic growth and jobs. Low income families in work would receive a guaranteed income which would make them better off than at present and better off than welfare beneficiaries who remained dependent on the state. Everybody would be required to save 7 percent of their income towards their retirement, pay for their own health care through private health insurance, and pay for their children's education. Government would meet or subsidise these costs for the poor.

A temporary 40 percent payroll tax on all wages, paid by employers, would cover superannuation for existing pensioners. Remaining pension costs and reduced debt servicing would be met by the sale of state assets (including all New Zealand's overseas reserves, 60,000 of the 70,000 state houses, Electricorp, NZ Post, Landcorp and Forestcorp) valued at $26 billion over the following eight years.[22] Core government spending and the size of government administration would be cut. Permanent immigration would be limited to 5000 places a year which would be auctioned to the highest bidder.

Despite the attempt to portray this as a bonanza for the poor,

ACT's strategy would continue to redistribute resources to the rich and intensify the crises facing the health, education and welfare systems. The real beneficiaries would be the owners and agents of finance capital, who would gain an enormous pool of funds for investment. There was no guarantee that these funds would be invested in New Zealand, that such investment would be labour-intensive and create jobs for other than an élite or at minimal wages, or that the profits from trans-national insurance corporations, their downstream investments, or entrepreneurial health and education companies would remain within the country. As competition law would be based on contestability rather than actual competition, trans-national monopolies would dominate the market and squeeze out or undercut more responsive, locally controlled alternatives.

ACT's policies had an initial appeal to many Maori, and were sold hard to communities in urban areas and on marae. While the social cost of structural adjustment had fallen most heavily on Maori, 'devolution' had provided more flexibility to tailor programmes to their needs which the centralised and monocultural welfare state had persistently ignored. ACT's model assumed, however, that Maori would compete from an equal position as consumers and commercial providers in the internationalised market-place. The possibility of restoring the resource base as a foundation for genuinely autonomous economic development was predictably ignored. So was the question of shared governance in the minimum state which, despite the rhetoric, would retain a significant degree of power.[23]

Those destined to profit most from the new economic order and to whom ACT primarily appealed were less likely to find problems with its logic. They were what journalist and Alliance politician Bruce Jesson called the 'Young Right'—well educated, in business or professions, mobile, not yet 40, without attachment to a particular firm, community or even city, competitive, ambitious and protective of their personal freedom of choice.[24] But they were a small minority. People still had strong memories of life after 1984. By mid-1995 ACT was stalled only halfway to the threshold of 5 percent voter support it needed to secure a single list seat.

National Party

National's blueprint for the future was set out in its 1993 pre-election document *Path to 2010*. This was fleshed out and updated in 1994 and 1995. The message was simple: by building on the current economic recovery National would create strong communities and a cohesive society. This required:

- further improvements in the government's financial position;
- a dynamic business sector with reduced costs and increased investment;
- strong trade and links with the global economy;
- breaking the cycle of disadvantage by early intervention in education and training, families and social skills, and preventing crime;
- fair and affordable settlement of Treaty of Waitangi claims; and
- balancing economic growth with the needs of the environment.

Net public sector foreign debt would be reduced to zero by 1997, with public sector debt between 20 and 30 percent of GDP.

National was prepared to share some of the credit for the economic recovery with Labour, notably low inflation, the competitive enterprise economy and trade deregulation. But it claimed the ECA, government expenditure restraint and a focused new strategy for education and training as its own. 'As a small and open trading nation, New Zealand will never be free from major changes to the international environment. Our aim should be to ensure that we can confront these changes from a position of strength.'[25] The key to that was a steady hand on the tiller with 'the great helmsman' Jim Bolger in the lead. With ACT and the moral-right parties as potential coalition partners, National could leave the extreme positions to them.

To carry it through, National was relying on the momentum of an economic recovery which appeared to have peaked by early 1995, the perception of National's policies and presence in government as the norm, and the inability of its competitors to mount a coherent, saleable alternative programme.

Prospects under MMP

After a decade of structural adjustment a paradigm shift had clearly taken place. National and Labour had repositioned themselves within its bounds, offering variations in form and detail but skirting around the longer-term implications of the internationalised market-driven economy. The re-emergence of party differences in the 1990s created an illusion of political choice while stabilising the change. Ultimately the new regime would survive if either of them controlled the reins of power.

Given this, popular expectations of MMP seemed quite inflated. Its supporters assumed that electoral reform would restore accountability and representation to the political system and help moderate, if not reverse, the structural adjustment programme. Yet it seemed increasingly likely that nothing would change, or worse. The polls suggested that the only party which could secure an outright majority was National. If no party did so, there was a strong possibility that a coalition of extreme libertarians, conservative moralists, pro-market Progressive Greens, the centre-right National Party and other centrist forces would hold power. Voters who believed that they could secure real change through MMP would have to wait three more years to try again.

A coalition government of the centre-left would almost certainly include Labour, and it was likely to insist that key elements of the structural adjustment programme were retained. If Labour's hand was forced, the previously unthinkable National/Labour alliance was a genuine prospect. Alternatively, Labour's centrist MPs could peel off to join the other side, leaving Labour in a minority coalition with the Alliance and maybe New Zealand First.

Even if a genuine centre-left coalition was elected, the entrenched nature of the changes would seriously limit what a more responsive and representative government, especially one working through a coalition, could do. As Alan Bollard explained: 'New Zealand is now a more open economy checked not only by the "arm's length" regulation of domestic markets, but also by international capital markets, trade and treaty undertakings, and international credit agencies. There is less scope for discretionary government action under either electoral system.'[26] The moderating effect of coalitions meant major policy swings and significant new structural reforms were also unlikely. To make sure of this, Bollard suggested shifting further key economic decisions beyond the control of the state: the 'idea of government relinquishing some direct interventionist powers in such a way becomes important under MMP and might be envisaged in other areas of economic policy as an insurance against an overly short-term coalition government.'[27]

This conservative assessment was shared by many of the technocrats and their allies. The time lapse between the 1993 referendum and the first MMP election had offered them three further years in which to finish the job. Most of the existing technocrats would remain in control of the state machinery for several years after that. An inexperienced, hostile coalition government would find it enormously difficult to neutralise their power. Treasury officials seemed confident that MMP would make the new regime more secure, reasoning that any party within a coalition government would have to negotiate a compromise and make commitments to which it would be bound. This would induce a cautious approach to ensure that the coalition remained intact and prevent any extreme reversal of the new status quo.[28]

Despite forebodings from opponents of MMP, and general wariness about the Alliance, the credit rating agencies also viewed the new regime as safe. Following the 1993 election Moody's indicated that a hung Parliament and a vote for proportional representation were not fundamentally negative from its point of view. It saw little to choose between the Labour and National parties on the 'fundamentals': 'We are reasonably comfortable that the types of changes with potential to improve New Zealand's credit rating are not likely to be undone.'[29]

The consolidation of the structural adjustment programme through the internationalisation of the New Zealand economy had imposed real constraints on subsequent governments. To make informed political decisions about the future direction of their lives, voters would need to know the likely costs of continuing down the current path, going back, or heading in a new direction, and on whom the costs and benefits of those options would fall. None of the political parties seemed willing or able honestly to engage in that debate.

The Maori political challenge

The theorists assumed that, once the initiation and consolidation phases were complete, the new regime would prove almost impossible to dislodge. Haggard and Kaufman, however, acknowledged that those who received no benefits from, and felt no commitment to, the new economic order might seek to bring it down. Pakeha presented no such risk. But Maori politics afforded a very different scenario. Maori had traditionally been defined, and had defined themselves, in opposition to the colonial state. They had periodically, but only ever partially, been incorporated into its hegemonic realm. While the impact of structural adjustment fell most heavily and disproportionately on them, many Maori viewed it as a variation on a long-standing theme. It was not surprising, then, that the most (some would say the only) sustained political resistance to the structural adjustment programme had come from them.

By 1984 the resurgence of Maori activism, centred on the Treaty of Waitangi, was potentially explosive. To defuse this threat, the new Labour government promised to address outstanding grievances.[30] The locus of treaty politics moved from the streets, police stations and prisons into the courts, the specialist Waitangi Tribunal and the negotiating rooms of the new 'treaty-friendly' state. But Labour's promises also created expectations and reinforced the determination of many Maori to resecure what was theirs before, and under, the treaty.

Many Maori initially sought to work alongside the new Labour government. As the implications of Rogernomics became clearer, they were forced to take the offensive. The suffering created by Labour's economic policies was distressing in itself. But Labour's attempt to corporatise and privatise disputed resources would have made it impossible for the Crown to restore those resources to Maori control. While the interests of capital would have been more secure, Maori would remain dispossessed and destitute. The outcome of court-ordered negotiations enabled the government to complete its programme (except for the privatisation of Coalcorp); Maori secured almost no tangible benefits in return.

Ironically, Labour's attempt in the late 1980s to devolve—or more accurately decentralise—delivery of Maori services through the tribes intensified debate on traditional authority structures and strengthened the revival of the tribal base.[31] Maori demands increasingly centred on tino rangatiratanga—the constitutional authority of the tribes to exercise independent political, legal and economic, as well as cultural, power.

As the political and economic contradictions of its treaty policy emerged in the late 1980s, Labour faced the extraordinary difficulty of convincing Maori that major advances were being made, while convincing Pakeha and capital that such changes would not reduce their own economic and political power. It could satisfy neither. Once its treaty policy became an economic and political liability, the Labour government attempted to relegate the issue to its previous peripheral place. Such a move sparked tensions between the judicial and executive arms of the state, which were each driven by their own internal and external imperatives.[32] After six years of Labour's promises, virtually no settlement of grievances had been achieved.

National continued Labour's failed settlement policies and floundered in treaty negotiations for the first four years. The backlog of claims before the Waitangi Tribunal reached 500 by May 1995. The tribunal's stretched human and financial resources[33] had seen it produce an average of seven reports a year since 1990.[34] Secretly, however, in September 1992 the National Cabinet had adopted a policy to settle all treaty claims by the year 2000 through a lump sum allocation known as the 'fiscal envelope'. After numerous denials, the government finally announced this publicly in December 1994—along with an admission that the fiscal cap had already been operating for several years.

The policy had its genesis in a purported full and final settlement of Maori fisheries claims in 1992.[35] The government funded certain Maori interests into a joint-venture purchase of the Sealord fishing company, which owned 22 percent of the privatised quota rights over fish. In return, all tribes' treaty rights to the fisheries were rendered unenforceable at law and placed beyond the Waitangi Tribunal's jurisdiction. The traditional relationship of Maori to the fisheries had been spiritual, collective, reciprocal, perpetual and sustainable. Their claims over the resource had been partly a reassertion of that relationship, and largely an attempt to restore tribal members' rights to fish. What they received was a financial interest in a commercial undertaking, jointly owned with a trans-national investment corporation (BIL), which sought to maximise profit from the exploitation of commodity rights in fish. The resulting controversy and inter-tribal division spread from the domestic courts to the United Nations. The Sealord experience should have convinced any sensible government that lasting settlements would not be achieved by negotiating with an élite of Maori entrepreneurs and imposing market economic models on Maori economic development.

The 'fiscal envelope' policy was the Sealord deal writ large. A notional $1 billion would be set aside over ten years to reach a full and final settlement of all outstanding treaty claims. Deducted from this sum would be the research costs of claimants already paid out by the government's treaty unit, lawyers' and consultants' fees and commissions, the Sealord payment and other undisclosed settlements. What remained would be used as cash compensation in itself or to enable tribes to buy land and resources back from the Crown or private owners. In return for an as yet unknown share of the envelope, a negotiating tribe would be required to concede for ever all its outstanding claims.

The fiscal envelope, its architects claimed, would resolve all outstanding grievances in a durable but fiscally responsible way. The treaty could then be removed from the political stage and everyone could get on with life. Either the government had seriously miscalculated, or it had set the scheme up to secure short-term credit knowing that in the longer term the policy would fail. The economic model it embodied, the commodification of nature, the inadequacy of the amount, its unilateral origins, and its imposition in the face of trenchant opposition made rejection inevitable. The attempt to exploit the envelope's appeal to entrepreneurs and vested interests among Maori was seen as a cynical exercise in divide and rule. It also represented a foolishly myopic reading of the treaty by reducing it to one generation's property rights. Grievances over the theft of resources were symptomatic of deeper resistance to the usurpation of tribal control over their people, resources and way of life which under the treaty Maori had been guaranteed to retain.

The fiscal envelope was unanimously rejected at a series of meetings between the government and tribes throughout the country. Yet the government persisted with the policy and reaffirmed it in the 1995 budget. A landmark settlement with the major Tainui tribe, the victim of large-scale confiscations during the wars of the 1860s, was concluded in May 1995 and hailed by government as proof that its strategy would work. The deal provoked intense controversy within the tribe. While Tainui negotiators denied that they were buying into the fiscal envelope, the government made it clear that they were. Moreover, the government insisted that the fiscal envelope was the only deal around and that Maori were likely to secure even less from coalition governments under MMP. Pressure then came on other tribes to negotiate a settlement, or miss out.

The government's arrogance and intransigence again radicalised Maori positions and fired up militant action. High-profile and broad-based protests were revived at the annual treaty celebrations at Waitangi in February 1995. Occupations subsequently erupted in a central city park in Wanganui, an Auckland school being sold to a Chinese church, the Maori Arts and Crafts Institute at Whakarewarewa in Rotorua, the marae at the University of Waikato, and elsewhere. Most politicians and media portrayed the protest leaders as militant hot-heads on ego trips of their own. But these were historically sourced grievances acted upon by young and old with a clear and consistent base—sovereignty over these resources vested in them, not in the Crown.

The occupations represented a potent threat to the new economy. The Chinese buyers withdrew from the Auckland school purchase, expressing anger at the government's failure to explain the situation fully in advance, at the damage to already tense Chinese/Maori relations, and at the behaviour of the police towards the occupiers. Word was bound to spread to potential Asian investors in New Zealand and overseas. Foreign tourist operators at Whakarewarewa sought to tighten their contracts to compensate for any fall-off in trade should protest action recur. Again, tourism networks were likely to keep a watching brief. National's blueprint *Toward 2010* had identified the economic risk of Maori dissent: 'Legitimate grievances that remain unresolved create an obstacle to race relations. In some circumstances the existence of unresolved Treaty claims creates uncertainty that deters investment.'[36] Yet the government's persistence with the fiscal envelope intensified these risks. The resurgence of militant activity and the consolidation of Maori demands in recent years suggested that any precipitate action on the part of future governments could provoke outright rebellion against the state.

CHAPTER THIRTEEN

The Cultural Deficit

In 1986, as the experiment gained momentum, one of its disciples observed: 'It's generally accepted that we in New Zealand are going through a period of revolution, in the sense that the old order is being replaced with a new order which has not just an infrastructure, but more importantly an ideology, beliefs and value system' which ranged across all domains. It featured pain on the part of those whose political, economic and psychological well-being was being cut away; and a feeling of exhilaration and excitement for those with opportunities in the turbulence of change 'to grow, to achieve and to increase their political and economic and . . . psychological well being'.[1] This was a revolution led by those who benefited—and left the mass of the people behind.

Social values

Canadian journalist Murray Dobbin observed in a documentary on New Zealand in 1994 that 'any grand social experiment not grounded in the citizenry or the culture goes awry because it has no natural limits'.[2] The findings of the Royal Commission on Social Policy in 1988, followed by two major surveys of social values in 1989 and 1993, show that most New Zealanders supported policies very different from those so uncompromisingly pursued by National after 1990 and Labour before it.

Drawing on eighteen months of research and consultation, the royal commission identified three main principles for future social policy: *voice, choice* and *safe prospect*. 'Underlying it all . . . is a uniquely New Zealand statement of the good society; it is one in which one had a say and a chance to determine one's own destiny, where there is opportunity to express a choice, but where in the end there is a sense of community responsibility and collective values that provide an environment of security.'[3]

The New Zealand Study of Values in late 1989 and the International Social Science Programme survey in 1993[4] provide a valuable indication of attitudes at the end of Labour's period in power, and near the end of National's first three-year term (see Tables 13.1, 13.2). Using exactly the same questions, more than 1000 people were asked to give their views on increasing government spending in each of nine areas, even if it meant paying higher taxes. The 1993 survey confirmed support for increased spending on education, health, job training and assistance, and pensions at levels even higher than in 1988. Even the traditionally unpopular area of the DPB attracted additional support for an increase, while the number of those wanting cuts to it fell significantly. The only area where support for cuts grew marginally was assistance to Maori and Pacific Islanders—justifying Maori cynicism that they would not benefit from a resurrected welfare state.

TABLE 13.1 **Increasing or cutting government spending meaning higher taxes, 1989, 1993**

Topic	year	strong yes	weak yes	neu- tral	weak no	strong no	can't choose
Education system	1989	30.1	48.3	14.7	3.1	2.0	1.8
	1993	45.9	42.8	9.4	0.6	0.3	0.9
Pensions	1989	12.0	39.9	39.4	5.8	1.6	1.3
	1993	14.6	50.4	30.6	2.0	0.3	2.1
DPB	1989	3.1	10.2	39.1	31.1	13.4	3.1
	1993	2.9	20.9	45.4	20.5	6.9	3.5
Protecting the	1989	21.5	41.6	28.4	4.4	2.6	1.5
environment	1993	19.9	49.9	26.2	1.5	0.5	2.1
Special assistance to	1989	1.8	10.7	37.4	24.7	24.0	1.4
Maori & Pacific Islanders	1993	2.5	10.0	32.8	29.4	20.6	4.8
Job training & assistance	1989	15.9	45.0	27.2	6.9	3.8	1.2
for the unemployed	1993	26.6	47.2	21.0	3.0	0.7	1.5
Health	1989	38.6	43.9	12.9	2.2	1.6	0.8
	1993	50.0	38.2	9.8	0.7	0.2	1.2
Special sports events	1989	4.1	18.3	39.8	20.4	16.0	1.4
	1993	2.3	14.3	46.2	21.4	13.0	2.8
Military, armaments	1989	3.0	11.9	36.0	26.6	18.8	3.7
& defence	1993	2.2	9.3	41.7	26.3	17.8	2.6

Source: adapted from P. Perry and A. Webster, 'Against the Tide: A government failure in popular persuasion', unpublished paper, Massey University, April 1994, Table 3. Sample: 1991: 1000; 1993: 1249.

A remarkable feature of the 1993 survey was the degree of concern about the unregulated economic environment and the lack of controls over big business. There was a relatively low level of support for government ownership of big business, but even that moved up slightly. Redistributing income and wealth to the less well-off was strongly endorsed, while the numbers opposed to such a move fell. Support for protecting the environment, even at some cost to economic growth, remained strong, although a small decline from 1989 probably reflected growing demands on social services at the time.

TABLE 13.2 Percentage responses on views of government action 1989, 1993

Topic	year	strong yes	weak yes	neu- tral	weak no	strong no	can't choose
Increase police powers	1989	41.4	40.2	6.9	7.5	3.4	0.6
to fight crime	1993	51.7	31.5	7.3	6.0	2.7	0.8
Stricter controls	1989	35.3	32.8	17.8	10.2	3.4	0.5
on pornography	1993	52.9	20.4	17.0	6.0	2.7	0.8
Govt owning big	1989	5.2	25.3	26.7	31.0	9.3	2.5
industries in NZ	1993	11.0	22.6	24.5	19.2	19.2	3.4
Tighter gov't regulation of	1989	13.8	41.3	24.6	15.0	3.0	2.3
big companies & multinat'ls	1993	28.5	35.1	19.4	8.0	3.8	5.1
Redistribute income &	1989	8.0	34.0	22.0	24.8	9.4	1.8
wealth to the less well off	1993	19.4	29.9	20.7	16.6	10.7	2.7
Stronger environ'l protect'n	1989	23.9	44.8	17.3	11.2	1.9	0.9
if it hurts economic growth	1993	18.6	46.0	19.1	10.7	2.8	2.8
Special rights to Maori to	1989	3.4	13.3	16.5	35.0	31.3	0.5
make up for past injustices	1993	7.0	13.4	12.8	22.5	42.0	2.3
Declare NZ a republic—	1989	5.3	10.9	21.2	34.8	26.3	1.5
no Queen	1993	14.6	12.7	22.8	15.4	31.6	2.8

Source: Adapted from Perry and Webster, Table 1. Sample 1989:1000, 1993:1264.

Analysing the two surveys, sociologists Paul Perry and Alan Webster conclude:

> the picture presented here is very striking. In most realms a clear majority of New Zealanders do not support the direction that successive governments have carried this country [in] over the last nine years. It is also evident that the National government's attempt to educate us about the correctness of its policies has failed, since most people in 1993 have views even farther removed from government policy than was the case in 1989.

This appears to contradict opinion polls which showed support for the general direction of the country at between 42 and 56 percent during 1993–95.[5] That support could be attributed in part to the economic recovery. Yet other polls showed a deep level of unhappiness about specific areas of social policy and government expenditure which were traditionally seen as part of the social contract.[6] Assuming all these polls were accurate, people seem to have been torn between upholding the welfare ethos to which most were instinctively committed, and internalising constant messages about what kind of economy New Zealand needed to succeed. The polls also indicated increasing polarities between different parts of New Zealand society. The director of AGB McNair explained this with reference to their survey of media target audiences. The grouping classed as 'lonely and dissatisfied' had grown from 16 percent of the population in 1991 to 24 percent in 1995. He concluded: 'There is a clear perception that the economy is in recovery and things are getting better, but a growing number are hurting badly.'[7]

Reshaping social values

Disdain for popular opinion was a feature of the Douglas and Richardson years. This was interspersed with short periods of pragmatism and appeals to voter support by Labour and National leadership. Even then, maintaining the confidence of the markets had remained equally important. By 1992, after eight years of stagnation and recession, rising unemployment and visible poverty, a deep sense of alienation had emerged and the advocates of the new regime had become concerned.

In the foreword to its blueprint *Budgetary Stress*, released at the height of the recession, the Business Roundtable urged the government to adopt a more systematic and sensitive approach to selling the new order, 'as any government is ultimately dependent on community understanding and support for its actions. These requirements have not always been present in the reform programme of recent years, and as a consequence it has at times faltered.'[8] The Roundtable was not advocating greater public scrutiny of the structural adjustment programme and debate over alternatives—merely that government market the new agenda more energetically and effectively.

Similar sentiments were expressed by the report of the Porter project on New Zealand's international competitiveness. New Zealand's only constraint on achieving its potential would be the 'people's inability or unwillingness to adapt, change and thus compete successfully in the global economy'.[9] Essential norms and attitudes towards business 'grow out of the educational system, social and religious history, family structures and other unique national conditions. The socio-political environment structure and context tends to have a distinct impact on the kinds of industries [with] which a nation achieves international pre-eminence.'[10] It was for the government to build 'a broadbased national consensus about the general thrust of the changes required'[11]—and to manipulate the hearts and minds of all New Zealanders to embrace this new ideal.

Changes to the key conduits of national identity, values and culture—education, media and the family—were of supreme ideological importance to the consolidation of the project. The immediate effect would be to neutralise potential sources of criticism. Their longer-term goal was to instil the neo-liberal ethos in the minds of the future generation, the 'children of the market' who had known no other way.

Education
In 1982, the OECD identified the most significant values informing the provision and practice of education in New Zealand as full employment, equality of treatment, multiculturalism, a consensual approach to education, consultation and participation, and individual freedom and social justice.[12] The changes to compulsory education that began in the late 1980s sought, with limited success, to redirect those values towards the free market society. The Porter report urged the government and the schools to 'expand our notion of education to include economic goals as well as social and academic goals'.[13] Roundtable director Roger Kerr expressed disdain for a society where 'the chattering classes appear to despise the sector that keeps a million New Zealanders in work and schools do not see it as their job to teach business values'.[14]

The rationale for restructuring tertiary education reinforced this goal. In addition to their educational role, universities had served a range of public service functions: the creation and expansion of knowledge, research and publication; advisory and servicing functions for the state and professions; repositories and transmitters of historical, cultural and social knowledge; and (rather too rarely) as social critics. The neo-liberal model sought to reduce that role to production of education and training—commodities which would be bought and sold in an artificially constructed education market and driven by the forces of supply and demand. Education could then be defined as a private good, with the burden of funding increasingly shifted from the state to the student. Research functions could be separated and funded from a contestable pool. The public good functions of universities, termed 'spillovers', might simply disappear. SSC officials explained the rationale in August 1992:

> The assumption is that academics must demonstrate their utility to society by placing themselves in an open market and accordingly competing for students who will provide the bulk of core funding through tuition fees. If academic research has a value it can stand up to the rigours of competition for limited funds.[15]

This shift to market-driven education was accompanied, somewhat paradoxically, by proposals for state control of degree accreditation and governance. Universities had to become accountable to their owner for the wise use of government assets. Objections that this was incompatible with the critical social function of the university carried no weight. According to Treasury:

> Choice, as well as cost, is best harboured with the party benefiting; in the case of social benefits not captured by individuals, with the government department most closely concerned. Government choice raises the questions of academic freedom from government interference. . . . The amount of academic time producing social benefits through discharge of the entrepot [storehouse] or research functions and funded directly by government departments is likely to be very limited. The issue of academic freedom will only be of significance for a part of that very limited sub-set. Historically universities may have acted as a key source of free information and discussion on political and other sensitive issues. In the information age this is no longer the case and the very multiplicity of information sources is itself a form of protection—as modern totalitarian states have found.[16]

The implications of this development were profound. New Zealand academics had never been in the forefront of struggles over social justice, and were slow to grasp the magnitude of structural change and play their role as public critics after 1984. But they remained one of the few potential sources of independent analysis and critique. Increasing numbers had already become captives of the commercialised world of consultancies, performance-based indicators, contestable research grants and short-term employment contracts. Neo-liberal sympathisers colonised the halls of academe while social critics struggled to survive in an increasingly hostile environment.

The implications for students were equally severe. The model presaged an élite student body, under heavy pressure to recoup the costs of their education and repay their loans, who would make instrumental demands on course availability and curriculum content. Student choice of training options would be driven by speculative labour market signals and pursuit of careers which they considered most likely to rescue them from debt, rather than subjects they were interested in or best equipped for. High-prestige, high-cost professional courses were predicted to become the domain of an even narrower élite. Courses which offered intellectual interest or social value, but no immediate prospect of employment, would become luxuries for all but the wealthy. Women, Maori and Pacific Island students whom market forces served least would be left with a particularly invidious choice.

Concern at the erosion of educational values was reinforced when the New Zealand government included education in its offer to the services agreement of the GATT. This guaranteed non-discrimination between foreign and domestic education providers. While the government's offer applied only to private primary, secondary and tertiary education, that assumed a meaningful distinction between public and private. A market-driven, fully contestable education system, funded by vouchers which students could use in public or private institutions, would erode that distinction, and with it the guarantee of local control. Because the GATT was a one-way street, once these commitments had been made they became virtually impossible to withdraw.

Neo-liberal economist Girol Karacaoglu confidently predicted in late 1994: 'Education will increasingly become a vehicle for employment creation rather than a device for creating well-rounded individuals.'[17] Education was once seen as a vital repository of unique identities and cultural values, a source of much-needed contest and critique, and a valued activity irrespective of market demand. In the hands of the zealots, that era seemed almost to have passed.

The media
The second major conduit of knowledge, values and critique was the media. The historically weak New Zealand press and broadcast media were blunted further after 1984 by the privatisation and concentration of ownership, commercialisation and Americanisation of programming, self-censorship of editorial content and journalistic

style, and government intolerance of those who adopted a fourth estate role.

By 1995 news and current affairs were in a bad way. In the print media, conglomeration and near-monopoly control had narrowed editorial perspectives and reduced journalistic critique. This placed the onus of investigative journalism on broadcasting. But that, too, was a victim of commercialism. Joe Atkinson describes the 'morselisation and depoliticisation' of television news content as stories were dissected into saleable segments and packaged into a tabloid format. Hard stories on domestic politics and foreign and defence policy gave way to emotionally and visually appealing items on human interest, disasters and crime. The moral of a story was conveyed to viewers through presenters' non-verbal cues. In-depth studio interviews and investigative journalism were replaced by populist crusades, group encounters and evasive or rigidly combative interviews. Analysis of complex issues became structurally impossible. By 1992, more than three-quarters of all interviews had been reduced to ten-second sound bites.[18] The privileged status that political and business élites continued to enjoy as 'authoritative sources' gave them powerful leverage over the language, agenda and perspectives that were capable of being heard.

Rare excursions into investigative journalism met an often hostile response. TVNZ's *Eyewitness* current affairs programme produced some critical investigations into specific issues in the later 1980s. But a documentary linking the Labour government with big business drew a number of defamation writs. This, and TVNZ's lack of support for the producer and journalists involved, forced television critique back underground. Some of the best television and radio journalists moved offshore, producing more pungent critiques than their homebound colleagues.

Radio provided more sustained critique, especially of National's assault on the welfare state. In 1992 the government blamed the media, and left-wing journalistic bias, for its poor opinion poll ratings. Politicians and their advisors directly pressured management of state-owned media to bring specified critics into line and recommended journalists they would prefer to see used. Government's plans to privatise commercial state radio and make non-commercial programmes contestable were linked to political displeasure at such criticism. Delays in progress over the sale were later attributed to anti-government campaigns run by private talkback radio, notably

Radio Pacific, which provided a vent for the populist and often red-neck frustrations of the disenfranchised populace. The *NBR*'s media commentator observed: 'Talkback radio is only filling a vacuum created by the lack of an effective parliamentary Opposition for the past eight years. As a result, it has converted the natural democratic process of dissent for its own—commercial—use. It has become Parliament with ad breaks and race results.'[19] Other journalists came under attack, with actual or threatened exclusion from press conferences and media events.[20] All this came, as media commentator Paul Smith observed, from a government 'which believes in the free market for everything but ideas, especially embarrassing ones'.[21]

Overt political pressure was not new, and after the 1993 election it declined. But the climate of commercialisation, deregulation and constant restructuring meant that it could be manifested in subtle and less visible ways. Many journalists, senior executives and funding agencies were aware that their personal futures and those of their agencies were constantly on the line. The relationship between press gallery journalists and politicians often seemed too close for comfort. Many of these journalists subsequently took up contracts in politicians' offices or as public relations consultants for newly created Crown agencies or corporate lobby groups.

A rare exception was the respected economic journalist Simon Collins, who left the *New Zealand Herald* and helped to found a weekly giveaway newspaper *City Voice*. This provided analysis of macro-issues at the micro-level of life in the capital city. The paper promoted campaigns against the sale of the local electricity company and user charges in the public library, alongside coverage of local activities and cultural events for a wide range of community tastes. In the harsh economic climate of the 1990s its financial survival remained fragile.

At the other end of the scale came Radio Liberty. The local broadcasting rights for the BBC World Service, bought by Alan Gibbs in the early 1990s, took on a new life when the frequency was sold to a Christchurch-based consortium in 1994. New station manager and former TVNZ journalist Lindsay Perigo saw it as his mission to 'promote individual liberty and be business-friendly and recovery-supportive', in contrast to Radio New Zealand's *Morning Report* and Pam Corkery programmes, 'which are full of that ghastly nonsense about profit-making being evil'.[22]

By 1995 a new intolerance of critique was evident in parts of the mainstream media. Campaigns were levied against 'political correctness', while individuals, agencies and programmes which were identified with human rights, anti-racism and social justice came under attack. The good-news machine which heralded the economic recovery seemed to harden its stance, rationalising the social costs of the experiment as an inevitable price 'the country' had to pay. According to the *New Zealand Herald* end-of-year editorial in 1994:

> hardly anybody believes in 'trickle-down' in the sense that only the antagonists use it. . . . An economy geared to enterprise and effort cannot reward the lack of them. Much public discourse in 1994 still encouraged people to imagine that the benefits of the new economy would come as a social gift to those who lie and wait. The growing disparity of incomes, though much maligned in discussion, was smaller this year than might have been expected.[23]

This increasingly hard-line approach was accompanied by a gloves-off attitude to social critics. The desire to discredit or intimidate such critics may have reflected the right-wing media's insecurity about the economic recovery, or a supreme confidence that they were now firmly in control.

The family

A third major conduit of social and cultural values is the family. The innate moralism and gender bias of the neo-liberal agenda were reflected in rhetorical attacks on the welfare state and moves to force 'responsibility' back onto the family. Underpinning this was the need to normalise the monocultural, nuclear and patriarchal family structure—one which denied gender power within the family, detached Maori from their whanau (families), turned its back on widespread evidence of domestic violence and dysfunction, and allowed only (some) men the freedom to choose.

In its 1987 briefing papers, Treasury identified the breakdown of the nuclear family as a major concern: 'The increasing incidence of marriage breakdown and the increasing proportion of families headed by a sole parent mean that many children are growing up in a family environment very different from the traditional family structure, and our schools, police and social agencies are facing large numbers of children suffering significant stress from their home environment.'[24] Social welfare minister Jenny Shipley, who helped oversee the dismantling of the welfare state, expressed similar sentiments in 1992: 'I believe that for a long time there have accumulated many serious disturbances in the role and function of families and other historic institutions such as the Church, law and education systems. A consequence of these disturbances is that the welfare state itself, through its mechanisms, produces young illiterates, juvenile delinquents, alcoholics, substance abusers, drug addicts and rejected people at an accelerated speed.'[25]

The quest to re-establish family values received a boost with the Year of the Family in 1994. Leading entrepreneur and ideologue Alan Gibbs, in a speech on the impact of the changing economy on families, laid the blame squarely on the decline of individual responsibility:

> We have had many great civilisations in the world and they have all come up against the problem that the nature of man is not terribly conducive to looking after women and children. . . . Every single significant civilisation adopted the institution of marriage as the basis for the socialising of men. . . . A practice that for thousands of years societies have said was fundamentally important to make sure that men did their cultural duty and took responsibility for a woman and her children we largely threw out. We decided we wouldn't bother with men, we'd get the state to do it for us. So we swapped husbands for benefits. I don't blame the DPB for the breakdown of marriage because the DPB came only halfway through the period of change. . . . I think the pill was most important because it relaxed the pressures that mothers put on their daughters to hold this cultural norm together. It also went along with other social changes that have occurred in the world in the last 30 years. Most of the problems the poor families have today are the result of that huge social change. They have little to do with the state of the economy. . . . Normally families react to external stress by pulling together, not falling apart. Human beings and their institutions are far too strong to fall apart from a bit of economic and social pressure.[26]

State support was systematically withdrawn from those who digressed from this 'norm' in an attempt to force human relations back into an economically optimal mode. That usually meant economic independence for men in the market and economic dependence for women within the home. The ultimate expression of this was contained in a paper from Infometrics Business Services in April 1991— when National's major benefit cuts took effect. Its primary author was neo-liberal economist and *NBR* columnist Gareth Morgan. Entitled 'Mitigating Misery—A Preliminary Assessment of New Zealanders' Capacity to Absorb Cuts in Real Income', the paper co-opted feminist arguments on valuing women's unpaid work to the neo-liberal cause. The basic premises, as summarised by economist Prue Hyman, were that 'earners of lower second incomes (usually women) would be more productive at home, and it would be economically rational for them to return there'. Further, 'efficiency in home production should be encouraged [and] such efficiency should be assumed, with some benefits able to be lowered still further'.[27]

Morgan argued that reduction of state support would provide incentives to increase household efficiency, especially for the poor: 'at the low end of the income scale there are significant gains in efficiency that households could capture as a counter to the falls in real market incomes. Further, we expect that it will be necessary for them to do so in order to prevent the income falls producing unnecessary hardship.'[28] Those on low incomes, especially benefits, Hyman explains, 'will, can and should have to manage on less by substituting cheaper goods and their labour for purchases, with women reverting to elbow grease, bottling and making the family clothes. Government should have the guts to make them do this by cutting benefits further.'[29] Morgan accepted that the polarity between the wealth and poverty of families would become worse as a result:

> The necessary shift of market income towards firms and away from households . . . will likely accentuate the differences in material wealth between those households fully participating in the market economy, and those who become more dependent upon home production. While the political and economic ramifications will be significant, it is likely that a dual economy will develop with the behaviour of one group of households driven by market economy forces, while the other group becomes increasingly immune to market cycles.[30]

In addition to challenging Morgan's 'back-of-envelope' calculations, dubious assumptions about the price of domestic production and the inequity of the results, Hyman condemned his attempt to disguise gender bias in the language of economic rationality. Rosie Scott went further:

> Morgan's language reflects the heartlessness at the centre of economic rational thought, the arid landscape of the cost accounting mentality, a world where ordinary people's lives, national institutions, cultural treasures, rights that have been painfully gained over generations, compassion for the poor, the dispossessed and the sick are all squashed flat by the bulldozer of profit and loss.[31]

Market newspeak

The ethos of the market pervaded daily life. Even the language had been captured. In the new (market) cultural revolution, words once familiar to advocates of democratic and social justice were turned into catch-cries of liberal individualism. Treasury's *Government Management* had its own market-speak. 'Freedom' no longer meant liberation from enforced economic, racial or social inequality. Instead, it meant 'freedom of the individual to achieve objectives free of constraining conditions'.[32] 'Devolution' meant the government retaining power over essential resource and policy decisions, while delegating delivery to the voluntary or private sector. This dominant/subordinate relationship was termed a 'partnership'. 'Accountability' would be achieved through market efficiency measures of profit or contractual performance criteria. All this would 'empower' individuals to take control of their lives as free and equal actors on the 'level playing field' of life. 'Liberation' was defined by Treasury to mean 'the promotion of the dignity of people through direction of their own lives'.[33] There was no room for putting altruism ahead of self-interest, compassion ahead of efficiency, or mutual obligations and collective identity ahead of individual benefit. Nor was there any doubt about the intrinsic superiority of the market-place.

The new vocabulary disguised the intentions and effects of the structural adjustment programme, and dehumanised the people and communities it affected. When talking about workers, Scott observed: 'There is "shedding workers", as if they were so much dead skin, there is demanning, cutting staff, retrenchment, labour rationalisation and restructuring . . . permanent downsizing and . . . reducing duplication through release of resources.'[34] Cutting wages becomes 'flexible wage rates'; continued high unemployment is 'persistent labour market slack'; 'incentives' equates with cutting benefits to force people into very low-paying jobs; 'broadening the tax base' involves shifting the tax burden from the rich to the poor; 'freeing up the market' means removing all impediments to making a profit; 'realigning resources to their most valued use' means forcing even profitable firms to close if more money can be made elsewhere; 'deinstitutionalisation' makes closing state institutions and transferring responsibility to families and communities sound progressive, whether or not they are adequately resourced; 'transparency' means exposing financial details to the scrutiny of an élite; 'an open economy' welcomes foreign companies to buy control of the country's key assets and resources; 'international competitiveness' means lowering local standards to the level of countries whose economies are premised on grinding poverty and environmental degradation; and so on.

Even sports, the icon of New Zealand culture that united (almost) everyone, did not escape the revolution unscathed. By the 1980s sport was big business, especially for promoters of alcohol and cigarettes, who were otherwise barred from advertising. In one of the decade's supreme ironies, the combination of sporting fervour and corporate enterprise saw the country unite around one of the world's most élite and extravagant sports—the unsuccessful challenge for the America's Cup in 1986 and the successful campaign in 1995. Politicians eagerly jumped on the bandwagon. Bill Birch's 1995 budget even extolled the win as an example of how New Zealand could take on and lead the world. 'Team New Zealand's success in the America's Cup is an example to us all of Kiwi innovation and dedication to skills, hard work and team spirit, succeeding against the best the world can offer'. Almost no one asked who would actually benefit from 'New Zealand' winning the event,[35] nor what the cost to local ratepayers would be of staging the cup's defence in Auckland. But 'bread and circuses' had always been a valuable diversion in controversial economic and political times.

Becoming Asian

Within a decade the country of New Zealand and the lives of its peoples had been turned upside down. This revolution—bloodless, but devastating for those who became its victims—had been prosecuted in the name of the 'nation as a whole'. Constant references to national wealth, national economy, national well-being and the national interest sought to submerge structural inequalities into an amorphous, consensual whole. In the process, the nation-state in whose name the experiment was carried out was irreversibly changed.

New Zealand's national identity since the mid-1930s had been constructed around the monocultural, interventionist and centralised welfare state. From 1984 the foundations of that identity were systematically undermined. Economic, social and political power became internationalised, diffused, individualised and increasingly uncontrolled. The centralised paternalist bureaucracy and corporatist alliance of old was replaced by a selectively coercive limited state, driven by market ideologues and a corporate élite. This rapid and dramatic shift provoked a crisis of identity among many Pakeha. Their reaction was in part nostalgia for the comfortable welfare years, and in part a xenophobic response to foreign ownership and Asian immigration. Both reflected a growing fear that people had lost control over their lives.

From 1993 National set about moulding a new national identity. Prime Minister Bolger's key-note address to the National Party conference in 1993 was entitled 'Succeeding in the World, Secure at Home'. Bolger reached back to the pre-welfare state ethos of the rugged risk-taking individual who succeeded on his (and, in recognition of the centennial year of women's franchise, her) own merits and who received his or her just deserts. He proclaimed:

> This recovery is about New Zealand and New Zealanders; about how we see ourselves. For a while New Zealand lost its way. We forgot the pioneer spirit, the sense of independence, and the community's responsibility for those who fell by the wayside. We said the state can look after this—and that—and eventually we expected the state to look after everything. And we ignored the fact that we were bankrupting the country. Eventually a Government has to have the courage—the guts— to say 'This simply can't go on.' . . . What we are dealing with here is nothing more nor less than the renaissance of the Kiwi spirit. The pulse of New Zealand is beating again. And with it we are seeing the return of the true spirit of New Zealand: proud, independent, hard-working and caring for your neighbour.

After a decade of sacrifice, a 'resurgence of the New Zealand spirit' was now 'flowing from New Zealand's farms, forests and factories. From the heartland of our country.' This national renewal had, Bolger claimed, been built on individual self-sacrifice for the advancement of the common good, the wealth of the nation and the national interest. Increasing polarities of wealth and poverty were transitional costs on the way to securing an emancipatory society for all, or resulted from personal inadequacy or lack of drive. Those in need, Bolger insisted, had not been abandoned. They were now being cared for in a fairer, more appropriate and fiscally responsible way.

Bolger attempted to invoke the nineteenth-century colonial identity to justify severing links with the twentieth-century welfare state. But global political and economic realities in the 1990s meant leaving the 'motherland' behind and relocating identity in the geopolitical and economic space to which New Zealand now supposedly belonged. A historical identity, steeped in European supremacism and

Enlightenment ideology, had somehow to be grafted onto the Asian region.

Redirecting the country's economic priorities and cultural identity towards Asia involved an eight-year strategic plan. *Asia 2000* had three objectives. The first two were economic: to develop a framework for New Zealand's relations with Asia by the year 2000, and excite New Zealand firms about business opportunities in East and South-east Asia. The third involved a conscious strategy to reorient New Zealand's dominant culture and identity away from the anachronistic colonial past towards its new economic destiny within the Asian region. Foreign affairs minister Don McKinnon described the transition in a July 1993 speech entitled 'Forward to the Year 2000':

> I was in a plane coming down through the Pacific from Tokyo where I had just seen economic growth like I'd never seen it before. And it struck me that, here we were as a nation in the bottom of the South Pacific—largely with a history as Europhiles mixed with Polynesians, now with North American influences, and neither fully reflecting where New Zealand really stands. In a nutshell, we needed a foreign policy initiative which would fundamentally realign New Zealanders' views about (a) what our neighbourhood is all about, beyond Australia and our South Pacific Home Region; and (b) where our economic future largely lies. It was not a matter of renouncing our history and heritage or devaluing the lasting importance of Europe and North America. But it did seem to me that we needed to make a giant, dramatic leap into Asia, and needed to do it now.[36]

This vision went well beyond redirecting New Zealand's trade priorities. It required 'a community-wide appreciation of the economic, political, strategic and cultural associations that we will need to develop with Asia'. Bolger even talked of developing a 'true Asia consciousness' with a 'sense of community for the region as a whole'.[37] National subsequently retreated from making New Zealand Asian to a middle ground which portrayed the country as part of the Asia–Pacific community, sharing a common history and heritage, but maintaining its own identity, social norms and values.

Immigration was integral to the new international economy, and portrayed as an unquestioned good, a vital source of capital and skills. The Muldoon years had seen a marked human exodus from New Zealand. After a brief respite, net outflows had resumed under Labour. These averaged 11,000 a year between 1985 and 1991, seriously depleting the pool of skilled labour. In late 1991 National introduced a four-tiered targeted immigration regime with general, business investment, family and humanitarian categories. This produced a net inflow of around 5000 a year between 1991 and 1993, mainly of professionals and technicians, with many from Asia and newly democratised South Africa. New Zealand was importing the skilled labour and capital that it was unable to provide from within. Both Labour and National enthusiastically promoted Asian immigration, but failed to establish effective settlement programmes. Wealthy business migrants and their families were accused of making excessive demands on scarce school places and resources, while their investments remained passive and short-term.

At the other extreme came reports of immigrant workers being paid below-subsistence wages and forced to live in sub-human conditions. Exploitation of guest workers, especially overstayers, was nothing new.[38] But high unemployment, combined with the Employment Contracts Act, encouraged employers to play off local workers against migrant labour to drive the costs of both down. The immigration service disclaimed responsibility for checking the validity of job guarantees, but said it would investigate the living and working conditions of job offers if somebody complained.[39] When cases of exploitation were exposed, some employers protested that they were unable to find local labour to take on such arduous work.[40]

Popular reaction to Asian immigration reflected a deep-seated racism. An *NBR* poll in April 1992 showed that over half those questioned believed there were too many Asian immigrants in the country, even though two-thirds of them thought the migrants made a positive contribution. Prejudice was strongest among women, young people aged 18 to 24 years and people earning $15,000 or less a year—those most likely to feel deserted by the state, and at risk of being overtaken in the quest for jobs, houses and life opportunities by the new migrants.[41] In November 1994, polls showed that 42 percent still believed that Asian immigration was too high.[42]

There was little opportunity for rational debate. Fears of an Asian economic takeover confused the racial origins of investment with the basically non-cultural operation of finance capital, wherever it originated. The reality that most foreign investment was sourced from Australia and the US was obscured by the sudden, visible influx from Asia. Politicians shared this ambivalence—Asian money was welcome, but the government would rather the immigrants came from elsewhere. In 1992 immigration minister Bill Birch expressed the need for a more 'balanced migration flow'[43] and subsequently announced a promotion in Britain to attract 'quality migrants' to New Zealand, along with a modified general migrants point-scoring system.

McKinnon rejected suggestions 'that New Zealand has turned into some sort of economic animal, ready to sell its heritage for pieces of silver'.[44] Yet that was what many believed successive governments had done. Historically grounded racism had targeted Asians, along with Maori, as the perpetrators of Pakeha dispossession. Pakeha felt that they were losing control of *their* identity, *their* economy, *their* country. The government understood the Pakeha problem: 'The anti-Asian tensions in New Zealand aren't about racism. They are about perceptions of control, particularly economic control. So much of the anti-Asian tension stems from fears about being overwhelmed by Asian money, numbers, technology and so on.' Its solution was to build a better 'understanding [of] what we as a nation want. As New Zealanders we need to be confident that we know where we are going and why. That is why we need a strategic framework. By debating and developing a framework, we retain clear and focused control of our national goals in the Asia–Pacific region.'[45]

When Maori expressed similar anger about losing control they attracted little sympathy or support. Professor Ranginui Walker describes the Treaty of Waitangi as the original immigration charter for New Zealand, any variation of which had to be renegotiated with the tribes. The treaty had allowed the presence of people from Europe, Australia and the United Kingdom on condition that the independent authority of the tribes was retained; in return, Maori would gain access to trade and economic benefits. At first those hopes had been realised. But once the immigrants achieved numerical superiority, and political and economic dominance, Maori became second-class citizens in their own land. The recent Asian immigration policy compounded this effect, leaving the largely poor and unemployed Maori population even more marginalised than before.[46]

The Labour government rejected demands, backed by the Human Rights Commission, that the treaty should be considered in decisions on immigration policy.[47] A Business Roundtable report by Australian Wolfgang Kaspar argued that Maori had nothing to fear from becoming a smaller minority. 'They could instead live in a nation of many minorities where the Maori minority fitted in much better as an equal social group.'[48] Walker countered that the report reflected the 'ignorant naivety of the outsider who knows nothing of the 150-year struggle of the Maori against an unjust colonial regime'.[49]

The failure of successive governments to involve Maori in making immigration policy, and to inform migrants of the treaty and its implications, was only part of the problem. The real objections were rooted in the government's obsession with securing economic growth through increasing foreign control, the effect of immigration on quality of life and the environment, and the further marginalisation of Maori in numerical, economic and cultural ways. A counter-move in 1993 to issue passports in the name of Aotearoa symbolised the determination of Maori to reassert control over *their* future in *their* land.

Foreign control

Opposition to Asian immigration reflected a deeper resentment of foreign control. This had been building among Pakeha for some time, fuelled by state asset sales to overseas buyers, the Asian buy-up of prime commercial and residential property, the ease of foreign takeovers of 'New Zealand' firms, and the creeping acquisition of rural land by overseas interests. It was brought to a head by the government's plan to extend the Overseas Investment Commission's jurisdiction to rural land in 1995. An *NBR*/Consultus poll in May 1995 showed that half of those surveyed did not want land sold to foreigners and would support a law to ban foreign ownership of land in New Zealand. Opposition was strongest among women, students, retired people and the unemployed. But even 37 percent of professionals, managers, technicians and associates said that foreign land ownership should not be allowed, and 44 percent wanted it banned. Over 40 percent of National voters were opposed to such sales.[50]

During 1995 New Zealand First and the Alliance campaigned aggressively on the issue of foreign control, although polls showed that the Alliance reaped most of the benefit. While reversing the level of foreign investment was not realistic in the short term, there was a strong determination at least to stem the tide. Labour sat uncomfortably on the fence, welcoming foreign investment generally but drawing the line at rural land. The intense popular reaction suggested that foreign investment and foreign control could pose the first serious Pakeha challenge to the structural adjustment programme. Yet this resistance was reactive, not creative, and seemed likely to be played out through party politics. The result would be, at best, an uneasy stalemate, given the country's deep infiltration by and dependence on foreign capital and an international profile premised upon the 'openness' of its foreign investment regime. The debate also carefully avoided the contradictions in the Pakeha argument. Opposition to immigration and foreign investment, coming from descendants of relatively recent immigrants who had themselves dispossessed Maori, raised a fundamental problem of where, when and against whom they could ethically draw the line, and on what grounds.

Concerns about foreign control were being voiced even more vigorously among Maori. These were Maori resources which were being sold off. They were hard enough to recover when held by the Crown. Once ownership moved offshore, they would be lost for ever. Governments needed to settle the internal debt to Maori before selling the country's treasures overseas and repaying their foreign creditors. The carefully nurtured image of New Zealand as a haven for foreign investors and immigrants came under attack at a press conference of Maori nationalists during the Asian Development Bank meeting in Auckland in May 1995. Lawyer Annette Sykes declared:

> Perhaps the most poignant message we wish to give development bankers and those wishing to invest in New Zealand is that it's about time you sat down and talked to us because the present illegal government has no warrant to deal with resources, neither for the past, nor the present and certainly not for the future. . . . It's about time world governments and New Zealand in particular woke up to the fact that as of right tangata whenua [first nations] should have representation at these conferences and not be marginalised to the outside where we are in confrontation with the police. If they do not acknowledge the status we enjoy nationally and internationally within law, then they will be facing extreme acts of terrorism and activism amongst us, and it is about time they changed.

The government reacted with threats to charge Sykes and fellow nationalist Mike Smith with sedition. It was wisely advised not to proceed with the charges. To proceed would have provided a rallying point, unprecedented in this century, for reassertion of Maori sovereign authority and for the unilateral exercise of that authority by various tribes and groups of Maori throughout the land. Even without such provocation, that was beginning to take place.

Constitutional reform
A decade of Waitangi Tribunal claims, court cases and negotiations had bought the Labour and National governments time. In 1995 they were served notice that Maori patience had run out. There were mounting demands for constitutional dialogue to establish a system

of governance in which Maori would exercise sovereignty and self-determination over their lives and their lands. This was what the 1835 Declaration of Independence had recognised, and the 1840 Treaty of Waitangi with the English Crown confirmed. For some, this meant sovereign Maori authority over the entire country; for others, it meant complete Maori independence from the colonial state; for the more moderate, it still required co-existent and co-operative polities of equal status within one nation. There was vigorous debate over the relationship between tribes and urban Maori, and over the economic models to be pursued. But these involved variations within a generally agreed theme: Maori had to exercise control over their own.

Until 1995 the National government's official line on the constitutional status of the treaty, as Labour's before it, had been placatory. The fall-out from the Sealord deal, electoral reform, the fiscal envelope, Waitangi protests and the rash of land occupations heightened divisions within the Cabinet. Those who espoused an uncompromisingly hard line appeared to capture control, producing a significant and potentially inflammatory shift in the government's public position. Any claims to the high ground of good faith and morality were abandoned. While the National Party still recognised the treaty as the founding document of the nation, in practice this was displaced by a new assertion of raw power.

In a syndicated newspaper column in May 1995, technopol Simon Upton resurrected the essence of a speech from a retired law professor delivered some eighteen months before. This conceded that something less than sovereignty had been acquired by the English Crown through the treaty. But, said Upton approvingly,

> whatever legitimacy the Crown failed to derive from the treaty, it acquired through the effective and durable assertion of power. To not put too fine a point upon it . . . the British Crown and subsequently the New Zealand Parliament, effected a revolutionary seizure of power. . . . [T]he passage of time and the effective extension of government power have made the idea of parallel sovereign states within the same land practically and politically unworkable.[51]

Revolution, Upton continued, 'rests upon what is done, not what is legal, or necessarily moral or just'. Minister in Charge of Treaty Negotiations, Doug Graham, ran the same line in a speech two days later. This was unflinching in its assertion of European supremacy and completely devoid of the appeasement which had previously characterised Graham's speeches.[52] All arguments in support of Maori sovereignty, whether based on the 1835 Declaration of Independence, the fact that some tribes had never signed the treaty, the treaty's guarantee of tino rangatiratanga (independent authority) or the government's subsequent failure to honour the treaty, were peremptorily dismissed. Graham made it clear that the English Crown had seized power by revolution and that power had since prevailed. The hypocrisy of the government's position was highlighted by prominent Maori.[53] Here were two ministers of the Crown legitimising revolution—indeed, privileging it over other constitutional processes. Yet the same Crown was claiming the moral and legal authority to indict for sedition those Maori who promoted 'revolutionary' means to recover what the colonial state had forcibly taken away.

Recent Maori assertions of sovereignty were portrayed by Graham as uncomfortable outbursts which every country with an indigenous minority experienced from time to time. The concept of shared sovereignty was deemed 'quite untenable' in a 'fully integrated society'. In settling treaty grievances, the Crown would provide redress for the confiscations made last century. Other events which might be difficult for the Crown to justify could be left to the Waitangi Tribunal, which Graham tellingly described as 'a valuable safety valve in allowing these matters to be aired'. As far as it would go on the constitutional front was a heavily subordinated form of self-determination amounting to self-management. This was consistent with references by Prime Minister Bolger to the possibility of greater Maori self-management or co-management, and a 'new voice of Maoridom' through some form of elected Maori advisory body. Graham's speech was clearly calculated to reassure National's supporters that it had turned its back on appeasement, and to show Maori that the iron fist would, where necessary, replace the velvet glove.

Despite the government's new assertive stance, it was clear by 1995 that the issue of constitutional power was not going away, and that this was a debate the government could not control. The form which a treaty-based constitution might take was the subject of growing interest and debate.[54] Those reasserting tino rangatiratanga insisted that there were benefits for both Maori and Pakeha, and that they were willing to share. At a stage in the country's history when many Maori and Pakeha felt alienated and disempowered, having lost control of their lives, their futures and their land, there was an unprecedented common bond. If this mood was harnessed and built upon, any future government which turned its back on the issues or sought to repress those advocating self-determination could face rebellion of a more embracing kind.

Constitutional change could be grappled with by Pakeha institutions and power-brokers as part of a constructive dialogue, or it could be deferred yet again in pursuit of short-term electoral pragmatism—at grave risk to the political and economic stability and future well-being of the country and its peoples. The latter looked increasingly likely. In the past politicians, officials, journalists and other Pakeha commentators had ignored warnings that their refusal to address tino rangatiratanga would provoke a more militant response. National was still not prepared to tackle the question seriously. Labour made vague promises of constitutional dialogue, but this was difficult to reconcile with its economic and political programme. The Alliance and New Zealand First, working from a policy base of economic sovereignty and anti-foreign investment, and with a stronger rhetorical commitment to the treaty, were better equipped to engage with the debate. But selling it to their Pakeha supporters would be an uphill task. In a Radio New Zealand/MRL poll in June 1995, 81 percent of those interviewed, who were predominantly Pakeha, believed that Maori should receive no special rights. Only a quarter believed that Maori should receive compensation for past losses—57 percent believed they should not. And over half remained committed to the historic 'we are one people' line.[55]

Republicanism

The constitutional issue was bound to arise via another route anyway. In March 1994 Prime Minister Bolger had unexpectedly floated the idea that New Zealand should become a republic. Widespread speculation on his political and personal motives largely missed the point. Replacing the economic, cultural and political links of the colonial past with a forward-looking, internationalist identity was an imperative of the new world order. Republicanism would help sharpen people's sense of independence and self-reliance, and their drive to succeed in the competitive global economy. Bolger suggested that the transition could be achieved with minimal constitutional upheaval. The Governor-General would become an elected or appointed Head of State. A new domestic court of final appeal would be created in place of the Privy Council. A local version of the Queen's Honours list would be devised.[56] Others suggested that a formal constitution might also be required. But that was about all.

The shift to a republic was presented as a natural evolutionary process. But there was little enthusiasm for change. Opinion polls in April 1993 had shown 27 percent in favour of becoming a republic, 56 percent opposed and 17 percent unsure. Following Bolger's speech in March 1994, poll results remained much the same: 28 percent in support, 46 percent against, and 26 percent who did not know or care.[57] Support for the status quo reflected Pakeha ambivalence more than pro-royal sentiments. Populist hysteria during periodic visits by English royalty had declined in recent years, although the royal family remained essential to the commercial survival of glossy women's magazines. Trappings of Empire, such as the uninspiring flag and the honours list, were of peripheral interest and concern. Debate about the future of appeals to the Privy Council touched the lives of lawyers, academics and politicians. But that was not about to set popular royalist or republican sentiment on fire.

Bolger's attempt to promote republicanism sought to sidestep the Treaty of Waitangi. Yet the treaty was an inescapable part of the debate. Republicanism meant formally cutting colonial ties and creating a post-colonial state. It was fundamentally an exercise in decolonisation. Successive New Zealand governments had supported decolonisation elsewhere. But they showed a chronic inability, intrinsic to New Zealand's origin as a settler colony, to apply the logic to indigenous sovereignty at home. Maori rights were defined as human rights based on cultural self-identity, not rights to sovereignty and self-government—despite the explicit guarantee of continued independent authority in the Maori text of the treaty itself.

Diverse Maori responses to Bolger's republicanism speech highlighted a consistent underlying position: republicanism could not be addressed without the treaty. There were three inter-related arguments. First, the treaty was an agreement between Maori and the English Queen sealed with her personal mana (prestige and authority) and that of the rangatira (chiefs). These links could not be amended, and certainly not severed, unilaterally without destroying the very basis for non-Maori presence in Aotearoa in the past or present day. Second, the promotion of republicanism was viewed by many Maori as a device to remove their access to the Privy Council as a court of last resort. By linking the future of the Privy Council to the republican debate, the government invited suspicion, resentment and confrontation. Third was the insistence that constitutional reform must precede or be an integral part of any move towards a republic. This meant constructing a new constitutional framework which reflected the treaty relationship of co-existing independent nations—the tribes and the Crown.

Rather than grappling with these fundamental questions, the National government sought to wipe the colonial slate clean. But the crucial issue for resolution had always been Maori sovereignty. However much colonial governments and courts might try to redefine the treaty guarantees and indulge in divide and rule they could not change that political fact. Any attempt to close the door on the treaty and create a post-colonial republic without addressing the issues of sovereignty and constitutional power was doomed to fail.

Towards the future

The decade of structural adjustment had provoked a crisis of identity in Aotearoa New Zealand. National's 'heartland' and Asianisation strategies assumed that the people's minds were malleable and responsive to the needs of international capital, and would passively internalise those needs as their own. Both Maori and Pakeha opinion proved largely unmoved.

Many Pakeha felt that first the Labour, then the National, governments had sold out democracy and sold off their country to big business. The dominant national (Pakeha) identity, fostered by the political and legal institutions of the colonial state, had combined settler supremacism with the complacency of welfare democracy. The global free market threatened that identity. After almost a decade of passive acquiescence, some Pakeha looked as though they might begin to fight back. But the deeply racist nature of their identity meant that most found it difficult to understand and identify with Maori nationalist expression of the same concerns.

By 1995 it was clear that the sharp end of politics, and potentially the future direction of the country, would lie in Maori hands. This was an element which the structural adjustment blueprints failed to factor in, just as with the Zapatistas in Mexico. There, a sectoral coalition of Spanish Mexicans had joined cause with the indigenous peoples of Chiapas against a common foe. The critical question in New Zealand was whether those Pakeha who now found themselves victims of the neo-liberal regime would continue to side with the state and international capital against Maori, or whether enough would change sides and seek out a complementary vision and strategy for the future.

CHAPTER FOURTEEN

There Are *Alternatives*

AT THE INSTITUTE FOR INTERNATIONAL ECONOMICS (IIE) colloquium in 1993, New Zealand economist Alan Bollard observed that there was now less appetite for continued radical reform, but that the changes which had been made would not easily be reversed. Elements locked in place included 'repeal of the executive powers, the undertakings on trade policy to international agencies such as the GATT, the reduction in the strength and lobbying ability of many special interest groups, the reduction in union power, the deregulated financial markets, and the role of international money markets'. Bollard found it 'ironic that, in 1993, as the country is at last starting to feel the benefits of liberalization, the public appears to have lost its appetite for further reform'.[1] This book questions whether the *country* had any such appetite to begin with, what the costs and benefits of structural adjustment have been and to whom, and how people are likely to respond when they find the policies of the past decade have been embedded, in some cases irreversibly, to prevent them from being changed.

The neo-liberal revolution
In the space of a decade a strong central state authority, operating with almost total disregard for democratic process and pluralist politics, and abetted by a private sector élite, revolutionised New Zealand's economy and its peoples' lives. The strategy of the technocrats and technopols fitted the IIE's manual for structural adjustment almost perfectly. Without the foreign exchange crisis in July 1984, provoked partly by Douglas himself, they would have found it much more difficult to begin. The country's economic problems would have been subject to more leisurely assessment, and a more prag-

matic response would probably have been endorsed. Once the justification existed for urgent and radical change, and after a short honeymoon that bought them more time, the blitzkrieg began.

The convergence of ideology and strategy between the Labour government in the 1980s and National in the 1990s enabled the revolution to continue almost unimpeded, whichever party was in power. Initiation of the project by a party of the social-democratic left served to disarm potential critics, especially the organised labour and social movements within Labour's ranks. By 1990 what could readily be achieved under Labour was done. National's election was vital to remove the remaining barriers to labour market deregulation and erosion of the welfare state. The project's beneficiaries shifted their political allegiances accordingly. The re-emergence of political pragmatism in 1993 and the partial paralysis in the lead-up to MMP were minor inconveniences in the overall scheme.

This truly was an experiment. Economic theories which had never been tried, let alone proved, anywhere else in the world became New Zealand government policy. Through their abstract and static view of the economy and society those responsible for the programme detached themselves from the real-life context in which they worked. Indeed, a willingness to take such considerations into account was seen as a weakness. With the conviction of religious zealots, they claimed that they knew best and that people would appreciate the benefits of change only after it had been made. Manifest empirical failures were blamed on the government's refusal to move fast enough, on political prevarication over aspects that were incomplete, or on technical problems of a temporary kind. Adverse effects were frequently ignored.

The discourse of empowerment, accountability and transparency conveyed the antithesis of what really took place. Information on policies and outcomes was made accessible to those with the technical skills and 'need to know', who then repackaged it for popular consumption. Information which exposed the deficiencies and negative impact of restructuring and deregulation in labour markets, education, health, corporate activity and foreign investment was no longer collected or became extraordinarily difficult for outsiders to gather and analyse.

Both governments were reckless as to the economic and social damage they caused. Stagnation, recession and instability dominated economic life. Poverty and inequality deepened as unemployment and the gap between rich and poor grew. The capture of both major parties, their public embrace of economic fundamentalism, and the enthusiasm with which they prosecuted the 'reforms', left them deeply implicated in the process. This cast traditional party allegiances, political forms of opposition and the legitimacy of the democratic state into disarray. Alienation, social dis-ease and a deep sense of betrayal took hold. Maori once more began to rebel.

By 1995, after a decade of radical structural change, New Zealand had become a highly unstable and polarised society. Its underskilled, under-employed, low wage, low inflation, high exchange rate, export-driven economy was totally exposed to international economic forces. The victims of the market were forced to depend on a shrinking welfare safety net or private charity. What were once basic priorities—collective responsibility, redistribution of resources and power, social stability, democratic participation and the belief that human beings were entitled to live and work in security and dignity—seemed to have been left far behind.

Were there no alternatives?

Few would disagree that the New Zealand economy required remedial attention when Labour came to power in 1984, or that the country needed to respond to global economic change. Yet the claim that there was 'no alternative' to this extreme form of neo-liberalism achieved, by sheer repetition, the status of received truth. This was not the only option available to the New Zealand government and peoples in 1984. It was just the only option which had been systematically formulated at the time, and which enjoyed the patronage of the political, bureaucratic and business élite.

Neo-Keynesians have argued that a gentler combination of liberalisation with a managed mixed economy, welfare state and corporatist labour policy would have sufficed.[2] Some preferred the pragmatism of the Australian federal government, which gradually and selectively shifted the balance in favour of the market while retaining positive economic growth and sectoral and social support throughout the decade. Even the chief executive of Fletcher Challenge, Hugh Fletcher, publicly argued that this more pragmatic approach would have caused less damage to the economy and people's lives along the way. A comparative review of the Australian Labor and New Zealand Labour governments over the same period seems to bear that out.[3] Brian Easton and Rolf Gerritsen note that social democratic governments were subject to the same globalisation-induced pressures for economic policy convergence as non-Labour Western governments.

Yet Australian Labor resisted implementing pure more-market policies. It generally eschewed contradictory fiscal policies, even expanding social welfare and regulatory wages policy initiatives . . . and—contrary to its public rhetoric—conducted an active industry policy. In other words, like some European Social Democratic governments, Australian Labor was willing to forgo some efficiency gains in the name of distributing the social costs of economic adjustment. In that sense, it behaved in a manner traditionally associated with social democratic governments.

This reflected its corporatist strategy and a deep personal and institutional relationship with the trade union movement: 'in the early 1980s the ALP had decided it could get superior economic performance, in additional growth and jobs without additional inflation, if the unions would restrain their wage demands in exchange both for enhanced social wage outcomes and social welfare benefit levels and for a fuller role in national decision-making. . . . In return for the wage restraint, the unions negotiated increases in the social wage, which together with the rise in employment appears to have satisfied most workers.'

The New Zealand Labour government, by contrast, adopted a commercialist/monetarist approach. Early promises of consultation quickly evaporated. Institutional links between the party and unions were more distanced, and personal connections with the Cabinet almost non-existent.

So the New Zealand Labour government was left to reduce inflation by a monetary disinflation, while maintaining a large government deficit. This generated an overvalued exchange rate as capital flooded in seeking the high interest rates, which depressed domestic prices by squeezing the tradeable sector, and thence the economy as a whole. Import penetration rose sharply, but there was not a compensating lift in the export effort because of the deteriorating profitability of exporting. The costs of the policy were lost output, jobs, and investment, which may well be irrecoverable in the long run.

The economic performance of the two countries offered a stark contrast. Australia's GDP growth between 1985 and 1992 was 16.8 percent; the OECD average was 19.7 percent; New Zealand's was -1 percent. Employment growth in Australia during that time was 14.6 percent, the OECD 8.4 percent, and New Zealand -5.6 percent. Unemployment rates rose more rapidly in New Zealand, although by 1992 the countries were pretty much on a par. New Zealand's inflation rate was marginally lower, having started from a higher level. In 1994 New Zealand's GDP growth finally exceeded Australia's and unemployment fell more rapidly. But that did nothing to diminish the economic, social and political legacy of the preceding decade. Nor was it proof that the New Zealand economy would outperform its stronger, more diverse Australian counterpart in the years ahead.

Other economists and social analysts saw the Australian and New Zealand models as variations within the 'Washington consensus'. They argued that policies which achieved the goals of social justice, collective responsibility, human dignity, environmental sustainability and self-determination required a more fundamental rethink of economic assumptions and goals.[4] But alternative models that reflected these values were neither available nor tenable in the political and economic environment of 1984.

A decade on, ruminating on 'what might have been' is a rather fruitless exercise for New Zealanders. It is an historical, irreversible fact that the technocrats and technopols were able to impose the structural adjustment programme by default. Other countries, governments and peoples being sold the New Zealand model would do well to learn from that most basic failure. The question facing many New Zealanders in the mid-1990s is where they can move from here.

Barriers to change

There is no doubt that the technocrats and technopols set out to implement the changes as rapidly and comprehensively as possible, and to make each element difficult, if not impossible, to reverse. Both Labour and National faced the prospect of being single-term, three-year governments. In their haste, those who were driving the experiment allowed neither political, administrative and ethical constraints nor theories about optimal sequencing to get in their way. The goal was to move as fast as possible to the point of no return. By 1995 it appeared that the initiation and consolidation of structural change had been largely 'successful' in neo-liberal terms, although the extent to which each of the 'fundamentals' had been entrenched differed in form and degree.

At the level of policy, a coherent set of norms, premised on unfettered market forces and limited government, had displaced those of the centralised, interventionist welfare state. Such shifts were not new, and on their own could be expected to give way to another set of norms when economic, political and social conditions changed. Yet each element of the structural adjustment programme was deeply integrated in both a conceptual and an operational sense. While some aspects might appear easier to change than others, altering one element would not substantially alter the paradigm. Consciously realigning all the fundamentals would require an exercise as coherent, well planned and ruthlessly executed as the structural adjustment programme itself. Such a conjunction of personalities, economics, politics and prevailing ideology is rare. Having happened once in recent times, the chances of that being able or allowed to recur, either by those who oversaw the previous change or those who suffered it, seems remote. Aside from the logistics, the risk of failure would be a significant restraint in itself. The alternative of piecemeal reform and adjustments to detail would leave the neo-liberal paradigm unstable and riddled with contradictions, but largely intact.

These policy norms were underpinned by a powerful ideology binding each element together. The internal incoherence and fallible assumptions of much neo-liberal theory were shielded by an unshakeable, often evangelical, faith. This was bolstered by constant mutual reinforcement and the marginalisation of dissent. 'Free market' ideology was propagated directly and indirectly through media whose ownership, commercial imperatives, weak commitment to investigative journalism and ideological sympathies frequently undermined their 'fourth estate' role. Fellow-travellers in academia reinforced the new orthodoxy and indoctrinated future generations of economists and policy analysts. Critics were forced to respond within those terms. Many became marginal, discredited and harassed; others 'collapsed into careerism or subordination'.[5]

But ideological capture would not in itself shield the new order from change. Economic ideas are never frozen. They are part of a dynamic, on-going debate. They had changed in the past. They would change again, despite the assumption of economic fundamentalists that theirs was the only way. Critical intellectuals would regroup and new voices emerge. Increased familiarity with and understanding of the concepts, and the techniques of power, would open both to sharper critique. Visible failure of the model would cast doubt on basic premises and accepted truths. New ideas would gradually render the new orthodoxy into the old.

At the administrative level, statutory authority had conferred on key technocrats, agencies and private actors a high degree of autonomy from political interference, and enabled them to deflect interests other than those the market favoured. Their institutionalised control over economic policy-making, implementation and information made them potentially indispensable and difficult to dislodge. Any moves to dismantle this administrative framework or fundamentally alter its direction would be strongly contested. But the tenure of the technocrats and government appointees was limited. Future ministers would have the power to replace the guardians of the new regime with those who held different views. How effectively they could wrest back control of government's administrative machine would depend on how systematically and thoughtfully that strategy was pursued.

Incorporating the changes into legislation had erected a further barrier to change. The use of legislation was not in itself exceptional. None of these Acts was constitutionally entrenched; they could be amended or repealed by a simple majority in the current or future Parliament. Only the international obligations under CER and the World Trade Organisation, brought into play by an act of state, were effectively beyond Parliament's reach. Even commitments to the WTO, in theory, could be wound back in subsequent negotiating rounds, by the exercise of emergency powers to protect the balance of payments,[6] or by withdrawing from the organisation altogether.

Yet the use of legislation was significant. Most of these Acts contained explicit policy principles and norms that were intended to restrain future amendment or repeal. Neo-liberal 'orthodoxy' had been made the reference point within which future policy arguments had to be framed, and against which alternatives would be measured. Any deviations from or future changes to the legislation would have to be justified politically in explicit policy terms, and secure majority support in a Parliament governed by MMP.

Complementing the legislative machine was the coercive power of the common law. Its most fundamental concept, the inviolability of private property rights, was bound to be invoked to protect the interests of capital against any reassertion of collectivism, whether on the part of indigenous peoples or the central state.

How far these factors deterred future governments from overturning the new status quo would depend partly on the political climate and economic and social conditions of the time. Yet domestic politics was not the only consideration. The most powerful forces which had embedded the new regime were not personal, ideological, legal, political or structural. They were economic. New politicians could be elected. New bureaucrats could be appointed. New policy norms could be developed. Laws could be repealed and new ones passed. But only with enormous difficulty and great cost could the changes to the economy be reversed.

The deep infiltration of the New Zealand economy by international capital had been a clear and deliberate strategy. As economists David Harper and Girol Karacaoglu observed:

> Despite apparent attempts at financial re-regulation across the OECD there are good reasons to believe that the process of financial deregulation, once started, is very difficult to reverse. The same fundamental factor, namely, the fungibility of financial capital, that explained the scope and the speed of financial policy reform, will frustrate any attempt to reintroduce regulation. By deregulating the financial sector first and so quickly, the [Labour] government (maybe deliberately) has forced all future administrations into a very tight corner.[7]

Through the restructuring of New Zealand's economy trans-national capital, especially finance capital, could dictate the terms of any policy which had implications for international competitiveness, profitability and economic stability. That would include Treaty of Waitangi, environment and social policy. Attempts to nationalise, to restrict the operations and movements of capital, to renege on the bindings in the GATT, to significantly increase taxes, to re-regulate the labour market, or to require a balance of economic, social and environmental goals, would invite a potentially devastating backlash. It was this threat that stood as the ultimate barrier to change.

Yet even the seemingly irrepressible power of trans-national capital would never be secure. The neo-liberal economy has never been the smooth-working and self-adjusting model its theorists make out. The free market economies which existed in the nineteenth century collapsed partly through their own inadequacies and internal contradictions, and partly because people struggled against the devastation that the free market wreaked on their lives. History could repeat itself on both counts.

At the global economic level, the frenzy of unregulated and amoral finance markets could lead to them to self-destruct and bring the entire economic system to its knees. The WTO and the free trade regime could collapse under the weight of self-interest among the major powers as they reassert a pragmatic mix of protection and open trade to their own advantage. The inability of the ecosystem to sustain the depletion of nature's resources and destruction of the biosphere could reach such a crisis that exploitative economic growth simply has to end. All these are real possibilities that would force the global economic system to change. The effect would potentially be catastrophic, not only for international capital, but also for those whose lives have been involuntarily locked into the 'free market' mode.

Less spectacularly, the chasm between the pure theory on which New Zealand's experiment was based and economic and social reality could bring about the programme's demise. The abdication of state responsibility for health, education, housing and basic utilities might bring these services to the brink of collapse, requiring the state to intervene once more to correct the failures of the market and re-establish control. Rampant abuses of monopoly power might stem from the failure of contestability theory and light-handed regulation. State regulation of corporate activities might be needed once more to ensure that essential services were accessible to the poor and that economic efficiency was maintained. If the contradictions between low inflation and economic growth prove irresolvable, or the costs unsustainable, the obsession with price stability might give way to a more balanced approach. The failure of capital to invest in the long-term research and skills training that were once provided by government might require it to resume an active role.

Numerous other adjustments could be made if a government had the political will. The Reserve Bank could be required to pursue social development and full employment as well as price stability goals. Active support of the kind given to exports could be directed to the domestic market. The post-1996 round of tariff cuts could be cancelled. The Employment Contracts Act could be replaced by legislation that recognises workers' rights to organise and bargain collectively. Industrial democracy and employment equity could be put back on the agenda. An end could be called to privatisation, with regulations introduced to govern essential services that are currently in private hands. Controls on foreign investment could channel funds towards genuinely productive enterprise. Commitments to the WTO could be frozen at their present level with genuine multi-sectoral consultation before and during future negotiations. Relationships with Asian countries could become more responsible in attitudes to Asian peoples, whether as targets of New Zealand corporate investment or as immigrants, while the costs that immigration imposes on

Maori and Pakeha could be acknowledged and addressed. Marginal income tax could be increased, with essential items removed from GST. Research and development could become tax-deductible again. Crown Research Institutes could be required to service economic, social and cultural goals. The health 'reforms' could be undone by reinstating elected boards to manage centralised funds, or the CHEs could be required to give equal weight to health, economic and social outcomes. The government's housing stock could be made responsive to genuine housing needs, with subsidised rentals restored. Educational curriculum and management could restore the value placed on social skills, knowledge, professionalism and critique. Local authorities could be encouraged to redevelop their community services, including housing, recreational facilities and the conservation estate. Rebuilding the neglected infrastructure could create jobs, and feed the domestic economy. Public service broadcasting could be re-established by cross-subsidising from a commercial state-owned TV2 to a non-commercial TV1. And so on.

Local economists have suggested other institutional strategies to restore some balance to government's economic programme. Dennis Rose from the BERL economic consultancy has proposed a separate slim-lined Ministry of Economic Development to monitor the impact of government actions and policies on economic growth, analyse key determinants of growth and recommend appropriate policies to government.[8] Suzanne Snively advocates a Governor of Employment and Savings to complement the role of the Governor of the Reserve Bank. The two governors could deliver a 'balanced economy where there is full employment and low inflation'. The new office would enjoy a structure and level of statutory autonomy, and a single statutory objective, on the same model as the bank. 'What we need is an organisation equally resourced with equally skilled and competent staff driven to over-achieve on the employment front in the same way the Reserve Bank is driven to over-achieve on its inflation targets. Then, this organisation needs a Government mandate to work towards a target of reducing unemployment to 0–2% as soon as realistically possible.'[9]

Rethinking economic values

These are piecemeal adjustments within the prevailing paradigm, although cumulatively they could seriously destabilise its foundations. Others have urged a fundamental rethink of assumptions, values and goals. Social policy analyst Ian Shirley has described the neo-liberal version of economy and society as a caricature of reality. Dynamic parts of people's lives which are experienced and contested are reduced to technical elements in an equation. The only vibrant feature is the interplay of market forces. Shirley insists that the economy cannot be detached from people's realities in this way. Life is not an abstract model, nor an aggregation of atomised transactions. It involves complex, interactive economic, political, cultural and social relationships. Nor is the society, tribe, community or family simply a conglomeration of isolated individuals who lack any source of cohesion, identity, sense of obligation and motivation beyond self-interest. Individual desires are themselves the product of their shared environment.

> When we define ourselves as atomised individuals we deny a significant part of our humanity. As members of the human race we have legitimate claims on one another simply because of the humanity we share. To view human beings as 'consumers' or 'commodities' is to deny their human qualities and potential. . . . It follows that the 'welfare' of a nation cannot be reduced to a narrow economic construct such as the level or rate of economic growth. . . . Social development is about participating in life . . . how we enhance human potential and how we accept social responsibility.[10]

Economic policy should reflect the values people want to live by. The neo-liberal goal of ever-increasing economic growth, secured by efficient use of scarce resources and fuelled by the quest for profit, reflects only one narrow view of progress. Scarcity presumes there are insufficient resources to satisfy all needs; those that are locked into inefficient uses must be liberated before the resource pool, and hence wealth, can grow. Economist Petrus Simons explains the implications of this:

> We must first [travel] through a tunnel of austerity before we are able to satisfy more needs. . . . There is ever a need for more and longer tunnels to secure a more prosperous future in which more needs can be satisfied. Another word for this tunnel complex is 'progress'. Progress means that the future is more authoritative than the present. The present is always inadequate, because tomorrow we will have progressed to something more and better.[11]

The inexorable quest for economic growth (often equated with GDP) through internationally competitive markets presumes there is an 'efficient' level of unemployment, inequality, human pain and environmental degradation. For those concerned about the quality of social life, this obsession with increasing economic output is misguided and perverse. Only transactions within the market-place are deemed productive. People's lives from cradle to grave are telescoped into time spent in the paid workforce. Many, especially women whose work in the family, voluntary sector and informal economy is unpaid or in kind, are deemed to spend totally unproductive lives.[12] The more fortunate who participate in the market-place have perhaps a 30-year 'productive' life. As opportunities to participate in this market shrink, so does people's economically valued contribution to the society. Shirley argues: 'Although we continue to assign great significance to [GDP] as if it were somehow a measure of our productive capacities as a nation, it neither reflects the country's standard of living nor its quality of life.'[13]

Economist Prue Hyman points out that the market is merely one means of production, distribution and exchange: 'the notion that market price is the only measure of value [is] crass, offensive and contrary to human beliefs and actions'. Price based on scarcity does not reflect value to human life, as 'the low valuation of water and the high valuation of inessential but scarce diamonds' shows. Profits from militarism, unsafe pharmaceuticals and pesticides, and other environmental destruction, are recorded as growth. By transferring public sector activities to the private sector, whether businesses (like telecommunications, railways and forestry), financial services (such as superannuation, accident compensation and health insurance), or social provision of education, health and housing, they instantly stop being drains on state expenditure and become positive productive growth.

Orthodox economics, Hyman argues, reflects values and preferences which are important to some men. A more complete theory of economics would encompass concepts like co-operation, loyalty and reciprocity: 'a positive feminist economics is to see well-being less in terms of a neoclassical utility function and more in terms of access and capability to be and do many things, such as eat, be adequately and warmly sheltered, read, write, be free of violence and take an active role in one's community.'[14]

Similar flaws affect the concept of choice. Market allocation is based not on relative efficiency but on relative power. 'Those who see outcomes largely as the consequences of choice and individual responsibility, rather than constraints and systems, will be able to justify the resulting inequalities to themselves.'[15] The claim that market equilibrium leaves everyone better off deflects attention from economic and social outcomes which frequently leave some absolutely or relatively worse off. Hence, small and specific efficiency gains may be made from welfare cuts at the cost of widening distributive imbalances. The effect is an abdication of human ethical responsibility. The challenge is to find ways that human endeavours and attributes which are not priced in the market, like control of one's life and self-esteem, can be recognised as values and taken into account.[16]

During the 1990s creative models for economic development emerged which reflect these alternative values. Nationalist, community and Maori economic perspectives all represent interests whom economic fundamentalism sought to silence and exclude. At the least, they provide a complementary basis for adaptation and/or co-existence with a mixed market economy, giving a more positive and empowering meaning to the concept of a dual economy. But, to varying degrees, their premises also challenge neo-liberalism at its roots.

Economic nationalism

Economist Tim Hazledine has argued that in the 1960s a give-and-take, or synergy, bound New Zealanders together—workers and employers belonged to communities about which they cared. Many of those synergies, which were driven by the private sector, have been demolished by the brutalising effect of market forces and the preoccupation with efficiency and growth. 'When people care about each other, anonymous markets are not efficient. . . . If "demanders" have some interest in the well-being of "suppliers", then it is wrong to force demands and supply to keep apart from each other.' Attacking the obsession with comparative economic growth, he goes on to suggest that:

> a free and stable society ends up getting roughly the rate of growth that it wants, according to the pace at which its people want to perform in their workplaces, and on their attitude towards monetary rewards as opposed to things which are not well-captured by measured Gross National or Domestic Product. Love and friendship; work and play; security and autonomy—these are the things that count in life. They have a lot to do with not being poor, but they have very little to do with being rich. And they truly have nothing at all to do with whether the

Singaporeans now have an official GDP per capita that exceeds New Zealand's. Good luck to those poor downtrodden folk. Would you really want to *live* there?[17]

Hazledine urges the revival of domestic production for domestic consumption. 'The salvation-by-exports approach has been oversold. . . . [W]e'd do much better to export less (and get a better price for it) and turn our attention more to supplying the domestic market.'[18] Import competition, he argues, offers fewer productivity benefits than domestic competition, which produces 'network synergies' and skills development with on-going economic and social benefits for the community. Added value in the form of transport, distribution, marketing and retailing provides more work. This is reflected in turn through more household spending. Wages and profits earned in the country can be spent in the country, maintaining demand.

This approach would require a revival of nationalist attitudes— manufacturers feeling good about domestic production for domestic consumption, consumers buying New Zealand-made. New Zealand governments would need to end their obsession with leading the world in unilateral tariff reduction, and inject an equivalent amount of government funding into development of domestic markets as they invest in promoting exports. In something of a heresy for the time, Hazledine concludes, 'I have read that "the future of New Zealand is in Asia". I disagree. I think that the future of New Zealand is in New Zealand.'

Community economic model

The Aotearoa Network of Unemployed and Beneficiaries (ANUB) has raised other options. Their moral imperative is to get people into work, which in its broadest sense embraces socially necessary labour of caring for children, household tasks, voluntary community work and other unwaged productive activities usually left out of the employment equation. They argue that the sale of strategic assets has hindered the return to full employment in the public sector, with the government losing a significant income flow and much of its ability to influence the direction of the economy. But there is still considerable scope for job creation in the public sector and services. Local government has a vital role in promoting new jobs, forming creative partnerships with central government, the community economic sector, the private sector and funded programmes.

In the private sector, small businesses, which often have commitments to local communities, workers and lifestyles, are potential sources of real job growth. These could be fostered through revolving venture-loan capital, backed by advice and support. Underemployed skilled people could then move into their own businesses, releasing their jobs for the unemployed and creating new ones. Other options to increase paid work include a shorter working week. Protection of workers' interests would require the revitalisation of strong independent unions, and adequate compensation for job loss and developing new skills.

ANUB insists that those not in full paid employment should not be forced to depend on the broken-down social welfare system. Drawing on work by economist Keith Rankin,[19] they have promoted the idea of a universal basic income (UBI). A tax credit/rebate of $7650 per year, automatically paid to every adult, would replace social welfare benefits, national superannuation, student loans, family support and other state-financed cash benefits. Additional payments would be made for adults over 60 and single adult households. Supplementary benefits for high accommodation costs or disability would apply. Young people aged 16 to 18 would receive the UBI through a nominal affiliation with an educational or training institution, community organisation or other provider of post-secondary training or work.

The UBI is seen as an equitable alternative to the outmoded welfare state. 'It costs little more than the current [income support] systems, while doing away with all the iniquities of poverty traps, means testing, the blaming of those forced to rely on benefits and the many restrictions on their personal freedoms.' It would streamline tax and social welfare bureaucracy. Disincentives for part-time and transitional work would be removed. And wealth would be redistributed from the very rich to the poor. The level of payment would not encourage an exodus from paid work; but it would enable people to spend more time on unpaid work within families and communities without forfeiting income security.

Under the ANUB proposal, this could be funded by a tax on private income of 52 percent rising to a maximum of 68 percent, an effective company tax rate of 50 percent, plus taxes on assets, energy use and currency exchange transactions. Other assessments suggest that a 45 percent tax rate, with a maximum EMTR of 60 percent, would suffice. Greater numbers in paid work would increase revenue, while lower social welfare administration costs and improved social stability and health would decrease government expenditure. These strategies could be complemented by work in the community economic sector for those who are excluded from, or opt out of, the market economy. While profits are generally lower, community benefit is high, with value placed on human worth, environmental sustainability and mutuality. This sector is generally ignored in the polarisation of public and private sectors, except where it threatens to escape the Inland Revenue net.[20] ANUB's proposals for government support in the community economic sector include:

- a community development banking facility managed with assistance from those experienced in the community economic sector;
- a social responsibility tax of 1 percent on all financial institutions and multi-national companies to help finance community economic projects;
- regional community development agencies, independent of government, operating in genuine partnership with the community sector and accountable to both;
- a working party, with a majority drawn from the community economic sector, to identify how to build its infrastructure and release its employment creation potential, backed by a genuine government commitment to act.

The underlying philosophy of the community economic model is a form of democracy through which people can genuinely participate in the economic decisions that affect their lives. Communities can seek out their own solutions to social and economic problems through strategies that combine financial and social goals. While minimal financial resources can be recycled efficiently, some base level of public income support is still required. Working examples include community house-building projects, green dollar exchanges, credit co-operatives, information resource networks and community newspapers. Perhaps the most sophisticated, the Auckland People's Centre, provides members with quality health, dentistry, legal advocacy and other services for a minimal weekly fee. The centre combines its economic and social programmes with political action targeted at local and international patrons of structural adjustment, and the genesis of a training school for community activists.

These kinds of initiative form part of an integrated programme of people-based development that was endorsed by sectoral and community groups during the 'Building Our Own Futures' programme, funded by the churches in 1994. Those who participated in the

National People's Assembly adopted a People's Charter to guide future Pakeha strategies for change.[21]

The community economic model can be extended into the international market-place in a way that harnesses the benefits of globalisation and minimises the economic, social and environmental costs. Efficient international business is not inherently bad. It can offer economies of scale and access to technological advances, improve the quality and range of products available, and provide opportunities to diversify or specialise. The problem lies with who owns and controls the commercial vehicles through which the internationalised economy operates. The trend towards decentralised control, franchising and sale of branch operations to management and staff can create opportunities for co-operative-based enterprise, enabling the local to interface with the international in a way that maximises the benefits of each.

Maori economic development

Maori economic alternatives are based on the fundamental right to tino rangatiratanga or self-determination.[22] Rob Cooper, in a paper prepared for the Maori Council of Churches, describes 'true Maori development' as 'an enterprise of justice. For it has as its goals the restoration and reconciliation of we Maori people with our lands and the promotion of our self-determined advancement in life, according to our own Maori human values and ideals.' Cooper distinguishes between modernisation and development. Modernisation represents 'an intense level of economic seduction' which has the potential to corrupt completely or totally destroy Maori customs and values. It elevates individualism and self-interest above all else, and reduces natural and human resources to mere commodities exploited for commercial gain.

True development involves an integrated and harmonious balance of socio-economic factors in a way that serves Maori social, cultural, material, environmental and spiritual needs. It is sourced in traditional values of reciprocity, a sense of collective responsibility that endures through past, present and future generations, and a spiritual relationship that binds people, nature and cosmology together. Its form constantly adapts to, and takes advantage of, changing times.[23] This is what the Treaty of Waitangi promised: access to the benefits of Western knowledge and technology which Maori could adapt selectively according to traditional ethics and values. In the

1840s and 1850s tribes had dominated key sectors of the New Zealand economy through collective entrepreneurship, until their political power and economic resources were eroded by force, fraud and guile. If even some of the resources stolen from Maori were returned and employed on ethical Maori lines, genuine economic development could be restored.

The key to 'true Maori development' therefore lies in control over resources—land, forestry, fisheries, ngawha (geothermal) and waterways—and the transmission of knowledge, culture and values. The political struggles waged over a century and a half, and particularly over the past three decades, have been dedicated to securing back that control. In the 1990s, with minimal assistance and frequent obstruction by the state, a number of tribes are successfully rebuilding their economic and political base, and translating the treaty ethos of self-determination into their daily lives.

Land, either retained or regained, now provides a place to stand and an economic base for many young and middle-aged Maori women and men returning home. Consultation has been sought, and increasingly direct action taken, to protect sacred sites or reclaim resources taken by the Crown. Some pay their taxes and rates to the tribe instead of central and local government. In some areas, tribal laws have displaced the resource management, fisheries and criminal laws of the Crown. Tribal education, health and development programmes focus on rebuilding language, culture, spiritual well-being and identity. Whanau- and marae-based enterprises are taking advantage of niche markets, such as tourism, which integrate economic, social and cultural goals. Whanau trusts operate as credit co-operatives. A growing market for authentic services reflects a reassertion of control over Maori resources, identity, culture, artefacts, souvenirs, music, films and arts.

Refocusing on the tribal base is not without its tensions. The mass of Maori still live in the cities. Most are aged under 30, and many are unemployed. Urban Maori authorities offer a range of services, training programmes and small business opportunities adapted on cultural lines. This sits uncomfortably with the revival of a tribally-centred world, and tribally-based treaty settlement policies of which urban Maori legitimately demand a share.

This traditionalist approach to Maori development also challenges the modernisation line promoted by a number of Maori entrepreneurs who seek to locate tribal structures and traditional values within the global market-place. Some of their commercial operations use existing tribal resources. Others result from settlements negotiated with government that have locked Maori resources into corporate ventures, which the entrepreneurs often help to run at considerable personal gain. In line with 'free-market' thinking, the benefits are meant to trickle down to the people as financial dividends over time.

These nationalist, community and Maori economic models place priority on people-centred development over market-driven economic growth, and offer varying roles for the market and the central state. All celebrate what is unique about Aotearoa New Zealand. All believe that the future of economic development lies in the hands of the people themselves. All seek to address, in different ways and degrees, the inequalities which are compounded by the structural adjustment programme. All recognise that political and economic self-determination, combined with a strong sense of identity, vision and ethics, hold the key to meaningful change.

In isolated pockets these alternatives can be tolerated and accommodated by the neo-liberal regime. But attempts to promote them as alternative visions for the future will pit the economic imperatives and vested interests of the global market-place against the political determination of peoples and communities to achieve social justice, and to reassert some control over their lives. That will produce resistance from both sides.

Reclaiming sovereignty

The political question for those seeking to change the economic paradigm is how this can be achieved. That, in turn, depends on how much power—or sovereignty—the New Zealand state, government and people still exercise over their domain. Reclaiming sovereignty has become the catchcry among many Maori and Pakeha. But their exact meaning remains unclear. *Black's Law Dictionary* defines *sovereignty* as:

> The supreme, absolute and uncontrollable power by which any independent state is governed; supreme political authority; the supreme will; paramount control of the constitution and frame of government and its administration; the self-sufficient source of political power, from which all specific political powers are derived; the international independence of a state, combined with the right and power of regulating its internal affairs without foreign dictation; also a political society, or state, which is sovereign and independent.[24]

All these definitions treat the central state as the principal actor, the principal centre of power and the principal object of interest. Its 'subjects' are invisible. They are assumed under a liberal democracy to be passive consensual participants who share equally in the political and economic power of the nation-state, and are equally represented within the state-defined national identity, national economy and national interest. The sovereign state is then treated by the outside world as self-contained, inviolate and supreme.

This conceptualisation of unitary state-centred sovereignty reflects many of the tensions facing New Zealand in the 1990s. It champions a colonial state which is premised on the suppression of Maori sovereignty. It claims a universality which denies the visible inequality of economic and social power. It assumes a gender neutrality based on formal rights of participation in the electoral process, while it renders invisible the gendered power of both the public and private spheres. It ignores the historical dependence of the colonial state on the economic, political and military patronage of external powers, and the enduring reality of superpower influence over the country's affairs.

If sovereignty is to be a helpful vehicle for change, its precise meaning and potential benefits need to be much more clearly defined. The concept of *legal sovereignty* refers to the supreme authority of the state and the legal order, which is conferred internally by a written or unwritten constitution, and recognised externally in international law and legal instruments. This authority exists irrespective of the degree of political legitimacy the state enjoys, or the moral and ethical source of its claim to power. Parts of the state's legal authority can be given away by consent. But consent is narrowly defined. Entry into international agreements and obligations by New Zealand governments is deemed an act of state which does not need ratification through domestic political processes. As occurred with the GATT, elected representatives and citizens are effectively denied a right of input into that decision.

Every reduction of legal authority limits future domestic political control over those matters, denies the right of parliamentary and citizen input, and exposes governments who wish to change direction to potentially crippling economic, legal and moral sanctions. The international agencies and forums to which this authority is ceded are dominated by major powers who generally protect their own interests. These may or may not coincide with those of weaker and dependent states such as New Zealand.

So there are sound reasons for concern about the erosion of legal sovereignty. At the same time, there is a danger of romanticising its merits. Legal sovereignty confirms the constitutional status quo. It reinforces the position of the central colonial state as the sole recognised authority to speak on behalf of 'its subjects', even where it has usurped their own sovereign authority or failed to represent their interests in the past. If the state does retain its legal sovereignty, there is no guarantee that domestic political processes will produce different, and better, results from those negotiated in the international arena. On occasion, the reverse might be true. The value of retaining state legal sovereignty is therefore contingent upon a constitutional framework and law- and policy-making procedures which will ensure substantive outcomes that are socially just.

The erosion of *economic sovereignty* has significantly greater impact. This involves restrictions on the ability of the state to control economic activities which take place within, or impact on, the country. These include currency flows, exchange rates, levels and sources of foreign debt, taxation, imports and exports, interest rates, money supply, labour costs, investment strategies, levels of state and foreign ownership, exploitation of natural resources, control of essential utilities, and so on. Full economic sovereignty ceased to exist in New Zealand when Maori authority over their resources was usurped by the British in 1840. The colonial economy was always controlled by external economic powers, both state and corporate. What the New Zealand state, though not necessarily the people, did exercise some authority over was the regulatory framework for the economy and key infrastructural resources and activities.

The residual authority of most states has been eroded over the past three decades through globalisation. International capital seeks out favourable regulatory regimes for its capital, labour, resource use and operational activities; cheap and plentiful access to raw materials, infrastructural facilities and services; a compliant, competent and flexible labour supply; and a stable social and political environment. But this need not take the form of neo-liberalism, and certainly not the extreme New Zealand kind. International capital is far more pragmatic than the theorists like to suggest. While it can employ powerful leverage over a domestic economy, it is primarily concerned about securing sustainable long-term profits. A looser monetary and fiscal policy and a more co-operative labour market, accompanied by full employment, may offer a more fertile economic environment than recessionary high interest and exchange rates, structural unemployment and low consumer demand. An abrupt abandonment of 'free market' policies would probably provoke short-term capital flight, but the introduction of alternative policies that are consistent and sustained, and promote stability and balanced growth, would convince many investors to remain.

At the same time, global capital is not autonomous and its needs are not self-executing. They require the continued co-operation of domestic governments. And even where the government is accommodating, they still require a sustainable ecosystem and the acquiescence of the populace. The globalisation of national economies is, at least for the meantime, a fact of life. But there is choice in how far a particular state embraces it, and how much room that leaves for manoeuvre if (or when) the expansion of trans-national enterprise proves ecologically, economically, politically or socially unsustainable.

So national governments are not totally redundant, and they are important to fight over. They still serve significant functions of state direction, planning and management, within restricted perimeters. They can still be pressured to pass legislation to regulate the economic, social, political, cultural and environmental activities of natural and corporate entities within their jurisdiction, provided those laws accord with their external obligations. They can and do redistribute social income through fiscal and welfare strategies, although again of a different degree and kind. National economies also continue to exist. But they are now so deeply imbricated in the global or trans-national economy that any future vision has to take account of the nature and extent of that restraint.

As a result of the changes since 1984, New Zealand governments have even less room to exercise this form of economic autonomy than before. Those who advocate alternatives of the neo-Keynesian or more radical kind need to examine carefully how far the state can realistically reassert effective economic control, how damaging sanctions, capital flight or interest rate hikes might be, and the risks involved in calling their bluff. Before any precipitate moves are made, people are entitled to an assessment of the price.

Traditionally, pressures to change economic direction in New Zealand have focused on the exercise of *political sovereignty* by way of electoral democracy. When a government proved unresponsive to demands for change, people could in theory vote that party out of power. When such behaviour becomes endemic to the political system, however, the system itself comes into disrepute. In 1993, a majority of New Zealand people reflected that sentiment by voting the electoral system out. They replaced it with a system which they believed would better promote their interests, values and preferred policies in the future. But the potential for a truly accountable, representative, participatory and effective government to be elected under MMP, which can articulate and pursue a less-market approach, seems extremely low.

If this attempt to reassert political sovereignty does fail, people may lower their expectations accordingly. Popular acquiescence, backed by a consensus among political leaders, élite lobby groups, corporate actors and the media, could then limit economic debate and demands within what they consider to be acceptable bounds. Benefactors and beneficiaries of the new regime could hold the line until the next generation, the children of the market, take their place.

But not everyone is likely to accept the new social order as a *fait accompli*. If the traditional political channels prove futile, those who are committed to change will be left to exercise *popular sovereignty* through alternative non-state strategies, alliances and forums. The challenge will be to construct new forms of economics, politics and identity at the tribal, community, sectoral, national, regional or international levels which will enable people to be collectively, co-operatively and creatively reassertive.

The sovereignty of the state is therefore limited. How far the residual legal authority of the state benefits the people will depend on constitutional arrangements, openness and accountability. Legal sovereignty will be further constrained by limits on economic autonomy. Government still has some important regulatory powers. How it exercises them will depend on political will, an assessment of the risk, and pressure from the electorate. If governments are unwilling to test the boundaries, people might acquiesce. Alternatively, political strategies premised on popular sovereignty might emerge.

People can therefore challenge economic fundamentalism; but it will not be easy, there may be no mainstream political channels to work through, and it will come at a price. New Zealand's structural adjustment programme since 1984 is intended to be irreversible. That has not made it humanly acceptable. Nor has it closed off channels for innovation and struggle. People still have a choice. They can fall into line, and become creatures and victims of the global market within a divided and polarised society. Or they can seek out new identities, new economic strategies and new decolonised forms of politics, which eschew nostalgia for an irretrievable past and respond creatively to a rapidly changing world. Ultimately, the peoples of New Zealand have to decide the kind of society in which they want to live. Many Maori seem to have made their choice. It remains for the mass of Pakeha to work out where they—we—wish to stand.

Appendix: A Manual for Counter-technopols

IF THE ARCHITECTS OF structural adjustment are pooling their experiences in a manual for technopols to help them impose their agenda on the rest of the world, those who want to stop them should do the same. A preliminary checklist of potential pitfalls and strategies for resistance, drawn from New Zealand's experience, might include the following:

• *Take economic fundamentalism seriously*—what initially appears like extremism, if not effectively challenged and discredited, may in a short time be considered orthodox.

• *Nip it in the bud*—early changes can be the most fundamental and deliberately difficult to undo; once the structural adjustment agenda is under way, its internal logic has a domino effect on all policies and programmes.

• *Be sceptical about 'crises'*—anticipate a 'crisis' in the making, and move quickly to examine the real nature of the problem, who defines it as a crisis, and who stands to gain. Demand to know the range of possible solutions, and the costs and benefits of each to whom. If the answers are not forthcoming, burn the midnight oil to produce the answers for yourselves.

• *Watch for the blitzkrieg*—constantly monitor, document and expose what is going on behind the scenes. Act on instinct and anticipate the logical next step. Waiting until all the facts can be documented will probably be too late.

• *Remember the Tories are not always the worst*—social democratic parties and governments can neutralise potential opponents and initiate vital changes which provide the thin end of the wedge. Fighting to prevent a party's capture by zealots is important. But once the party has been taken over, maintaining solidarity on the outside while seeking change from within merely gives them more time. When the spirit of the party is dead, shed the old skin and create something new.

• *Take economics seriously*—economic fundamentalism pervades everything. There is no boundary between economic, indigenous, social, foreign, environmental or other policies. Those who focus on narrow sectoral concerns and ignore the pervasive economic agenda will lose their own battles and weaken the collective ability to resist. Leaving economics to economists is fatal.

• *Expose the illogic of their theory*—neo-liberal theories are riddled with dubious assumptions and internal inconsistencies, and often lack empirical support. Agency and public choice theories in particular need to be exposed as self-serving rationalisations which operate in the interests of the élites whom the policies empower.

• *Evaluate the arguments carefully*—acknowledge the valid aspects of arguments for change and meet them with alternatives which address the substance of the concern.

• *Challenge hypocrisy*—ask who is promoting a strategy as being in the 'national interest', and who stands to benefit most. Document cases where self-interest is disguised as public good.

• *Expose 'stacking of the deck'*—name the key players behind the scenes, document their interlocking roles and allegiances, and expose the personal and corporate benefits they receive.

• *Maximise every political obstacle*—federal systems of government, written constitutions, bicameral parliaments, complex voting systems, supra-national institutions and strong local governments provide barriers which can neutralise the blitzkrieg approach and slow the pace of, if not prevent, undesirable change.

• *Maintain a strong civil society and popular sector*—extra-parliamentary politics are essential to complement resistance through traditional party channels, and may become the front line once institutional politics fall captive.

• *Work hard to maintain solidarity*—avoid the trap of divide and rule; sectoral in-fighting is self-indulgent and everyone risks losing in the end.

• *Do not compromise the labour movement*—build awareness of the structural adjustment agenda at union branch and workplace level, so union members can demand accountability from their leadership. Openly debate the pros and cons of political party ties, and the costs and benefits of compromise. Concessions intended to forestall more radical change tend to deepen co-option and weaken the ability to resist the next step. Publicly challenge the failure of union bureaucrats to defend the interests of workers and the unemployed. If the leadership doesn't listen, disobey.

• *Employ the politics of international embarrassment*—if the forums of institutional politics have been taken and local resistance neutralised, marginalised or suppressed, the most potent political arena may be the international stage. Neo-liberal governments and free market economies depend on foreign investment and international approval. Image is everything. The international sphere is one arena they cannot effectively control.

• *Reinforce the concept of an independent public service*—undercut attempts to discredit, sideline and colonise the public service by acknowledging deficiencies and promoting pro-active models for change. Create a constituency of support among client groups and the public which stresses the need for independence and professionalism, the obligations of public service, and the risks of the managerial approach.

• *Encourage community leaders to speak out*—public criticism from civic and church leaders, folk heroes and other prominent 'names' makes governments uncomfortable and people think. The fewer public critics there are, the easier they are to discredit, harass and intimidate. Remind community leaders of their social obligations, and the need to look themselves in the mirror in the morning.

• *Avoid anti-intellectualism*—a pool of critical academics and other intellectuals who can document and expose the fallacies and failures of a structural adjustment programme, and develop viable alternatives in partnership with community and sectoral groups, is absolutely vital. They need to be supported when they come under attack, and challenged when they fail to speak out or are co-opted or seduced.

• *Establish well-resourced critical think-tanks*—neo-liberal and libertarian think-tanks have shown the importance of well-resourced and internationally connected institutes which can develop an integrated analysis and foster climates favourable to change. Unco-ordinated research by isolated critics can never compete.

• *Develop alternative media outlets*—once mainstream media are captured it is difficult for critics to enter the debate, and impossible to lead it. Alternative media and innovative strategies must be in place before people and financial resources come under stress. Effective communication and exchange of information between sectoral groups and activists are essential, despite the time and resources involved.

• *Raise the levels of popular economic literacy*—familiarise people with the basic themes, assumptions and goals of economic fundamentalism. Insist that economic policy affects everyone, that everyone has a right to participate in the debate, and that alternatives do exist.

• *Educate popular and sectoral groups in advance*—draw on international experience, networks, publications, speakers and examples to put people on the alert. Identify the likely strategies, policies and effects of structural adjustment for sectors like labour, education, health, local government, community work, public service and the media. Encourage sectors to workshop counter-strategies in advance. There will be little time for this when people are struggling just to survive.

• *Resist market-speak*—maintain control of the language, challenge its capture, and refuse to convert your discourse to theirs. Insist on using hard terms that convey the hard realities of what is going on.

• *Be realistic and avoid nostalgia*—recognise that the world has changed, in some ways irreversibly, and the past was far from perfect. Avoid being trapped solely into reaction and critique. Many neo-liberal criticisms of the status quo are justified and will strike a chord with people. Defending the past for its own sake adds credibility to their arguments and wastes opportunities to work for genuine change.

• *Be pro-active and develop real alternatives*—start rethinking visions, strategies and models of development for the future. Show that there are workable, preferable alternatives from the start. This becomes progressively more difficult once the programme takes hold.

• *Rethink identity and alliances*—combine a critical analysis of economic, political, cultural and social models of the past with a forward-thinking vision of what a socially just future might look like. Recognise that the legitimate expectations, insights and vision of indigenous peoples are not just a matter of social justice, but offer the foundation for an alliance which can forge a new way ahead.

It is impossible to tell in retrospect how far these strategies would have hindered, let alone prevented, the onset of economic fundamentalism in New Zealand. They most certainly would have made the 'successful' implementation of the structural adjustment programme more difficult, and given time for opponents to rethink, regroup and resist.

Sadly, the time for many of these strategies has passed. It is going to be enormously difficult and costly to bring about changes which genuinely empower people in Aotearoa New Zealand to take control of their lives, within communities where they can play an active, equal and valued part. Yet the potential is still there for alternative forms of economics, politics and identity to emerge, and there are strategies which can exploit the soft underbelly of the new regime to bring them into effect. The beginnings of a manual for counter-technopols in this post-structural adjustment phase might include the following:

• *Challenge the TINA syndrome*—convince people individually and collectively that there *are* alternatives. Carefully analyse present barriers and future trends to produce options that combine realism with the prospect of meaningful change. Actively promote them and have them ready to be implemented when the market fails.

• *Promote informed debate and critique*—build a constituency for change through alternative information networks and media; use tribal, community, workplace, women's, church, creche, union and similar outlets, and harness technology where available, to balance the good-news machine with critical analysis of the economic and social costs.

• *Promote participatory democracy*—encourage people to take back control; empower them with knowledge to understand the forces affecting them and the points at which they can intervene. Stress that no one has a fail-safe recipe for change, and that everyone has a contribution to make. Recognise the skills, resources and insights of tribes, individuals, communities, sectoral groups and civil society, and the right to act both separately and in concert.

• *Embrace the Treaty of Waitangi as a liberating force*—moving forward means facing up to the past. Healing the wounds from over 155 years means restoring to Maori their economic and political power. Constructive debate on a treaty-based republican constitution can provide a liberating framework within which Maori and Pakeha can co-exist.

• *Encourage progressive counter-nationalism*—celebrate diversity rather than uniformity; work to build identities and values which replace xenophobia, racism and nostalgia with multiple identities and progressive visions for the future.

• *Develop multi-level strategies*—take action at local, sectoral, regional, national and international levels, and co-ordinate those activities through informal networks and formal linkages.

• *Hold the line*—the structural adjustment programme is not yet complete; the state still plays an active role in providing social services and public goods. Sustained and co-ordinated action in communities, sectors and national politics can effectively hold the line.

• *Localise politics*—recognise the power held by regional and local authorities and the ability to secure information and influence decisions at that level. Encourage accountability of local officials and participation in local politics. Continue local struggles to maintain services which provide for local needs; build solidarity, political awareness and a belief in the possibility of change.

• *Ginger up party politics*—maintain pressure on political parties through popular mobilisation and public education campaigns, document failed policies and unacceptable practices, and use the politics of embarrassment at home and overseas to complement the work of party activists within.

• *Invest in the future*—provide financial, human and moral support to sustain alternative analysis, publications, think-tanks, training programmes and people's projects that are working actively for change. Create alternatives to state dependency by providing financial, personal and moral support for alternative economic developments.

• *Support those who speak out*—intimidation and harassment of social critics works only if the targets lack personal, popular and institutional support. Withdrawing from public debate leaves those who remain more exposed.

• *Promote ethical investment*—support overseas and local investors who genuinely respond to indigenous, ecological and social concerns. Expose and attack unethical investors who don't. Boycotts have proved a powerful force internationally and in New Zealand, including anti-apartheid, anti-nuclear, environmental and safe product campaigns. 'New Zealand' companies can be most easily embarrassed and called to account. 'Foreign' companies are often targets of co-ordinated campaigns overseas that welcome information, participation and support.

• *Think global, act local*—develop an understanding of the global nature of economic, political and cultural power, and those forces which drive current trends. Draw the links between global forces and local events. Target local representatives, meetings and activities which feed into and on the global economic and political machine.

• *Think local, act global*—actively support international strategies for change, such as people's tribunals, non-state codes of conduct, non-governmental forums, and action campaigns against unethical companies, practices and governments. Recognise that international action is essential to counter the collaboration of states and corporations, and to empower civil society to take back control.

Notes and References

Abbreviations

EM   *Economic Management*
GM   *Government Management: Brief to the Incoming Government 1987*
IIE   Institute for International Economics, Washington, DC
NBR   *National Business Review*
NZPD   *New Zealand Parliamentary Debates*
NZULR   *New Zealand University Law Review*

Introduction

1 OECD, *New Zealand Country Report 1993*, OECD, Paris, 1993, p.13.
2 OECD, 1993, pp.14-15.
3 OECD, 1993, p.15.
4 Moody's Investors Services, *New Zealand Sovereign In-Depth Analysis*, New York, 1994, pp.4, 7 & 8.
5 *Economist*, 1 June 1985, p.19.
6 *Economist*, 5 Mar. 1988, p.74.
7 *Economist*, 8 Aug. 1988, p.45.
8 *Economist*, 3 Nov. 1990, p.19.
9 *Economist*, 15 June 1991, p.72.
10 *Economist*, 13 Nov. 1993, p.155.
11 *Economist*, 13 Nov. 1993, p.155.
12 *Economist*, 13 Oct. 1993, p.128.
13 *Economist*, 10 July 1993, p.75.
14 *Economist*, 16 Oct. 1993, p.20.
15 22 June 1992, 'New Zealand strides down the hard road to economic recovery'.
16 24 July 1992, 'Blueprint for a shrinking state'.
17 Aug. 1994, 'Radically sensible New Zealand', reported in *NZ Herald*, 20 Sept. 1994.
18 14 Dec. 1994, 'Kiwi School of Economics'.
19 E.g. *Toronto Star*, 29 Mar. 1993; *Canadian Forum*, Apr. 1995, p.10.
20 Notably 'The Remaking of New Zealand', *Ideas*, CBC, 12 Oct. 1994.
21 *Independent on Sunday*, 13 Mar. 1994.
22 *OECD Outlook*, OECD, Paris, 1993.
23 See synopsis in *Evening Post*, 3 & 4 Apr. 1995. For a more detailed account, see pp.273–90.

1 Setting the Scene

1 J. Camilleri & J. Falk, *The End of Sovereignty? The Politics of a Shrinking and Fragmenting World*, Edward Elgar, Aldershot, 1992, p.26.
2 Camilleri & Falk, p.132.
3 As encapsulated in the United Nations Charter, 1945.
4 A. Smith, *An Inquiry into the Nature and Causes of the Wealth of Nations*, Modern Library, New York, 1937.
5 E. J. Hobsbawm, *Nations and Nationalism Since 1780*, Cambridge University Press, 2 edn, 1992, p.38.
6 J. Williamson, 'In Search of a Manual for Technopols', in J. Williamson (ed.), *The Political Economy of Policy Reform*, IIE, 1994, p.18.
7 Williamson, Appendix, pp.26-28.
8 Williamson, pp.17-18.
9 See R. Garnaut, 'Australia', in Williamson (ed.). Note, however, that Garnaut's account reflects his position as advisor to Prime Minister Bob Hawke in 1983-89. See also B. Easton & R. Gerritsen, 'Economic Reform: Parallels and Divergences', in F. Castles et al. (eds), *The Great Experiment: Labour Parties and Public Policy Transformation in Australia and New Zealand*, Allen & Unwin, Sydney (forthcoming).
10 See J. Kelsey, 'Restructuring the Nation: The Decline of the Colonial Nation-State and Competing Nationalisms in Aotearoa/New Zealand', in P. Fitzpatrick (ed.), *Nationalism, Racism and*

the Rule of Law, Dartmouth, Aldershot, 1995, pp.177, 183-5.

11 N. Haworth, 'Neo-Liberalism, Economic Internationalisation and the Contemporary State in New Zealand', in A. Sharp (ed.), *Leap into the Dark: The Changing Role of the State in New Zealand Since 1984*, Auckland University Press, Auckland, 1994, p.19.

12 B. Jesson, *Fragments of Labour: The Story Behind the Labour Government*, Penguin, Auckland, 1989, p.17.

13 The traditional Maori name for the North Island, which is now generally used as the Maori name for the three main islands that make up New Zealand.

14 Those who identified partly or solely as Maori in 1994 numbered around 435,000, or 13% of the population, and rising. Statistics New Zealand, *New Zealand Now: Maori*, Wellington, Dec. 1994, p.3. This is based on 1991 census figures. However, these census questions provoked considerable criticism from Maori, with calls for a boycott of them, so the returns may be unreliable.

15 J. Nagel, 'Market Liberalization in New Zealand. The Interaction of Economic Reform and Political Institutions in a Pluritarian Democracy', paper delivered to the 1994 Political Science Association annual meeting, New York, Sept. 1994, p.15.

2 Capturing the Political Machine

1 J. Williamson (ed.), *The Political Economy of Policy Reform*, IIE, 1994.

2 J. Williamson, 'In Search of a Manual for Technopols', pp.9, 11.

3 Williamson, 'In Search of a Manual', p.23.

4 J. Williamson & S. Haggard, 'The Political Conditions for Economic Reform', in Williamson (ed.), pp.527, 589.

5 *Ideas*, CBC.

6 *NBR*, 11 July 1986.

7 His background as an accountant, rather than an economist, led to suggestions in the IIE study that Douglas was not a real technopol. However, the term is used in a broad sense throughout this book.

8 R. Douglas, *Unfinished Business*, Random House, Auckland, 1993, p.7.

9 S. Collins, *Rogernomics: Is There a Better Way?*, Pitman, Auckland, 1987, p.7.

10 R. Douglas & L. Callen, *There's Got to Be a Better Way!*, Fourth Estate, Wellington, 1980.

11 R. Douglas & L. Callen, *Towards Prosperity: People and Politics in the 1980s — A Personal View*, David Bateman, Auckland, 1987, p.30.

12 H. Schwartz, 'Can Orthodox Stabilization and Adjustment Work? Lessons from New Zealand 1984–90', *International Organizations*, 45,2 (1991), pp.221, 251.

13 E.g. Jim Anderton, as reported in B. Jesson, *Fragments of Labour*, Penguin, Auckland, 1989, p.62.

14 Douglas & Callen, *Towards Prosperity*, p.38.

15 Treasury, *EM*, Wellington, 1984.

16 A. Bollard, 'New Zealand', in J. Williamson (ed.) *The Political Economy of Policy Reform*, IIE, 1994, p.89.

17 Economic Summit Conference Communiqué, 1984, para.1.

18 Douglas & Callen, *Towards Prosperity*, p.74.

19 *NZ Herald*, 30 Mar. 1991.

20 B. Easton, 'How did the Health Reforms Blitzkrieg Fail?', *Political Science*, 4,2 (1994), p.215.

21 A. Bollard, 'New Zealand', in J. Williamson (ed.), p.97.

22 Nagel, 'Market Liberalization in New Zealand.', p.21.

23 *Ideas*, CBC.

24 Douglas, *Unfinished Business*, pp.220-1.

25 Douglas, *Unfinished Business*, p.225.

26 Douglas, *Unfinished Business*, p.218.

27 Douglas, *Unfinished Business*, p.229.

28 Treasury, *EM*, p.133.

29 R. Prebble, speech to Wellington Society of Accountants, 20 Mar. 1988.

30 Seventeen of the 20 members of the 1984 Cabinet were from professional or semi-professional backgrounds, including eight former teachers and six with law degrees. Caucus representation followed similar lines. B. Gustafson, 'The Labour Party', in H. Gold (ed.), *New Zealand Politics in Perspective*, 3 edn, Longman Paul, Auckland, 1992, pp.263, 276.

31 Gustafson, 'The Labour Party', p.276.

32 Schwartz, p.251.

33 Douglas, *Unfinished Business*, p.39.

34 Gustafson, 'The Labour Party', p.281.

35 CBC, *Ideas*.

36 B. Gustafson, *The First 50 Years: A History of the New Zealand National Party*,

Reed Methuen, Auckland, 1986, p.180.

37 *Listener*, 19 Aug. 1989.

38 While nineteen National MPs were farmers or had farming interests, there were fifteen MPs from business and commerce, ten were lawyers, four accountants, three from the armed forces, and ten from the public sector including the police. G. A. Wood, 'The National Party', in Gold (ed.), pp.289, 295.

39 *NZPD*, Vol. 458, 6 Nov. 1984, p.1313.

40 Ruth Richardson, John Luxton, Jenny Shipley, Maurice Williamson, Simon Upton, Rob Storey, Paul East, John Falloon, Lockwood Smith, Denis Marshall, Doug Kidd & Doug Graham.

41 *NZ Herald*, 23 Jan. 1992 & 21 Feb. 1992.

42 M. Loughlin, 'Law, Ideologies and the Politico-juridical System', in A. Gamble & C. Wells (eds), *Thatcher's Law*, GPC Books, Cardiff, 1989, pp.37-38.

43 See below, pp.236-7.

44 *NZPD*, Vol. 522, 5 Mar. 1992, pp.6653-4 & 6658 especially.

45 Social Security Amendment Bill (No. 6) 1992.

46 *NZPD*, Vol. 522, 5 Mar. 1992, p.6657, per McCully.

47 NZPD, Vol. 522, 5 Mar. 1992, p.6654.

48 Williamson & Haggard, p. 592.

3 *Empowering the Technocrats*

1 R. Bates & A. Krueger, *Political and Economic Interactions in Economic Policy Reform*, Blackwell, 1993, pp.462-3.

2 A. Bollard, 'New Zealand', in J. Williamson (ed.), p.91.

3 *Report of the Hospital and Related Services Taskforce: Unshackling the Hospitals* (Gibbs Report), Dept of Health, Wellington, 1988.

4 See Chapter 13.

5 *Listener*, 4 May 1992, p.14.

6 R. Polaschek, *Government Administration in New Zealand*, Oxford University Press, Wellington, 1958 edn, p.252.

7 *EM*, Wellington, pp.125-6.

8 Douglas & Callen, *Towards Prosperity*, p.129.

9 J. Roberts, *Politicians, Public Servants and Public Expenditure: Restructuring the New Zealand Government Executive*, VUP, Wellington, 1987, p.33.

10 B. Easton, 'The Commercialisation of the New Zealand Economy', in Easton (ed.), *The Making of Rogernomics*, AUP, Auckland, 1989, pp.114, 127.

11 E1.5 d(i) Cabinet Office Manual, quoted by J. Boston, 'The Treasury: Its Role, Philosophy and Influence', in H. Gold (ed.), *New Zealand Politics in Perspective*, pp.194, 206.

12 J. Boston, 'Reorganizing the Machinery of Government: Objectives and Outcomes', in J. Boston et al (eds) *Reshaping the State: New Zealand's bureaucratic revolution*, OUP, Auckland, 1991, p.245.

13 See Chapter 6.

14 Brian Picot; see Report of the Taskforce to Review Education Administration, *Administering for Excellence: Effective Administration in Education*, GP, Wellington, Apr. 1988 (Picot Report).

15 Gary Hawke; see *Report of the Working Group on Post Compulsory Education and Training in New Zealand*, GP, Wellington, July 1988 (Hawke Report).

16 Harold Titter; see *School Property for Better Education: The Report of the Taskforce on the Development of Long-Term Policy for School Property*, Ministry of Education, Wellington, 1993.

17 Jeff Todd; see *Report on Funding Growth in Tertiary Education*, Education Department, Wellington, 1994 (Todd Report).

18 *Private Provision for Retirement: The Way Forward. Final Report of the Task Force on Private Provision for Retirement*, GP, Wellington, 1992 (Todd Report on Superannuation).

19 Bollard, 'New Zealand', p.94.

20 G. Bertram, 'Keynesianism, Neoclassicism, and the State', in B. Roper & C. Rudd (eds) *State and Economy in New Zealand*, OUP, Auckland, 1993, pp.26, 37-38.

21 Bertram, p.39.

22 Easton, p.88.

23 Bernard Galvin, reported by A. Bollard, 'Introduction', in A. Bollard (ed.), *The Influence of United States Economics on New Zealand: The Fulbright Anniversary Seminars, 1988*, Res. Monograph 42, NZIER, Wellington, 1988, pp. 6-7.

24 Bryce Wilkinson, reported by Bollard, 'Introduction', p.6.

25 Grant Spencer, reported by Bollard, 'Introduction', p.8.

26 'The Remaking of New Zealand', *Ideas*, CBC, 12 October 1994.

27 For example, Bryce Wilkinson, one of the authors of *Economic Management*, was a Harkness Fellow at Harvard 1977-78; Graham Scott, who took over as Secretary to the Treasury in 1987,

was at Harvard Business School in 1985; Rob Cameron, a co-author of *Economic Management*, has also been a fellow at Harvard.

28 Grant Spencer was seconded to the IMF 1881–84. Deane had been alternate executive director with the IMF 1974-76.

29 Bollard, 'Introduction', p.10.

30 Treasury, *EM*, Wellington, July 1984, p.[iii].

31 *EM*, p.104.

32 *EM*, p.103.

33 *EM*, p.106.

34 *EM*, pp.107-8.

35 *EM*, p.111.

36 *EM*, p.112.

37 *EM*, pp.113-14, 122-33.

38 *EM*, pp.125-6.

39 Treasury, *Government Management: Brief to the Incoming Government 1987*, Treasury, Wellington, 1987, Vol. 1, p.31.

40 *GM*, p.32.

41 *GM*, p.33.

42 *GM*, p.47.

43 *GM*, p.44.

44 *GM*, p.46.

45 *GM*, annex especially pp.416-26.

46 *GM*, pp.424-6.

47 S. Goldfinch & B. Roper, 'Treasury's Role in State Policy Formulation during the Post-war Era', in Roper & Rudd (eds), pp.50, 64.

48 P. Dalziel, 'The Rhetoric of Treasury: A Review of the 1990 Briefing Papers', *New Zealand Economic Papers* 25, 2 (1991), pp.259, 266.

49 *1990 Treasury Briefing Papers*, Treasury, Wellington, 1990, p.142.

50 Dalziel, 'The Rhetoric of Treasury', p.267.

51 P. Dalziel, 'The April 1st Benefit Cuts', unpublished paper, 1991.

52 M. Prebble, *Information, Privacy and the Welfare State: An Integrated Approach to the Administration of Redistribution*, Institute of Policy Studies, Wellington, 1990.

53 F. Holmes & C. Falconer, *Open Regionalism? NAFTA, CER and a Pacific Basin Initiative*, Institute of Policy Studies, Wellington, 1992.

54 G. Hawke (ed.), *A Modest Safety Net?*, Institute of Policy Studies, Wellington, 1991.

55 Personal communications.

56 Bertram, 'Keynesianism', p.41. See also R. Buckle (ed.), *Inflation and Economic Adjustment: Proceedings of a Seminar*, Department of Economics, Victoria University of Wellington, Wellington, 1983.

57 For a detailed discussion see H. Oliver, 'The Labour Caucus and Economic Policy Formation, 1981–84', in B. Easton (ed.), p.11.

58 G. Zanetti et al, 'Opening the Books: A Review Article', *New Zealand Economic Papers* 18 (1984), pp.13, 28.

59 Bertram, 'Keynesianism', p.46.

60 B. Easton, 'From Reaganomics to Rogernomics', in Bollard (ed.), pp.69, 89.

61 S. Snively, 'Labour Markets and Social Policy: Reversing the Roles', in Bollard (ed.), pp.136, 142.

62 Easton, 'Reaganomics', p.77.

63 Easton, 'Reaganomics', p.85.

64 Easton, 'Reaganomics', pp.87-88.

65 Bertram, 'Keynesianism', pp.36-37.

66 Snively, 'Labour Markets', p.148.

67 Bertram, 'Keynesianism', p.30.

68 Bertram, 'Keynesianism', p.47.

4 Embedding the New Regime

1 S. Haggard & R. Kaufman, 'Institution and Economic Adjustment', in S. Haggard & R. Kaufman (eds), *The Politics of Economic Adjustment*, Princeton UP, New Jersey, 1992, p.19.

2 Haggard & Kaufman, pp.19-20.

3 Haggard & Kaufman, p.36.

4 T. Moe, 'Political Institutions: The Neglected Side of the Story', *Journal of Law, Economics, and Organization*, 6 (1990), pp. 213, 243.

5 Moe, 'Political Institutions', p.244.

6 R. Bates, 'Comment', in Williamson (ed.), pp.29, 32.

7 M. McCubbins, R. Noll & B. Weingast, 'Structure and Process, Politics and Policy: Administrative Arrangements and the Politial Control of Agencies', *Virginia Law Review*, 75 (1989), pp.431, 443.

8 M. McCubbins, R. Noll & B. Weingast, 'Administrative Procedures as Instruments of Political Control', *Journal of Law, Economics and Organization*, 6 (1990), pp.243, 261, orig. emphasis.

9 Moe, pp. 213, 228.

10 Williamson & Haggard, p.587.

11 Williamson & Haggard, p.588.

12 A. Hawkins & G. McLaughlan, *The Hawk*, Four Star Books, Auckland, 1989, p.126.

13 H. Schwartz, 'Can Orthodox Stabilisation and Adjustment Work? Lessons from New Zealand, 1984–90', *International Organizations*, 45, 2 (1991), p.221.
14 *NZ Herald*, 26 Feb. 1992.
15 *NBR*, 19 June 1992.
16 J. Vowles, 'Business, Unions and the State: Organising Economic Interests in New Zealand', in H. Gold (ed.), pp.342, 346; D. McLoughlin, 'Nights of the Roundtable', *North and South*, Sept. 1992, p.76.
17 *NZ Herald*, 26 Mar. 1992.
18 *NZ Herald*, 30 Mar. 1991.
19 N. Haworth, 'National Sovereignty, Deregulation and the Multinational: New Zealand in the 1980s', in J. Deeks & N. Perry (eds), *Controlling Interests: Business, the State and Society in New Zealand*, AUP, Auckland, 1992, pp.16, 28.
20 B. Roper, 'A Level Playing Field? . . .', in Roper & Rudd (eds), pp.147, 163.
21 Vowles, 'Business', p.346.
22 R. Bremer & T. Brooking, 'Federated Farmers and the State', in Roper & Rudd (eds), p.125.
23 *NZ Herald*, 18 Jan. 1993.
24 Easton, 'Reaganomics', pp.69, 76.
25 *NZ Hansard Supplement*, Vol. 12, pp.3629-32, 3870-88. See also *NZPD Question Supplement*, Vol. 16, pp.6824-7.
26 Information provided by the Treasury, Dec. 1994.
27 *NZ Herald*, 6 Jan. 1993.
28 B. Jesson, 'Lobbying and Protest: Patterns of Political Change at the Informal Level', in Gold (ed.), pp.365, 371.
29 Jesson, 'Lobbying', p.377.

5 *Market and Trade Liberalisation*

1 A. Bollard, 'More Market: The Deregulation of Industry', in A. Bollard & R. Buckle (eds), *Economic Liberalisation in New Zealand*, Allen & Unwin, Wellington, 1987, pp.25, 38.
2 A. Bollard, 'New Zealand', in J. Williamson (ed.), *The Political Economy of Policy Reform*, IIE, 1994, pp.106-10.
3 *EM*, pp.296-7.
4 *GM*, ch. 1.
5 *GM*, p.41.
6 *GM*, pp.258-9.
7 *Financial Policy Reform*, RBNZ, Wellington, 1986, pp.39-40.
8 D. Harper & G. Karacaoglu, 'Financial Policy Reform in New Zealand', in Bollard & Buckle (eds), p.206.
9 See *NBR*, 10 June 1994 & 12 May 1995; *Listener*, 21 May 1994.
10 P. Fitzsimons, 'The New Zealand Securities Commission: The Rise and Fall of a Law Reform Body', *Waikato Law Review*, 2 (1994), pp.87, 104.
11 *GM*, p.248.
12 *Business Review Weekly*, 7 Sept. 1990.
13 *Ideas*, CBC.
14 *GM*, pp.16, 20-21, 254-66.
15 K. Vautier, 'Competition Policy and Competition Law in New Zealand', in Bollard & Buckle (eds), pp.46, 52.
16 D. Greer, 'Contestability in Competition Policy: Replacement, Supplement or Impediment?', in Bollard (ed.), pp.39, 55. See also *NBR*, 19 July 1988, 2 Aug. 1988 & 18 Aug. 1988.
17 Greer, 'Contestability', p.56.
18 Vautier, 'Competition Policy', p.63.
19 Ministry of Commerce, *Review of the Commerce Act 1986*, Aug. 1989.
20 Justice Department, *Report of the Review Committee of the Commerce Act 1986*, Jan. 1993.
21 See also the Court of Appeal's balancing approach between efficiency and competition in *Telecom Corporation of New Zealand v Commerce Commission* [1992] 3 NZLR 429, 435.
22 *Telecom Corporation of New Zealand v Clear Communications* [1995] 1 NZLR 385.
23 Quoted in Fitzsimons, p.100. See also J. Farrar, 'Company Takeovers—A Critical Examination of the Securities Commission's Report', *NZULR*, 13 (1989), p.312.
24 *Securities Commission Report on Company Takeovers*, Securities Commission, Wellington, Oct. 1988.
25 *1990 Briefing Papers*, p.169.
26 *1990 Briefing Papers*, p.168.
27 J. Farmer, 'The Harmonisation of Australian and New Zealand Business Laws', in K. Vautier et al. (eds), *CER and Business Competition: Australia and New Zealand in a Global Economy*, CCH, Auckland, 1990, p.67.
28 Farmer, 'Harmonisation', p.63.
29 *NZPD*, Vol. 251, 17 Dec. 1991, p.6351.
30 P. Speakman, paper to IBC seminar on 'Capital Raising in the New Zealand Market', reported in *NBR*, 9 Dec. 1994.
31 *EM*, p.315.
32 L. Evans, 'Farming in a Changing Eco-

nomic Environment', in Bollard & Buckle (eds), p.102.

33 *1990 New Zealand Official Yearbook*, GP, Wellington, 1990, pp.682-3.

34 R. Bremer & T. Brooking, 'Federated Farmers and the State', in Roper & Rudd (eds), pp.108, 121, 125.

35 Evans, p.120.

36 Bremer & Brooking, 'Federated Farmers', p.116.

37 *EM*, pp.303, 325.

38 P. Wooding, 'Liberalising the International Trade Regime', in Bollard & Buckle (eds), pp.86, 98.

39 For a detailed account, see Wooding, 'Liberalising'.

40 Bollard, 'More Market', pp.25, 45.

41 *GM*, pp.250-1.

42 *GM*, p.250.

43 *GM*, p.250.

44 *GM*, p.242.

45 *GM*, p.242.

46 A. Bollard & B. Easton (eds), *Markets, Regulation and Pricing: Six Case Studies*, Research Paper 31, NZIER, Wellington, 1985.

47 Bollard, 'More Market', p.45.

48 *NZ Herald*, 23 June 1992.

49 *NZ Herald*, 17 Dec. 1994.

50 Minister of Finance, *Finance Focus*, Dec. 1994.

51 *GM*, p.244.

52 E.g. A. O. Krueger, 'Global Trade Prospects for the Developing Countries', *The World Economy*, 15, 4 (1993), pp.459, 472-3; J. Bhagwati, 'The Threats to the World Trading System', *The World Economy*, 15, 4 (1993), pp.449, 451-6; C. Raghavan, *Recolonization: GATT, the Uruguay Round and the Third World*, Third World Network, Penang, 1990.

53 P. Krugman, 'Does the New Trade Theory Require a New Trade Policy?', *The World Economy*, 15, 4 (1993), pp.423, 438.

54 G. Allen, 'The Deal on Services—a Necessary Step to Integration', in Vautier et al. (eds), pp.165, 171.

55 Allen, 'Services', p.175.

56 Farmer, 'Harmonisation', p.48.

57 *Sunday Star-Times*, 27 Nov. 1994.

58 Christchurch *Press*, 1 July 1992.

59 *NZPD*, Vol. 541, 13 July 1994, p.2847.

60 *Australian Financial Review*, 7 Apr. 1995.

61 Ministry of Foreign Affairs and Trade, *Trading Ahead. The GATT Uruguay Round: Results for New Zealand*, Min-

istry of Foreign Affairs & Trade, Wellington, 1994, p.12.

62 See Table 10.3.

63 New Zealand Law Commission, 'The Making and Implementation of Treaties: Three Issues for Consideration', Aug. 1993.

64 Article XII and XVIII:B of the GATT 1994, and Understanding on the Balance-of-payments Provisions of the General Agreement on Tariffs & Trade 1994.

65 Personal communication.

66 National Maori Congress, press release, 29 Nov. 1994.

67 Report of the Eminent Persons Group to APEC Ministers, *A Vision for APEC: Towards an Asia Pacific Economic Community*, APEC, Singapore, Oct. 1993, p.36.

68 *NZ Herald*, 17 Nov. 1994.

69 *Sunday Star-Times*, 27 Nov. 1994.

70 Figures supplied by Bill Rosenberg, based on annual listing in *Management Magazine*, Dec. 1994.

71 *Financial Times*, 27 Aug. 1993.

72 R. Chung, 'Foreign Investment in New Zealand Commercial Property', Ernst & Young, Auckland, Aug. 1994.

73 *NBR*, 10 June 1994.

74 *Foreign Control Watchdog*, 76, Sept. 1994, pp.24-30.

75 Statistics New Zealand now produces a regular update on 'New Zealand's International Investment Position' which is somewhat more informative, and at times diverges from the information released by the OIC.

76 Report of the Ombudsman for the year ended June 1993, p.135,.

77 *Foreign Control Watchdog*, 76, Sept. 1994, p.31.

78 Overseas Investment Commission Officials Report to Select Committee, 20 Mar. 1995.

79 *Foreign Control Watchdog*, 77, Dec. 1994, pp.1-2.

80 *NZ Herald*, 7 Dec. 1994.

81 *NBR*, 4 Aug. 1995.

82 *GM*, p.265

83 *1990 Briefing Papers*, pp.166-7.

84 *1990 Briefing Papers*, p.167.

85 *Environment 2010 Strategy*, Ministry for the Environment, Wellington, Oct. 1994, pp.10, 14.

86 Speech to the Magazine Publishers' Association, Auckland, 24 May 1988, quoted in A. Cocker, 'Broadcasting De-

regulation and Content Diversity: The New Zealand Experience', paper for the International Conference Association, Sydney, July 1994.

87 J. Atkinson, 'The State, the Media, and Thin Democracy', in Sharp (ed.), pp.146, 148.

88 J. Farnsworth, 'Mainstream or Minority: Ambiguities in State or Market Arrangements for New Zealand Television', in Deeks & Perry (eds), pp.191, 202-3.

89 Cocker, 'Broadcasting'.

90 Research by Avon Adams, 'Local Content in New Zealand Television', unpublished research essay, Dept of Political Studies, University of Auckland, 1992, quoted in Atkinson, 'The State', p.150.

91 *Attorney-General* v *New Zealand Maori Council* [1991] 2 NZLR 129; *Attorney-General* v *New Zealand Maori Council* (No 2) [1991] 2 NZLR 147; *New Zealand Maori Council* v *Attorney-General* [1994] 1 NZLR 513; *Report of the Waitangi Tribunal on the Broadcasting Claim*, WAI-150, Nov. 1990.

6 *Limiting the State*

1 *EM*, pp.293-4.

2 *GM*, p.55.

3 Public Service Association, 'Discussion Paper on Privatisation', Jan. 1989.

4 *GM*, p.113.

5 *GM*, pp.233-4.

6 *GM*, p.117.

7 *GM*, p.119.

8 For further discussion, see J. Kelsey, *Rolling Back the State: Privatisation of Power in Aoteroa/New Zealand*, Bridget Williams Books, Wellington, 1993, ch.2.

9 R. Birchfield & I. Grant, *Out of the Woods: The Restructuring and Sale of New Zealand's State Forests*, GP Books, Wellington, 1993, p.66.

10 Birchfield & Grant, pp.44-47.

11 *New Zealand Maori Council* v *Attorney-General* [1987] 1 NZLR 641; *New Zealand Maori Council* v *Attorney-General* [1989] 2 NZLR 142; *Tainui Maori Trust Board* v *Attorney-General* [1989] 2 NZLR 513.

12 Treaty of Waitangi (State Enterprises) Act 1988; Crown Forest Assets Act 1989.

13 See below, pp.224-7.

14 *NZ Herald*, 13 Apr. 1992.

15 *NZ Herald*, 22 July 1992.

16 G. Campbell, 'R for Chaos', *Listener*, 25 Nov. 1991, p.14.

17 I. Duncan & A. Bollard, *Corporatization and Privatization: Lessons from New Zealand*, OUP, Auckland, 1992, p.168.

18 Duncan & Bollard, Preface.

19 Information from Crown Company Monitoring Advisory Unit.

20 Ministerial Cabinet Committee, MCC/SOE, nos 59, 59a, 59b, 87, 239.

21 Duncan & Bollard, p.113.

22 Duncan & Bollard, p.155.

23 *Dominion*, 18 Aug. 1994.

24 Ministerial Cabinet Committee, MCC/SOE, 13 Aug. 1986.

25 Birchfield & Grant, p.103.

26 Duncan & Bollard, p.67, Table 6.2.

27 Commerce and Marketing Select Committee, 'Report on the Inquiry into the Proposed Increases of Wholesale and Retail Electricity Prices', Feb. 1992.

28 *NBR*, 1 July 1994.

29 For a detailed discussion, see Kelsey, ch.12.

30 Ombudsman to the Minister of Justice, 'Submission on the SOEs and the Ombudsman', Aug. 1986.

31 Submission to the SOEs (Ombudsman and Official Information Acts) Committee 1990.

32 Auditor-General, 'Discussion Paper: Accountability Requirements for SOEs', 16 Mar. 1988.

33 Auditor-General, Annual Report, 1988.

34 *Federated Farmers of New Zealand* v *New Zealand Post Ltd* (unreported), Wellington High Court, 1 Dec. 1992.

35 *Auckland Electric Power Board* v *Electricity Corporation of New Zealand* [1994] 1 NZLR 551, 558-9.

36 *New Zealand Maori Council* v *Attorney-General* [1994] 1 NZLR 513, 519.

37 *Mercury Energy* v *Electricity Corporation of New Zealand* [1994] 2 NZLR 385, 388.

38 *NBR*, 8 July 1994, 22 July 1994.

39 *NZPD*, Vol. 525, 2 June 1992, p.8421, per Luxton.

40 For further discussion, see Kelsey, ch.3.

41 R. Deane, 'Reforming the Public Sector', in S. Walker (ed.), *Rogernomics: Reshaping New Zealand's Economy*, GP Books, Wellington, 1989, pp.116, 125.

42 *NZPD*, Vol. 474, 30 Sept. 1986, p.4731, per Prebble.

43 Assets for sale included Government Property Services, Shipping Corpora-

tion, PostBank, Tourist Hotel Corporation, Bank of New Zealand, financial assets of Landcorp, non-core railways assets, and the Crown's commercial forestry holdings.

44 *NZ Herald*, 20 July 1990.

45 *Budgetary Stress*, New Zealand Business Roundtable, Wellington, 1992, p.45, original emphasis.

46 Fletcher Challenge bought Petrocorp, Rural Bank, Liquid Fuels Investment, Synfuels stocks and a quarter of the state forest cutting rights; Fay Richwhite secured a quarter of the BNZ, a large share of Housing Corporation mortgages, 5% of Telecom, and a share of NZ Rail; Brierley Investments Ltd bought an initial 65% of Air New Zealand; National Australia Bank bought the BNZ from the government and Fay Richwhite, and the Rural Bank from Fletcher Challenge; ANZ Bank bought Postbank and some Housing Corporation mortgages; Rank Group bought the Government Printing Office; Carter Holt Harvey bought over a third of the forestry cutting rights; Freightways bought 5% of Telecom. Roundtable membership also included chief executives of privatised businesses, notably Telecom, BNZ, NZ Rail, Tower Corporation (formerly State Insurance), and several SOEs and LATEs, notably Mercury Energy, Ports of Auckland, Forestry Corporation, NZ Post and Electricorp.

47 Among the major beneficiaries were financial advisors Jarden Morgan ($7.4m), CS First Boston and First Boston ($34.9m), Fay Richwhite ($7.66 million), Buttle Wilson ($24.7m), Goldman Sachs ($17.2m) and Bankers Trust ($3.4m); law firms Chapman Tripp ($3m), Bell Gully ($1.3m), and Kensington Swan ($1.3m); accountants Coopers & Lybrand ($3.76 million), with lesser sums to Peat Marwick, Price Waterhouse, Arthur Young, Touche Ross, and Ernst & Young. Figures provided by Treasury, Mar. 1995.

48 *NZ Herald*, 10 Dec. 1994.

49 The most extreme example was Comalco, owned by mining trans-national CRA, which enjoyed exclusive access to 16% of the country's total electricity output. Until 1993 it paid almost half the rate of other large industrial users and less than a quarter of domestic rates. Under a new contract with ECNZ in 1994 the price of power would rise to 90% of commercial rates by 2010, but increase only 10% over the first ten years.

50 *NZ Herald*, 24 Oct. 1992.

51 *NBR*, 19 Nov. 1993.

52 Government Administration Committee on the Inquiry into the Sale of the GPO, 1991.

53 See above, p.112

54 *Foreign Control Watchdog*, 77, Dec. 1994, p.3

55 *NBR*, 24 Mar. 1995.

56 *NZ Herald*, 24 July 1989.

57 Birchfield & Grant, p.163.

58 *NZPD*, Vol. 490, 28 July 1988, pp.5545-50, per Douglas.

59 Birchfield & Grant, p.228.

60 Treasury, 'Information for Ministers-designate with State-owned Enterprises Responsibilities', Feb. 1990, Part III, pp.2-3.

61 M. Taggart, *Corporatisation, Privatisation and Public Law*, Legal Research Foundation, Auckland, 1990, p.24.

62 *NZ Herald*, 3 June 1992.

63 For further discussion, see Kelsey, *Rolling Back the State*, ch.4.

64 'SteeringGroup Review of State Sector Reforms, *Review of the State Sector Reforms*, 29 Nov. 1991, SSC (1991), p.1 (Logan Report).

65 G. Scott, 'What's wrong with Managerialism?', *Public Sector*, 16, 1, p.2.

66 G. Scott & R. Blakeley, 'Professionalism in the Public Service', *Public Sector*, 16, 4, p.24.

67 J. Boston , 'Reorganizing the Machinery of Government: Objectives and Outcomes', in J. Boston et al. (eds), *Reshaping the State: New Zealand's Bureaucratic Revolution*, OUP, Auckland, 1991, pp.233, 237.

68 Clause 22, State Sector Bill 1987.

69 Discussed in J. Boston, 'Chief Executives and the Senior Executive Service', in Boston et al. (eds), pp.81, 85-87.

70 Boston, 'Chief Executives', pp.92-93.

71 E.g. J. Roseveare, 'Chief Executives and Statutory Independence', *Public Sector*, 17, 4, p.8; M. Probine, 'The State Sector Act: Lessons from the Recent Past', *Public Sector*, 17, 4, p.12; J. Boston, 'On the Sharp Edge of the State Sector Act: the Resignation of Perry Cameron', *Public Sector*, 17, 4, p.2.

72 Probine, 'State Sector Act', p.14.
73 M. Durie, 'Maori and the State: Professionalism and Ethical Implications for a Bicultural Public Service', *Public Sector*, 17, 1, pp.20, 23-24.
74 PSA Presentation to the ILO Delegation, Sept. 1994, App. 2.
75 *PSA Journal* 81, 7, Sept. 1994, p.7, especially in relation to the customs department.
76 D. Bradshaw, 'Professionalism in the Public Service', *Public Sector* 17, 1, pp.13, 14.
77 Section 2, Public Finance Act 1989.
78 J. Pallot, 'Financial Management Reform', in Boston et al. (eds), pp.166, 189.
79 *Report of the Controller & Auditor-General*, Third Report for 1994, pp.15-41.
80 Boston, 'Reorganizing the Machinery', p.263.
81 D. Rose, 'Redistribution, Employment and Growth: A Briefing Paper for the New Zealand Council of Christian Social Services', Nov. 1993, p.17.
82 J. Martin, 'The Role of the State in Administration', in A. Sharp (ed.), pp.41, 44.
83 Logan Report, ch.4.
84 Boston, 'Chief Executives', p.102.
85 J. Martin, 'Ethos and Ethics', in Boston et al. (eds), pp.367, 370.
86 Martin, 'The Role of the State', pp.60-61.
87 Boston, 'Reorganizing the Machinery', p.260.
88 See also Logan Report, pp. 66-67.
89 'Review of the Purchase of Policy Advice from Government Departments', SSC, Wellington, 1991.
90 A. West, 'Public Service Is Independent of Public Servants', *Public Sector*, 17, 2, pp.26, 28.
91 J. Boston, 'Purchasing Policy Advice: the Limits to Contracting Out', *Governance*, 17, 1 (1994), pp.1, 28.
92 Boston, 'Purchasing Policy Advice', p.28.
93 Martin, 'The Role of the State', p.63.

7 *Monetary Policy*

1 Reserve Bank, *Financial Policy Reform*, RBNZ, Wellington, 1986, pp.39-40.
2 *EM*, p.144.
3 P. Dalziel, 'The Reserve Bank Act', in Roper & Rudd (eds), *State and Economy in New Zealand*, pp.74, 84-85.

4 *GM*, p.194
5 *GM*, p.202.
6 *GM*, p.202.
7 *GM*, pp.199-200.
8 *GM*, p.16.
9 *GM*, pp.203, 199.
10 *GM*, p.210.
11 D. K. Sheppard, 'The 1989 Reserve Bank Bill as a Charter for Price and Financial Sector Stability: A Review of its Defacto Performance', unpublished paper, 1989, p.2.
12 J. Whitwell, 'Monetary Policy with a Deregulated Financial Sector', in Bollard & Buckle (eds), *Economic Liberalisation*, pp.261, 270.
13 R. Buckle, 'Sequencing and the Role of the Foreign Exchange Market', in Bollard & Buckle (eds), pp.236, 243.
14 Figures from D. K. Sheppard, 'The 1989 Reserve Bank Bill', p.4.
15 Whitwell, 'Monetary Policy', p.277.
16 Reserve Bank, *Post-Election Paper to the Minister of Finance on the Areas of Responsibility of the Reserve Bank*, RBNZ, Wellington, 1984.
17 Whitwell, 'Monetary Policy', pp.278-9.
18 Whitwell, 'Monetary Policy', p.280.
19 Reserve Bank, 'Critique of the Submission to the Finance and Expenditure Select Committee made by the New Zealand Manufacturers' Federation', 1989, para.23.
20 *GM*, pp.205-6.
21 Reserve Bank, 'Critique', para.28.
22 Buckle, 'Sequencing', p.249.
23 Brian Easton, for example, had raised the issue in the *Listener*, 3 Dec. 1983, p.84.
24 G. Harper & G. Karacaoglu, 'Financial Policy Reform in New Zealand', in Bollard & Buckle (eds), p.215.
25 *GM*, p.199.
26 OECD, *New Zealand Country Report, 1994*, OECD, Paris, 1994, p.77.
27 *The Banker*, Nov. 1987, p.4.
28 Dalziel, 'Reserve Bank Act', p.77.
29 Dalziel, 'Reserve Bank Act', p.84.
30 Dalziel, 'Reserve Bank Act', p.87.
31 Reserve Bank, 'Critique of the Submission', para.14.
32 Treasury, 'Reserve Bank Bill: Background Note for the Finance and Expenditure Select Committee', 3 Aug. 1989.
33 Reserve Bank, 'Critique of the Submission', para.7.
34 Memorandum for the Cabinet Legisla-

tion Committee on the Reserve Bank Bill, 3 June 1988.

35 This argument is explained more fully in Dalziel, 'Reserve Bank Act', pp.87-88.

36 Reserve Bank Brief to the Select Committee on the Reserve Bank Bill, 28 June 1989.

37 CTU submission on the Reserve Bank Bill 1989.

38 *EM*, p.147.

39 Treasury, 'Reserve Bank Reform: Summary', 27 Apr. 1988.

40 Report of the Finance and Expenditure Committee on the Reserve Bank of New Zealand Bill, 1989, p.5.

41 OECD, p.52.

42 *Economist*, 26 June 1993.

43 Reserve Bank, *Monetary Policy Statement*, June 1992, p.6.

44 *NZ Herald*, 31 Dec. 1994.

45 *NBR*, 16 Sept. 1994.

46 OECD, p.21.

47 *NZ Herald*, 8 Nov. 1994.

48 *NZ Herald*, 29 Dec. 1994.

49 *NBR*, 16 Sept. 1994.

50 Reserve Bank, *Monetary Policy Statement*, June 1992, p.7.

51 Reserve Bank, *Monetary Policy Statement*, June 1994, p.28.

52 Media release, Jan. 1995.

53 J. Anderton, press statement, 28 June 1994.

8 *Labour Market Deregulation*

1 Unqualified preference provisions had been repealed in 1983 when Jim Bolger was Minister of Labour in the Muldoon National government.

2 *EM*, pp.235-6.

3 *EM*, p.237.

4 *GM*, p.279.

5 *GM*, p.284.

6 *GM*, pp.280-1.

7 Labour was preparing to reintroduce a mild version of final offer arbitration when it lost the 1990 election.

8 P. Walsh, 'A Family Fight? Industrial Relations Reform under the Fourth Labour Government', in Easton (ed.), p.168.

9 R. Harbridge & K. Hince, *A Sourcebook of New Zealand Trade Unions and Employee Organisations*, Industrial Relations Centre, Victoria University of Wellington (IRC/VUW), Wellington, 1994, p.4.

10 K. Douglas, 'Organising Workers: The Effects of the Act on the Council of Trade Unions and Its Membership', in R. Harbridge (ed.), *Employment Contracts: New Zealand Experiences*, VUP, Wellington, 1993, pp.197, 207.

11 Walsh, 'A Family Fight?', p.167.

12 O. Harvey, 'The Unions and the Government: The Rise and Fall of the Compact', in Deeks & Perry (eds), pp.59, 70.

13 J. Vowles, 'Business, Unions and the State: Organising Economic Interests in New Zealand', in Gold (ed.), pp.342, 348.

14 J. Deeks, 'Introduction: Business, Government and Interest Group Politics', in Deeks & Perry (eds), pp.1, 6.

15 M. Wilson, 'Employment Equity Act 1990: A Case Study in Women's Political Influence 1984-90', in Deeks & Perry (eds), p.113.

16 *1990 Briefing Papers*, p.157.

17 For a detailed discussion, see P. Walsh, 'The Employment Contracts Act', in J. Boston & P. Dalziel (eds), *The Decent Society?: Essays in Response to National's Economic and Social Policies*, OUP, Auckland, 1992, p.59.

18 Walsh, 'The ECA', p.67.

19 Walsh, 'The ECA', p.59.

20 Walsh, 'The ECA', p.74.

21 Department of Statistics, *Key Statistics*, Dec. 1992, Wellington, Table 4.04.

22 Walsh, 'The ECA', p.71.

23 *NBR*, 9 May 1992.

24 A Survey of Labour Market Adjustment under the Employment Contracts Act 1991 prepared for the Department of Labour by Heylen Research Centre, Oct. 1992.

25 *PSA Journal*, 79, 5, June 1992.

26 Case no.1698, Complaint against the Government of New Zealand presented by the New Zealand Council of Trade Unions (NZCTU), International Labour Organisation, Nov. 1994 (ILO Final Report), para.154.

27 R. Harbridge, A. Honeybone & P. Kiely, *Employment Contracts: Bargaining Trends and Employment Law Update: 1993/94*, VUW Industrial Relations Centre, Wellington, 1994, pp.2-3.

28 Harbridge & Hince, *A Sourcebook*, Preface.

29 R. Harbridge, K. Hince & A. Honeybone, *Unions and Union Membership in New Zealand: Annual Review for 1994*,

IRC/VUW, Working Paper 2/95, 1995, pp.10-13.
30 *NBR*, 30 Oct. 1992.
31 *NZ Herald*, 17 Nov. 1992.
32 *Ideas*, CBC.
33 Douglas, 'Organising Workers', p.207.
34 R. Reid, 'Crushing Labor in New Zealand, *Multinational Monitor*, June 1992, p.12.
35 Harbridge & Hince, *A Sourcebook*, p.14.
36 *Dominion*, 4 Dec. 1993.
37 *NZ Herald*, 17 Sept. 1992.
38 Information provided by the Employment Institutions, 25 July 1995.
39 *Port of Wellington* v *Longwith* [1995] 1 ERNZ 87.
40 *Grant* v *Superstrike Bowling Centres Ltd* [1992] 1 ERNZ 727. See also *New Zealand Resident Doctors Assoc* v *Otago Area Health Board* (1991) 4 NZELC 95,334.
41 *Paul* v *New Zealand Society for the Intellectually Handicapped* (1992) 4 NZLEC 95,528.
42 *PSA* v *DesignPower* (unreported), Employment Court, 16 Apr. 1992, WEC 17A/92; W 29/92.
43 Sections 62 & 64 of the Employment Contracts Act had been sections 232 and 233 of the Labour Relations Act 1987. My thanks to Bill Hodge for this point.
44 *Adams* v *Alliance Textiles (NZ) Ltd* (1992) 4 NZELC 95,423.
45 *Adams* v *Alliance Textiles* at 95,462.
46 *Adams* v *Alliance Textiles* at 95,464.
47 See the discussion of section 59(3) Employment Contracts Act in *Paul* v *New Zealand Society for the Intellectually Handicapped Inc* (1992) 4 NZELC 95,528 and *Adams* v *Alliance Textiles (NZ) Ltd* (1992) 4 NZELC 95,423.
48 *Northern Local Government Officers Union Inc* v *Auckland City* [1992] 1 ERNZ 1109.
49 *NZ Herald*, 1 Oct. 1992.
50 W. Hodge, 'Employment Law', *NZ Recent Law Review*, 1992, p.111.
51 Hodge, 'Employment Law', p.118.
52 *NBR*, 8 May 1992.
53 Hodge, 'Employment Law', p.112.
54 *Report of the Minority of the Labour Select Committee on the Inquiry into the Effects of the Employment Contracts Act on the New Zealand Labour Market*, 21 Sept. 1993.
55 ILO Final Report, para.153.
56 *Report of the Select Committee on the Inquiry into the Effects of the Employment*

Contracts Act on the New Zealand Labour Market, 1993, p.87.
57 *NZ Herald*, 23 Dec. 1994.
58 ILO, 292nd Report of the Committee on Freedom of Association, Case no. 1698, Mar. 1994 (ILO Interim Report), para 741.
59 *NBR*, 22 July 1994.
60 *NBR*, 22 July 1994.
61 *NBR*, 23 Sept. 1994.
62 ILO Final Report, para.155.
63 ILO Final Report, para.163.
64 *Eketone* v *Alliance Textiles*, Court of Appeal, 5 Nov. 1993, per Cooke P., p.6.
65 *Eketone* v *Alliance Textiles*, per Gault J., pp.15-16.
66 *Mineworkers Union of New Zealand* v *Dunollie Coal Mines*, Employment Court, Christchurch, 18 Feb. 1994.
67 *New Zealand Medical Laboratory Workers Union* v *CapitalCoast Health Ltd*, Employment Court, Wellington, 12 Aug. 1994.
68 ILO Final Report, Annex: 'Report of the Direct Contacts Mission to New Zealand concerning Case No. 1698', para.41.
69 ILO Final Report, paras 248-9.
70 ILO Final Report, para.252.
71 ILO Final Report, para.205.
72 ILO Final Report, para.259.
73 ILO Final Report, paras 254-5.
74 *NBR*, 25 Nov. 1994.
75 N. Haworth & S. Hughes, 'New Zealand and the ILO: Current Debates and Future Directions', unpublished paper, Feb. 1995.
76 Other cases which showed a moderating of position include *Hobday* v *Timaru Girls' High School Board of Trustees*, CEC 16/94, 10 June 1994 [procedural fairness in personal grievance]; *Kitchen Pak Distribution Ltd* v *Stoks* [1993] 2 ERNZ 401 & *Jones* v *Schindler Lifts Ltd* [1993] 2 ERNZ 300 [notice of redundancy & compensation]; *Pugmire* v *Good Health Wanganui Ltd* WEC 6/94, 8 Mar. 1994 & *Duggan* v *Wellington City Council* WEC 9/94, 21 Mar. 1994 [interim reinstatement]; *Witihera* v *Presbyterian Support Services (Northern)* AEC 31/94, 17 June 1994 [partial lockout]; *Labour Inspector* v *Telecom Networks and Operations Ltd* [1993] 1 ERNZ 492 [statutory holidays].
78 R. Kerr, 'Appeals to the Privy Council', New Zealand Bar Association, 22 July 1995.

77 Notably the split decision of the Court of Appeal in *Brighouse Ltd* v *Bilderbeck* [1995] 1 NZLR 158.

78 R. Kerr, 'Appeals to the Privy Council', New Zealand Bar Association, 22 July 1995.

79 *GM*, p.265.

80 Bill Birch, press release, 14 Aug. 1991.

81 Minister of Labour to CTU, 27 July 1994.

82 Report of the Select Committee on the ECA, pp.97-98.

83 Submission of CTU on Regulations under the HSEA 1992, Aug. 1994.

84 E.g. *Peter Baker Transport (1989) Ltd*, Auckland High Court, 28 Feb. 1994; *Kaitaia Intermediate School Board of Trustees*, Kaitaia District Court, 26 Apr. 1994.

85 G. Duncan, 'The ACC: Costs and Benefits', unpublished paper, 8 June 1994.

86 *1990 Treasury Briefing Papers*, p.115.

87 D. Farlow, 'An Employer Viewpoint', paper to COAC Conference, 8 June 1994.

88 *Submission to the Policy Statement 'Accident Compensation: A Fairer Scheme'*, NZ Business Roundtable, Wellington, 1991.

89 *Report of the Ministerial Working Party on the Accident Compensation Corporation and Incapacity*, 1st report, 1990.

90 See B. Birch, *Accident Compensation: A Fairer Scheme*, Wellington, July 1991.

91 *Report of the Regulations Review Committee on Complaints Relating to the Accident Rehabilitation and Compensation Insurance (Social Rehabilitation) Regulations 1992*, 1993, para.39.

92 *Report of the ACC Regulations Review Panel*, Aug. 1994; *Report of the Inquiry into the Procedures of the Accident Compensation Corporation* (Trapski Report), Aug. 1994.

93 ACC Annual Report, Dec. 1993, pp.20-21.

94 Duncan, 'The ACC'.

95 R. Wilson, 'Providing Solutions: The COAC View—Compensation, Injury Prevention, and a Structural Framework', unpublished papers, 8 June 1994.

96 Duncan, 'The ACC'.

97 *NZ Herald*, 4 Apr. 1992.

98 *NZ Herald*, 26 Feb. 1992.

9 *Fiscal Restraint*

1 *EM*, p.251.

2 *EM*, p.194.

3 B. Stephens, 'Social Policy Reform: In Retrospect and Prospect', in Bollard & Buckle (eds), *Economic Liberalisation in New Zealand*, pp.299, 313.

4 *EM*, p.217.

5 Stephens, 'Social Policy Reform', p.328.

6 Warrant, Report of the Royal Commission on Social Policy, *New Zealand Today*, Apr. 1988, Vol. 1, Wellington, pp.vi-vii.

7 B. Jesson, *Fragments of Labour: The Story Behind the Labour Government*, Penguin, Auckland, 1989, chs 6-8.

8 R. Stephens, 'Radical Tax Reform in New Zealand', *Fiscal Studies*, 14, 3 (1993), pp.45, 59, table 7.

9 *GM*, p.7.

10 J. Martin, 'Devolution and Decentralisation', in J. Boston et al. (eds), *Reshaping the State*, pp.268, 289-90.

11 SSC Task Group, 'Devolution: Initial Report to the Steering Group of Permanent Heads from the Task Group on Devolution', June 1987, p.17.

12 Martin, 'Devolution', p.268, original emphasis.

13 *GM*, p.147.

14 T. Ashton, 'The Purchaser/Provider Split in New Zealand: The Story so Far', unpublished paper, Dec. 1994.

15 G. Fougere, 'The State and Health-care Reform', in A. Sharp (ed.), *Leap into the Dark* p.110.

16 S. Upton, *Your Health and the Public Health*, Ministry of Health, Wellington, 1991.

17 *NZ Herald*, 18 Nov. 1992.

18 *NZ Herald*, 29 July 1992.

19 *NZ Herald*, 22 Dec. 1992.

20 *Consumer*, 295, July 1991, p.3; 338, June 1995, p.26.

21 *NZ Herald*, 29 Dec. 1994.

22 B. Easton, 'How Did the Health Reforms Blitzkrieg Fail?', pp.215, 225-6.

23 *Budgetary Stress*, Business Roundtable, Wellington, 1992, p.37.

24 *NZ Herald*, 19 Jan. 1995.

25 Fougère, 'The State', p.107.

26 OECD, *The Reviews of National Education Policy: New Zealand*, OECD, Paris, 1983, p.10.

27 Report of the Taskforce to Review Education Administration, *Administering for Excellence: Effective Administration in Education*, GP, Wellington, 1988.

28 J. Jesson, 'Curriculum in New Zealand: Is it Policy by Dodgems?', unpublished paper, 1994.

29 For Wellington figures, see *City Voice*, 15 Dec. 1994.
30 Founded in 1991; its members included the CEO of the Employers' Federation, former president of Federated Farmers, former principal of Auckland Boys' Grammar, and director of the Business Roundtable.
31 *Budgetary Stress*, p.39.
32 K. Hawk & J. Hill, *Teacher Salaries Grant (TSG) Scheme Trial Education*, Massey University Education Development and Research Centre, 1995, p.iii.
33 J. Jesson, 'Curriculum in New Zealand'.
34 Cabinet Committee on Education, Training & Employment, 'Proposed Legislation Changes: NZQA', 4 July 1995.
35 For a detailed account, see R. Butterworth & N. Tarling, *A Shakeup Anyway: Government and the Universities in New Zealand in a Decade of Reform*, AUP, Auckland, 1994.
36 Figures from Ministry of Education, Mar. 1995.
37 Report of the Ministerial Consultative Group, 'Funding Growth in Tertiary Education and Training', Ministry of Education, May 1994.
38 J. Boston, 'The Funding of Tertiary Education: Rights and Wrongs', in J. Boston & P. Dalziel (eds), *The Decent Society?*, pp.186, 198.
39 S. St John, 'Costing the State', Social Policy Conference, Wellington, Dec. 1992.
40 E. McLeay, 'Housing Policy', in Boston & Dalziel (eds), pp.169, 171-2.
41 See above, p.120.
42 *NZ Herald*, 31 Dec. 1992.
43 Reported in *Jobs Letter*, 4, 7 Nov. 1994.
44 Ministry of Housing, 'Serious Housing Need', 51/94, 11 Mar. 1994.
45 *NZ Herald*, 10 Aug. 1992.
46 C. Rudd, 'The Changing Structure of Public Expenditure', in Boston et al. (eds), *Reshaping the State*, pp.140, 143, Table 1.
47 Rudd, pp.149-54.
48 *Sunday Times*, 4 Mar. 1990.
49 *1990 Briefing Papers*, p.2.
50 *NZ Herald*, 20 Dec. 1990.
51 D. Rose, 'Redistribution, Employment and Growth', briefing paper for the New Zealand Council of Christian Social Services, Nov. 1993.
52 *NZ Herald*, 20 Dec. 1990.
53 *NBR*, 8 July 1994.

54 *NBR*, 1 July 1994.
55 *NZPD*, Vol. 536, 1 July 1993, p.16525.
56 Treasury, 29 May 1993, Budget Report no. 61, Annex C, para.22.
57 Treasury, 31 Mar. 1993, Budget Report no.35, para.2.
58 Treasury, 25 May 1993, Budget Report no. 58, para.6.
59 Report by the Treasury on the Fiscal Responsibility Bill, undated, paras 75-76.
60 *NZPD*, Vol. 538, 16 Sept. 1993, p.18065.
61 Treasury, T94/142, 4 Feb. 1994, para.3.
62 Minister of Finance to Chair, FEC, 21 Apr. 1994.
63 *NZPD*, Vol. 250, 26 May 1994, p.1143.
64 Minister of Finance, Memorandum to Cabinet, 9 Mar. 1994, para.4.
65 M. A. Collins, 'Review of the Treasury Costings of Labour Party Policies', State Services Commission, Wellington, 1994.
66 *NBR*, 8 July 1994.
67 OECD, *Country Report: New Zealand*, OECD, Paris, 1993, p.45, Table 11.
68 Treasury, 29 May 1993, Budget Report no. 61, Annex C, para.8.
69 *NZPD*, Vol. 540, 26 May 1994, p.1151 per Simich.
70 *New Zealand Report 1994*, Moody's Investor Service, New York, 1994, p.5.
71 *NZPD*, Vol. 540, 26 May 1994, p.1143, per Cullen.
72 *NZ Herald*, 23 Mar. 1994.

10   The Economic Deficit

1 *OECD Outlook*, OECD, Paris, 1993.
2 *Economic Surveys: New Zealand*, OECD, Paris, 1994, p.11 & Fig. 1.
3 *NZ Herald*, 25 Aug. 1995.
4 *Listener*, 17 Dec. 1994.
5 Raising more funds domestically than needed for government expenditure to fund repayment of external debt.
6 OECD 1994, p.63.
7 OECD 1994, p.53 &Table 9.
8 OECD 1994, p.58 & Table 13.
9 Economic briefing to the Alliance by Integrated Economic Services, Feb. 1995.
10 *Dominion*, 13 Sept. 1994.
11 OECD, 1994, p.115, note 53.
12 G. Malcolm, *Business Dynamics in New Zealand 1987–1991: Entry, Growth and Decline in the Business Sector*, Res. Monograph 61, 1993, NZIER, Wellington, p.62.

13   Malcolm, *Business Dynamics*, p.64.
14   Malcolm, *Business Dynamics*, p.65.
15   *Independent*, 5 May 1995.
16   *Independent*, 5 May 1995.
17   Infometrics Economic Forecasts, Sept. 1993, p.3. See also P. Saunders, 'Rising on the Tasman Tide: Income Inequality in New Zealand and Australia in the 1980s', *Social Policy Journal of New Zealand*, 2 (1994), p.97; K. Rankin, 'Are New Zealanders Getting Poorer', *New Zealand Political Review*, 2, 1 (1993), p.11; K. Rankin, 'Who's Getting What? Income Distribution in Godzone', *NZ Political Review*, 4, 2 (1995), p.11.
18   P. Simons, 'Tunnel or Tree? Social Justice in a Technistic Society', paper for symposium on the Church Leaders' Statement on Social Justice, 19 Nov. 1993, Wellington, pp.14-15.
19   B. Easton, 'Poverty in New Zealand 1981-1993', unpublished paper, p.9.
20   Seminar, 'Investment in New Zealand', 25 Nov. 1994.
21   *Dominion*, 24 Sept. 1994.
22   Village meeting place or surrounds.
23   *Listener*, 17 Sept. 1994.
24   *Key Statistics*, Jan. 1995.
25   *Independent*, 3 Mar. 1995.
26   Although it reasserted itself during the period of economic recovery.
27   *Jobs Letter*, 7, 20 Dec. 1994.
28   In November 1994, for example, TrustBank announced a record profit of $44.5m and continued restructuring which could see another 400 jobs gone in six months' time.
29   R. Deane, 'Reforming the Public Sector', in S. Walker (ed.), *Rogernomics: Reshaping New Zealand's Economy*, GP Books, Wellington, 1989, p.133.
30   See Table 6.1. In December 1994, a further 1000 Telecom workers were asked to consider 'redeployment' in yet another round of restructuring.
31   *Independent*, 5 May 1995.
32   The Prime Minister opened a new forestry processing plant in 1992 with promises of 265 jobs and massive profits; two years later 97 staff were being laid off.
33   OECD, 1994, p.16.
34   OECD, 1994, p.18.
35   *Listener*, 12 Mar., p.62.
36   *Jobs Letter*, 4, 7 Nov. 1994.
37   In December 1994, 26,335 were in employment schemes and subsidised jobs.

38   *Jobs Letter*, 1, 26 Sept. 1994.
39   OECD, 1994, p.110.
40   *NBR*, 18 June 1993, 2 Sept. 1994, 23 June 1995; *NZ Herald*, 23 June 1992, 18 June 1993.
41   D. Hayward & M. Salvaris, 'Creating the Conditions of Their Own Existence: Credit Rating Agencies and Australian Social Policy', paper to the Social Policy Conference, University of New South Wales, 14–17 July 1993.
42   'The Remaking of New Zealand', *Ideas*, CBC, 12 Oct. 1994.
43   New housing permits from local authorities increased 25% in the 1994 year. Construction was up 16.6%, trade restaurants and hotel industry up 8.7%, transport, communications and services up 6.9%, manufacturing 5.8% and farming 5.5%.
44   *NZ Herald*, 29 Dec. 1994.
45   *NZ Herald*, 10 Jan. 1995.
46   Auckland Manufacturers' Association, press release, 8 May 1995.

11   The Social Deficit

1   *Economist*, 5 Nov. 1994, p.19.
2   *NZ Herald*, 16 Mar. 1995.
3   Report of the Royal Commission of Inquiry, *Social Security in New Zealand*, Mar. 1972, Government Printer, Wellington, p.65, original emphasis.
4   Report of the Royal Commission on Social Policy, *New Zealand Today*, Vol. 1, Apr. 1988, Wellington, p.vi.
5   J. Shipley, *Social Assistance: Welfare that Works*, DSW, Wellington, July 1991, pp.15-16.
6   'Whanau' is the Maori word for what is known in English as 'family'. It has a wider meaning than nuclear family, referring to what would best be described in English as an 'extended family'.
7   M. Prebble, 'Critical New Elements in Government Thinking', in G. Hawke (ed.), *A Modest Safety Net?*, pp.1, 3-4.
8   E.g. *Neither Freedom nor Choice: The Report of the People's Select Committee*, 1992; *Poverty and Hardship*, Manukau City Council, Manukau, 1992; *Passing the Buck*, Wellington Downtown Ministry, Wellington, Dec. 1994.
9   *NZ Herald*, 27 Aug. 1992.
10   UNHDP, *Human Development Report 1994*, OUP, New York, 1994, p.104, Table A5.2.
11   B. Easton, 'Poverty in New Zealand

1981-1993' See also *Evening Post*, 3 & 4 Apr. 1995.

12 Easton, 'Poverty', p.18.

13 B. Easton, 'Properly Assessing Income Adequacy in New Zealand', Working Paper 94/10, Economic and Social Trust on New Zealand, 1994; P. Hyman, *Women and Economics: A New Zealand Feminist Perspective*, Bridget Williams Books, Wellington, 1994, pp.71-74.

14 R. Stephens, 'The Incidence and Severity of Poverty in New Zealand 1990-1991', Working Paper 12/94, Victoria University of Wellington, cited in Easton, 'Poverty', pp.6-7.

15 I. Shirley, 'Social Development in New Zealand', Social Development Seminar, 5 Aug. 1994.

16 M. Mowbray & N. Dayal, 'The Fall and Rise(??) of Household Incomes', *Social Policy Journal of New Zealand*, 2 (1994), pp.114, 120.

17 C. Waldegrave, 'The 1990/91 National Budgets: A Social Assessment', Report to the Sunday Forum, Oct. 1991, pp.57-62.

18 Aotearoa Network of Unemployed and Beneficiaries, press statement, 13 Jan. 1995.

19 *Listener*, 25 Mar. 1991, p.16.

20 *NZ Herald*, 3 Oct. 1994.

21 *Dominion*, 16 Oct. 1994.

22 *Dominion*, 21 Dec. 1994.

23 *Dominion*, 4 Oct. 1994.

24 S. St John & A. Heynes, 'The Welfare Mess', Dept of Economics Policy Discussion Paper, 15, University of Auckland, Oct. 1994.

25 P. Simons, 'Tunnel or Tree? Social Justice in a Technistic Society', paper for symposium on the Church Leaders' Statement on Social Justice, 19 Nov. 1993, Wellington, p.16, Table 3.

26 Statistics New Zealand, press release, 8 May 1995.

27 Hyman, *Women and Economics*, p.188.

28 *NZ Herald*, 2 Jan. 1995. From 1988 to 1995 the number on invalid benefits increased 46 %, and on sickness benefits more than doubled.

29 *GM*, p.404.

30 *Dominion*, 20 Feb. 1991.

31 St John & Heynes, 'Welfare Mess', p.4.

32 Hyman, *Women and Economics*, p.21.

33 Hyman, *Women and Economics*, p.192.

34 *Dominion Sunday Times*, 20 Mar. 1988.

35 *NZ Herald*, 19 Jan. 1992.

36 C. Dann & R. du Plessis, *After the Cuts: Surviving on the Domestic Purposes Benefit*, Dept of Sociology Working Paper 12, University of Canterbury, 1992, pp.1, 65.

37 Dann & du Plessis, *After the Cuts*, p.66.

38 Waldegrave, pp.61-62.

39 Statistics New Zealand, *New Zealand Now: Maori*, Wellington, Dec. 1994, pp.44-45.

40 *New Zealand Now: Maori*, p.18.

41 *NZ Herald*, 7 Apr. 1990.

42 *Feeling Stretched: Women and Families in Transition*, West Auckland Women's Centre, 1994.

43 *Status of New Zealand Women 1992: Second Periodic Report on the Convention on the Elimination of all Forms of Discrimination Against Women*, Ministry of Women's Affairs, Wellington, 1992, p.39.

44 Hyman, *Women and Economics*, p.150.

45 R. Harbridge, 'Service Workers Union Women Members Survey', Report to SWU, 1993, cited in Hyman, pp.138-9.

46 L. Hill & R. du Plessis, 'Tracing the Similarities, Identifying the Differences: Women and the ECA', *New Zealand Journal of Industrial Relations*, 18, 1, pp.31-43.

47 St John & Heynes, pp.11-13.

48 Statistics New Zealand, press release, 8 May 1995.

49 Statistics New Zealand, press releaase, 8 May 1995.

50 S. St John, 'Delivering Financial Assistance to Families: An Analysis of New Zealand's Policies and the Case for Reform', Dept of Economics Policy Discussion Paper 18, University of Auckland, Dec. 1994.

51 *Poverty and Hardship*.

52 *NZ Herald*, 24 Oct. 1994.

53 K. Rankin, 'Are New Zealanders Getting Poorer', *New Zealand Political Review*, 2, 1 (1993), pp.11, 15

54 For further discussion, see J. Kelsey, *Rolling Back the State*, ch.24.

55 *NZ Herald*, 5 Feb. 1992.

56 *NZ Herald*, 19 Feb. 1992.

57 J. Boston, 'Redesigning the State in the New Zealand Economy', in M. Holland & J. Boston (eds), *The Fourth Labour Government*, pp.83, 95-96.

58 T. Hazledine, 'Taking New Zealand Seriously', inaugural lecture, University of Auckland, Aug. 1993, p.12.

59 *Passing the Buck*, Wellington Down-

town Ministry, Wellington, Dec. 1994.
60 Social Policy Agency, 'Foodbanks in New Zealand: Patterns of Growth and Usage', Department of Social Welfare, Oct. 1994, para.7.2.
61 Social Policy Agency, 'Foodbanks', para.18.4.
62 See Kelsey, *Rolling Back the State*, ch.25.
63 Convictions for violent crime increased 50% between 1982 and 1991. Police crime statistics show a 13.7% increase in reported violent crime and a 13% increase in reported serious offences for 1992–93. For 1993–94 the number of reported dishonesty offences fell, but reported violence increased.
64 New Zealand Law Commission, *Criminal Evidence: Police Questioning—A Discussion Paper*, Preliminary Paper 21, Law Commission, Wellington 1992.
65 Ministerial Review Team to the Minister of Social Welfare, *Review of the Children, Young Persons and Their Families Act 1989*, Wellington, 1992; section 30, Children, Young Persons & Their Families Amendment Act 1994.
66 *NZ Herald*, 4 Mar., 5 Mar., 11 Mar. & 15 Mar. 1993.
67 Reported in *Jobs Letter*, 2, 10 Oct. 1994.
68 M. Jackson, *He Whaipaanga Hou: Maori and the Criminal Justice System*, Justice Dept, Wellington, 1988.
69 *NZ Herald*, 10 Apr. 1992.
70 R. Busch et al, *Domestic Violence and the Justice System: A Study of Breaches of Protection Orders*, Justice Dept, Wellington, 1992. Note that this is the government's edited version.
71 Shirley, 'Social Development'.
72 *Ideas*, CBC.
73 *NZHerald*, 8 Aug. 1992.

12 The Democratic Deficit

1 *Ideas*, CBC.
2 *Ideas*, CBC.
3 The churches sponsored a number of reports, including S. Jackman (ed.), *Windows on Poverty*, NZCCSS, Wellington, 1992; P. Dalziel, *Taxing the Poor*, NZCCSS, Wellington, 1993; S. Jackman, *Child Poverty in Aotearoa/New Zealand*, NZCCSS, Wellington, 1993.
4 J. Vowles, 'Nuclear Free New Zealand and Rogernomics: The Survival of a Labour Government', *Politics*, 25, 1 (1990), pp.81, 82, Table 1.
5 But note the changed composition of

Labour voters in 1987, see above, pp.300–2.
6 G. A. Wood, 'The National Party', in Gold (ed.), *New Zealand Politics in Perspective*, pp.289, 293.
7 P. Aimer, 'The Changing Party System', in Gold (ed.), p.334.
8 J. Nagel, 'Market Liberalization in New Zealand: The Interaction of Economic Reform and Political Institutions in a Pluritarian Democracy', paper delivered to the 1994 Political Science Association annual meeting, New York, Sept. 1994, p.27.
9 Nagel, 'Market Liberalization', p.30.
10 Vowles, 'Nuclear Free', p.81.
11 Nagel, 'Market Liberalization', p.32.
12 *NZ Herald*, 4 Jan. 1992.
13 *NZ Herald*, 10 Jan. 1992.
14 *NZ Herald*, 11 Jan. 1993.
15 *North and South*, July 1993; *New Zealand Business*, July 1993.
16 *Ideas*, CBC.
17 Aimer, 'Changing', p.332.
18 Labour's Economic Policy, 'A Working Future', Oct. 1994.
19 *NZ Herald*, 7 Apr. 1995.
20 ACT's unofficial manifesto is Douglas's book, *Unfinished Business*, Random House, Auckland, 1993.
21 *NZ Herald*, 6 Apr. 1995.
22 *City Voice*, 9 Mar. 1995.
23 As purer libertarians pointed out, ACT's scheme was heavily state-directed. Contributions to a set amount for education, health and superannuation would be compulsory, and the state would approve these private providers according to its own criteria, and oversee their operation.
24 B. Jesson, 'Republicanism', public lecture, Christchurch, 14 Apr. 1994.
25 National Party, *The Next 3 Years*, 1994, p.12.
26 A. Bollard, *The Economic Consequences of Electoral Reform*, Discussion Paper 38, NZIER, Wellington, 1993, p.34.
27 Bollard, *Economic Consequences*, p.31.
28 Treasury, 29 May 1993, Budget Report no.61, Annex C, para.8.
29 *NZ Herald*, 10 Nov. 1993. See also Moody's Investors Services, *New Zealand Sovereign In-Depth Analysis*, New York, 1994, p.8.
30 For further discussion, see J. Kelsey, *Rolling Back the State:*, ch.19.
31 Kelsey, ch.20.
32 Kelsey, chs 15, 21.

33 The tribunal's budget was actually cut in 1992–93, then increased to $2.6m in 1993–94 and $3.95m in 1994–95.
34 Information provided by the Waitangi Tribunal, May 1995.
35 Kelsey, pp.260-9.
36 National Party, *Toward 2010*, National Party, Wellington, 1993, p.15.

13 The Cultural Deficit

1 N. Marsh, 'Theory K—Can Culture Change?', in A. von Tunzelmann and J. Johnston (eds), *Responding to the Revolution*, NZ Institute of Public Administration, GP, Wellington, 1987, p.70.
2 'The Remaking of New Zealand', *Ideas*, CBC, 12 Oct. 1994.
3 *New Zealand Today*, Vol. 2, p.454.
4 Summarised in P. Perry & A. Webster, 'Against the Tide: A Government Failure in Popular Persuasion', unpublished paper, Massey University, Apr. 1994.
5 *NBR/Insight* opinion polls published monthly in *NBR* from 1993–95.
6 E.g. *NBR*, 10 June 1994: over 80% believed funding in health, education and training should be increased; 37% felt social welfare benefits should be increased while 40% felt they should stay the same. *NBR*, 27 Jan. 1995: 61% preferred local body ownership of electricity supply, 21% private sector ownership. *NBR*, 16 Sept. 1994: 51% disapproved the ECA, 32% approved and 17% were unsure.
7 *NBR*, 10 Feb. 1995.
8 *Budgetary Stress*, New Zealand Business Roundtable, Wellington, 1992, p.2.
9 G.Crocombe et al., *Upgrading New Zealand's Competitive Advantage*, OUP, Auckland, 1991 (Porter Report), p.157.
10 Porter Report, p.30.
11 Porter Report, p.168.
12 R. Dale, 'The State and Education', in A. Sharp (ed.), *Leap into the Dark*, pp.68, 69.
13 Porter Report, p.168.
14 R. Kerr, 'What Kind of Country?', Queen's High School Winter Lecture, Dunedin, June 1992.
15 State Services Commission, paper to the Taskforce on Capital Charging of Tertiary Institutions, 'Governance of Tertiary Institutions', 18 Aug. 1992.
16 *GM*, p.178.
17 Seminar, 'Investment in New Zealand', 25 Nov. 1994.

18 J. Atkinson, 'The State, the Media, and Thin Democracy', in Sharp (ed.), pp.146, 152.
19 *NBR*, 30 Oct. 1992.
20 *NBR*, 3 Apr. 1992.
21 *NBR*, 10 Apr. 1992.
22 *NZ Herald*, 10 Dec. 1994.
23 *NZ Herald*, 29 Dec. 1994.
24 *GM*, Vol. 1, p.397.
25 *NZ Herald*, 20 July 1992.
26 A. Gibbs, 'The Impact of the Changing Economy on Families', *Transcript of the International Year of the Family Conference*, Nov./Dec. 1994, pp.264-65.
27 P. Hyman, *Women and Economics:*, p.65.
28 Quoted in Hyman, p.71.
29 Hyman, p.71.
30 Quoted in Hyman, p.75.
31 R. Scott, 'The Dark Abyss of Pish: The Language of Economic Rationalism', *New Zealand Political Review*, 4, 1 (1995), pp.17, 21.
32 *GM*, p.33.
33 *GM*, p.423.
34 Scott, 'Dark Abyss', p.20.
35 See *NBR*, 19 May 1995.
36 D. McKinnon, speech at launch of the Asia 2000 Seminar, 16 July 1993.
37 J. Bolger, 'New Zealand in the Asia-Pacific Community', speech to the Asia Society Conference, Tokyo, May 1993.
38 For further discussion see J. Kelsey, *Rolling Back the State*, pp.306-8.
39 *NZ Herald*, 31 Jan. 1995
40 *NZ Herald*, 29 Mar. 1994.
41 *NBR*, 3 Apr. 1992.
42 *NBR*, 11 Nov. 1994.
43 *NZ Herald*, 14 Feb. 1992.
44 D. McKinnon, speech to the Asia Society, New York, 29 Sept. 1993.
45 McKinnon, 'Asia 2000—The Next Steps', International Conference on Asian Studies, Wellington, 9 July 1993.
46 R.Walker, 'The Government's Economic Mantra of BIP Immigration', unpublished paper, Sept.1991.
47 'Report to the Prime Minister on Migrant Workers', Human Rights Commission, Auckland, 1990, p.19.
48 W. Kaspar, *Populate or Languish: Rethinking New Zealand's Immigration Policy*, Business Roundtable, Wellington, 1990, p.49.
49 Walker.
50 *NBR*, 26 May 1995.
51 *Dominion*, 1 May 1995.
52 D. Graham, speech to the Waikanae/Kapiti Rotary Clubs, 3 May 1995.

53 *NZ Herald,* 6 May 1995.

54 Notably Chris Trotter's attempt to draft a treaty-based constitution for a post-colonial New Zealand republic. See C. Trotter, 'The Struggle for Sovereignty', *New Zealand Political Review,* 4, 2 (1995), p.16.

55 *Radio NZ/MRL* poll, 8 June 1995.

56 *NZPD,* Vol. 539, 8 Mar. 1994, pp.120-21.

57 *Sunday Star-Times,* 20 Mar. 1994. Greatest support for a republic came from those under 30, with those over 60 and women more opposed to the idea.

14 There Are *Alternatives*

1 A. Bollard, 'New Zealand', in J. Williamson (ed.), *The Political Economy of Policy Reform,* pp.73, 103-4.

2 E.g. L. Bayliss, *Prosperity Mislaid: Economic Failure in New Zealand and What Should Be Done About It,* GP Books, Wellington, 1994. See also S. Collins, *Rogernomics: Is There a Better Way?,* Pitman, 1987, ch.15.

3 B. Easton & R. Gerritsen, 'Economic Reform: Parallels and Divergences', in F. Castles et al. (eds), *The Great Experiment: Labour Parties and Public Policy Transformation in Australia and New Zealand,* AUP, Auckland, 1995.

4 See below, pp.357–66.

5 This phrase was used by Noam Chomsky to describe the demise of left intelligentsia in the US, and is equally applicable to New Zealand.

6 However, similar emergency powers were not available under CER, which affected the bulk of New Zealand's trade.

7 D. Harper & G. Karacaoglu, 'Financial Policy Reform in New Zealand', in Bollard & Buckle (eds), pp.206, 235.

8 D. Rose, 'Briefing paper for New Zealand Council of Christian Social Services', November 1993.

9 S. Snively, 'Treating Unemployment Seriously: Balancing the Inflation Objective', *Signpost,* 1994.

10 'The Remaking of New Zealand', *Ideas,* CBC, 12 October 1994.

11 P. Simons, 'Tunnel or Tree? Social Justice in a Technistic Society', paper for symposium on the Church Leaders' Statement on Social Justice, 19 November 1993, Wellington, p.16.

12 See M. Waring, *Counting for Nothing: What Men Value and What Women are Worth,* Allen & Unwin, Wellington, 1988.

13 *Ideas,* CBC.

14 P. Hyman, *Women and Economics,* 1994, p.59.

15 Hyman, p.17.

16 Hyman, p.16.

17 T. Hazledine, 'Taking New Zealand Seriously', Inaugural Lecture, University of Auckland, Aug. 1993.

18 T. Hazledine, 'The Exporter as Hero?', address to the Manufacturers' Federation, Wellington, Sept. 1993.

19 K. Rankin, Department of Economics Policy Discussion Paper, 12, Auckland University.

20 Aotearoa Network of Unemployed and Beneficiaries, 'Employment: Issues and Solutions', July 1994, p.6. The Inland Revenue Department has sought ways to include the green economy in calculating tax and benefit entitlement.

21 *Building Our Own Future: People's Assemblies Project,* Auckland Unemployed Workers' Rights Centre, Auckland, Aug. 1994.

22 For further discussion, see J. Kelsey, *Rolling Back the State,* ch.18.

23 R. Cooper, 'A Maori Socio-economic Perspective', paper for the World Council of Churches Programme on Justice and Service, February 1988.

24 *Black's Law Dictionary,* 6 edn, West Publishing Co, St Paul, Minnesota, 1990, p.1396.

Select Bibliography of Published Works

Aimer, P. 'The Changing Party System', in H. Gold (ed.), *New Zealand Politics in Perspective*, 3 edn, Longman Paul, Auckland, 1992.

Allen, G. 'The Deal on Services—a Necessary Step to Integration', in K. Vautier et al. (eds), *CER and Business Competition: Australia and New Zealand in a Global Economy*, Commerce Clearing House, Auckland, 1990.

Atkinson, J. 'The State, the Media, and Thin Democracy', in A. Sharp (ed.), *Leap into the Dark: The Changing Role of the State in New Zealand Since 1984*, Auckland University Press, Auckland, 1994.

Bates, R. 'Comment', in J. Williamson (ed.), *The Political Economy of Policy Reform*, Institute for International Economics, Washington DC, 1994.

Bates, R. & A. Krueger, *Political and Economic Interactions in Economic Policy Reform*, Blackwell, Oxford, 1993.

Bayliss, L. *Prosperity Mislaid: Economic Failure in New Zealand and What Should Be Done About It*, GP Books, Wellington, 1994.

Bertram, G. 'Keynesianism, Neoclassicism, and the State', in B. Roper & C. Rudd (eds), *State and Economy in New Zealand*, Oxford University Press, Auckland, 1993.

Bhagwati, J. 'The Threats to the World Trading System', *The World Economy*, 15, 4 (1993).

Birch, B. *Accident Compensation: A Fairer Scheme*, Wellington, July 1991.

Birchfield, R. & I. Grant, *Out of the Woods: The Restructuring and Sale of New Zealand's State Forests*, GP Books, Wellington, 1993.

Bollard, A. 'More Market: the Deregulation of Industry', in A. Bollard & R. Buckle (eds), *Economic Liberalisation in New Zealand*, Allen & Unwin, Wellington, 1987.

Bollard, A. 'Introduction', in A. Bollard (ed.), *The Influence of United States Economics on New Zealand: The Fulbright Anniversary Seminars 1988*, Research Monograph 42, NZIER, Wellington, 1988.

Bollard, A. *The Economic Consequences of Electoral Reform*, Discussion Paper 38, NZIER, Wellington, 1993.

Bollard, A. 'New Zealand', in J. Williamson (ed.), *The Political Economy of Policy Reform*, Institute for International Economics, Washington DC, 1994.

Bollard, A. & B. Easton (eds), *Markets, Regulation and Pricing: Six Case Studies*, Research Paper 31, NZIER, Wellington, 1985.

Boston, J. 'Redesigning the State in the New Zealand Economy', in M. Holland & J. Boston (eds), *The Fourth Labour Government: Politics & Policy in New Zealand*, Oxford University Press, Auckland, 1990.

Boston, J. 'Chief Executives and the Senior Executive Service', in J. Boston et al. (eds), *Reshaping the State: New Zealand's Bureaucratic Revolution,* Oxford University Press, Auckland, 1991.

Boston, J. 'Reorganizing the Machinery of Government: Objectives and Outcomes', in J. Boston et al. (eds), *Reshaping the State: New Zealand's Bureaucratic Revolution,* Oxford University Press, Auckland, 1991.

Boston, J. 'The Funding of Tertiary Education: Rights and Wrongs', in J. Boston & P. Dalziel (eds), *The Decent Society?: Essays in Response to National's Economic and Social Policies,* Oxford University Press, Auckland, 1992.

Boston, J. 'The Treasury: Its Role, Philosophy and Influence', in H. Gold (ed.), *New Zealand Politics in Perspective,* 3 edn, Longman Paul, Auckland, 1992.

Boston, J. 'Purchasing Policy Advice: The Limits to Contracting Out', *Governance,* 17, 1 (1994).

Boston, J. 'On the Sharp Edge of the State Sector Act: The Resignation of Perry Cameron', *Public Sector,* 17, 4.

Bradshaw, D. 'Professionalism in the Public Service', *Public Sector* 17, 1 (1994), p.13.

Bremer, R. & T. Brooking, 'Federated Farmers and the State', in B. Roper & C. Rudd (eds), *State and Economy in New Zealand,* Oxford University Press, Auckland, 1993.

Buckle, R. (ed.), *Inflation and Economic Adjustment: Proceedings of a Seminar,* Department of Economics, Victoria University of Wellington, Wellington, 1983.

Buckle, R. 'Sequencing and the Role of the Foreign Exchange Market', in A. Bollard & R. Buckle (eds), *Economic Liberalisation in New Zealand,* Allen & Unwin, Wellington, 1987.

Building Our Own Future: People's Assemblies Project, Auckland Unemployed Workers' Rights Centre, Auckland, August 1994.

Busch, R. et al., *Domestic Violence and the Justice System: A Study of Breaches of Protection Orders,* Justice Department, Wellington, 1992.

Butterworth, R. & N. Tarling, *A Shakeup Anyway: Government and the Universities in New Zealand in a Decade of Reform,* Auckland University Press, Auckland, 1994.

Camilleri, J. & J. Falk, *The End of Sovereignty? The Politics of a Shrinking and Fragmenting World,* Edward Elgar, Aldershot, 1992.

Collins, S. *Rogernomics: Is There a Better Way?,* Pitman, Auckland, 1987.

Crocombe, G. et al., *Upgrading New Zealand's Competitive Advantage* (The Porter Report), Oxford University Press, Auckland, 1991.

Dale, R. 'The State and Education', in A. Sharp (ed.), *Leap into the Dark: The Changing Role of the State in New Zealand Since 1984,* Auckland University Press, Auckland, 1994.

Dalziel, P. 'The Rhetoric of Treasury: a Review of the 1990 Briefing Papers', *New Zealand Economic Papers* 25, 2 (1991).

Dalziel, P. *Taxing the Poor,* NZCCSS, Wellington, 1993.

Dalziel, P. 'The Reserve Bank Act', in B. Roper & C. Rudd (eds), *State and Economy in New Zealand,* Oxford University Press, Auckland, 1993.

Deane, R. 'Reforming the Public Sector', in S. Walker (ed.), *Rogernomics: Reshaping New Zealand's Economy,* GP Books, Wellington, 1989.

Deeks, J. 'Introduction: Business, Government and Interest Group Politics', in

J. Deeks & N. Perry (eds), *Controlling Interests: Business, the State and Society in New Zealand,* Auckland University Press, Auckland, 1992.

Douglas, K. 'Organising Workers: The Effects of the Act on the Council of Trade Unions and Its Membership', in R. Harbridge (ed.), *Employment Contracts: New Zealand Experiences,* Victoria University Press,Wellington, 1993.

Douglas, R. *There's Got to Be a Better Way!,* Fourth Estate, Wellington, 1980.

Douglas, R. *Unfinished Business,* Random House, Auckland, 1993.

Douglas, R. & L. Callen, *Towards Prosperity: People and Politics in the 1980s— A Personal View,* David Bateman, Auckland, 1987.

Duncan, I. & A. Bollard, *Corporatization and Privatization: Lessons from New Zealand,* Oxford University Press, Auckland, 1992.

Durie, M. 'Maori and the State: Professionalism and Ethical Implications for a Bicultural Public Service', *Public Sector,* 17, 1 (1994).

Easton, B. 'From Reaganomics to Rogernomics', in A. Bollard (ed.), *The Influence of United States Economics on New Zealand: The Fulbright Anniversary Seminars 1988,* Research Monograph 42, NZIER, Wellington, 1988.

Easton, B. 'The Commercialisation of the New Zealand Economy', in B. Easton (ed.), *The Making of Rogernomics,* Auckland University Press, Auckland, 1989.

Easton, B. 'How Did the Health Reforms Blitzkrieg Fail?', *Political Science,* 46, 2 (1994).

Easton, B. & R. Gerritsen, 'Economic Reform: Parallels and Divergences', in F. Castles et al. (eds), *The Great Experiment: Labour Parties and Public Policy Transformation in Australia and New Zealand,* Allen & Unwin, Sydney (forthcoming).

Environment 2010 Strategy, Ministry for the Environment, Wellington, October 1994.

Evans, L. 'Farming in a Changing Economic Environment', in A. Bollard & R. Buckle (eds), *Economic Liberalisation in New Zealand,* Allen & Unwin, Wellington, 1987.

Farmer, J. 'The Harmonisation of Australian and New Zealand Business Laws', in K. Vautier et al. (eds), *CER and Business Competition: Australia and New Zealand in a Global Economy,* Commerce Clearing House, Auckland, 1990.

Fitzsimons, P. 'The New Zealand Securities Commission: The Rise and Fall of a Law Reform Body', *Waikato Law Review,* 2 (1994).

Fougere, G. 'The State and Health-care Reform', in A. Sharp (ed.), *Leap into the Dark: The Changing Role of the State in New Zealand Since 1984,* Auckland University Press, Auckland, 1994.

Gibbs, A. 'The Impact of the Changing Economy on Families', *Transcript of the International Year of the Family Conference,* November/December 1994.

Goldfinch, S. & B. Roper, 'Treasury's Role in State Policy Formulation during the Post-war Era', in B. Roper & C. Rudd (eds), *State and Economy in New Zealand,* Oxford University Press, Auckland, 1993.

Greer, D. 'Contestability in Competition Policy: Replacement, Supplement or Impediment?', in A. Bollard (ed.), *The Influence of United States Economics on New Zealand: The Fulbright Anniversary Seminars 1988,* Research Monograph 42, NZIER, Wellington, 1988.

Gustafson, B. *The First 50 Years: A History of the New Zealand National Party,* Reed Methuen, Auckland, 1986.

Gustafson, B. 'The Labour Party', in H. Gold (ed.), *New Zealand Politics in Perspective*, 3 edn, Longman Paul, Auckland, 1992.

Haggard, S. & R. Kaufman, 'Institution and Economic Adjustment', in S. Haggard & R. Kaufman (eds), *The Politics of Economic Adjustment*, Princeton University Press, New Jersey, 1992.

Harbridge, R. & K. Hince, *A Sourcebook of New Zealand Trade Unions and Employee Organisations*, VUW Industrial Relations Centre, Wellington, 1994.

Harbridge, R., A. Honeybone & P. Kiely, *Employment Contracts: Bargaining Trends and Employment Law Update: 1993/94*, VUW Industrial Relations Centre, Wellington, 1994.

Harper, D. & G. Karacaoglu, 'Financial Policy Reform in New Zealand', in A. Bollard & R. Buckle (eds), *Economic Liberalisation in New Zealand*, Allen & Unwin, Wellington, 1987.

Harvey, O. 'The Unions and the Government: The Rise and Fall of the Compact', in J. Deeks & N. Perry (eds), *Controlling Interests: Business, the State and Society in New Zealand*, Auckland University Press, Auckland, 1992.

Hawkins, A. & G. McLaughlan, *The Hawk*, Four Star Books, Auckland, 1989.

Haworth, N. 'National Sovereignty, Deregulation and the Multinational: New Zealand in the 1980s', in J. Deeks & N. Perry (eds), *Controlling Interests: Business, the State and Society in New Zealand*, Auckland University Press, Auckland, 1992.

Haworth, N. 'Neo-Liberalism, Economic Internationalisation and the Contemporary State in New Zealand', in A. Sharp (ed.), *Leap into the Dark: The Changing Role of the State in New Zealand Since 1984*, Auckland University Press, Auckland, 1994.

Hill, L. & R. du Plessis, 'Tracing the Similarities, Identifying the Differences: Women and the ECA', *New Zealand Journal of Industrial Relations*, 18, 1.

Hobsbawm, E. J. *Nations and Nationalism Since 1780*, Cambridge University Press, 2 edn, 1992.

Holmes, F. & C. Falconer, *Open Regionalism? NAFTA, CER and a Pacific Basin Initiative*, Institute of Policy Studies, Wellington, 1992.

Hyman, P. *Women and Economics: A New Zealand Feminist Perspective*, Bridget Williams Books, Wellington, 1994.

Jackman, S. (ed.), *Windows on Poverty*, NZCCSS, Wellington, 1992.

Jackman, S. *Child Poverty in Aotearoa/New Zealand*, NZCCSS, Wellington, 1993.

Jackson, M. *He Whaipaanga Hou: Maori and the Criminal Justice System*, Justice Department, Wellington, 1988.

Jesson, B. *Fragments of Labour: The Story Behind the Labour Government*, Penguin, Auckland, 1989.

Jesson, B. 'Lobbying and Protest: Patterns of Political Change at the Informal Level', in H. Gold (ed.), *New Zealand Politics in Perspective*, 3 edn, Longman Paul, Auckland, 1992.

Justice Department, *Report of the Review Committee of the Commerce Act 1986*, January 1993.

Kaspar, W. *Populate or Languish: Rethinking New Zealand's Immigration Policy*, Business Roundtable, Wellington, 1990.

Kelsey, J. *Rolling Back the State: Privatisation of Power in Aotearoa/New Zealand*, Bridget Williams Books, Wellington, 1993.

Kelsey, J. 'Restructuring the Nation: The Decline of the Colonial Nation-State and Competing Nationalisms in Aotearoa/New Zealand', in P. Fitzpatrick (ed.), *Nationalism, Racism and the Rule of Law*, Dartmouth, Aldershot, 1995.

Krueger, A. 'Global Trade Prospects for the Developing Countries', *The World Economy*, 15, 4 (1993).

Krugman, P. 'Does the New Trade Theory Require a New Trade Policy?', *The World Economy*, 15, 4 (1993).

Loughlin, M. 'Law, Ideologies and the Politico-juridical System', in A. Gamble & C. Wells (eds), *Thatcher's Law*, GPC Books, Cardiff, 1989.

Malcolm, G. *Business Dynamics in New Zealand 1987–1991: Entry, Growth and Decline in the Business Sector*, Res. Monograph 61, 1993, NZIER, Wellington.

Marsh, N. 'Theory K—Can Culture Change?', in A. von Tunzelmann & J. Johnston (eds), *Responding to the Revolution*, New Zealand Institute of Public Administration, GP Books, Wellington, 1987.

Martin, J. 'Devolution and Decentralisation', in J. Boston et al. (eds), *Reshaping the State: New Zealand's Bureaucratic Revolution*, Oxford University Press, Auckland, 1991.

Martin, J. 'Ethos and Ethics', in J. Boston et al. (eds), *Reshaping the State: New Zealand's Bureaucratic Revolution*, Oxford University Press, Auckland, 1991.

Martin, J. 'The Role of the State in Administration', in A. Sharp (ed.), *Leap into the Dark: The Changing Role of the State in New Zealand Since 1984*, Auckland University Press, Auckland, 1994.

McCubbins, M., R. Noll & B. Weingast, 'Structure and Process, Politics and Policy: Administrative Arrangements and the Political Control of Agencies', *Virginia Law Review*, 75 (1989).

McCubbins, M., R. Noll & B. Weingast, 'Administrative Procedures as Instruments of Political Control', *Journal of Law, Economics and Organization*, 6 (1990).

Ministerial Review Team to the Minister of Social Welfare, *Review of the Children, Young Persons and Their Families Act 1989*, Wellington, 1992.

Ministry of Commerce, *Review of the Commerce Act 1986*, August 1989.

Ministry of Foreign Affairs and Trade, *Trading Ahead: The GATT Uruguay Round: Results for New Zealand*, MFAT, Wellington, 1994.

Moe, T. 'Political Institutions: the Neglected Side of the Story', *Journal of Law, Economics and Organization*, 6 (1990).

Moody's Investors Services, *New Zealand Sovereign In-Depth Analysis*, New York, 1994.

Mowbray, M. & N. Dayal, 'The Fall and Rise (??) of Household Incomes', *Social Policy Journal of New Zealand*, 2 (1994).

National Party of NZ, *Toward 2010*, National Party, 1993, Wellington.

National Party of NZ, *The Next 3 Years*, National Party, 1994, Wellington.

Neither Freedom nor Choice: The Report of the People's Select Committee, 1992.

New Zealand Business Roundtable, *Submission to the Policy Statement 'Accident Compensation: A Fairer Scheme'*, Business Roundtable, Wellington, 1991.

New Zealand Business Roundtable, *Budgetary Stress*, Business Roundtable, Wellington, 1992.

New Zealand Law Commission, *Criminal Evidence: Police Questioning—A Discussion Paper*, Preliminary Paper 21, Law Commission, Wellington, 1992.

New Zealand Treasury, *Economic Management*, Treasury, Wellington, 1984.

New Zealand Treasury, *Government Management: Brief to the Incoming Government 1987*, 2 vols, Treasury, Wellington, 1987.

New Zealand Treasury, *1990 Treasury Briefing Papers*, Treasury, Wellington, 1990.

OECD, *The Reviews of National Education Policy: New Zealand*, OECD, Paris, 1983.

OECD, *Economic Surveys: New Zealand*, OECD, Paris, 1993; 1994.

Oliver, H. 'The Labour Caucus and Economic Policy Formation, 1981–84', in B. Easton (ed.), *The Making of Rogernomics*, Auckland University Press, Auckland, 1989.

Pallot, J. 'Financial Management Reform', in J. Boston et al. (eds), *Reshaping the State: New Zealand's Bureaucratic Revolution*, Oxford University Press, Auckland, 1991.

Passing the Buck, Wellington Downtown Ministry, Wellington, December 1994.

Polaschek, R. *Government Administration in New Zealand*, Institute of Public Administration, Wellington, 1958.

Poverty and Hardship, Manukau City Council, Manukau, 1992.

Prebble, M. *Information, Privacy and the Welfare State: An Integrated Approach to the Administration of Redistribution*, IPS, Wellington, 1990.

Prebble, M. 'Critical New Elements in Government Thinking', in G. Hawke (ed.), *A Modest Safety Net? The Future of the Welfare State*, Institute of Policy Studies, Wellington, 1991.

Private Provision for Retirement: The Way Forward. Final Report of the Task Force on Private Provision for Retirement, GP Books, Wellington, 1992.

Probine, M. 'The State Sector Act: Lessons from the Recent Past', *Public Sector*, 17, 4 (1994).

Raghavan, C. *Recolonization: GATT, the Uruguay Round and the Third World*, Third World Network, Penang, 1990.

Rankin, K. 'Are New Zealanders Getting Poorer?', *New Zealand Political Review*, 2, 1 (1993).

Rankin, K. 'Who's Getting What? Income Distribution in Godzone', *New Zealand Political Review*, 4, 2 (1995).

Reid, R. 'Crushing Labor in New Zealand', *Multinational Monitor*, June 1992.

Report of the ACC Regulations Review Panel, August 1994.

Report of the Eminent Persons Group to APEC Ministers, *A Vision for APEC: Towards an Asia Pacific Economic Community*, APEC, Singapore, Oct. 1993.

Report of the Hospital and Related Services Taskforce: Unshackling the Hospitals, Department of Health, Wellington, 1988.

Report of the Inquiry into the Procedures of the Accident Compensation Corporation, August 1994.

Report of the Ministerial Working Party on the Accident Compensation Corporation and Incapacity, 1st report, 1990.

Report of the Regulations Review Committee on Complaints Relating to the Accident Rehabilitation and Compensation Insurance (Social Rehabilitation) Regulations 1992, 1993.

Report of the Royal Commission of Inquiry, *Social Security in New Zealand*, March 1972, Government Printer, Wellington.

Report of the Royal Commission on Social Policy, *New Zealand Today*, Vol. 1, April 1988, Royal Commission on Social Policy, Wellington.

Report of the Select Committee on the Inquiry into the Effects of the Employment Contracts Act on the New Zealand Labour Market, 1993.

Report of the Taskforce to Review Education Administration, *Administering for Excellence: Effective Administration in Education*, Government Printer, Wellington, April 1988.

Report of the Working Group on Post Compulsory Education and Training in New Zealand, Government Printer, Wellington, July 1988.

Report on Funding Growth in Tertiary Education, Education Department, Wellington, 1994.

Reserve Bank, *Post-Election Paper to the Minister of Finance on the Areas of Responsibility of the Reserve Bank,* RBNZ, Wellington, 1984.

Reserve Bank, *Financial Policy Reform,* RBNZ, Wellington, 1986.

Roberts, J. *Politicians, Public Servants and Public Enterprise: Restructuring the New Zealand Government Executive,* Victoria University Press, Wellington, 1987.

Roper, B. 'A Level Playing Field? Business Political Activism and State Policy Formation', in B. Roper & C. Rudd (eds), *State and Economy in New Zealand,* Oxford University Press, Auckland, 1993.

Roseveare, J. 'Chief Executives and Statutory Independence', *Public Sector,* 17, 4 (1994).

Rudd, C. 'The Changing Structure of Public Expenditure', in J. Boston et al. (eds) *Reshaping the State: New Zealand's Bureaucratic Revolution,* Oxford University Press, Auckland, 1991.

Saunders, P. 'Rising on the Tasman Tide: Income Inequality in New Zealand and Australia in the 1980s', *Social Policy Journal of New Zealand,* 2 (1994).

School Property for Better Education: the Report of the Taskforce on the Development of Long-Term Policy for School Property, Ministry of Education, Wellington, 1993.

Schwartz, H. 'Can Orthodox Stabilization and Adjustment Work? Lessons from New Zealand 1984-90', *International Organizations,* 45, 2 (1991).

Scott, G. 'What's Wrong with Managerialism?', *Public Sector,* 16, 1 (1993).

Scott, G. & R. Blakeley, 'Professionalism in the Public Service', *Public Sector,* 16, 4 (1993).

Scott, R. 'The Dark Abyss of Pish: The Language of Economic Rationalism', *New Zealand Political Review,* 4, 1 (1995).

Securities Commission Report on Company Takeovers, Securities Commission, Wellington, October 1988.

Shipley, J. *Social Assistance: Welfare that Works,* DSW, Wellington, July 1991.

Smith, A. *An Inquiry into the Nature and Causes of the Wealth of Nations,* Modern Library, New York, 1937.

Snively, S. 'Labour Markets and Social Policy: Reversing the Roles', in A. Bollard (ed.), *The Influence of United States Economics on New Zealand: The Fulbright Anniversary Seminars 1988,* Research Monograph 42, NZIER, Wellington, 1988.

Snively, S. 'Treating Unemployment Seriously: Balancing the Inflation Objective', *Signpost,* 1994.

Statistics New Zealand, *New Zealand Now: Maori,* Wellington, December 1994.

Status of New Zealand Women 1992: Second Periodic Report on the Convention on the Elimination of All Forms of Discrimination Against Women, Ministry of Women's Affairs, Wellington, 1992.

Steering Group Review of State Sector Reforms, *Review of the State Sector Reforms,* 29 November 1991, SSC, 1991.

Stephens, B. 'Social Policy Reform: In Retrospect and Prospect', in A. Bollard & R. Buckle (eds), *Economic Liberalisation in New Zealand,* Allen & Unwin, Wellington, 1987.

Stephens, R. 'Radical Tax Reform in New Zealand', *Fiscal Studies*, 14, 3 (1993).

Taggart, M. *Corporatisation, Privatisation and Public Law*, Legal Research Foundation, Auckland, 1990.

Trotter, C. 'The Struggle for Sovereignty', *New Zealand Political Review*, 4, 2 (1995).

UNHDP, *Human Development Report 1994*, Oxford University Press, New York, 1994.

Upton, S. *Your Health and the Public Health*, Ministry of Health, Wellington, 1991.

Vautier, K. 'Competition Policy and Competition Law in New Zealand', in A. Bollard & R. Buckle (eds), *Economic Liberalisation in New Zealand*, Allen & Unwin, Wellington, 1987.

Vowles , J. 'Nuclear Free New Zealand and Rogernomics: The Survival of a Labour Government', *Politics*, 25, 1 (1990).

Vowles, J. 'Business, Unions and the State: Organising Economic Interests in New Zealand', in H. Gold (ed.), *New Zealand Politics in Perspective*, 3 edn, Longman Paul, Auckland, 1992.

Walsh, P. 'A Family Fight? Industrial Relations Reform under the Fourth Labour Government', in B. Easton (ed.), *The Making of Rogernomics*, Auckland University Press, Auckland, 1989.

Walsh, P. 'The Employment Contracts Act', in J. Boston & P. Dalziel (eds), *The Decent Society?: Essays in Response to National's Economic and Social Policies*, Oxford University Press, Auckland, 1992.

Waring, M. *Counting for Nothing: What Men Value and What Women are Worth*, Allen & Unwin, Wellington, 1988.

West, A. 'Public Service is Independent of Public Servants', *Public Sector*, 17, 2.

Whitwell, J. 'Monetary Policy with a Deregulated Financial Sector', in A. Bollard & R. Buckle (eds), *Economic Liberalisation in New Zealand*, Allen & Unwin, Wellington, 1987.

Williamson, J. 'In Search of a Manual for Technopols', in J. Williamson (ed.), *The Political Economy of Policy Reform*, Institute for International Economics, Washington DC, 1994.

Williamson, J. (ed.), *The Political Economy of Policy Reform*, Institute for International Economics, Washington DC, 1994.

Williamson, J. & S. Haggard, 'The Political Conditions for Economic Reform', in J. Williamson (ed.), *The Political Economy of Policy Reform*, Institute for International Economics, Washington DC, 1994.

Wilson, M. 'Employment Equity Act 1990: A Case Study in Women's Political Influence 1984-90', in J. Deeks & N. Perry (eds), *Controlling Interests: Business, the State and Society in New Zealand*, Auckland University Press, Auckland, 1992.

Wood, G. A. 'The National Party', in H. Gold (ed.), *New Zealand Politics in Perspective*, 3 edn, Longman Paul, Auckland, 1992.

Wooding, P. 'Liberalising the International Trade Regime', in A. Bollard & R. Buckle (eds), *Economic Liberalisation in New Zealand*, Allen & Unwin, Wellington, 1987.

Zanetti, G. et al., 'Opening the Books: A Review Article', *New Zealand Economic Papers*, 18 (1984).

Index